THE
MUSIC
FESTIVAL
GUIDE

THE MUSIC FESTIVAL GUIDE

for Music Lovers and Musicians

JON PRUETT
and MIKE McGUIRK

CHICAGO
REVIEW
PRESS

An A Cappella Book

Library of Congress Cataloging-in-Publication Data

Pruett, Jon.
  The music festival guide : for music lovers and musicians / Jon Pruett and
Mike McGuirk.—1st ed.
      p. cm.
  Includes index.
  ISBN 1-55652-515-X
  1. Music festivals. I. McGuirk, Mike. II. Title.
  ML35.P78 2004
  780'.79—dc22

                                                            2003015964

∞

The authors have made every effort to ensure that all the listing information
is correct and current at the time of publication.

You can contact the authors at musicfestivalguide@yahoo.com with
festival updates.

Jon Pruett and Mike McGuirk swear on their mothers' graves that the people
they interviewed for this book agreed to be interviewed and to have their words
printed in *The Music Festival Guide*.

∞

Cover and interior design: Monica Baziuk

©2004 by Jon Pruett and Mike McGuirk
All rights reserved
First Edition
Published by A Cappella Books
An imprint of Chicago Review Press, Incorporated
814 North Franklin Street
Chicago, Illinois 60610
ISBN 1-55652-515-X
Printed in the United States of America
5 4 3 2 1

CONTENTS

ACKNOWLEDGMENTS

JON PRUETT

I would not have been able to do the work that you find in this book without the support and assistance of dozens of festival promoters and organizers (especially within the city of New Orleans), not to mention the various nonjaded musician types, cynical music fans, and other folks who were willing to help out. Did I forget my seventh-grade teacher who taught me how to type? Well, thanks for that, too. Also, the music of the Velvet Underground and the Beach Boys' *Smile* sessions got me by in the wee hours. Most important, my mother and sister and the amazing Kara Jo and Ruby Isobel, because they get it. And Jackson Harper, I'm sure you will too.

MIKE MCGUIRK

Thank you to Lila Holland, Stephen LaChance, Jason Boronski, William York, Henry Bono, and Tim Quirk without whom this possible would not have been book.

THE BIG, BAD, BOLD FESTIVAL BOOK

Gentle Reader,

What you hold in your hands is the finished product of more than 666 million, zillion hours of living and breathing music festivals: attending, researching, eating, drinking, sweating in the sun, and freezing in the cold. We hope you'll find the listings in *The Music Festival Guide* informative and interesting. We've included festivals that happen all over the world—festivals of all manner, shape, and form—from the largest gathering of German techno fans (see page 233) to Tulsa's annual whistling festival (see page 184).

This book is a resource guide for the festivalgoer, with dates, locations, and the makeup of events galore. But we felt it was just as important for this book to be useful to the performer, so we've provided contact information for booking agents (whenever we could dig it up), deadlines for submissions, and in some cases, warnings for when you may be dealing with a labyrinth of intrigue in order to get on the bill.

We learned a great deal about the internal workings of festivals while compiling this guide. And we hope that this book will lead you to festivals you never knew existed and are glad to find. Here are a few things you should know about the way this book is constructed.

- Admission price is a tricky thing. Prices change from year to year. There are single day rates, advance and at-the-gate rates, full weekend pass rates, and camping-included rates. And some festivals don't charge a dime. To attempt to simplify all these variables we have devised a pricing key for each entry. One dollar sign means admission is cheap, two means it's reasonable, and three means it's anywhere from a little pricey to the "holy moley, and a bottle of water costs six bucks to boot?" range. Like so:

  FREE Free
  $ $20.00 and under for full weekend pass/admission
  $$ $20 to $50
  $$$ $50 and up

  Again, these guidelines are approximate, and, like we said, prices can change drastically from year to year, so be sure to check the Web site or call for more information before setting out.

- The larger the festival, the more automated your experience is going to be. This fact mostly concerns musicians looking to perform at festivals that only accept artist submissions online. In these cases we have provided a URL so that you may visit the Web site at your convenience.

- If we have not given specific artist submission instructions it does not necessarily mean that the festival is closed to applications. If you still wish to apply, you can use the other information we've included, such as phone number or e-mail address, to contact the festival's organizers.

- Festival dates are not to be banked upon. It's more than likely that the event will be rescheduled and revamped by the time you pack up the car. We definitely advise contacting the festival beforehand to confirm the dates.

- We tried to define the festivals by basic genres, but there is really no way to categorize a festival that presents traditional Senegalese folk songs alongside a grindcore band from New Jersey. There's always going to be some crossover. Use these categories as simple guidelines.

- Many festivals offer travel packages and deals with specific hotels. We've tried to include that hotel's information with each entry. In any case, be sure to contact the hotel to see if it offers a festival deal before you make a reservation.

- While we're on the subject, let's talk about hotels. There are many of them. Some are part of faceless multinational corporations. Some are family owned and operated. Depending upon the surrounding area, you'll find a few of both. In all cases, we have tried to include a variety of reasonably priced places for you to stay.

- Many festivals taking place in larger cities have few or no hotel accommodations listed; this is because there are too many hotels available to choose from. Your own judgment is probably going to be the best call.

- Campers should also plan ahead. While many festivals offer large camping areas with unlimited space, many have only a few available spots. RV campers especially should plan ahead. You wouldn't want to lug the steel behemoth across five states only to be given a thumbs-down by a teenage volunteer.

- Volunteers are always needed. If you know of a festival in your area, you should be down there helping them right now.

- For the big outdoor events there are usually many guidelines and rules you'll be expected to abide by. For the most part you might want to leave your pet, your weapons, your recording equipment, your whiskey bottles (glass bottles, that is), and (for reasons we have yet to get a straight answer on) your Frisbee at home. For more information, see our "Twelve Things You'll Need (Or Need to Know)" section on page xiii.

Our selection process combined meticulous Internet research with some very helpful word of mouth from friends, friends of friends, and the many festival promoters we talked to during the course of compiling all this information. We also gained much indispensable insight from a number of books about festivals that you will find listed in our resource guide.

There are sure to be a great many festivals that we've missed here. If your particular favorite, or a festival you help organize, is not included, we're sorry. We would like to include it in future editions of this guide. Please feel free to send any helpful suggestions, angry complaints, or good old put-downs to musicfestivalguide@yahoo.com and we will certainly do our best to make the next edition of *The Music Festival Guide* as comprehensive as possible.

We hope you find this book useful, informative, and well written. If you find it absolutely spellbinding from the first page to the last—well, then that's all right, too.

TWELVE THINGS YOU'LL NEED (OR NEED TO KNOW)

Researching and attending so many *great* festivals has taught us a few things, such as when to leave the dog at home, how handy a lawn chair can be, and that cockroaches in New Orleans can *fly*. To help you maximize your quality time at the festival of your choice, we've compiled a list of vital information (some dos and don'ts, a few things to bring) we recommend you take care of before you pack.

1. Invest in a low-to-the-ground lawn chair. The rule here is that if you can roll a basketball underneath your chair, then it is too high and will block the view of people behind you.

2. Pack some bug spray. Why? Because bugs carry disease. Didn't your parents teach you anything?

3. Always ask "Is my dog allowed?" before you get to the festival. Because, if Fido isn't allowed, you'll have to leave him in the car, and people who leave their animals to bake in the car for six hours while they eat corn dogs and candy apples should have their eyes gouged out with hot spikes.

4. You may also want to ask, "What about my out-of-control teenager? Are there going to be any teenager-related activities and/or areas that will help me keep my teenage son or daughter from running off with those nice people who showed up on Harleys?"

5. Many festivals that provide camping areas have been smart enough to separate the people who want to party all night from the people who want to get to sleep as soon as the sun goes down so they can be first in line for the face-painting booth on Sunday morning. If the latter scenario applies to you, then always be sure to ask, "Where's the quiet camp?"

6. If it doesn't, and you're the type of person who thinks the Clancy Brothers just sound *better* when you've got an eight ball of cocaine in your tent, then you may want to ask, "Where's the camp where I can party all night?"

7. Bring along a flashlight and some batteries. As you might imagine, flashlights can be very useful at night. In daytime . . . not so much. If you plan on staying the night, bring one. Without one, a simple trip to the bathroom could turn into a painful slapstick routine without the humor. Also, batteries are always useful. Carry a few in your pocket or place them around the brim of your hat in a humorous fashion.

8. Come prepared with a first aid kit—because one simple, misguided attempt to pass a flaming marshmallow skewer could result in a Dario Argento–esque display of unplanned gore. Well, in that case, you'd be better off calling an ambulance. But for the most part, dealing with a dazed, flashlightless camper ankles-deep in your campsite's smoldering embers is the kind of trauma you'll be most likely to deal with. This is why a first aid kit is a good idea. Granted, the chances of injury are pretty slim if you're just spending an afternoon at the park with Peabo Bryson and friends, but for longer, more remote excursions, it's always good to pack the Neosporin.

9. If you're allowed to bring it in, a lot of bottled water is highly recommended for the simple reason that, despite what you may have been taught in school, man and woman cannot exist on microbrewed blueberry-almond ale alone. You need water. A lot of water. Not only does it taste good, but it's also good for you and severely decreases your chances of waking up in a drum circle.

10. Don't forget to bring your Canadian-to-English dictionary!

11. Remember your rain gear. You've heard the phrase "rain or shine," correct? If you haven't, this could spell bad news for anyone not packing some sort of formless plasticwear to shield off any unexpected wetness.

Have you ever driven down the street and seen those people exiting a just-rained-on outdoor event who have been forced to wear garbage bags? Do you really want to be the guy who has to wear a garbage bag? No, no, you don't. Bring a slicker.

12. Festivals are *always* in need of volunteers and donations, so help out if you can. Your help, both physically and monetarily, can keep a much-loved annual event from folding. Also, when you volunteer, you get in for free.

THE
MUSIC
FESTIVAL
GUIDE

BLUES, R&B, and GOSPEL

♪ BALTIMORE BLUES FESTIVAL

Two days in May
Baltimore, Maryland
www.baltimorebluesfestival.com
Admission: *FREE*

The Baltimore Blues Festival features a variety of local and national acts ranging from classic, house-rocking rhythm and blues to down-home Southern soul to swampy folk-blues. With an abundance of locally brewed beer on-site and a variety of arts and crafts vendors providing everything from gourd art to handmade ceramics, you're likely to enjoy your days in the park.

Artist Submissions

Baltimore Blues Festival Music Committee
P.O. Box 231
Glyndon, MD 21071
info@baltimorebluesfestival.com

Camping: No

Accommodations

■ **Radisson Hotel at Cross Keys**
100 Village Sq.
Baltimore, MD 21210
(410) 532-6900

■ **Inn at Henderson's Wharf**
1000 Fell St.
Baltimore, MD 21231
(410) 522-7777

BATTLE OF THE BLUES HARPS

One day in November
Long Beach, California
www.southlandblues.com/harpbattle.htm
Admission: $$

The Battle of the Blues Harps takes place at the Best Western Golden Sails Hotel in Southern California on Thanksgiving Eve. The event is organized by the folks at Southland Blues Festival and shows off some of the most fiery practitioners of blues harmonica you're likely to find. They've had more than 13 years of experience in putting this festival together, so there's no doubt you're going to experience some extreme levels of excitement.

Camping: No

For more information: (562) 498-6942

Accommodations

■ **Best Western Golden Sails Hotel**
6285 E. Pacific Coast Hwy.
Long Beach, CA 90803
(800) 762-5333

■ **Queen Mary Hotel**
1126 Queens Hwy. N.
Long Beach, CA 90802
(800) 437-2934

BAYFRONT BLUES FESTIVAL

Three days in August
Duluth, Minnesota
www.bayfrontblues.com
Admission: $$

The organizers of the Bayfront Blues Festival have more than a dozen years of experience running this event, so it should come as no surprise that it draws some very high-profile acts such as Little Milton, Blues Traveler, and Dr. John. Bayfront also organizes a highly anticipated "blues cruise" during the festival for fans looking for something a bit out of the ordinary. There's also a postfestival party for those who just can't get enough. If you're itching to explore other parts of the city, a variety of local clubs also offer events during the duration of the festival.

For more information: bayfrontbluesfest@aol.com

Camping: No

Accommodations

■ **Hampton Inn**
310 Canal Park Dr.
Duluth, MN 55802
(218) 720-3000

■ **Comfort Inn West**
3900 W. Superior St.
Duluth, MN 55807
(218) 628-1464

BLIND WILLIE MCTELL BLUES FESTIVAL

One day in May
Thomson, Georgia
www.blindwillie.com
Admission: $

Mention the music of William Samuel McTell to any true blues fan and you'll undoubtedly be faced with a moment of silent reverence. One of the most distinctive of all the country blues players, Blind Willie's tracks "Statesboro Blues" and "Southern Can Is Mine" are key to understanding just how important the prewar blues sound is to popular music as we know it today. The first festival in his honor was held in Thomson, Georgia—his birthplace—in 1993. A few thousand people show up every year to explore the area and hear music by the likes of Peter Case, the Blind Boys of Alabama, and Junior Kimbrough.

Camping: No

Accommodations

■ **Best Western White Columns Inn**
1890 Washington Rd.
Thomson, GA 30824
(800) 528-9765
bestwest@whitecolumnsinn.com

■ **Howard Johnson Express Inn**
1847 Washington Rd.
Hwy. 78 & I-20
Thomson, GA 30824
(800) 446-4656

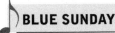

BLUE SUNDAY

Labor Day weekend
Johannesburg, Michigan
www.farmhousemusic.org/blue.html
Admission: $$

Blue Sunday is a Labor Day weekend event arranged by the Farmhouse Music Organization, a nonprofit organization dedicated to the promotion of the arts in the Johannesburg area. The two stages mix up a wide array of local talent with well-respected bluesmen such as Honeyboy Edwards. Harp aficionados can look forward to the Blow Your Face Off harmonica contest.

Artist Submissions

Farmhouse Music Organization

P.O. Box 525

Johannesburg, MI 49751

For more information: info@farmhousemusic.org

Camping: No

Accommodations

■ **Elk View Cabins**

16645 Elkview Trl.

Johannesburg, MI 49751

(517) 785-4896

BLUES ON THE RANGE

Two days in June

Chisholm, Minnesota

www.bayfrontblues.com

Admission: $$

Blues on the Range takes place at the Ironworld Discovery Center, a theme park of sorts dedicated to the preservation of Minnesota history. In addition to the music and food provided by the festival, the venue provides visitors with perks such as a mini golf course, a playground for the children, and trolley rides (which can also be used by on-site campers to get to the festival). Combined attendance rates for past festivals have pushed the 10,000-person mark, so be sure to plan ahead.

For more information: bayfrontbluesfest@aol.com

Camping: Yes. Tent and RV camping are available on-site. For off-site camping that's in the general vicinity, call (800) 777-8497.

Accommodations

■ **Super 8 Motel**

1411 E. 40th St.

Hibbing, MN 55746

(218) 263-8982

■ **Hibbing Park Hotel**

1402 E. Howard St.

Hibbing, MN 55746

(800) 262-3481

♪ BLUES WEEK

One week in July
Elkins, West Virginia
www.augustaheritage.com/blues.html
Admission: $$$

The title does not mislead. The town of Elkins offers up an entire week of concerts and other blues-related activities for the whole family—and for a few second cousins, if necessary. This celebration is in its twentieth year and prides itself on its ability to educate as well as entertain. The days are filled with classes for the young, inexperienced, and technically inept, providing basic instrument instruction that places an emphasis on the pre-World War II acoustic style. With a staff that has grown to more than two dozen teachers —many of them noted blues players—the students can expect a unique, inspiring education. As the sun sets with each day of the event, scheduled performers take the stage, and players both young and old learn firsthand how to use the techniques they've learned.

For more information: augusta@augustaheritage.com
Camping: No
Accommodations

■ **Elkins Days Inn**
1200 Harrison Ave.
Randolph Center
Elkins, WV 26241
(304) 637-4667

■ **Elkins Travelodge**
Routes 219/250 S.
P.O. Box 1879
Elkins, WV 26241
(304) 636-7711

♪ BOSTON BLUES FESTIVAL

End of September
Boston, Massachusetts
www.bluestrust.com
Admission: FREE

The Boston Blues Festival takes place on the last Saturday in September and is the only free blues festival you'll find in this area all year. This jam-packed weekend fest bills itself as part of a larger Blues Week during which participating clubs book blues-related events and offer free or discounted entry fees for festival attendees. Honeyboy Edwards, Susan Tedeschi, and harmonica favorite Jerry Portnoy have been some of the past participants.

Artist Submissions

Blues Trust Productions

75 Altamont Ave.

Melrose, MA 02176

For more information: greg@bluestrust.com

Camping: No

Accommodations

■ **Seaport Hotel**
One Seaport Ln.
Boston, MA 02210
(877) SEAPORT
www.seaporthotel.com

■ **Copley Square Hotel**
47 Huntington Ave.
Boston, MA 02116
(800) 225-7062
www.copleysquarehotel.com

BUDWEISER LOWCOUNTRY BLUES BASH

One week in February
Charleston, South Carolina
www.bluesbash.com
Admission: $–$$

Since its inception in 1991, the Lowcountry Blues Bash has gained a reputation as an event where well-respected blues musicians can perform in more intimate surroundings. The festival lasts several days and nights and often spills into bars and clubs all over the historic city of Charleston. Robert Lockwood, Mighty Sam McClain, and Honeyboy Edwards have all made appearances during festivals past.

For more information: emusic@mindspring.com

Camping: No

Accommodations

■ **Howard Johnson Inn**
250 Spring St.
U.S. 17 S.
Charleston, SC 29403
(843) 554-4140

■ **Elliot House Inn**
78 Queen St.
Charleston, SC 29401
(800) 729-1855

♪ BURNABY BLUES FESTIVAL

One day in July
Burnaby, British Columbia, Canada
www.jazzvancouver.com/concerts_details.cfm?event_id=994
Admission: $$

The Burnaby Blues Festival is a straightforward, single-day blues event that emphasizes quality over quantity. You can expect to hear a mixture of smoking guitar work with some of the more subdued, down-home elements of the blues. Slow-burning odes to love gone wrong and updates on the pursuance of the carnal arts come courtesy of acts like Ike Turner and Eddie Cotton. The festival provides activities for the children when the tight musicianship fails to hold their interest.

For more information: cjbs@coastaljazz.ca
Camping: No
Accommodations

■ **Radisson Hotel**
4331 Dominion St.
Burnaby, BC V5G 1C7
Canada

■ **Happy Day Inn**
7330 6th St.
Burnaby, BC V3N 3L3
Canada
(800) 665-9733

♪ CHICAGO BLUES FESTIVAL

Last weekend in May
Chicago, Illinois
www.ci.chi.il.us/SpecialEvents
Admission: FREE

Many of the artists that currently make up blues royalty have called Chicago home at one time or another. So it should come as no surprise that the Chicago Blues Festival manages to both match and exceed blues lovers' expectations. Known as the largest free blues festival in the world (more than 650,000 people attend), the festival has seen some of the genre's key players pass across its stages. Ray Charles, Stevie Ray Vaughan, and Chuck Berry represent just a fraction of the names.

For more information: SpecialEvents@cityofchicago.org

Camping: No
Accommodations
- City Suites Hotel
933 W. Belmont
Chicago, IL 60657
(800) 248-9108

- Chicago Marriott Downtown
540 N. Michigan Ave.
Chicago, IL 60611
(312) 836-0100

CHICAGO GOSPEL MUSIC FESTIVAL

Early June
Chicago, Illinois
www.ci.chi.il.us/SpecialEvents
Admission: FREE

A celebration of one of America's greatest musical forms, Chicago's Gospel Music Festival usually draws more than 150,000 people into downtown Chicago's Grant Park over the course of three days. This free event pays tribute to the modern forms of gospel music while also giving top billing to the traditional styles associated with legends such as the Pilgrim Jubilee Singers and the Mighty Clouds of Joy.

Camping: No
Accomodations
- City Suites Hotel
933 W. Belmont
Chicago, IL 60657
(800) 248-9108

- Chicago Marriott Downtown
540 N. Michigan Ave.
Chicago, IL 60611
(312) 836-0100

CISCO SYSTEMS BLUESFEST

Ten days in July
Ottawa, Ontario, Canada
http://ottawa-bluesfest.ca
Admission: $$$

Cisco Systems Bluesfest originated in the mid-nineties as a modest, strictly blues-and-gospel affair but has grown exponentially since then and opened its doors to notable performers such as Sting and Melissa Etheridge. Spanning ten days and five stages, the Bluesfest is one of the most well-attended blues events in Canada.

Artist Submissions: artisticdirector@ottawa-bluesfest.ca
Camping: No

Accommodations

■ **Gasthaus Switzerland Inn**
89 Daly Ave.
Ottawa, ON K1N 6E6
Canada
(888) 663-0000

■ **Howard Johnson Ottawa City Center**
123 Metcalfe St.
Ottawa, ON K1P 5L9
Canada
(613) 237-9300

DALLAS FESTIVAL OF ARTS AND JAZZ

Early September
Dallas, Texas
www.meifestivals.com/dalfest.html
Admission: $

If you spend Labor Day weekend at this festival in downtown Dallas, you can enjoy plenty of both shade and sunshine in City Hall Plaza. The Dallas Festival of Arts and Jazz is nearing its ten-year anniversary and can count artists such as Chaka Khan and the Fabulous Thunderbirds among its past performers. Come early—anyone who arrives before 6:00 P.M. gets in free.
For more information: mei@meifestivals.com
Camping: No
Accommodations

■ **Ramada Hotel Downtown**
1701 Commerce St.
Fort Worth, TX 76102
(817) 335-7000

■ **Holiday Inn Dallas Aristocrat**
1933 Main St.
Dallas, TX 75201
(800) 231-4235

DENVER BLUES & BONES

Two days in May
Denver, Colorado
www.denverfestivals.com/blues/blueshome.html
Admission: $

A Memorial Day weekend event that takes place just outside Mile High Stadium, the Blues & Bones festival takes its barbecue as seriously as it does its blues. In addition to a fine array of talent featuring folks such as Taj Mahal and Dr. John, this festival also provides a forum for any would-be barbecuers to flaunt their skills during the Backyard BBQ Challenge and the Mile High BBQ Championship.

For more information: piman@performanceintl.org
Camping: No
Accommodations

■ **Comfort Inn Downtown**
401 17th St.
Denver, CO 80202
(800) 221-2222

■ **Loews Hotel**
4150 E. Mississippi Ave.
Denver, CO 80246
(800) 235-6397

DOGWOOD BLUES FESTIVAL

Mid-April
Charlottesville, Virginia
www.cvilledowntown.org/blues.shtml
Admission: :FREE:

With barely five years of history behind it, the Dogwood Blues Festival is getting its sea legs fairly early. Originally just a collection of local all-stars getting together for a few nights of fun, the festival is gaining international status remarkably quickly now that artists such as Corey Harris and John Mayall are stopping by to perform. An old-fashioned chili cook-off and a Sunday morning gospel show ensure a good time will be had by all.

Camping: No

■ **Accommodations**
2000 Morton Dr.
Charlottesville, VA 22901
(800) 786-5400

■ **Best Western Cavalier Inn**
105 N. Emmett St.
Charlottesville, VA 22903
(434) 296-8111

DOHENY BLUES FESTIVAL

Two days in May
Dana Point, California
www.omegaevents.com/blues/index.html
Admission: $$–$$$

Doheny State Beach in southern California becomes home base for the blues for the duration of this two-day festival. Not far from Los Angeles, this locale provides a scenic backdrop for enjoying a great selection of earthy, soulful blues. Past performers have included Mavis Staples, Charlie Musselwhite, and Bobby "Blue" Bland. The festival offers a wide selection of foods and lawn seating only—so bring your wallet and a chair. A variety of local businesses and shops provide discounts for visitors; just be sure to keep your ticket stub if you want to shop around the town.

For more information: (949) 262-2662

Camping: Yes. Call (800) 444-PARK to reserve a spot at Doheny State Beach.

Accommodations

■ **Double Tree Hotel**
34402 Pacific Coast Hwy.
Dana Point, CA 92629
(949) 661-1100

■ **Harbor Inn**
25325 Dana Point Harbor Dr.
Dana Point, CA 92629
(949) 493-5001

FESTIBLUES INTERNATIONAL DE MONTRÉAL

Mid-August
Montreal, Quebec, Canada
www.festiblues.com
Admission: $$

The Festiblues International lures upwards of 60,000 people to its musically diverse events, which begin early in the day and stretch well into the night. Expect to see a mixture of blues veterans and young Canadian upstarts all vying for the audience's attention during this four-day festival.

For more information: info@festiblues.com

Camping: No

Accommodations

■ **Auberge Bonaparte**
447 St. François Xavier
Montreal, QC H2Y 1Z5
Canada
(514) 844-1448

■ **Hotel du Fort**
1390 rue du Fort
Montreal, QC H3H 2R7
Canada
(514) 938-8333

HARD KNOX BLUES FEST AND RIB COOK-OFF

June
Knoxville, Tennessee
Admission: *FREE*

This one-day festival in eastern Tennessee's Great Valley showcases a series of fine regional blues acts until the early evening. As if this weren't enough, the rib cook-off guarantees someone will come home with his or her very own "Big Rib" trophy to display on the mantel.

For more information: (865) 573-4042

Camping: No

Accommodations

■ **Knoxville Hilton**
501 W. Church Ave.
Knoxville, TN 37902-2591
(865) 523-2300

■ **Hyatt Regency**
500 Hill Ave. SE
Knoxville, TN 37915
(800) 233-1234

JULY JAMM

End of July
Lincoln, Nebraska
www.julyjamm.org
Admission: $

Three days of live music, fine food, and arts and crafts: this is what the Lincoln, Nebraska, July Jamm is all about. Guitarist Gary Hoey and blues favorites Roomful of Blues are some of the performers you can expect to hear on either the blues stage or the jazz stage.

Artist Submissions: rhawthorne@digitalims.com

Camping: No

Accommodations

■ **Chase Suites by Woodfin**
200 S. 68th
Lincoln, NE 68510
(402) 483-4900

■ **The Cornhusker**
333 S. 13th St.
Lincoln, NE 68508
(800) 793-7474

KALAMAZOO BLUES FESTIVAL

Mid-July
Kalamazoo, Michigan
www.kvba.org/fest02
Admission: $

Here we have three days of the blues in the fine town of Kalamazoo. The emphasis is on classic electric blues and blues-rock; regional acts take up the majority of the stage time. Workshops are offered, and Lobo the Hobo Clown will be on hand for face painting.

Camping: No

Accommodations

- Radisson Plaza Hotel at the
  Kalamazoo Center
100 W. Michigan Ave.
Kalamazoo, MI 49007
(616) 343-3333

- Best Western Hospitality Inn
3640 E. Cork St.
Kalamazoo, MI 49001
(616) 381-1900

KANSAS CITY BLUES & HERITAGE FESTIVAL

Two days in early April
Kansas City, Missouri
www.kcbluesandheritage.com
Admission: $$

This popular two-day event gathers together some of the most well-known and well-respected names in modern blues. You can expect to hear the likes of Robert Cray, Otis Rush, and John Mayall on the main stage. Some of the finest food in the Midwest will be available for concession for audience members relaxing out on the grass.

For more information: info@kcbluesandheritage.com
Camping: No
Accommodations

- Hyatt Regency Crown Center
2345 McGee St.
Kansas City, MO 64108
(816) 421-1234
http://crowncenter.hyatt.com

- Hotel Phillips
106 W. 12th St.
Kansas City, MO 64105
(816) 221-7000

LIMESTONE CITY BLUES FESTIVAL

End of August
Kingston, Ontario, Canada
www.kingstonblues.com
Admission: $

The Limestone City Blues Festival throws together big names such as Rod Piazza and the Holmes Brothers on a variety of different stages to create an atmosphere that combines daytime festival activities with nightclub entertainment. Visitors can relax in the sun during the day in Confederation Park or they can carouse through downtown Kingston's many bars and pubs, sampling a variety of blues-related evenings scheduled as a part of the festival.

For more information: downtown@kingston.org

Camping: No

Accommodations

■ **Howard Johnson Hotel Kingston**
237 Ontario St.
Kingston, ON K7L 2Z4
Canada
(613) 549-6300

■ **LaSalle Travelodge Hotel**
2360 Princess St.
Kingston, ON K7M 3G4
Canada
(800) 578-7878

MISSISSIPPI DELTA BLUES & HERITAGE FESTIVAL

Mid-September
Greenville, Mississippi
www.deltablues.org
Admission: $$

If anyone has the right to put together a blues festival, it's the folks at the Mississippi Delta Blues & Heritage Festival. The original artists from the Delta helped to define the genre as we know it today, and although most of those artists have long since passed on, their illegitimate sons and daughters continue to prosper. And for three days in Greenville, you can see it for yourself. The main stage usually features folks such as Robert Cray and Charlie Musselwhite, while the gospel stage brings the great American jubilee style to the masses with performances from legends such as the Mighty Clouds of Joy.

For more information: bluesfest@tecinfo.com

Camping: Yes. RV parking is allowed on-site.

Accommodations

■ **Comfort Inn Greenville**
3080 US 82 E.
Greenville, MS 38702
(662) 378-4976

■ **Fairfield Inn**
137 N. Walnut St.
Greenville, MS 38701
(662) 332-0508

MISSISSIPPI VALLEY BLUES FESTIVAL

Early July
Davenport, Iowa

www.mvbs.org/fest.htm

Admission: $$

Organized by the Mississippi Valley Blues Society, this yearly festival is dedicated to the pursuit of the best of the blues. The society also seeks to educate those who might not have a firm grasp on the topic, so they provide children with their own "BluesSkool" in addition to sponsoring artist-in-residency programs and publishing books. The event itself boasts three days of excellent food and top-notch performers (Sun Ra Arkestra, R.L. Burnside, and Susan Tedeschi have appeared in the past).

For more information: mvbs@revealed.net

Camping: No

Accommodations

■ **Abbey Hotel**
1401 Central Ave.
Bettendorf, IA 52722-6034
(563) 355-0291
www.theabbeyhotel.com

■ **Jumer's Castle Lodge**
900 Spruce Hills Dr.
Bettendorf, IA 52722-1698
(563) 359-7141
www.jumers.com/documents/
iowa-hotels.htm

♪ MOHICAN BLUES FESTIVAL

Mid-August

Loudonville, Ohio

www.mohicanentertainment.com

Admission: $

Set in the Mohican River Valley at the Mohican Reservation Camp Grounds, this lush region is perfect for those hoping to set up camp for a few days. Families are more than welcome to come and enjoy the laid-back atmosphere and competent musicianship. Nearby Mohican Castle provides shelter for those who enjoy a bit of the medieval with their bluesfests.

Artist Submissions

Mohican Entertainment Ltd.
316 Twp. Rd. 2352
Loudonville, OH 44842-9615
(419) 368-3090 or (877) NEW-FEST

For more information: info@mohicanbluesfestival.com

Camping: Yes. Call (800) 766-CAMP or visit www.mohicanreservation.com.

Accommodations

■ **Mohican River Inn**
16024 C. R. #23
Loudonville, OH 44842
(800) 228-5118
www.mohicanriverinn.com

■ **Landoll's Mohican Castle**
561 Twp. Rd. 3352
Loudonville, OH 44842
(800) 291-5001
www.landollsmohicancastle.com

MONTEREY BAY BLUES FESTIVAL

Late June
Monterey, California
www.montereyblues.com
Admission: $$$

The coastal city of Monterey provides a great background for this high-profile event. Three different stages present a wide variety of blues over the course of three days. With 17 years of event planning behind them, the folks who run the festival have the right idea when it comes to arranging the lineup. You can expect everything from the classic soul of the O'Jays and Teddy Pendergrass to blues staples such as John Mayall and Coco Montoya.

For more information: mbbf@montereyblues.com

Camping: No

Accommodations

■ **Best Western Monterey Beach Hotel**
2600 Sand Dunes Dr.
Monterey, CA 93940
(800) 242-8627

■ **Merritt House**
386 Pacific Ave.
Monterey, CA 93940
(831) 646-9686

NATCHEZ BLUFF BLUES FEST

End of April
Natchez, Mississippi
http://ncvb.natchez.ms.us/NATCHEZ%20BLUFF%20BLUES%20FEST.htm
Admission: FREE

Great food and great music abound at the Natchez Bluff Blues Festival. Located only a few hundred feet above the Mississippi River, Natchez is the oldest city on the river. This historic location provides a great backdrop for experiencing the many regional acts that provide music over this three-day weekend. As far as food goes, anyone with an inclination toward crawfish is likely to find much to rejoice over.

For more information: (601) 442-2988 or eglatzerl@aol.com

Camping: No

Accommodations

■ **Ramada Inn Hilltop**
130 John R. Junkin Dr.
Natchez, MS 39120
(888) 298-2054

■ **The Natchez Eola Hotel**
110 Pearl St.
Natchez, MS 39120
(601) 445-6000 or (866) 445-EOLA
eolahotel@natchezeola.com

♪ NATCHITOCHES JAZZ/R&B FESTIVAL

Early April
Natchitoches, Louisiana
www.natchitoches.net/jazzfest
Admission: $

The Natchitoches Jazz/R&B Fest, situated along the banks of the Cane River Lake, has welcomed down-home folk such as Irma Thomas, Percy Sledge, and Delbert McClinton to its stages. Gospel, soul, and a heap of authentic, southern-style blues play a large part in the all-day festivities. The event maintains a reasonable price and allows those under the age of 12 in free. All in all, if you're searching for a good introduction to both creole food and music, this is the place.

For more information: (800) 259-1714

Camping: No

Accommodations

■ **Days Inn**
1000 College Ave.
Natchitoches, LA 71457
(800) 544-8313

■ **Comfort Inn**
5362 SR 6 W.
Natchitoches, LA 71457
(318) 352-7500

♪ NORTH ATLANTIC BLUES FESTIVAL

Late July
Rockland, Maine
www.northatlanticbluesfestival.com
Admission: $$

This event, which takes place in Maine's Harbor Park, right above Rockland Harbor, combines daily outdoor stages with an evening club crawl for a mid-July weekend full of the blues. Expect a number of well-known acts like Susan Tedeschi, Pinetop Perkins, and Tab Benoit to mix in with acts from the New England area.

For more information: (207) 593-1189

Camping: No

Accommodations

■ **Limerock Inn**
96 Limerock St.
Rockland, ME 04841
(800) 546-3762

■ **Captain Lindsay House**
5 Lindsey St.
Rockland, ME 04841
(800) 523-2145

♪ PITTSBURGH BLUES FESTIVAL

Three days in July
Pittsburgh, Pennsylvania
www.pghblues.com
Admission: $

The Pittsburgh Blues Festival started off strong back in 1995 and has since grown into a well-respected, high-profile festival that attracts critically acclaimed artists such as Steve Earle, the Brian Setzer Orchestra, and South-side Johnny & the Asbury Jukes. The event is held each year at the Pittsburgh Brewing Company so you can expect an ample stream of the devil's bath-water to flow here.

For more information: (412) 460-BLUE

Camping: No

Accommodations

■ **Radisson Hotel Green Tree**
101 Radisson Dr.
Pittsburgh, PA 15205

■ **Country Inn & Suites**
5311 Campbells Run Rd.
Pittsburgh, PA 15205
(800) 456-4000

♪ POCONO BLUES FESTIVAL

Two days in early August
Lake Harmony, Pennsylvania

www.big2resorts.com/blues-festival-2003.asp
Admission: $$

Outdoor sports take the side stage for a few days in the Poconos while the blues take center stage. This award winning festival takes place at the Jack Frost Mountain and Big Boulder Resort and continually offers up an exhilarating lineup of blues mainstays such as Robert Cray and Clarence "Gatemouth" Brown while occasionally booking acts such as the recently rediscovered soul legend, Howard Tate. Those looking to do a little vicarious skiing can take a free ride on the chair lift, but please be advised that skiing in Pennsylvania in the summer might be a bit rugged.

For more information: (800) 468-2442
Camping: Yes. Call (570) 646-CAMP.
Accommodations

■ **Split Rock Resort**
One Lake Dr.
Lake Harmony, PA 18624
(717) 722-9111

■ **Ramada Inn**
Route 940 P.O. Box 809
Lake Harmony, PA 18624
(888) 298-2054

♪ PORT TOWNSEND BLUES AND HERITAGE FESTIVAL

Early August
Port Townsend, Washington
www.centrum.org/events/blues.html
Admission: $$

Port Townsend mixes things up a bit by providing daylong, open-air concert events along with plenty of shows at participating nightclubs that provide entertainment late into the night. The wharf downtown provides the setting for a free dance that's sure to kick the weekend off right. The daytime events promise plenty of traditional-style blues but since there's no reserved seating, plan on getting there early for the best spots.

For more information: peter@centrum.org
Camping: No
Accommodations

■ **Palace Hotel**
1004 Water St.
Port Townsend, WA 98368
(800) 962-0741

■ **Tides Inn**
1807 Water St.
Port Townsend, WA 98368
(800) 822-8696

QUEEN CITY BLUES FEST

Mid-July

Cincinnati, Ohio

http://cincyblues.org/fest.htm

Admission: FREE

The Queen City Blues Fest (QCBF), a free festival set along the banks of the Ohio River, is put together by a group of volunteers dedicated to blues preservation and education. The QCBF places an emphasis on family by providing a series of workshops for kids, setting up a high school art gallery dedicated to the blues, and much more. Adults can look forward to a lineup that usually draws acts like Alvin Youngblood Hart and Duke Robillard to the stage.

For more information: gcbs@compuserve.com

Camping: No

Accommodations

■ **Crown Plaza Hotel**
15 W. 6th St.
Cincinnati, OH 45202
(888) 279-8260

■ **Vernon Manor**
400 Oak St.
Cincinnati, OH 45219
(513) 281-3300

RED, WHITE & BLUES

Fourth of July weekend

Asheville, North Carolina

www.biltmore.com/visit/events/summer_holiday_weekends.html

Admission: $$

The Biltmore Estate Winery hosts this Fourth of July event, which is not just a celebration of America and the blues but of the art of winemaking as well. In addition to live performances, visitors can enjoy wine tasting and guided tours. There are plenty of activities to keep the kids busy, too.

For more information: (828) 255-1798

Camping: No

Accommodations

■ **American Court Motel**
85 Merrimon Ave.
Asheville, NC 28801
(828) 253-4427

■ **Albemarle Inn**
86 Edgemont Rd.
Asheville, NC 28801
(800) 621-7435

RITZVILLE BLUES FESTIVAL

July
Ritzville, Washington
www.ritzvilleblues.com
Admission: $$

The town of Ritzville turns very busy for one day each July. Beginning at noon, more than two dozen acts perform at more than seven different venues and don't stop until last call. Visitors can carouse around the local watering holes or just sit tight and enjoy the outdoor stage. Bo Diddley, Robert Junior Lockwood, and Charlie Musselwhite have all spent time at this event.

Artist Submissions
Ritzville Area Chamber of Commerce
W. 111 Main
Ritzville, WA 99169
For more information: info@ritzvilleblues.com
Camping: Yes. RV camping is available. Call (509) 659-1936 for details.
Accommodations

■ Best Inn & Suites
1513 Smitty's Blvd.
Ritzville, WA 99169
(509) 659-1007

■ Colwell Motor Inn
501 W. First Ave.
Ritzville, WA 99169
(506) 659-1620

RIVER CITY BLUES FESTIVAL

Mid-March
Marietta, Ohio
www.bjfm.org/bluesfestival.html
Admission: $–$$

A multitude of fine musicians use this two-day event to explore the many varieties of the blues. The River City Blues Festival has featured the old-time Piedmont sounds of Cephas & Wiggins as well as the ever-evolving Roomful of Blues.

For more information: bjfm@bjfm.org
Camping: No

Accommodations

■ **The Lafayette**
101 Front St.
Marietta, OH 45750
(740) 373-5522

■ **Econo Lodge**
702 Pike St.
Marietta, OH 45750
(740) 374-8481

♪ RIVERHEAD BLUES FESTIVAL

Three days in July
Riverhead, New York
www.riverheadblues.com
Admission: FREE

Billed as the largest musical event on Long Island, this free festival officially takes place over three days, but related events in the area last throughout the week. In addition to a parade and rides for the kids, Riverhead Blues Festival also offers educational workshops and a scenic blues cruise at sunset. You can expect to hear the excellent acoustic blues of Woody Mann and the classic blues-rock of Savoy Brown.

For more information: tgahan@optonline.net

Camping: No

Accommodations

■ **Budget Host Inn**
30 East Moriches Rd.
Riverhead, NY 11901
(516) 727-6200

■ **Best Western Riverhead East End**
1830 Route 25
Riverhead, NY 11901
(631) 369-2200

♪ ROCHESTER MUSIC FEST

Mid-July
Rochester, New York
http://rochestermusicfest.com
Admission: $$

This weeklong extravaganza takes place all over Rochester and mixes contemporary R&B with soul greats and international rock acts. A bevy of contemporary artists of faith kicked off the 2002 event in a gospel celebration in Highland Park. Ashanti, Al Green, the Isley Brothers, and the Smithereens also took to the stage.

For more information: mdonovan@rbtl.org

Camping: No
Accommodations

■ **Four Points Sheraton**
120 E. Main St.
Rochester, NY 14604
(888) 596-6400

■ **Rochester Riverside Hotel**
120 Main St.
East Rochester, NY 14604
(585) 546-6400

RUSSIAN RIVER BLUES FESTIVAL

Late June
Guerneville, California
www.russianriverbluesfest.com/blues
Admission: $$–$$$

The Russian River Blues Festival is a must-see for those who enjoy the beauty of the outdoors mixed in with their slide guitar. The city of Guerneville is found right in the middle of the northern California redwoods, and the fest itself takes place along the river that gives it its name. Bring a camera and get ready to enjoy a premiere selection of artists like Robert Cray and Bobby "Blue" Band.

For more information: rrfestivals@rcn.com
Camping: No
Accommodations

■ **Rio Inn**
4444 Wood Rd.
Guerneville, CA 95446
(800) 344-7018

■ **Ridenhour Ranch House Inn**
12850 River Rd.
Guerneville, CA 95446
(888) 877-4466

SALMON ARM ROOTS AND BLUES FESTIVAL

Mid-August
Salmon Arm, British Columbia, Canada
www.rootsandblues.ca
Admission: $$$

It's been around for more than 10 years, but the Salmon Arm Roots and Blues Festival has made some major inroads in the past few years. The festival takes on the appearance of a small village for three days every summer now that it's relocated to an outdoor venue. Five stages provide ample entertainment, and a variety of craftspeople and cooks provide arts and nourishment.

For more information: safms@sunwave.net

Camping: Yes. Contact (877) 725-6667 for more information.

Accommodations

■ **Best Western Villager West Motor Inn**
61 10th St. SW
Salmon Arm, BC V1E 1E4
Canada
(800) 528-1234

■ **Holiday Inn Express Salmon Arms**
1090-22nd St. NE
Salmon Arm, BC V1E 2V5
Canada
(250) 832-7711

♩ SAN FRANCISCO BLUES FESTIVAL

End of September
San Francisco, California
www.sfblues.com
Admission: $$

The San Francisco Blues Festival is a massive gathering in San Francisco's posh Marina District on the grounds of Fort Mason, down by Fisherman's Wharf. Five stages bustle with nearly constant musical activity over the course of what can be a hot weekend in the Bay Area's unpredictable but enjoyable fall weather. The aroma of food from the four corners of the earth (even vegans eat well in San Francisco!) fills the air as this municipal institution gains momentum. Lesser-known bluesmen work the crowd in the afternoon, but the heavyweights come out in the evening to bring the house down.

At the 2002 festival, long-missing soul singer Howard Tate gave a devastating set that culminated with his heartbreaking version of "Get It While You Can," a song made famous by Janis Joplin but never rendered as beautifully as it was on that day. Other highlights include James Cotton's truly smoking harmonica playing and classic rock's elder statesman Steve Miller playing a full set of spaced-out boogie. Over the years, Etta James, Albert Collins, and Taj Mahal have all played the San Franciso Blues Festival as well.

For more information: (415) 979-5588

Camping: No

Accommodations

■ **Hayes Valley Hotel**
417 Gough St.
San Francisco, CA 94102
(415) 431-9131

■ **Layne Hotel**
545 Jones St.
San Francisco, CA 94102
(415) 441-9317

■ **Inn on Castro**
321 Castro St.
San Francisco, CA 94114
(415) 861-0321

SANTA CRUZ BLUES FESTIVAL

End of May
Aptos, California
www.santacruzbluesfestival.com
Admission: $$

The Santa Cruz Blues Festival, already ten years in the running, usually brings about 3,000 people to this coastal town and into the redwood-spotted natural amphitheater where the fest is held every Memorial Day weekend. Tommy Castro, Koko Taylor, and Dr. John are just some of the musical guests you can hope to see in this beautiful setting.

For more information: info@santacruzbluesfestival.com

Camping: Camping is not available on-site, but many of the surrounding beaches provide overnight tent camping spots. Call (831) 763-7063 for information.

Accommodations

■ **Apple Lane Inn**
6265 Soquel Dr.
Aptos, CA 95003
(800) 649-8988

■ **Bayview Hotel**
8041 Soquel Dr.
Aptos, CA 95003
(800) 422-9843

SOUND ADVICE BLUES FESTIVAL

Three days in early November
Fort Lauderdale, Florida
Admission: $

The beginning of November signals the annual Sound Advice Blues Festival in Fort Lauderdale. For the past thirteen years, the festival has put together a creative lineup that places as much emphasis on nationally touring artists as it does the local heroes. Alvin Youngblood Hart and New Orleans favorite Tab Benoit are a few of the names you can expect on the main stage.

For more information: debbied@ci.fort-lauderdale.fl.us

Camping: No

Accommodations

- **Hampton Inn Cypress Creek**
720 East Cypress Creek Rd.
Fort Lauderdale, FL 33309
(954) 776-7677

- **La Quinta Inn Cypress Creek**
999 W Cypress Creek Rd.
Fort Lauderdale, Florida 33309
(954) 491-7666

SOUTH LOUP RIVER BLUES AND BARBEQUE

One day in July
Arnold, Nebraska
www.custercounty.com/blues
Admission: $

Held on the second Saturday of July, the South Loup festival takes place in Old Mill Park in Custer County, Nebraska. The beautiful outdoor setting is sometimes prone to unpredictable summer storms, so be prepared to move the party inside at a moment's notice. But, for one day, this scenic valley is home to an equally unpredictable mixture of renowned touring and regional blues acts.

For more information: kcnikbbn@neb-sandhills.net
Camping: No
Accommodations

- **Hotel Custer**
Hwy. 92
Arnold, NE 69120
(308) 848-3394

- **Arnold Motel and Trailer Court**
307 Hillcrest St.
Arnold, NE 69120
(308) 848-2223

SPRINGING THE BLUES FESTIVAL

First weekend in April
Jacksonville Beach, Florida
www.springingtheblues.com
Admission: FREE

This free three-day festival is widely regarded as one of the most popular in the country. Its oceanside views and dedication to the arts make this event a must-see for anyone visiting Florida during the first weekend of April. Past performers have included Clarence "Gatemouth" Brown, Coco Montoya, and Joe Turner. In addition to the actual festival, several clubs and restaurants in the area offer late-night events and blues brunches.

For more information: saveal@bellsouth.net

Camping: Yes. Camping is available five miles north of the festival grounds. Call (904) 249-4700 for details.

Accommodations

- **Sea Turtle Inn**
1 Ocean Blvd.
Atlantic Beach, FL 32233
(904) 249-7402

- **Seahorse Oceanfront Inn**
120 Atlantic Blvd.
Neptune Beach, FL 32266
(904) 246-2175

TAMPA BAY BLUES FESTIVAL

First weekend in April
St. Petersburg, Florida
www.tampabaybluesfest.com
Admission: $$

Some of the finest beaches in the United States act as a backdrop for this three-day blues festival. The event usually begins on a Friday night, with all-day concerts taking place over the weekend in scenic Vinoy Park. Past performers include the likes of Koko Taylor, the Fabulous Thunderbirds, and Charlie Musselwhite.

For more information: Editor@TampaBayBluesFest.com

Camping: No

Accommodations

- **Sunset Bay Inn**
635 Bay St. NE
St. Petersburg, FL 33701
(727) 896-6701

- **Holiday Inn**
11908 Gulf Blvd.
St. Petersburg, FL 33706
(727) 367-2761

TELLURIDE BLUES AND BREWS FESTIVAL

Mid-September
Telluride, Colorado
www.tellurideblues.com
Admission: $

You'd be hard-pressed to find a more scenic location for musical enjoyment than the Rocky Mountains. Visitors can call this amazing backdrop home for three days while they soak up the eclectic music mix and imbibe liquid refreshments from 50 of the finest local microbreweries. If you're staying in the Mountain Village, you should take advantage of the free gondola rides that will carry you to the festival site.

A word to the wise for those with pets: don't bring them. Thinking about bringing a Frisbee? Well, don't do that either.

For more information: info@tellurideblues.com

Camping: Yes. Call (866) 515-6166 to reserve a spot.

Accommodations

■ **The Ice House Lodge**
310 S. Fir
P.O. Box 2909
Telluride, CO 81435
(800) 544-3436

■ **Telluride Mountainside Inn**
333 S. Davis St., Box 2288
Telluride, CO 81435
(888) 728-1950
www.telluridemtnsideinn.com

♪ VANCOUVER ISLAND BLUES BASH

Labor Day weekend
Victoria, British Columbia, Canada
www.vicjazz.bc.ca/bluesbash
Admission: FREE

Help give a hearty farewell send-off to the summer at this weekend bash in Victoria's Inner Harbor in British Columbia. Although the main events in the evening require a paid ticket, the afternoon's festivities are as free as free can get. You can expect a fine blend of hard-hitting, old-fashioned R&B and electric blues. And as for food, Pescatore's Fish House makes sure attendees are stuffed to the gills with gills.

Artist Submissions
Darryl Mar, Program Director
Victoria Jazz Society
#250-727 Johnson St.
Victoria, BC V8W 1M9
Canada

Camping: No

Accommodations
642 Johnson St.
Victoria, BC V8W 1M6
Canada
(800) 663-7241

The Cherry Bank
825 Burdett Ave.
Victoria, BC V8W 1B3
Canada
(250) 385-5380

W. C. HANDY BLUES & BARBECUE FESTIVAL

Four days in June
Henderson, Kentucky
www.handyblues.org
Admission: *FREE*

Named after the man many consider to be the father of the blues, the W. C. Handy Blues & Barbecue Festival features musical tributes along with dance workshops and lectures on ragtime and stride piano. A multitude of family-oriented activities are held all week long, and a weekend bash winds things up with a plethora of national touring acts. Past performers have included Leon Redbone, Son Seals, and John Hammond.

Artist Submissions: (270) 827-1852
Camping: No
Accommodations

■ **Days Inn**
2044 US 41 N.
Henderson, KY 42420
(502) 826-6600

■ **Sleep Inn**
2224 US 41 N.
Henderson, KY 42420
(270) 830-6500

W. C. HANDY MUSIC FESTIVAL

July–August
Florence, Alabama
www.wchandyfest.com
Admission: $$

It was in Florence, Alabama, in 1876 that the father of the blues was born. And not too far from here, along the banks of the Tennessee River, W. C. Handy was probably first exposed to the folk songs that would course through his veins for the rest of his life. That William Christopher Handy was able to harness the essence of this tradition, put it into written form, and create songs such as "St. Louis Blues" and "Beale Street Blues" is not lost on the people of Florence. This weeklong celebration commemorates his contributions to the blues with a variety of events that range from musical performances to family-oriented barbecues to 5K races.

For more information: cdi@cdiweb.net
Camping: No

Accommodations

■ **Budget Inn**
1238 Florence Blvd.
Florence, AL 35630
(256) 764-7621

■ **The Cove Cottage Guest House**
102 W. Grandview Dr.
Muscle Shoals, AL 35661
(256) 314-4401

WATERFRONT BLUES FESTIVAL

Fourth of July weekend
Portland, Oregon
www.waterfrontbluesfest.com
Admission: $

This Pacific Northwest festival began in 1987 and usually takes place over the Fourth of July weekend. In addition to being a fine festival for blues fans, the event works in tandem with the Oregon Food Bank project, collecting food and money for hunger relief. Since its inception, the festival has raised more than one million dollars and donated over half a million pounds of food. Aside from the charity work, the festival itself is remarkable. It gathers blues notables such as Solomon Burke and Otis Rush along with young upstarts such as Johnny Lang to woo the crowds.

Artist Submissions: damray@europa.com
For more information: postoffice@oregonfoodbank.org
Camping: No
Accommodations

■ **RiverPlace Hotel**
1510 SW Harbor Way
Portland, OR 97201
(800) 227-1333
www.riverplacehotel.com

■ **Mallory Hotel**
729 SW 15th Ave.
Portland, OR 97205
(800) 228-8657

WESTERN MARYLAND BLUES FESTIVAL

End of May
Hagerstown, Maryland
www.blues-fest.org
Admission: $

Expect a mixture of high-profile and regional blues acts when visiting this event in historic Hagerstown (originally formed in 1762). Tourists and die-hard blues fans alike will be entertained when artists such as Blind Boys of Alabama, Hubert Sumlin, and Eddie Shaw take the stage. This festival normally takes place the weekend after Memorial Day, so you can expect large crowds—friendly, blues-loving crowds, to be sure.

For more information: kmg01@hagerstownmd.org

Camping: No

Accommodations

■ **Hampton Inn**
1716 Dual Hwy.
Hagerstown, MD 21740-6635
(301) 739-6100

■ **Motel 6**
11321 Massey Blvd.
Hagerstown, MD 21740
(I-81 at Exit #5/Halfway Boulevard)
(301) 582-4445

WINTHROP RHYTHM AND BLUES FESTIVAL

Three days in July
Winthrop, Washington
www.winthropbluesfestival.com
Admission: $$

The Winthrop Rhythm and Blues Festival, which actually takes place one mile outside the rustic town of Winthrop, has been going strong for more than 15 years. Former Rolling Stone Mick Taylor, the Blind Boys of Alabama, and Percy Sledge are just a few of the names that have graced the stages here. A street dance usually kicks off the festival, and, according to many festival-goers, it's usually one of the highlights of the weekend. The festival does allow on-site camping, so plan ahead.

For more information: carol@nwblues.com

Camping: Yes. Contact (877) 202-2999 for more information.

Accommodations

■ **Best Western Cascade Inn**
960 Hwy. 20
Winthrop, WA 98862
(800) 468-6754

■ **Sun Mountain Lodge**
Patterson Lake Rd.
Winthrop, WA 98862
(800) 572-0493

CLASSICAL, EARLY, CHAMBER, and CONTEMPORARY

2

♪ AMHERST EARLY MUSIC FESTIVAL

July–August
Location changes from year to year
www.amherstearlymusic.org
Admission: $

The Amherst Early Music Festival is a weekend of educational workshops with instruction in voice, viola, recorder, and harpsichord. The faculty presents a concert on the final night of the weekend. The festival travels to a different location each year (in 2002 it was held at the University of Connecticut), so check the Web site or call the front office for details.

For more information: (617) 744-1324 or info@amherstearlymusic.org
Camping: No
Accommodations: Provided with registration

♪ ARAB MUSIC FESTIVAL

November
Cairo, Egypt
Admission: $$

The newly renovated Cairo Opera House, located on an island in the middle of the Nile River, hosts this festival of traditional Arabic music, classical music, opera, and ballet. Orchestras, choirs, dance companies, and ensembles from the Middle East and beyond perform here each year.

For more information: (20) 2-339-8144 or info@cairooperahouse.org

Camping: No

Accommodations: See www.cairotourist.com.

 ## ASPEN MUSIC FESTIVAL

Mid-June to mid-August

Aspen, Colorado

http://aspenmusicfestival.com

Admission: $$–$$$

More than 200 concerts and other performances, featuring everything from orchestral standards to obscure works by medieval composers, are presented over the course of this nine-week summer celebration of classical music. Operas, contemporary premieres, symphonies, and concertos are complemented by lectures, classes, and workshops. In addition to these events, the daily concerts that take place at the Benedict Music Tent are, for the most part, free. The Aspen Music Festival is now more than 50 years old and has become one of the most prestigious festivals of its kind in the world. Each year it attracts the most distinguished guest conductors, symphony orchestras, and ensembles.

For more information: (970) 925-3254 or festival@aspenmusicfestival.org

Camping: No

Accommodations

■ **Alpine Lodge**
1240 E. Cooper St.
Aspen, CO 81611
(970) 925-7351

■ **Aspen Bed & Breakfast**
311 W. Main St.
Aspen, CO 81611
(970) 925-7650

■ **Aspen Alps**
P.O. Box 1228
Aspen, CO 81611
(970) 925-7820

ATHENS FESTIVAL

May–September

Athens, Greece

www.greekfestival.gr

Admission: $$$

For five months the Odeon of Herodes Atticus (the ancient, open-air amphitheater that is a major Greek destination in and of itself) plays host to a series of summer concerts. And the stakes just keep getting higher—at least when there's no danger of an appearance by Yanni. Instead, you'll be treated to classical and contemporary music, along with presentations of operas, ballets, and Shakespearean plays.

Artist Submissions: artisticdirector@greekfestival.gr

For more information: (30) 210-928-2900 or pr@greekfestival.gr

Camping: No

Accommodations

■ Athens Cypria Hotel

Diomias 5

Syntagma

Athens, Greece

(30) 01-323-8038

AUSTIN CHAMBER MUSIC FESTIVAL

Three weeks between June and July

Austin, Texas

www.austinchambermusic.org

Admission: *FREE*–$$$

Nine concerts, many of them free, are given at the Austin Chamber Music Center during June and July every year. You'll hear chamber music from all periods performed by the likes of the Austin Quartet and the current artist in residence (past artists in residence have included the Arundel Trio).

For more information: (512) 454-7562 or info@austinchambermusic.org

Camping: No

Accommodations

■ A B & R Corporate Suites

11902 Tobler Trl.

Austin, TX 78753

(512) 832-9592

■ Austin Chariot Resort Inn

7300 N. I H 35

Austin, TX 78753

(512) 452-9371

■ Austin Center

700 San Jacinto Blvd.

Austin, TX 78753

(512) 476-8423

BACH FESTIVAL

Fall, winter, and spring
Philadelphia, Pennsylvania
www.bach-fest.org
Admission: $$

The Bach Festival of Philadelphia brings together critically acclaimed classical musicians from around the world to perform a month of concerts. Their primary focus is celebrating the genius of baroque composer Johann Sebastian Bach, but they also touch on works by his followers and peers, such as Wolfgang Amadeus Mozart. Concerts are given at a number of churches and auditoriums throughout the city. Past festivals have featured Dutch cellist Anner Bylsma performing Bach's suites for solo cello and organist Michael Gailit performing the Toccata and Fugue in D Minor (arguably Bach's most popular composition).

For more information: bach@bach-fest.org
Camping: No
Accommodations

■ **Chestnut Hill Hotel**
8229 Germantown Ave.
Philadelphia, PA 19118
(215) 242-5905

■ **Best Western Center City**
501 N. 22nd St.
Philadelphia, PA 19130
(215) 568-8300

■ **Korman Suites Hotel**
2001 Hamilton St.
Philadelphia, PA 19130
(215) 569-7000

BARD MUSIC FESTIVAL

August
Annandale-on-Hudson, New York
www.bard.edu/bmf
Admission: $$

For years the Bard Music Festival was held outdoors on the campus of Bard College in New York. Many faithful attendees will undoubtedly be glad to hear that the festival has finally secured its own indoor venue, the Bard Performing Arts Center, thus eliminating the many trials that can befall an outdoor event (weather, mosquitoes, etcetera). Others may miss the sense of adventure past festivals had due to nature's unpredictability, but no one can deny the quality of each year's program selection and the skill of the school's orchestras. This is one of America's premier festivals and well worth attending.

For more information: (845) 758-7410 or bmf@bard.edu

Camping: No

Accommodations

■ **Joslen Motor Lodge**
320 Joslen Blvd.
Hudson, NY 12534
(518) 828-7046

■ **Sunset Motel**
P.O. Box 47
Hudson, NY 12534
(518) 851-3721

■ **St. Charles Hotel**
16 Park Pl.
Hudson, NY 12534
(518) 822-9900

BEETHOVEN FESTIVAL

One day in September
Oyster Bay, New York
www.friendsofthearts.com/beethoven
Admission: $$

In 2002 this Oyster Bay festival unveiled a Beethoven symphony that had never been heard before, an event that will probably never be repeated. The symphony was culled from unfinished orchestral transcriptions and completed by pianist Dalit Warshaw. This full day of Beethoven appreciation includes access to historical buildings on the grounds of Planting Fields Arboretum State Historic Park.

For more information: (516) 922-0061 or info@friendsofthearts.com

Camping: No

Accommodations

■ **Oyster Bay Manor**
150 South St.
Oyster Bay, NY 11771
(516) 624-0600

BEIJING MUSIC FESTIVAL

End of October/early November
Beijing, China
www.bmf.org.cn
Admission: $$–$$$

The first annual Beijing Music Festival was held in 1998 and originally show-cased China's wealth of opera talent. In subsequent years the festival has cultivated a more diverse program with performances ranging from piano concertos to jazz concerts to traditional ceremonial music. You can expect to hear large ensembles, soloists, and even vocal groups like the Swingle Singers.

For more information: editor@bmf.org.cn

Camping: No

Accommodations

■ **King Wing Hot Spring Hotel**
17 Nanlu of Dong
Sanhuan Chaoyang, Beijing
China
(86) 10-6766-8866

■ **China World Hotel**
No. 1 Jian Guo Men Wai Ave.
Beijing 1000004
China
(86) 10-6505-2266
cwh@shangri-la.com

BERKELEY FESTIVAL & EXHIBITION

One week in early June
Berkeley, California
http://bfx.berkeley.edu/bfx
Admission: $$

The Berkeley Festival & Exhibition features panel discussions and meet-and-greets with instrument craftsmen and musicians in addition to a full week of concerts given at the Zellerbach Hall on the UC Berkeley campus.

For more information: tickets@calperfs.berkeley.edu

Camping: No

Accommodations

■ **California Motel**
1461 University Ave.
Berkeley, CA 94702
(510) 848-3840

BERMUDA FESTIVAL OF THE PERFORMING ARTS

January to March
Bermuda
www.bermudafestival.com
Admission: $$–$$$

Classical, jazz, world, and folk music, dance exhibitions, and other performing arts are featured in concerts at venues all over the island during this two-month event.

For more information: (441) 295-1291
Camping: No
Accommodations
■ **Bermuda Tourist Office**
(441) 292-0023
tourbox@ibl.bm

BLOOMINGTON EARLY MUSIC FESTIVAL

Ten days in May
Bloomington, Indiana
www.blemf.org/index.htm
Admission: $$

In addition to offering opera performances and concerts of musical selections culled from both early and baroque periods, the Bloomington Early Music Festival has also been known to show films about the kind of music featured during the weekend. In 2002, Henry Purcell's semi-opera *King Arthur* was staged and the award-winning film *Nine German Arias: An Urban Baroque Film* was shown. Workshops are given throughout the weekend.

For more information: (812) 331-1263 or office@blemf.org
Camping: No
Accommodations

■ **Hampton Inn**
2100 N. Walnut St.
Bloomington, IN 47404
(812) 334-2100

■ **University Plaza Hotel**
1710 Kinser Pk.
Bloomington, IN 47401
(812) 334-3252 or (888) 406-4262

■ **Quality Inn**
1100 W. Rappel Dr.
Bloomington, IN 47404
(812) 323-2222

We caught up with ALAIN BARKER, executive director of the Bloomington Early Music Festival, just a couple days before the 2002 BEMF was scheduled to kick off. Although he was a bit harried, he was kind enough to answer some questions about the BEMF and festivals in general for us. In addition to acting as executive director of the festival, Barker is a trained musician, and he performs frequently both on and off the Indiana University campus.

Why the hell would you want to organize a music festival?

As a student of classical music and a professional performer (I've played in South Africa, England, and the United States), I found myself questioning the way the genre was being presented. I often felt that the experience of performing the music didn't gel with the way it was being promoted. Somehow, there was a disconnect between the ever changing and deeply meaningful relationship I had with the music and the staid and predictable way the music was being presented to audiences and the general public. In 1994, just as the Bloomington Early Music Festival started, I felt a need to involve myself in the promotion and production of classical music in an effort to experiment with new ways of presenting. The festival was looking for an executive director at the time—and the rest is history!

What is it about the music that inspires you to keep doing this?

Early music is a fascinating field that is continually reinventing itself. Very little is taken for granted in the field, and the musicians who perform it approach their art with an uncommon freshness. The music itself can be stunningly beautiful.

What do you mean by saying, "very little is taken for granted in the field?" That the styles of playing aren't as "set" as they are for playing Mozart or Beethoven?

That's partly right, although the field of early music covers Mozart and Beethoven too. In the early music field, historically informed performances continue to uncover technical, stylistic, and instrumental aspects of music that bring new life to what we're doing. The "modern" performance field tends to stay within interpretive styles for longer; more is taken for granted there.

What is the hardest part?

Finding the money to pay for the projects. This involves building a support base of individual contributors and businesses that would be in a position to underwrite the festival.

Is it worth it?

Absolutely. I wouldn't be in the field if I thought otherwise—especially with the remuneration available in the arts.

How much chance does an unknown performer/composer have of performing in some capacity at your festival?

We are very interested to know about emerging artists in the early music field and make a special effort to have them perform in the festival. We also include a number of students in our opera and orchestra productions, which gives them an opportunity to work with the invited professionals. Emerging composers who use elements of early music in their scores or instrumentation have also been featured in our festival.

Do any of the proceeds from the festival go to charity or a cause?

As a not-for-profit public organization, we consider the festival itself a charity and receive contributions from individuals, businesses, and foundations who believe in supporting the arts.

What are the three things you think set your festival apart from other festivals?

Innovation: We are very supportive of projects that push the envelope on what constitutes early music.

Diversity: We like to support as much difference in our performances as possible. We often include concerts that reveal early music concepts in nonwestern cultures.

Inclusiveness: We like to present upcoming talents alongside seasoned professionals. This is different from the way other festivals are organized around the country. In a field that is continually questioning the interpretation of style and technique, it makes sense to do so. Especially since part of our mission as a festival is to nurture young talent.

What is the strangest thing you've ever seen at your festival?

The "Genius of Winter" bass solo in the performance of Henry Purcell's semi-opera *King Arthur* at the 2002 festival. I'd never heard a singer sound as if he were a piece of ice before. The music depicts frozen notes unlike anything I would have thought possible.

Is there a particular performance from over the years that sticks out as a personal favorite for you?

Stanley Ritchie (baroque violinist extraordinaire) playing Vivaldi's concerto *The Four Seasons*. Ritchie is a poet unlike any other on the baroque violin. His talents combined with a wonderful score such as *The Four Seasons* gave our audiences an unforgettable treat.

What advice would you give to potential festival organizers?

If you have a concept that you really believe in, it will probably work. The one thing that usually stops a concept from becoming reality is a lack of consistency and follow-through. The implementation of a good idea is always much more difficult (and important) than the idea itself.

What hopes do you have for the festival's future?

I look forward to the Bloomington Early Music Festival establishing itself as one of the most important and interesting festivals in the midwestern United States. There are established, world-class festivals on the East and West Coasts (in Boston and Berkeley, respectively). I hope that, with our growing local and regional audiences, the Bloomington Early Music Festival will soon become a must-see for many who attend the other festivals.

BOSTON EARLY MUSIC FESTIVAL

Ongoing
Boston, Massachusetts
www.bemf.org
Admission: $$

With a concert series that runs practically year round, a tradition of excellence that goes back nearly a hundred years, and one of the most lauded symphony orchestras in the world, Boston is considered by many to be the center of the classical music universe. Each year the Boston Early Music Festival offers innumerable performances highlighting the music of the medieval, Renaissance, and baroque periods, often unearthing rare operas and obscure composers. The 2003 festival concentrated on Germany and included a staging of Johann Georg Conradi's opera *Ariadne* (1691).

For more information: (617) 661-1812 or david@bemf.org
Camping: No
Accommodations

■ **463 Beacon Street Guest House**
463 Beacon St.
Boston, MA 02115
(617) 536-1302

■ **Alexander Hotel**
15 Beacon St.
Boston, MA 02108
(617) 723-0323

■ **Bed & Breakfast Agency–Boston**
47 Commercial Wharf
Boston, MA 02110
(617) 720-3540

BUDAPEST SPRING FESTIVAL

Late March
Budapest, Hungary
Admission: $$

Traditional Hungarian folk music, classical music, film, arts, and dance are all celebrated during this two-week festival, the largest annual event in Hungary. The entire city opens its doors for the occasion: performances run almost around the clock in various locations and the streets blossom into an Eastern European marketplace. Ensembles and performers are primarily Hungarian but acts from abroad appear each year as well.

For more information: (36) 061-210-8301 or tickets@fesztivalvaros.hu

Camping: No

Accommodations

■ **Hungary Tourist Office**

(36) 01-355-1133

htbudapest@hungarytourism.hu

 ## CABRILLO FESTIVAL OF CONTEMPORARY MUSIC

End of July–early August
Santa Cruz, California
www.cabrillomusic.org
Admission: $$$

Lovely seaside Santa Cruz, California, hosts the Cabrillo Festival of Contemporary Music each year. The focus here is on contemporary music by artists such as Steve Reich, Mark Adamo, and Thea Musgrave. The program includes music, multimedia events, and educational workshops.

For more information: (831) 426-6966 or info@cabrillomusic.org

Camping: No

Accommodations

■ **Babbling Brook Bed & Breakfast**
1025 Laurel St.
Santa Cruz, CA 95060
(831) 427-2437

■ **Beach View Inn**
50 Front St.
Santa Cruz, CA 95060
(831) 426-3575

■ **Beach RV Park**
2505 Portola Dr.
Santa Cruz, CA 95062
(831) 462-2505

CARMEL BACH FESTIVAL

July
Carmel, California
www.bachfestival.org/home/frame.php
Admission: $$

A month of concerts and special performances highlighting the great composers (Mozart, Hayden, Bach) is held in beautiful Carmel, a favorite tourist destination on the California coast. The schedule of music will appeal to the larger body of classical music fans rather than the more specialized listener. Maestro Bruno Weil, a former student of Herbert von Karajan, has directed the festival for the past twenty years.

For more information: (831) 624-2046

Camping: No

Accommodations

■ **Adobe Inn Carmel**
P.O. Box 4115
Carmel, CA 93921
(831) 624-3933

■ **Candle Light Inn**
P.O. Box 1900
Carmel, CA 93921
(408) 624-6451

■ **Briarwood Inn**
P.O. Box 5245
Carmel, CA 93921
(831) 626-9056

♪ CENTRUM'S PORT TOWNSEND WINTER CHAMBER MUSIC FESTIVAL

Early February
Fort Worden State Park, Port Townsend, Washington
www.centrum.org/events/wchamber.html
Admission: $$

The music of Beethoven, Debussy, Brahms, and other major composers fills the stately Joseph F. Wheeler Theater each winter in the lovely coastal town of Port Townsend, Washington. In 2003 Cypress String Quartet of San Francisco was the festival's honored guest, and they performed selections from Haydn and Dvořák. In addition to the concerts, lectures are given by composers, conductors, and musicians.

For more information: (800) 733-3608 or (360) 385-5320

Camping: No

Accommodations

■ **Aladdin Motor Inn**
2333 Washington St.
Port Townsend, WA 98368
(360) 385-3747

■ **Port Townsend Inn**
2020 Washington St.
Port Townsend, WA 98368
(360) 385-2211 or (800) 216-4985

■ **Valley View Motel**
162 Hwy. 20
Port Townsend, WA 98368
(360) 385-1666 or (800) 280-1666

CHELTENHAM INTERNATIONAL FESTIVAL OF MUSIC

Three weeks in July
Cheltenham, United Kingdom
www.cheltenhamfestivals.co.uk
Admission: $$

For almost the entire month of July each year the city of Cheltenham is transformed into a bustling center for classical music. The celebration includes live performances, lectures, and workshops. Classical musicians from all over the world make the pilgrimage to Cheltenham to give concerts that represent a whole spectrum of periods and forms, ranging from operas to arias to concerti to works for solo instruments. The rambunctious Fringe Festival, which showcases street performers, clowns, and artists alongside nationally recognized pop, folk, and jazz acts, runs concurrently with the music festival. This is a giant event in England and has been well organized and well received every year since its inception.

For more information: JaneEg@Cheltenham.gov.uk
Camping: No
Accommodations

■ **Beechworth Lawn Hotel**
Cheltenham, Gloucestershire
  GL52 6ST
United Kingdom
(44) 1-242-522-583

■ **Stretton Lodge Hotel**
Western Road
Cheltenham, Gloucestershire
  GL50 3RN
United Kingdom
(44) 1-242-570-771

DUBLIN INTERNATIONAL ORGAN AND CHORAL FESTIVAL

Nine days in June
Christ Church Cathedral, Dublin, Ireland
www.dublinorganfestival.com
Admission: $$

The purpose of the Dublin International Organ and Choral Festival is simple: to bring organ music to the forefront of the Dublin early music scene for a full week. Choral concerts supplement the wide variety of virtuoso organ performances, and the special programs geared for children are a plus for families. A combination of local talent and distinguished musicians from abroad perform in a dozen different historic chapels and auditoriums around the city.

For more information: (353) 1-633-7392 or organs@diocf.iol.ie

Camping: No

Accommodations: www.visitdublin.com

FESTIVAL OF CLASSICAL MUSIC AT ST. BARRAHANE'S CHURCH

July–August

Castletownshend, County Cork, Ireland

http://homepage.eircom.net/~barrahane

Admission: $

This is a small, local classical music festival that concentrates on the talents of young artists and students from nearby Cork School of Music.

For more information: (353) 283-6193 or barrahane@eircom.net

Camping: No

Accommodations

▪ Tourist Information Offices, Cork City

(353) 0-214-273-251

FESTIVAL OF CONTEMPORARY MUSIC AT LOUISIANA STATE UNIVERSITY

Mid-February

Baton Rouge, Louisiana

http://festival.music.lsu.edu

Admission: $

The Louisiana State University Symphony Orchestra and its student and faculty ensembles perform a mix of original and traditional music during this four-day event. All manner of contemporary music is represented, and each year a different contemporary composer is appointed Director of the

Festival. The guest composer works with students and faculty during the week and shows his or her work throughout the festival.

For more information: (225) 578-5128 or sdbeck@lsu.edu

Camping: No

Accommodations

■ **Alamo Plaza Motel**
4243 Florida Blvd.
Baton Rouge, LA 70806
(225) 924-7231

■ **Brown's Motel**
2531 Airline Hwy.
Baton Rouge, LA 70805
(225) 355-7641

■ **Bellemont Hotel**
7370 Airline Hwy.
Baton Rouge, LA 70805
(504) 357-8612

FEZ FESTIVAL OF WORLD SACRED MUSIC

June–August
Fez, Morocco
www.fezfestival.org
Admission: $$$

The ancient walled city of Fez, in the international crossroads that is Morocco, is the setting for this month-long series of exhibitions, concerts, and lectures focusing on the various ways spirituality is expressed through music. Religious music from around the globe is represented, including the trancelike music of the Middle East and India, the gospel spirituals of the West, Celtic music, and Eastern European folk songs.

Camping: No

Accommodations: Included with admission

GALWAY EARLY MUSIC FESTIVAL

Five days in May
Galway, Ireland
www.galwayearlymusic.com/index.html
Admission: $

This festival is primarily an educational one. Workshops in music and dance are provided for primary and secondary schoolchildren as well as for adults at both beginning and intermediate levels. The three-day festival features works from all periods of classical music performed by local students, non-professionals, and the Seoda Galway Early Music Ensemble, a group that performs with authentic reproductions of Renaissance instruments such as lyre, recorder, and flute.

For more information: maireadk@eircom.net

Camping: No

Accommodations

■ **Galway Bay Hotel**
The Promenade
Salthill, Galway
Ireland
(353) 91-520-520

■ **Galway Hostel**
35 Eyre St.
Eyre Square, Galway
Ireland
(353) 091-566-959

GLEBE MUSIC FESTIVAL

Eight days in November
Sydney, Australia
www.glebemusicfestival.com
Admission: $$

In previous years the Glebe Society, Australia's premier classical music consortium, has offered performances of Donizetti's Trio in F Minor, the Goldberg Variations by Johann Sebastian Bach, and various works by other composers including Beethoven, Sibelius, and Telemann. The weeklong festival is held in Sydney at Margaretta Cottage, an early nineteenth century building, and seating is very limited, so early reservations are a must.

Camping: No

Accommodations: www.travelaustralia.com.au

HUDDERSFIELD CONTEMPORARY MUSIC FESTIVAL

November
University of Huddersfield, Huddersfield, United Kingdom
www.hcmf.co.uk/index.htm
Admission: $$$

The Huddersfield Festival specializes in debuting new works by both established and rising artists. More than 50 events are held in a number of venues around town and the range of musical styles covers everything from twentieth century classical to experimental electronica and jazz.

For more information: (44) 1-484-425-082/472103 or info@hcmf.co.uk

Camping: No

Accommodations

■ **Bagden Hall Hotel**
Wakefield Rd.
Scissett, Huddersfield, Yorkshire HD8 9LE
United Kingdom
(44) 01-484-865-330

INTERNATIONAL BEETHOVEN FESTIVAL

Autumn

Bonn, Germany, and surrounding region

www.beethovenfest-bonn.de

Admission: $$$

The general area of Ludwig van Beethoven's birth in Germany provides the backdrop for this fifty-concert festival. The largest events take place in venues around the city of Bonn and many of the performances are broadcast over the radio both locally and internationally. This massive festival brings together some of the most distinguished orchestras, conductors, and performers from around the world to pay tribute to Beethoven with song cycles, concertos, and performances of his more obscure works. Like the Bayreuth Wagner Festival, the festival in Bonn is an absolute must for any serious fan of Beethoven, if only for the experience of hearing his music performed in his birthplace.

For more information: (49) 022-820-1030 or info@beethovenfest-bonn.de

Camping: No

Accommodations

■ **Hilton Bonn**
Berliner Freiheit 2
Bonn, North Rhine-Westphalia 53111
Germany
(49) 228-72690

INTERNATIONAL MILITARY MUSIC FESTIVAL

November
Berlin, Germany
Admission: $

The sight of thousands of uniformed soldiers marching to triumphant brass music and moving in perfectly synchronized patterns may be a bit unsettling, especially in Berlin. But this autumn event is strictly for show and features the talents of more than 700 different military bands from around the globe. The parades are held in the Max Schmeling Halle, a new building that was named after the famed prizefighter and built after the Wall came down. It straddles the border between East and West Germany.

For more information: (49) 030-44-30-45 or info@velomax.de
Camping: No
Accommodations
■ Berlin Tourist Office
(49) 0-700-8623-7546

JUNE MUSIC FESTIVAL AND CHAMBER MUSIC AT THE SIMMS

Ongoing
Albuquerque, New Mexico
www.unm.edu/~shapiro/MUSIC/cma.html
Admission: FREE–$$

Concerts run year-round at the Simms Center for the Performing Arts in Albuquerque, New Mexico, thanks to the combined efforts of the June Music Festival and Chamber Music at the Simms. The June Music Festival has been in operation since 1942 and is one of the oldest music festivals in the country. World-class orchestras, ensembles, and soloists (both domestic and international) perform at Friday and Sunday evening concerts where no single style of classical music prevails. Past guests have included Kalichstein-Laredo-Robinson Trio, Shanghai Quartet, and Lydian String Quartet.

For more information: (505) 268-1990 or cma@cma-abq.org

Camping: No
Accommodations

■ **A-1 Motel**
1520 Candelaria Rd. NE
Albuquerque, NM 87107
(505) 345-2547

■ **Adobe Manor Motel**
7412 Central Ave. SW
Albuquerque, NM 87107
(505) 836-1617

■ **Albuquerque Convention & Visitors Center**
20 First Plaza Ctr. NW # 601
Albuquerque, NM 87107
(505) 842-9918

KILLINGTON MUSIC FESTIVAL

Last two weeks of June
Killington, Vermont
www.killingtonmusicfest.com/index.html
Admission: $$

Instructional workshops in violin, viola, cello, classical guitar, clarinet, and the repair of stringed instruments are offered to registered summer school students at this elevated event in the mountains of Killington, Vermont. Every Sunday night a concert is given in Ram's Head Lodge, alternately featuring the students and the professional musicians who have taken up residency for the season as instructors. The program differs from year to year.

For more information: (802) 773-4003 or kmfest@sover.net
Camping: No
Accommodations

■ **Alpenhof Lodge-Killington Camp**
RR 1 Box 2880
Killington, VT 05751
(802) 422-9787

■ **Butternut Motor Inn**
P.O. Box 306
Killington, VT 05751
(802) 422-2000

■ **Cascades Lodge**
RR 1 Box 2848
Killington, VT 05751
(802) 422-3731

♪ LAS VEGAS MUSIC FESTIVAL

August
Las Vegas, Nevada
www.unlv.edu/Colleges/Fine_Arts/Music/lvmf.html
Admission: $$

University of Nevada, Las Vegas hosts this two-week event showcasing the talents of young musicians who are just getting started. They perform both chamber and orchestral music in four different auditoriums around the campus.

For more information: (702) 895-3949

Camping: No

Accommodations

■ **Black Jack Motel**
2909 E. Fremont St.
Las Vegas, NV 89104
(702) 382-9366

■ **Jackpot Motel**
1600 S. Casino Center Blvd.
Las Vegas, NV 89104
(702) 384-7211

■ **Normandie Motel**
708 Las Vegas Blvd.
Las Vegas, NV 89101
(702) 382-1002

♪ LINCOLN EARLY MUSIC FESTIVAL

May–August
Lincoln, United Kingdom
www.lemf.org
Admission: $$

The Lincoln Early Music Festival, founded in 1995, takes place in England's East Midlands at the Bishop Grosseteste College chapel in the town of Lincoln. The event's hosts seek to accurately recreate the early music period by using authentic medieval instruments and giving performances in period-appropriate surroundings. A castle dating back to the eleventh century dominates the center of the city, so even Lincoln itself is part of the historical reenactment. This attention to detail also extends to the planning of the program each year; for example, in 2002 the schedule included works by contemporaries Antonio Vivaldi and Salomone Rossi.

For more information: (44) 1522-532213 or
richardstill605@netscapeonline.co.uk
Camping: No
Accommodations

■ **Mayfield Guest House**
213 Yarborough Rd.
Lincoln, Lincolnshire LN1 3NQ
United Kingdom
(44) 1522-533732

■ **Hillcrest Hotel**
15 Lindum Terrace
Lincoln, Lincolnshire LN2 5RT
United Kingdom
(44) 1522-510182

MAINLY MOZART FESTIVAL

June
Baja, California
www.mainlymozart.org/index.asp
Admission: $$$

This is a critically acclaimed festival that, as the name suggests, focuses on the works of Mozart. (Other selections are offered as well.) The majority of the concerts are given in the Neurosciences Institute in beautiful Baja, California, with a number of other performances offered in the surrounding area. An array of internationally known musicians are featured.

For more information: (619) 239-0100 or sales@mainlymozart.org
Camping: No
Accommodations

■ **Arena Inn**
3330 Rosecrans St.
San Diego, CA 92110
(619) 224-8266

■ **Atlas Hotels Inc.**
P.O. Box 85098
San Diego, CA 92186
(619) 291-2232

■ **Arlington Apartment Hotel**
701 7th Ave.
San Diego, CA 92101
(619) 231-2385

NEWPORT MUSIC FESTIVAL

Three weeks in July
Newport, Rhode Island

www.newportmusic.org/default.htm

Admission: $$

Presenting more than 60 concerts in less than a month, the Newport Music Festival is packed with events, from entertaining programs for kids to musical retrospectives of composers such as Chopin and Mozart. A number of works debut there each year and internationally known musicians such as Russian pianist Alexander Melnikov, French violinist Pierre Amoyal, and Bulgarian pianist Ludmil Angelov have been known to make appearances. Concerts take place in the many breathtaking mansions that have made Newport famous.

For more information: (401) 849-0700 or staff@newportmusic.org

Camping: No

Accommodations

■ **Admirals' Inns of Distinction**
8 Fair St.
Newport, RI 02840
(401) 846-4256

■ **Artful Lodger**
503 Spring St.
Newport, RI 02840
(401) 847-3132

■ **Anna's Victorian Connection**
5 Fowler Ave.
Newport, RI 02840
(401) 849-2489

OLYMPIC MUSIC FESTIVAL

June–September

Seattle, Washington

www.olympicmusicfestival.org/index.html

Admission: $$–$$$

This three-month-long series of concerts—held in a big barn on the Olympic Peninsula, just outside Seattle, Washington—is a very casual event. Musicians perform in jeans, and audience members are scattered about the grass lawn much the way they would be at a folk or jazz festival. This may be an ideal way to expose kids to the music of the great composers. While this is a laid-back affair, please be forewarned that dogs are not allowed.

For more information: (206) 527-8839 or info@olympicmusicfestival.org

Camping: No

Accommodations

■ **Foxbridge B&B**
30680 Hwy. 3 NE
Poulsbo, WA 98370
(360) 598-5599

■ **Greywolf Inn B&B**
395 Keeler Rd.
Sequim, WA 98382
(800) 914-9653

■ **Quilcene Hotel**
Maple Grove Rd.
Quilcene, WA 98376
(360) 765-3868

♩ SANTA FE CHAMBER MUSIC FESTIVAL

Mid- to late summer
Santa Fe, New Mexico
www.santafechambermusic.org
Admission: $–$$

The Santa Fe Chamber Music Festival does not restrict its program to any one genre of music; it often incorporates jazz and world music into the season, which usually kicks off in mid- to late summer. Founded in 1973, the festival has flourished over the years and today the program often includes up to 80 different events each season. The 2003 schedule was highlighted by the weeklong series "A Celebration of Schubert," which featured performances of his piano trios, works for solo cello, and the song cycle "Die Winterreise." Concerts are given at the Lensic Performing Arts Center and at St. Francis Auditorium in the heart of downtown Santa Fe.

For more information: (505) 982-1890 or denise@sfcmf.org
Camping: No
Accommodations

■ **Cactus Lodge Motel**
2864 Cerillos Rd.
Santa Fe, NM 87505
(505) 471-7699

■ **El Rey Inn**
1862 Cerrillos Rd.
Santa Fe, NM 87502
(505) 982-1931 or (800) 521-1349

■ **Camel Rock Suites**
3007 S. St. Francis Dr.
Santa Fe, NM 87505
(877) 989-3600

♪ SPOLETO FESTIVAL

May–June
Charleston, South Carolina
www.spoletousa.org
Admission: $$$

The Spoleto Festival is a celebration of music, dance, and theater held in venues all over Charleston, South Carolina, the gem of the South. In 2002 Ireland's Gate Theatre staged a production of *Pride and Prejudice*, and the musical program offered works by Mahler and Delibes.

For more information: jmcpherson@spoletousa.org

Camping: No

Accommodations

■ **Anchorage Inn**
26 Vendue Range
Charleston, SC 29401
(843) 723-8300

■ **Andrew Pinckney Inn**
199 Church St.
Charleston, SC 29401
(843) 937-8800

■ **Ansonborough Inn**
21 Hasell St.
Charleston, SC 29401
(843) 723-1655

♪ ST. BARTS MUSIC FESTIVAL

Three weeks in January
St. Barthelemy, French West Indies
www.stbartsmusicfestival.org
Admission: $$

This small-scale but acclaimed festival takes place on St. Barts, an island off the coast of the French West Indies, in the fourteenth century castle of Chateau d'Ainay-le-Vieil. The schedule changes every year; the 2003 program included an all-Mozart series, a staging of Gounod's opera *Faust*, and a performance of Brahms's Symphony No. 1. Selections geared for children are often performed as well. The festival has a sister program that takes place in Ainay, France, during the summer.

For more information: chateau.ainaylevieil@free.fr or Jill@StBartsMusicFestival.org

Camping: No

Accommodations: www.st-barths.com

♪ ST. PETERSBURG INTERNATIONAL EARLY MUSIC FESTIVAL

September–October

Pereulok, St. Petersburg, Russia

www.classicalmusic.spb.ru/early_music/index.htm

Admission: $$–$$$

This seasonal festival, held in St. Petersburg, Russia, covers everything from early Russian music to modern American composers. The St. Petersburg International Early Music Festival was founded as a tribute to the "Great Embassy," Tsar Peter I's historical visit to Britain in 1698.

For more information: (7) 812-327-0889 or demauny@earlymusic.ru

Camping: No

Accommodations: www.travel.spb.ru

♪ TANGLEWOOD

June–September

Lenox, Massachusetts

www.bso.org

Admission: $$$

For more than 60 years, the lauded Boston Symphony Orchestra has made its home in the deep woods of the Berkshires in western Massachusetts, and its summer concert series has become an American cultural tradition. Tanglewood is a required destination for avid classical music fans. The quietly stunning surroundings make this festival an unforgettable experience.

For more information: (413) 637-1600 or webinfo@bso.org

Camping: No

Accommodations

■ **Apple Tree Inn**
224 West St.
Lenox, MA 01240
(413) 637-1477

■ **Blantyre**
P.O. Box 995
Lenox, MA 01240
(413) 637-3556

■ **Brook Farm Inn**
15 Hawthorne St.
Lenox, MA 01240
(413) 637-3013

WAGNER FESTSPIELE BAYREUTH

Summer
Bayreuth, Bavaria, Germany
www.bayreuther-festspiele.de/Anfangsseite/deutsch.htm
Admission: $$–$$$

This is the largest, most acclaimed Wagner festival in the world—in other words, it's an absolute must for die-hard fans of the great German composer. His marathon operas are presented in the magnificent surroundings of the Festspielehaus, a massive and breathtaking building that's worth visiting regardless of whether or not a performance is scheduled. State-of-the-art stage techniques bring Wagner's music and librettos to vivid, sometimes crushing, life.

For more information: (49) 921-7878-0 or info@realtime.de
Camping: No
Accommodations

■ **Accent Hotel Bayreuth**
Kolpingstrasse 5
Bayreuth, Bavaria 95444
Germany

■ **Ramada Treff Bayreuth**
Erlanger Strasse 37
Bayreuth, Bavaria 95444
Germany

WEST CORK CHAMBER MUSIC FESTIVAL

One week in early July
Bantry, County Cork, Ireland
www.westcorkmusic.ie
Admission: $$

Each year since its inception in 1995, the West Cork Chamber Music Festival has offered attendees a thematic program. In 2002 Mozart was the main focus, but they also ran a concurrent series on lesser-known Polish composers. New works commissioned by the festival and composed by Irish artists debut there each year. The resident RTÉ Vanbrugh Quartet and guest musicians from around the globe give concerts at St. Brendan's Church in Bantry, a stunningly beautiful rural community in County Cork, Ireland.

For more information: (353) 027-52788 or info@westcorkmusic.ie

Camping: No

Accommodations

■ **Tourist Information Offices**

Cork City (353) 2142-73251

Bantry (353) 275-0229

YORK EARLY MUSIC FESTIVAL

July

York, United Kingdom

www.yorkearlymusic.org

Admission: $$

You can expect to see many internationally recognized performers, ensembles, and orchestras at this prestigious event. The York Early Music Festival, in operation since 1977, is an anticipated month of concerts where performances are given in the ancient churches and theaters that dot the mazelike city of York. Students from York University handle the lighting and staging duties for programs that normally consist of baroque, medieval, and romantic period music. Past performers include the Gabrieli Consort of Music, the Tallis Scholars, and the Consort of Musicke.

For more information: (44) 0190-465-8338 or boxoffice@yorkearlymusic.org

Camping: No

Accommodations

■ **Best Western York Pavilion Hotel**
45 Main St.
Fulford, York YO1 4PJ
United Kingdom
(44) 0190-462-2099

■ **St. George's Hotel**
6 St. George's Place
York, Yorkshire YO24 1DR
United Kingdom
(44) 0190-462-5056

■ **Grange Hotel**
1 Clifton
York, Yorkshire YO30 6AA
United Kingdom
(44) 0190-464-4744

COUNTRY, BLUEGRASS, and FOLK

3

♪ A-1 FESTIVAL OF MUSIC & DANCE

Mid-June
Thornhaugh, Peterborough, United Kingdom
www.a1festival.co.uk
Admission: $$

Unfortunately for steak-with-raisins-on-it lovers, the A-1 Festival of Music & Dance is not sponsored by the makers of the tangy American condiment. In this case, the "A-1" stands for quality. The A-1 Festival is a British event that takes place in Peterborough, at the Sacrewell Farm & Country Centre in Thornhaugh, showcasing traditional American country and folk music. Instructional workshops for beginner musicians and dancers are available, and there are a number of dances throughout the weekend, both organized and the result of rampant open jamming (and maybe a little drinking). Performers are primarily from Europe, performing American styles.

For more information: (44) 07904-439-164 or A1Festival@aol.com
Camping: Yes. On-site.
Accommodations

■ **Bell Inn**
Great North Rd.
Stilton, Peterborough,
  Cambridgeshire PE7 3RA
United Kingdom
(44) 01733-241-066

■ **Sacrewell Farm and Country Centre**
Sacrewell, Thornhaugh
Peterborough,
  Cambridgeshire PE8 6HJ
United Kingdom
(44) 01780-782-254

ALASKA FOLK FESTIVAL

Five days in April
Juneau, Alaska
www.juneau.com/aff
Admission: $

At this five-day event, performers come from all over Alaska and the Northwestern states to play 15-minute sets. A larger emphasis is placed on dance performances, to which both Thursday and Saturday nights are devoted. Performances range from school groups to professionals, traveling from hundreds or even thousands of miles away to participate.

For more information: (907) 463-3316 or fontjj@gci.net
Camping: No
Accommodations

■ **Admiralty View Bed & Breakfast**
16294 Point Lena Loop Rd.
Juneau, AK 99801
(907) 790-7277

■ **Auke Bay Inn Inc.**
11806 Glacier Hwy.
Juneau, AK 99801
(907) 789-7829

■ **Alaskan Hotel & Bar Inc.**
167 S. Franklin St.
Juneau, AK 99801
(907) 586-1000

AMBASSADOR CHARLIE RAY'S NASHVILLE MUSIC FESTIVAL

Late May
Nashville, Tennessee
www.radiocountry.org/Festival
Admission: $$$

This event was designed as a venue for musicians and songwriters to showcase their work, make contacts, and attend informative seminars on the Nashville music industry. Booth space and stage time are free with your ticket as long as you reserve in advance, and there is plenty of time and room for everyone to perform. Don't miss this one if you're looking to jump-start your music career.

For more information: (615) 252-8202 or c4promo@aol.com
Camping: No

Accommodations

■ **Red Roof Inn**
2460 Music Valley Dr.
Nashville, TN 37214
(615) 859-2537

■ **Guesthouse Inn**
1909 Hayes St.
Nashville, TN 37203
(615) 851-1067

■ **Econo Lodge**
893 Murfreesboro Rd.
Nashville, TN 37217
(615) 859-4988

♪ AMERICAN HERITAGE MUSIC FESTIVAL

Early June
Grove, Oklahoma
www.grandlakefestivals.com
Admission: $$

Taking place simultaneously with the American Heritage Clogging Contest (clogging is an old step-dancing tradition imported by Europe immigrants and perfected over the years by generation upon generation of Oklahomans), the folk festival features two stages with national and regional acts, food booths, and handcrafted arts vendors. Past performers include Ricky Skaggs, Texas Shorty, and the Whitewater Boys.

Artist Submissions
Grand Lake Festivals, Inc.
P.O. Box 451590
Grove, OK 74345-1590

For more information: (800) 526-2523 or mail@grandlakefestivals.com
Camping: Yes, at Honey Creek State Park. Call (918) 786-9447 for more information.

Accommodations

■ **Grand Motel**
2122 S. Main St.
Grove, OK 74344
(918) 786-6124

■ **Kristyl Inn**
10400 Highway 59 N.
Grove, OK 74344
(918) 786-9799 or (877) 868-9799

■ **Honey Creek Motel**
2511 S. Main St.
Grove, OK 74344
(918) 786-6113

■ **Outrigger Motel**
10603 Highway 59 N.
Grove, OK 74344
(918) 786-4456

♪ AMERICANA INTERNATIONAL

Fourth of July weekend
Newark, Nottinghamshire, United Kingdom
www.countrymusic.org.uk/americana/americana.php3
Admission: $$

Americana International is a festival for those of us who wish we were American, but simply aren't. Rock and country music is performed on five stages by bands from the United States and United Kingdom, line and jive dancing are de rigeur, and more than 40 awards are handed out to owners of the best American motorcycles, cars, trucks, and RVs. Don't forget your cowboy boots and American flag T-shirt!

Artist Submissions
Americana Promotions Ltd.
Jacksonville
1 Middle Orchard St.
Stapleford, Nottingham, NG9 8DD
United Kingdom

Camping: Yes

For more information
(44) 01159-390-595 or chris@americana-promotions.co.uk

Accommodations

■ **Cotswold Hotel**
330-332 Mansfield Rd.
Nottingham, Nottinghamshire
  NG5 2EF
United Kingdom
(44) 01159-551-070

■ **Eastwood Hall**
Mansfield Road
Eastwood, Nottinghamshire
  NG16 3AQ
United Kingdom
(44) 01773-532-532

♪ APPALACHIAN STRING BAND FESTIVAL

Late July
Clifftop, West Virginia
www.wvculture.org/stringband/index.html
Admission: $$

The preservation of America's old-time string band music is a service every music lover should be thankful for. And the Appalachian String Band Festival is deserving of some kind of medal for their wonderful annual event. Collecting string bands from all over the country and the world, this five-day festival held on a mountaintop in the heart of the Appalachians is a highly recommended destination for anyone with a love for mountain music and old-time country-folk of any kind. The festival features the best string bands you will hear anywhere and offers plenty of opportunities for folks to join in open jams and/or learn from the musicians.

Artist Submissions

Pat Cowdery

The Cultural Center

1900 Kanawha Blvd. E.

Charleston, WV 25305

pat.cowdery@wvculture.org

For more information: (304) 558-0220 or pat.cowdery@wvculture.org

Camping: Yes. On-site.

Accommodations

■ **Country Inn & Suites**

2120 Harper Rd.

Beckley, WV 25801

(304) 252-5100

■ **Green Bank Motor Inn**

505 S. Eisenhower Dr.

Beckley, WV 25801

(304) 253-3355

■ **Cutlip's Motor Inn**

1607 Bigley Ave.

Charleston, WV 25302

(304) 345-3500

APPALACHIAN UPRISING

Early June

Scottown, Ohio

www.earthproductions.net/appalachian-uprising.html

Admission: $$

Newgrass, jam rock, and traditional Appalachian folk bands get together for a weekend that reflects the spirit of rebelliousness that marks Appalachia and is such an integral part of that region's history, especially in light of the poverty suffered there by so many, even today. Put together by an awareness-promoting grassroots organization called Earth Productions, Appalachian Uprising occurs annually every June on Eden Valley Farm, a gorgeous 629-acre plot in Scottown, Ohio, which sits on the West Virginia border.

Artist Submissions

Robert Delong

1709 E. Long St.

Columbus, OH 43203

For more information: (614) 372-0539 or rdelong@earthproductions.net

Camping: Yes. Included with price of admission.

Accommodations

■ **Super 8 Gallipolis**

321 Upper River Rd. (State Route 7)

Gallipolis, OH 45631

(800) 800-8000 or (740) 446-8080

■ **Portsmouth Days Inn Wheelersburg**

8340 Ohio River Rd.

Wheelersburg, OH 45694

(740) 574-8431

APPEL FARM FESTIVAL

One day in June

Elmer, New Jersey

www.appelfarm.org/festival/index.htm

Admission: $$

Two stages, a crafts fair, an area for the kids called Children's Village, and food vendors are offered at this one-day-only fair in New Jersey. Past performers include Jackson Browne, Ani DiFranco, Arlo Guthrie, and Emmylou Harris.

Artist Submissions

Send press kit and demo to:

Sean Timmons, Artistic Director

Appel Farm Arts & Music Center

P.O. Box 888

Elmer, NJ 08318

For more information: (800) 394-1211

Camping: No

Accommodations

■ **Wellesley Inn & Suites**

517 S. Pennsville Auburn Rd.

Carneys Point, NJ 08069

(856) 299-3800

■ **Country Inn**

1125 Village Dr.

Millville, NJ 08332

(856) 825-3100

■ **Colonial Hotel**

76 W. Main St.

Penns Grove, NJ 08069

(856) 299-0077

APPLE & EVE NEWPORT FOLK FESTIVAL

Early August
Newport, Rhode Island
www.festivalproductions.net/folk/index.htm
Admission: $$–$$$

The legendary Newport Folk Festival—where Muddy Waters, Bill Monroe, Joan Baez, and Richard and Mimi Farina performed during the 1960s and where Bob Dylan was booed for making the switch to electric guitar—is a true American institution. Each year it brings a new generation into musical awareness with nothing but the best and often most important artists on the planet on the stage. Whether or not they play straight "folk music" has never been a concern for founder George Wein; the important thing has always been strength of vision and ability to touch others with musical expression. This tradition is kept alive today, with a continuing quality of performers—from Nanci Griffith and Jonatha Brook to gospel icons the Five Blind Boys of Alabama and the Hackberry Ramblers—all recent guests of the festival. The day-long concerts are given on a large stage on a jetty in Fort Adams State Park, which sits right on Newport Harbor—a forest of sails crowds the background and Newport's famous mansions are within walking distance. Food and beverages are plentiful, as are the handmade crafts you see at every festival, but the real reason to go to the Newport Folk Festival is the palpable air of history that hangs in the atmosphere the whole time you are there.

Artist Submissions
Attn: Newport Folk Festival
770 Aquidneck Ave.
Middletown, RI 02842
For more information: (401) 847-3700 or folkfest@fpiny.com
Camping: Yes
Accommodations

■ **Admirals' Inns of Distinction**
8 Fair St.
Newport, RI 02840
(401) 846-4256

■ **Artful Lodger**
503 Spring St.
Newport, RI 02840
(401) 847-3132

■ **Anna's Victorian Connection**
5 Fowler Ave.
Newport, RI 02840
(401) 849-2489

♪ ARCADIA BLUEGRASS FESTIVAL

Three days in August
Arcadia, Maryland
www.gotech.com/arcadia/homepg.htm
Admission: $$

Sponsored by the Arcadia Volunteer Fire Department for the past 20 years, the Arcadia Bluegrass Festival is a family-friendly outdoor gathering featuring three days of music and food, with over a dozen roots and bluegrass groups as well as a pancake breakfast served on Sunday morning included in the admission fee. You can expect a handful of the big names of contemporary bluegrass to perform alongside local acts and touring bands. In 2002, contemporary bluegrass lynchpins Larry Sparks and the Seldom Scene performed, with a smattering of lesser-known acts. The fairgrounds are situated off Route 30 in Maryland, at about the midpoint between historical Gettysburg, Pennsylvania, and Maryland's own state capitol, Baltimore. Lodging is available in nearby Westminster, 12 miles from the fairgrounds. Should you prefer a spot closer to the action, camping is offered on a first-come, first-served basis. This festival makes an excellent choice for parents interested in exposing their children to Americana music because there is no alcohol sold during the festival and an open-container law is enforced by festival security. It is suggested that festivalgoers bring their own lawn chairs.

For more information: (410) 374-2895
Camping: Yes
Accommodations
■ **The Boston Inn**
533 Baltimore Blvd.
Westminster, MD 21157
(410) 848-9095

♪ ARKANSAS FOLK FESTIVAL

Mid-April
Mountain View, Arkansas
www.ozarkfolkcenter.com
Admission: FREE

Blacksmithing, pottery making, and various other pioneer skills are on display at the Arkansas Folk Festival, with the intent of keeping alive the rich historic heritage of the Ozarks. Authentic mountain music, contemporary folk, and workshops in dance and gardening are offered.

For more information: (870) 269-3851 or ozarkfolkcenter@arkansas.com

Camping: No

Accommodations

■ **Best Western Fiddlers Inn**
601 Sylamore Ave., HC 72, Box 45
Mountain View, AR 72560
(870) 269-2828

■ **Country Charm Bed & Breakfast**
656 County Charm Rd.
Mountain View, AR 72560
(870) 269-2177

■ **Brickshy's Showboat**
P.O. Box 1254
Mountain View, AR 72560
(501) 585-2226

♪ AUCKLAND FOLK FESTIVAL

January
Keumu, New Zealand
homepages.ihug.co.nz/~ewildpt/aff
Admission: $$

The Auckland Folk Festival in New Zealand is held on a large campground in Auckland, at the very tip of New Zealand's North Island. Past performers include local personalities Brian Peters, Margaret Roadknight, and Joan Prior.

Artist Submissions
http://homepages.ihug.co.nz/~ewildpt/aff/application.htm

For more information: (025) 263-5733 or info@aucklandfolkfestival.org

Camping: Yes

Accommodations
www.purenz.com

♪ AVALON ANNUAL FOLKFEST

Three days in August
Paw Paw, West Virginia
www.avalon-nude.com/folkfest.html
Admission: $$$

For people looking for something a little, uh, *different*, we suggest the Avalon Folkfest, a clothing-optional event held at a nudist resort in Paw Paw, West Virginia. The weekend includes a dozen or so local acts playing contemporary and traditional folk (with their clothes on), songwriting seminars, instrumental workshops, and skin—lots of skin. Bring your sunscreen.

Artist Submissions

P.O. Box 369

Paw Paw, WV 25434

(304) 947-5600

For more information: (304) 947-5600 or vacation@avalon-resort.com

Camping: Yes. Naked.

Accommodations

■ **Belmont Motor Inn**

Bellview Blvd.

Fairmont, WV 26554

(304) 363-5300

■ **Country Club Motor Lodge**

1499 Locust Ave.

Fairmont, WV 26554

(304) 366-4141

■ **Budget Motel**

1101 Fairmont Ave.

Fairmont, WV 26554

(304) 366-1900

♪ BAKEAPPLE FOLK FESTIVAL

Early August

Labrador Straits, Canada

www.labradorstraits.net/festival.shtml

Admission: $

This folk festival is named for a delicious berry found in the Labrador region, the bakeapple, and features strictly homegrown musicians performing over the course of a weekend in August. Many games and activities for kids are incorporated into the schedule of events, which includes dancing, bake-offs, and tours of the local lighthouses.

For more information: info@labradorstraits.net

Camping: No

Accommodations

www.gov.nf.ca/tourism

♪ BEAN BLOSSOM BLUEGRASS FESTIVAL

Second week in July
Brown County, Indiana
www.beanblossom.com
Admission: $–$$$

Eight days and more than 40 bands, held at the Bill Monroe Memorial Music Park & Campground—this is *the* festival for bluegrass enthusiasts. Billing itself as the longest running bluegrass festival in the country, the Bean Blossom Festival has in fact been around for almost 40 years, and pretty much every major bluegrass figure has played here at one time or another, from the man who started the genre, Bill Monroe, to the duo that broke bluegrass to the masses, Flatt & Scruggs, to modern day keepers-of-the-flame J. D. Crowe and New South. The park and campgrounds offer free-range jamming, spread-out campsites, hiking, and fishing.

Artist Submissions

Bean Blossom Bluegrass
Attention: Dwight Dillman
5163 State Road 135 N
Bean Blossom, IN 46160

For more information: (800) 414-4677 or beanblossombg@hotmail.com
Camping: Yes
Accommodations

■ **The Seasons Lodge & Conference Center**
560 E. State Rd. 46
Nashville, IN 47448
(812) 988-2284 or (800) 365-7327
roomstsl@kiva.net

■ **The Nashville House**
15 S. Van Buren
Nashville, IN 47488
(812) 988-4554

■ **Brown County Inn**
51 E. State Rd. 46
Nashville, IN 47448
(812) 988-2291 or (800) 772-5249
roomsBCI@kiva.net

♪ BEDWORTH FOLK FESTIVAL

Late November
Warwickshire, United Kingdom

www.folkfax.net/folkday01/index.htm
Admission: $

Sing-alongs, storytelling, poetry, and various workshops round out the activities during this large-and-getting-larger-every-year festival, which boasts to have the "Ceilidh of the Year" (*ceilidh* is a traditional Scottish/Irish/British sort of riotous open dance gathering). Past performers include the Katherine Fear Band, Eddie Murphy (not the comedian), Derek Brimstone, and Cross O' th' Hands.

Artist Submissions

Bedworth Folk Festival
22, Juliet Close, Whitestone
Nuneaton, Warwickshire CV11 6NS
United Kingdom

For more information: (024) 7634-5568 or festival@folkfax.net
Camping: Yes
Accommodations

■ **Weston Hall Hotel**
Weston Lane, Bulkington
Nuneaton, Warwickshire CV12 9RU
United Kingdom

BIG VALLEY JAMBOREE

Early August
Camrose, Alberta, Canada
www.bigvalleyjamboree.com
Admission: $$–$$$

The largest event of its kind in Canada, the Big Valley Jamboree pulls out all the stops, each year transforming the Camrose Regional Exhibition Grounds into a massive country and western–themed expo center. With a trade show selling everything from spurs to saddles, a Saturday morning bull-riding competition, games, rides, and workshops geared for children and a mountain of BBQ and other foods, the three-day event is an exhaustive experience for some and an all-out bash for others. Festival headliners are always top flight (Dwight Yoakam, Alabama, Tammy Wynette, Tim McGraw, and Martina McBride are just some of the impressive guests Big Valley's had over the years) but there is still plenty of time allotted for less-established artists to gain a following.

For more information: (888) 404-1234 or (780) 672-0224 or bvj@bigvalleyjamboree.com

Camping: Yes. On-site.

Accommodations

- **Camrose Travelodge**
6216 48th Ave.
Camrose, AB T4V 0K6
Canada
(780) 672-3377 or (877) 672-3377

- **Camrose Motel**
6116 48th Ave.
Camrose, AB T4V 0K5
Canada
(780) 672-3364

- **Motel Stardust**
6009 48th Ave.
Camrose, AB T4V 0K2
Canada
(780) 672-1765

♪ BILL JORGENSON INVITATIONAL BLUEGRASS FESTIVAL

Mid-September
Door County, Wisconsin
www.bjorgensonbluegrass.com
Admission: $$

In its second year of operation in 2002, and held during a mid-September weekend from dusk on Friday to early evening on Sunday, local bluegrass enthusiast and musician Bill Jorgenson puts together a near continuous roster of musicians playing traditional, modern, and progressive styles of bluegrass. Artists are handpicked by Jorgenson himself and include both established guests of honor and local musicians just starting out. Sunday is devoted to gospel services and performance, a giant open jam, and a show just for the kids.

Artist Submissions: billj@doorpi.net

For more information: rbillings@new.rr.com

Camping: No

Accommodations

- **Wave Point Marina and Resort**
3600 County Rd. CC
Sturgeon Bay, WI 54235
(920) 824-5440 or (888) 882-WAVE
www.wavepointe.com/contact.shtml

BITTERROOT VALLEY BLUEGRASS FESTIVAL

Three days in July
Hamilton, Montana
www.bluegrassfestival.org
Admission: $–$$

This down-home get-together takes place less than an hour outside of Missoula, Montana, and features an array of workshops as well as acoustic bluegrass entertainment. International and local groups perform in the shade of a copse of birch trees as informal jam sessions pop up all over the place. The festival grounds are within a 30-minute drive from any number of hiking trails and fishing holes. While there may be no nationally known acts on the roster, remember that this is Montana, so you can expect a more rugged, authentic experience than you may encounter at some of the larger festivals.

Artist Submissions: Mark Dickerson: markd@bitterroot.com
For more information: (888) 592-2972 or mark@montananet.com
Camping: Yes
Accommodations

■ **Best Western Hamilton Inn**
409 S. 1st St.
Hamilton, MT 59840
(406) 363-2142

■ **Holiday Inn Express**
139 Bitterroot Plaza Dr.
Hamilton, MT 59840
(406) 375-2525

■ **Comfort Inn**
1115 N. 1st St.
Hamilton, MT 59840
(406) 363-6600
ask for Bluegrass Festival rate

■ **Super 8**
1325 N. 1st St.
Hamilton, MT 59840
(406) 363-2940

■ **Deffy's Motel**
321 S. 1st St.
Hamilton, MT 59840
(406) 363-1244

BLISTERED FINGERS FAMILY BLUEGRASS MUSIC FESTIVAL

June and August
Sidney, Maine

www.blisteredfingers.com

Admission: $–$$

IIIrd Tyme Out, the Misty Mountaineers, and Fiddlin' Tim Farrell are among the performers you'll see at this twice-a-summer event. The Open Stage is a perfect place for you to showcase your own talents, and possibly be hired to perform at next year's festival!

Artist Submissions

Blistered Fingers

263 Trafton Rd.

Waterville, ME 04901

For more information: (207) 873-6539 or blist-f@blisteredfingers.com

Camping: Yes

Accommodations

■ **Silver Fox Inn**

P.O. Box 358

Waterville Vly, NH 03215

(603) 236-3699

■ **Snowy Owl Inn**

P.O. Box 407

Waterville Vly, NH 03215

(603) 236-8383

■ **Valley Inn**

P.O. Box 1

Waterville Vly, NH 03215

(603) 236-8336

♪ BLUE MOUNTAINS ANNUAL MUSIC FESTIVAL

Three days in March

Blue Mountains, Katoomba, Australia

www.bmff.org.au

Admission: $$

Taking place within walking distance of the Katoomba Railway station, and within sight of the beautiful mountain range that names the event, the Blue Mountains Annual Music Festival offers innumerable Australian activities. One, Poet's Brunch, inspired this researcher to inquire, "what exactly is a poet's brunch?" The good people at the festival's Web site gave this answer: "A Poet's Brunch is a poet's breakfast for those bards who got too pissed the night before . . . perhaps it will end up as a poet's cocktail evening." Performances of American and world folk music, courtesy of local and imported talent performing on no less than six stages, round out the weekend.

For more information: (02) 800-651-322 or info@bmff.org.au

Camping: Yes

Katoomba Falls Caravan Park

Katoomba Falls Rd., Katoomba 2780

Australia

(02) 4782-1835

Accommodations

■ **Katoomba Hotel**

15 Parke St.

Katoomba 2780

Australia

(02) 4782-1106

■ **Town Centre Motel**

220 Katoomba St.

Katoomba 2780

Australia

(61) 024-782-1266

■ **Gearins Hotel**

273 Great Western Hwy.

Katoomba 2780

Australia

(02) 4782-4385

ALAN WARD: *musician, festival organizer, self-proclaimed useless document filing guru, and floor sweeper of the Blue Mountains Annual Music Festival in Katoomba, Australia. We got him to answer some questions about festivals, Australians, knives, and LSD.*

Why the hell would you want to organize a music festival?

It's one way to be sure of getting a gig. Seriously, it seemed like a logical way to keep contributing after 30 years in acoustic music.

What is Katoomba like? Rural? Urban? Is it very beautiful there?

Katoomba is a small town on a mountain ridge, surrounded by a World Heritage national park that includes the world's second biggest canyon (after the Grand Canyon). It's an amazingly beautiful place.

How much chance does an unknown act have to perform in some capacity at your festival?

Out of the hundreds who want to play, we only accept a handful of unknowns, so the odds aren't too good. We book about 40 acts and we need most of them to put bums on seats.

What are the three things you think set your festival apart from other festivals?

The physical environment. The size—it's perfect for artists and enthusiasts to mingle without the star tripping and drama that can go on at larger events. And the production values and thoughtful programming are consistently equal to what you expect at much larger festivals.

What is the strangest thing you've ever seen and/or done at your festival?

Me wearing shorts.

What is the best food to eat in Katoomba or at the festival itself—any favorite spots or tents?

There was a great paella stall last year. Otherwise a real variety of good tucker.

BONUS QUESTIONS:

How accurate a portrayal of Australian life and Australians in general are the Crocodile Dundee movies? Do all Australians carry giant knives?

Not very accurate. Most of us are less sophisticated and chatty. Not many large knives, but a lot of us carry vegetable peelers. (At our festival, all knives and vegetable peelers must be checked in at the box office.)

On a given day during your festival, about how many gallons of alcohol are consumed by the festivalgoers and performers? Does this often lead to knife fights?

There is a fair bit of recreational elbow tilting, but since the sharps are all at the box office, people fence with drinking straws.

Just how much of a factor is "drunken mayhem" at the Blue Mountains Festival?

Due to RSA regulations, all mayhem must be conducted off the festival site, unless one of the contracted performers is doing it.

It is often said on television in America that Australians go around licking toads to get high. Have you ever licked a toad and had a hallucinogenic experience as a result? Please describe.

I once licked a 45¢ stamp that sent me off. It was awful; I kept seeing Sammy Davis, Jr., singing "Mr. Bojangles."

How long are the lines for the bathrooms at your festival?

What lines?

Have you ever seen the film *Wendigo*, which is about a monster that is half-deer and half-tree? I would recommend it, but only after doing the toad thing.

Do you think it would be OK with a 45¢ stamp? Toads are hard to catch.

What advice would you give to potential festival organizers?

Oh boy. This is a big one. Be sure you know what you're going to do. Watch budgets and time lines. Delegate wisely. Stuff-ups happen . . . just keep moving ahead. Always debrief and write it all down. Folks come back to a happy festival.

Make a space where artists can mingle and catch up away from the punters. They'll perform better when they feel at home. Finally, don't panic! Remember, this was your idea.

What hopes do you have for the festival's future?

Longevity. Quality. More space for emerging acts. A reputation for great live audio and visual recordings. To be able to work more in the extraordinary natural environment. To have many more patrons from overseas who would include us in their Australian adventure.

BLUEBERRY BLUEGRASS FESTIVAL

Early August
Stony Plain, Alberta, Canada
www.blueberrybluegrass.com
Admission: $$

The Stony Plain Exhibition Park in Alberta hosts this bustling festival, which offers a variety of workshops during the day and over 20 bands performing from evening on over the course of two days and three nights. Look for a handful of nationally known acts (such as Rhonda Vincent and Jimmy Martin & the Sunny Mountain Boys) among the roster of fresh new bluegrass talent scheduled to perform.

Artist Submissions: info@blueberrybluegrass.com
For more information: (780) 963-4181
Camping: Yes
Accommodations

■ **Alberta Place Suite Hotel**
10049 103 St.
Edmonton, AB T5J 0X5
Canada
(780) 423-1565

■ **Best Western City Centre Inn**
11310 109 St.
Edmonton, AB T5J 0X5
Canada
(780) 479-2042

BLUEGRASS IN THE SMOKIES

Two days in August
Sevierville, Tennessee
www.bluegrassinthesmokies.com
Admission: $

Bluegrass in the Smokies is a two-day event organized by the Rogersville-based family bluegrass act, the Fritts Family. The Fritts Family has been a respected group for years; in 1999 the National Endowments for the Arts sponsored a national tour for the band. In the past the Fritts Family has taken the festival stage with such roots music stars as James Monroe and Rhonda Vincent.

For more information: (864) 583-6306 or gfr9818028@aol.com

Camping: Yes. Contact the Smoky Mountain Campground at (800) 864-2267 or (865) 933-8312.

Accommodations

■ **Best Western Dumplin Valley Inn**
3426 Winfield Dunn Pkwy.
Kodak, TN 37764
(865) 933-3467

■ **Days Inn**
3402 Winfield Dunn Pkwy.
Kodak, TN 37764
(865) 933-4500

■ **Quality Inn**
6712 Central Ave. Pike
Knoxville, TN 37912
(865) 933-REST

BOSTON FOLK FESTIVAL

Late September
Boston, Massachusetts
www.wumb.org/folkfest
Admission: $$

The Boston Folk Festival draws some big names, from folk-rock pioneer Richard Thompson and contemporary folk star Nanci Griffith to Aussie critical faves the Waifs and local country rockers the Swingin' Steaks. With three stages (one of which is an open mic), innumerable booths, an artisan market, and festival-sponsored cruises around Boston Harbor, this weekend affair has plenty going on for attendees.

Artist Submissions
Boston Folk Festival
c/o WUMB Radio
University of Massachusetts Boston
100 Morrissey Blvd.
Boston, MA 02125-3393
For more information: (617) 287-6911 or folkfest@umb.edu
Camping: No
Accommodations

■ **Cambridge-Harvard Square**
17 Russell St.
Somerville, MA 02143
(617) 354-3500

■ **YMCA**
101 Highland Ave.
Somerville, MA 02143
(617) 625-5050

BRAMPTON FOLK FESTIVAL

Mid-June
Brampton, Ontario, Canada
www3.sympatico.ca/bramptonfolk
Admission: $

Jam circles, performance workshops, hand-crafted arts, and a beer tent flowing with locally brewed lager make up this two-day festival in Ontario. Musicians are mainly local and in the past have included the comedic rock band Arrogant Worms, traditional Quebec band Matapat, and drumming ensemble Kiyoshi Nagata.

Artist Submissions

Deadline is December 31 each year.

Send press kit and demo to:

Brampton Folk Festival

Attn: Artistic Director

39 Windermere Ct.

Brampton, ON L6X 2L5

Canada

For more information: bramptonfolkfestival@sympatico.ca

Camping: No

Accommodations

■ **Best Western Brampton**
30 Clark Blvd.
Brampton, ON L6W 1X3
Canada
(905) 454-1300

■ **Holiday Inn Brampton**
30 Peel Centre Dr.
Brampton, ON L6T 4G3
Canada
(905) 792-9900

BRANTFORD FOLK CLUB OCTOBERFOLK FESTIVAL

One day in October
Brantford, Ontario, Canada
www.brantford.folk.on.ca
Admission: $$

In 2002 the traditional Irish group Danú headlined this well-attended Canadian festival featuring mainly Quebecois artists, including folksinger Valdy and country-soul musician Cindy Church. Instructional workshops, dancing, and food from around the world are also featured.

For more information: (519) 759-7676 or brantfordfolk@execulink.com

Camping: No

Accommodations

■ **Days Inn Brantford**
460 Fairview Dr.
Brantford, ON N3R 7A9
Canada
(519) 759-2700

■ **Holiday Inn Brantford**
664 Colborne St.
Brantford, ON N3S 3P8
Canada
(519) 758-9999

BREAUX BRIDGE CRAWFISH FESTIVAL

Early May
Breaux Bridge, Lousiana
www.bbcrawfest.com
Admission: $

Dubbed "a Crawfish Odyssey," the Breaux Bridge Festival is a good destination for folks looking to either eat between songs or listen to songs between eating. The fantastic food of the Deep South is a major attraction to this gathering, with such acts as zydeco king Boozoo Chavis and swamp blues guitarist Sonny Landreth playing among local musicians on four different stages. There is a whole tent devoted to open jamming so bring your instrument if you're a musician, amateur or professional.

For more information: Bbcrawfest@cs.com

Camping: No

Accommodations

■ **Best Western of Breaux Bridge**
2088B Rees St.
Breaux Bridge, LA 70517
(337) 332-1114

■ **Holiday Inn Express Breaux Bridge**
2942 H Grand Point Hwy.
Breaux Bridge, LA 70517
(337) 667-8913

DONA DEGATUR RICHARD, *organizer of the Breaux Bridge Crawfish Festival, answers our questions.*

Why the hell would you want to organize a music festival?

The Crawfish Festival provides one of the few venues that offers over 35 Cajun and zydeco bands in three days. This year 39 bands will be playing. No other festival around here offers that.

What is it about the music that inspires you to keep doing this?

It is our heritage. We grew up listening to it, maybe not embracing it like rock 'n' roll. But you cannot listen to Cajun or zydeco without tapping your foot or swinging some body part.

What is the hardest part?

The Crawfish Festival is held at the same time as the New Orleans Jazz and Heritage Festival and we have some musicians who play there too. So it's a matter of timing. Saturdays are the hardest because of the traffic.

Is it worth it?

Oh yeah! On Saturday afternoon, when the crowds are dancing, the music is flowing through you, and you're standing on stage watching, you realize that you're part of giving one of the best parties in the world. Makes a whole year of work worth it.

How much chance does an unknown act have of performing in some capacity at your festival?

We "discovered" Hunter Hayes. Hunter was a baby when he got on stage with Wayne Toups and just stole the crowd's heart with his performance.

Do any of the proceeds from the festival go to charity or a cause?

Most of our profits go to civic improvement, schools, other nonprofits. We provide mini-grants and scholarships to the schools. We've given away over $350,000.

. . . .

What are the three things you think set your festival apart from other festivals?

The music, the food, and the people.

What is the strangest thing you've ever seen at your festival?

Probably the weddings that have taken place at our festival.

Which act or acts stick out in your mind as providing the best performances at the Crawfish Festival?

Steve Riley and the Mamou Playboys, Beausoleil, Lil Band O' Gold, Nathan & the Zydeco Cha Chas, Bois Sec Ardoin—too many to name.

What advice would you give to potential festival organizers?

Be persistent in your vision.

What hopes do you have for the festival's future?

That we can continue to give such incredible entertainment at such a low cost ($5.00 per day). But, realistically, I don't see that happening.

What is the thing that everyone absolutely must try, food-wise, at your festival?

Either the crawfish étouffée, fried crawfish, or boiled crawfish—take your pick.

. . . .

♪ BREW GLASS

June
Terra Alta, West Virginia
www.sunshinedreams.com
Admission: $$

Brew Glass takes place on the grounds of Sunshine Daydream Camping Park, an event facility made specifically to house festivals and the crowds they come with. Like many of the events held there, Brew Grass is a post–Grateful Dead gathering of jam bands and country/folk figures highlighted by appearances from such stars as the David Grisman Quintet, Del McCoury Band, and Stewed Mulligan.

For more information: (304) 789-2292 or info@sunshinedreams.com

Camping: Yes. On-site.

Accommodations

■ **Alpine Lake Resort**

RR 2, Box 99D2

Terra Alta, WV 26764

(304) 789-2481

BRIDGETON FOLK FESTIVAL

June

Bridgeton, New Jersey

www.bridgetonfolkfestival.com

Admission: $

Steve Forbert, the great Commander Cody, and Janis Ian have performed at recent incarnations of this outdoor festival held in the Donald Rainear Amphitheatre by Sunset Lake in wonderful, wonderful New Jersey. Bridgeton also usually features a good dose of Cajun music and other purely American art forms with its mix of national and local musicians.

Artist Submissions

Bridgeton Folk Festival

P.O. Box 472

Bridgeton, NJ 08302

njbridge10@aol.com

For more information: (856) 451-9208 or (800) 319-3379

Camping: No

Accommodations

■ **Hiway 77 Motel**

1040 Pearl St. N.

Bridgeton, NJ 08302

(609) 455-2500

♩ BULK VALLEY MIDSUMMER FESTIVAL

Late July
Smithers, British Columbia, Canada
www.bvfms.org
Admission: $$

This small, local folk festival showcases homegrown talent and opens its doors to any number of unestablished musicians each year. Canadian acoustic comedy band the Arrogant Worms are regular guests, as is folksinger Valdy, but the focus is very much on a community getting together for a good time rather than on star power. Bulk Valley is a good festival for aspiring performers, as one of its stated aims is to support unknown musicians.

Artist submission: On-line only; go to web address listed above
For more information: festival@bvfms.org
Camping: Yes; located a short distance outside the fairgrounds.
Accommodations

■ **Fireweed Motor Inn**
1515 Main St.
Smithers, BC V0J 2N6
Canada
(250) 847-2208

■ **Sorrento Inn**
4435 Hwy. 16
Smithers, BC V0J 2N6
Canada
(250) 847-2601

■ **Hudson Bay Lodge**
3251 Hwy. 16
Smithers, BC V0J 2N6
Canada
(250) 847-4581

♩ CALGARY FOLK MUSIC FESTIVAL

Late July
Calgary, Canada
www.calgaryfolkfest.com
Admission: $$

The Calgary Folk Music Festival features many lesser-known musicians playing alongside such festival circuit mainstays as Sleepy LaBeef and Michael Franti. On top of that, the festival has in the past been host to British psychedelic popster Robyn Hitchcock, folk rock icons Fairport Convention, and sixties folk singer Buffy Sainte-Marie. Performers often join in informal jam sessions before and after playing on stage at this event.

Artist Submissions

Accepted *only* between September 1 and January 15 each year. Send CDs (with a labeled spine) and minimal printed materials (bio, press clippings, etc.):

Ms. Kerry Clarke, Associate Producer

Calgary Folk Music Festival

P.O. Box 2897, Station M

Calgary, AB T2P 3C3

Canada

(403) 233-0904

kerryc@calgaryfolkfest.com

For more information: (403) 233-0904 or folkfest@canuck.com

Camping: No

CAMP RUDE BLUEGRASS FESTIVAL

May

Parkfield, California

www.camprude.com/info/index.html

Admissions: $$–$$$

Camp Rude is in Parkfield, a central California town that sits on the San Andreas Fault, in the heart of earthquake country. Most of the earthquakes are so tiny, though, that no one notices, and the area is better known for the research done on the Fault than anything. Still you can occasionally feel a tremor here and there, which only adds to the fun at this party-friendly camping weekend event. Performers are almost exclusively from the region, with alternative rock band Nine Pound Hammer making an appearance in 2001.

For more information: pat@camprude.com

Camping: Yes. On-site.

Accommodations

- ■ Arbor Inn

  1058 Munras Ave.

  Monterey, CA 93940

  (831) 372-3381

- ■ Bay Park Hotel

  1425 Munras Ave.

  Monterey, CA 93940

  (831) 649-1020

■ **Ayres Motel**
2710 S. Orange Ave.
Fresno, CA 93940
(559) 264-4815

♪ CANMORE FOLK MUSIC FESTIVAL

Early August
Canmore, Alberta, Canada
www.canmorefolkfestival.com
Admission: $$

Held in the Canadian Rockies, this is a large festival that is getting larger every year. The Canmore Folk Music Festival is Canada's longest running folk festival, with three stages, a petting zoo, horse and pony rides, and a playground area with a climbing wall and rope challenges for the kids. Past performers have included Willie P. Bennett, Janis Ian, and Arlo Guthrie.

Artist Submissions
Send press kit and CD/cassette/video by February 14 to:
Ken Rooks, Festival Director
Box 8098
Canmore, AB T1W 2T8
Canada
(403) 678-2524

For more information: (403) 678-2524 or info@canmorefolkfestival.com
Camping: Yes. Contact Restwell Trailer Park at (403) 678-5111.

Accommodations

■ **Bow Valley Motel**
228 Bow Ave.
Canmore, AB T1W 2T8
Canada
(403) 678-5085

■ **Canmore Hotel**
738 8th St.
Canmore, AB T1W 2T8
Canada
(403) 678-5181

■ **Days Inn**
815 Bow Valley Trail
Canmore, AB T1W 2T8
Canada
(403) 609-0075 or (877) 609-6266

■ **Drake Inn**
909 Railway Ave.
Canmore, AB T1W 2T8
Canada
(403) 678-5131

♪ CANYON COUNTRY BLUEGRASS FESTIVAL

One day in July
Wellsboro, Pennsylvania
www.canyoncountrybluegrass.com/Bluegrass_Festival/bluegrass_festival.
html
Admission: $$

This small festival features quality regional acts. While you may not see the biggest names performing at the Canyon Country Festival, the roster of talent is nevertheless always of a quality true bluegrass fans will respect. Acts such as Mountain Heart and the North Fork Alliance are frequent performers at the single-day gathering.

For more information: (800) PA GRASS or info@canyoncountrybluegrass.com
Camping: Yes
Accommodations

■ **Canyon Motel**
18 East Ave.
Wellsboro, PA 16901
(570) 724-1681

■ **Sherwood Motel**
2 Main St.
Wellsboro, PA 16901
(570) 724-3424

■ **Penn Wells Lodge & Penn Wells Hotel**
62 Main St.
Wellsboro, PA 16901
(570) 724-2111

♪ CELTIC COLOURS INTERNATIONAL FESTIVAL

October
Cape Breton, Canada
www.celtic-colours.com/core.php
Admission: $$

The whole island of Cape Breton participates in this festival, which offers events including square dances, daytime workshops on Celtic culture, and evening folk music concerts in over 30 venues all over the island. Each year, more than 300 artists from all over Britain, the United States, and Canada perform.

For more information: (902) 562-6700 or (877) 285-2321 or info@celtic-colours.com

Camping: Yes

Accommodations

■ **Big Pond Housekeeping Cottages**
7671 Highway #4
Big Pond Centre
Cape Breton, NS B1J1Y8
Canada
(902) 828-2335
www.geocities.com/bigpondcottages
bigpondcottages@yahoo.ca

■ **Highland Motel**
530 Seaview Dr.
North Sydney, NS B2A 3N8
Canada
(902) 794-4530 or (877) 994-4530

■ **Piper's Guest House**
45929 Cabot Trail, Indian Brook
Cape Breton, NS BOC 1HO
Canada
(902) 929-2339

♪ CELTIC ROOTS FESTIVAL

Early August
Goderich, Ontario, Canada
www.celticfestival.ca
Admission: $$

Goderich, Ontario, celebrates its strong Celtic ties with this weekend event, collecting musicians from abroad and regionally to perform, instruct, and exhibit ancient Celtic arts as well as contemporary manifestations. The Celtic Roots Festival takes place in a wooded park overlooking Lake Huron. Performers have included the Reid-Taheny Band, Tony McManus, and the Canadian Celtic Choir.

Artist Submissions
20 Caledonia Terrace
Goderich, ON N7A 2M8
Canada

For more information: (519) 524-8221 or info@CelticFestival.ca

Camping: No

Accommodations
■ **Tourist Information Centre**
91 Hamilton St.
Goderich, ON N7A 1R1
Canada
(800) 280-7637

♪ CHAMPLAIN VALLEY FOLK FESTIVAL

Early August
Ferrisburgh, Vermont
www.cvfest.org
Admission: $$

Three days and nights of live music and contra dancing are featured at this local Vermont festival. The performers are decidedly homegrown, and this is a festival for people very interested in dancing: four hours of contra dancing is the main event each night.

For more information: info@cvfest.org
Camping: Yes. Contact Lone Pine at (802) 878-5447; Mallets Bay at (802) 863-6980; or Pinecrest at (802) 878-3351.

Accommodations

■ **Ho-Hum Motel**
1200 Shelburne Rd.
South Burlington, VT 05403
(802) 658-1314 or (802) 863-4551

■ **North Star**
2427 Shelburne Rd.
Shelburne, VT 05482
(802) 863-3421

■ **Lake View Inn**
1860 Shelburne Rd.
South Burlington, VT 05403
(802) 862-0230

■ **Shelburne Inn**
Route 7
Shelburne, VT 05482
(802) 985-3305

♪ CHARLES WELLS CAMBRIDGE FOLK FESTIVAL

Early August
Cambridge, United Kingdom
www.cam-folkfest.co.uk
Admission: $$

Going on 39 years in 2003, the Charles Wells Cambridge Folk Festival offers at least that many bands on multiple stages in downtown Cambridge. Despite the festival's name, many of the performers run in a more rock vein—an alternative one at that. The list of past performers reads like a true record geek's collection: Joe Strummer & the Mescaleros, X, Indigo Girls, North Mississippi All-Stars, Nick Cave, Taj Mahal, and Richard Thompson, to name just a few. Since its inception the three-day event has attracted nearly 10,000 people a year, making it one of the most widely acclaimed festivals in Europe. Countless workshops, kids' activities, campsite jams, and vendors are all part of the experience.

Camping: Yes

Accommodations

■ **Gonville Hotel**
Gonville Place
Cambridge, Cambridgeshire
  CB1 1LY
United Kingdom
(44) 0-1223-221-122

■ **Cambridge Lodge Hotel**
109 Huntingdon Rd.
Cambridge, Cambridgeshire
  CB3 0DQ
United Kingdom
(44) 0-1223-352-833

■ **Hotel Felix**
Whitehouse Lane, Huntingdon Rd.
Cambridge, Cambridgeshire CB3 OLX
United Kingdom
(44) 0-1223-277-977

CHELTENHAM FOLK FESTIVAL

February
Cheltenham, United Kingdom
www.cheltenhamfestivals.co.uk
Admission: $$–$$$

This four-day event is held inside the Edwardian Town Hall in downtown Cheltenham. It's beautiful, spacious, and historically significant (like everything else in England). Just outside the Hall, a crafts market bustles with activity and the aroma of ethnic foods from around the world. Inside the Hall, some of the major folk figures of the past 30 years mingle with lesser-known artists and perform for the crowd. The festival has been known to host premier screenings of films by local filmmakers during the weekend.

The great Fairport Convention has headlined in recent years, alongside Brass Monkey and the Old Rope String Band.

For more information: (44) 01242-227979 or JaneEg@Cheltenham.gov.uk

Camping: No

Accommodations

■ **Hotel on the Park**
38 Evesham Rd.
Cheltenham, Gloucestershire
  GL52 2AH
United Kingdom
(44) 01242-518-898

■ **Cheltenham/Gloucester Moat House**
Brockworth
Gloucester, Gloucestershire
Gloucester GL3 4PB
United Kingdom
(44) 01452-519988

♩ CHESTER FOLK FESTIVAL

May–June
Kelsall, United Kingdom
www.chesterfolk.freeserve.co.uk/festhome.htm
Admission: *FREE*

This small local festival in rural England features Irish and British folk groups, with such colorful names as His Worship & the Pig and the Old Rope String Band.

For more information: (44) 1352-762931 or festival@chesterfolk.freeserve.co.uk

Camping: No

Accommodations

■ **Crabwall Manor Hotel**
Parkgate Rd. Mollington
Chester, Cheshire CH1 6NE
United Kingdom
(44) 0-1244-851-666

■ **Northop Hall Country House Hotel**
Chester Rd. Northophall Village
Chester, Cheshire CH7 6HJ
United Kingdom
(44) 0-1244-816-181

♩ CHICAGO COUNTRY MUSIC FESTIVAL

Late June
Chicago, Illinois
www.ci.chi.il.us/SpecialEvents
Admission: $$

Often held concurrently with the giant food festival Taste of Chicago, the Chicago Country Music Festival is itself a large gathering, featuring top-flight acts such as Vince Gill and the Charlie Daniels Band performing alongside regional bands. Line dancing, square dancing, and workshops are scheduled throughout the weekend, but if you get a little overloaded with country music, there's always the Taste of Chicago happening right around the corner.

For more information: (312) 744-3370

Camping: No

Accommodations

(877) CHICAGO

www.877CHICAGO.com

CHIPPEWA VALLEY COUNTRY FEST

End of June

Cadott, Wisconsin

www.countryfest.com

Admission: $$$

Rough it in style at the Chippewa Valley Country Fest's first-rate campgrounds, participate in the local Leinenkugel brewery's beer-themed campsite decoration contest, and enjoy five days' worth of great country music. Neal McCoy, Tim McGraw, Dwight Yoakam, and Lee Ann Womack are a few of the top-quality acts that have performed at the fest in the past. VIP seating is available for folks who don't want to fight it out on the lawn.

For more information: (800) 326-FEST or info@countryfest.com

Camping: Yes

Accommodations

■ **Countryside Motel**
545 Lavorata Rd.
Cadott, WI 54727
(715) 289-4000

■ **Lake Aire Motel & Micro Mart**
5732 183rd St.
Chippewa Falls, WI 54729
(800) 236-223 or (715) 723-2231

■ **Edelweiss Steak House and Motel**
8988 Hwy. 124
Chippewa Falls, WI 54729
(715) 723-7881

♪ CHRISTOPHER RUN BLUEGRASS FESTIVAL

Early June
Mineral, Virginia
www.christopherrunbluegrass.com
Admission: $$–$$$

This rain-or-shine bluegrass festival is guaranteed to please the whole family. The music never stops. Acts such as the Lonesome River Band and Rhonda Vincent perform into the early evening, but the off-stage finger pickin' goes on around the clock. Swim, fish, or boat at the lovely Lake Anna, then retire to a campground with astonishingly convenient amenities such as real flush toilets, laundry machines, and hot showers.

For more information: (540) 894-4772 or (540) 894-4744 or kchilds569@aol.com

Camping: Yes. On-site.

Accommodations

■ **Anna Point Inn**
13701 Anna Point Ln.
Mineral, VA 23117
(540) 895-5900

■ **Sacra's Motel & Rest**
P.O. Box 340
Mineral, VA 23117
(540) 894-4706

♪ CITY STAGES: A WORLD-CLASS MUSIC FESTIVAL

Mid-May
Birmingham, Alabama
www.citystages.org/default.asp
Admission: $–$$

The lovely city of Birmingham, Alabama, hosts this festival every year during the third weekend in May. The name is no exaggeration and the diversity of the music is outstanding. Where else would you find country legends Alabama, rappers OutKast, crooner Dwight Yoakam, and R&B superstars the Isley Brothers on one bill? (They were among the 150 performers at the 2002 festival.) The *Chicago Sun-Times* told its readers that City Stages is "the best music festival you've never heard of." And it only seems to be getting better.

Artist Submissions
Deadline April 1
Local acts only, send e-mail to info@citystages.org
or send a CD or tape to:
Local Acts Programming Chairman
City Stages
P.O. Box 2266
Birmingham, AL 35201-2266
Camping: No
Accommodations

■ **Alta Vista Hotel**
260 Goodwin Crest Dr.
Birmingham, AL 35209
(800) 847-3716

■ **Comfort Inn**
2445 S. Acadian Hwy.
Birmingham, AL 35209
(800) 228-5150

■ **Courtyard South Colonnade**
4300 Colonnade Pkwy.
Birmingham, AL 35243
(800) 932-2198

CKCU OTTAWA FOLK FESTIVAL

Last weekend in August
Ottawa, Ontario, Canada
www.ottawafolk.org
Admission: $$

Since its inception in 1994, the CKCU Ottawa Folk Festival has opened its
gates during the last weekend in August, providing its loyal and laid-back
attendees with two days and three nights of the best touring Canadian,
American, and international folk, Cajun, Celtic, roots rock, blues, and even
alternative bands organizers Max Wallace and Chris White can come up
with. In addition to being a place for both musicians and fans to enjoy great
music, CKCU makes a point of including dance, the visual arts, and hands-
on craftsmanship in the weekend schedule. Past performers include Vance
Gilbert, Fred Eaglesmith, Odetta, Margo Timmons (of Cowboy Junkies), and
Trout Fishing in America.
For more information: (613) 230-8234 or festival@ottawafolk.org
Camping: No

Accommodations

■ **Chimo Ottawa**
1199 Joseph Cyr St.
Ottawa, ON K1J 7T4
Canada
(613) 744-1060

■ **Econo Lodge Ottawa East Orleans**
2098 Montreal Rd.
Ottawa, ON K1J 6M8
Canada
(613) 745-1531

■ **Delta Ottawa Hotel & Suites**
361 Queen St.
Ottawa, ON K1R 7S9
Canada
(800) 268-1133

♪ COLORADO RIVER BLUEGRASS FESTIVAL

First weekend in February
Bullhead City, Arizona/Laughlin, Nevada
www.coloradoriverbluegrassfestival.com
Admission: $

This reasonably priced festival (11 bands for under $20!) occurs over the course of three days, with all the usual trappings of a county fair rounding out the day's activities. Expect lots of food, some free-range jammers, and vendors selling everything from T-shirts to crystals. The list of performers will appeal to fans of more obscure bluegrass acts such as Front Range and the Schankman Twins. Every year a number of country gospel groups make an appearance as well.

For more information: (928) 768-5819
Camping: Yes
Accommodations

■ **Don Laughlin's Riverside Resort**
  Hotel & Casino
1650 S. Casino Dr.
Laughlin, NV 89029
(800) 227-3849

■ **Ramada Express Hotel & Casino**
2121 S. Casino Dr.
Laughlin, NV 89029
(800) 2-RAMADA

■ **Flamingo Hilton Hotel & Casino**
1900 S. Casino Dr.
Laughlin, NV 89029
(800) 352-6464

■ **Colorado Belle Hotel & Casino**
2100 S. Casino Dr.
Laughlin, NV 89029
(800) 458-9500

■ Harrah's Hotel & Casino
2900 S. Casino Dr.
Laughlin, NV 89029
(800) HARRAHS

COLUMBIA GORGE BLUEGRASS FESTIVAL

Late July
Stevenson, Washington
www.columbiagorgebluegrass.com
Admission: $$

The Columbia Gorge Festival offers a number of activities in addition to the dozen touring bands that perform on the main stage. You'll find arts and crafts booths, fiddle and vocal contests, and a band scramble. For this latter event, musicians are put together in random groups, given almost no time to rehearse, and then have to perform for the crowd. The results range from utterly brilliant to hilarious to tragic. Whatever the case, the tradition is a favorite activity of many of the folks both in the audience and onstage.

For more information: (509) 427-8146 or
bluegrass@columbiagorgebluegrass.com
Camping: Yes
Accommodations
■ Columbia Gorge Riverside Lodge
P.O. Box 381
Stevenson, WA 98648
(509) 427-5650 or (866) 427-5650

COOK FOREST FOLK GATHERING

Early September
Clarion, Pennsylvania
http://simplegiftsmusic.com/cookforest
Admission: $$$

The Cook Forest Folk Gathering, taking place on the campus of Clarion University in Pennsylvania, is a weekend of instructional workshops, open jamming, and onstage performances by artists such as John McCutcheon and the mountain music dulcimer band Sweetwater. Initially a dulcimer festival, in the past few years it's been branching out to include other folk instruments.

Artist Submissions: lrl@psu.edu

For more information: (814) 393-2227 or kstiglitz@clarion.edu

Camping: Yes. Contact Deer Meadow Campground at (814) 927-8125. Mention the Cook Forest Folk Gathering to receive a discount.

Accommodations

■ **Super 8**

135 Hotel Rd. (I 80 & Route 68)

Clarion, PA 16214

(814) 226-4550

■ **Days Inn**

225 Hotel Rd. (I 80 & Route 68)

Clarion, PA 16214

(814) 226-8682

COUNTRY FESTIVAL

First weekend in August

Skagastrond, Iceland

www.kantry.is/kantryfors.htm

Admission: $

You may not think of Iceland as a place to go for country music, but according to one Hallbjorn Hajartarsson, Iceland's lone country star and itinerant cowboy, the Country Festival held in the city of Skagastrond is one hootin', hollerin' good time. You may also be surprised to find that the festival, and country music itself, is very popular in Iceland as 10,000 people attended last year's event. You're not going to see Garth Brooks here, but a good time is almost guaranteed seeing as how it's too cold to sleep alone and there isn't much to do besides party.

For more information: hreppur@skagastrond.is

Camping: No

Accommodations: www.destination-iceland.com

COUNTRY RENDEZ-VOUS FESTIVAL

End of July

Craponne sur Arzon, France

www.ifrance.com/countryrdv

Admission: $$

Tune your radio dial to Country Rendez-Vous Radio, the event's own 24-hour country radio station, and get ready for a three-day party with 20,000 people and 14 bands. Set in the gorgeous mountains of central France, with concerts happening inside a natural amphitheater, these days the Rendez-

Vous boasts such popular American and European acts as Steve Earle, Bill Monroe, Kathy Mattea, and BR5-49. Remember to check out the music and dancing classes, American car parade, record exchange, and other "American cultural" facilities.

Artist Submissions

E-mail festival@festivaldecraponne.com and give your Web site URL or send a demo CD and a press kit to:

Georges Carrier

Festival Country Rendez-Vous

6 Place Croix de Carle

43500 Craponne sur Arzon

France

For more information: (33) 0-471-03-25-52 or festival@festivaldecraponne.com

Camping: Yes

Accommodations: For hotel reservations anywhere in the world call Interhotel at (34) 902-180-743.

COUNTRY STAMPEDE (MANHATTAN)

Late June

Manhattan, Kansas

http://countrystampede.com

Admission: $$$

As much as some people might like to see 300 head of cattle stampeding through the streets of the Lower East Side, the Country Stampede of Manhattan takes place in Tuttle Creek State Park in Manhattan, Kansas, not New York. And a good thing, too; those city folk could not handle the rodeo atmosphere and nonstop country music pouring from a giant stage with huge video monitors arranged throughout the crowd to allow just about everyone a front row seat. Eleven thousand people pass through the gates of the festival each year, so these may not be the most intimate of performances, but there is plenty of informal jamming to be joined in or witnessed in the adjacent campground. Like the Country Thunder Festivals, Country Stampede occurs twice during the summer. The other event happens in Sparta, Kentucky.

For more information: (800) 795-8091 or stampede@kansas.net

Camping: Yes

Accommodations

■ **Holiday Inn**
530 Richards Dr.
Manhattan, KS 66502
(785) 539-5311

■ **Super 8 Motel**
200 Tuttle Creek Blvd.
Manhattan, KS 66502
(785) 537-8468

■ **Best Western/Continental Inn**
100 Bluemont Ave.
Manhattan, KS 66502
(785) 776-4771

■ **Hampton Inn**
501 E. Poyntz Ave.
Manhattan, KS 66502
(785) 539-5000

■ **Days Inn**
1501 Tuttle Creek Blvd.
Manhattan, KS 66502
(785) 539-5391

■ **Motel 6**
510 Tuttle Creek Blvd.
Manhattan, KS 66502
(785) 537-1022

■ **Fairfield Inn**
300 Colorado St.
Manhattan, KS 66502
(785) 539-2400

COUNTRY STAMPEDE (SPARTA)

Early June

Sparta, Kentucky

http://countrystampede.com

Admission: $$$

A giant festival similar to the Country Thunder Festivals of Arizona and Wisconsin, Country Stampede features the biggest names in pop country performing in front of stadium-sized crowds.

For more information: (800) 795-8091 or stampede@kansas.net

Camping: Yes

Accommodations

■ **K & T Motel**
1590 Owenton Rd.
Williamstown, KY 41097
(606) 824-4371

■ **The Fountain Inn**
517 S. Main St.
Williamstown, KY 41097
(606) 823-1211

COUNTRY THUNDER USA (ARIZONA)

Late April
Queen Creek, Arizona
www.countrythunder.com
Admission: $$$

This is a major-league country music festival with two events that take place in both Arizona and Wisconsin a couple months apart from each other. So, if you really enjoy it the first time, there's nothing stopping you from catching the second one (except maybe a couple thousand miles). Both festivals feature the biggest names in country—John Michael Montgomery, Brooks & Dunne, Willie Nelson, and Colin Raye, among many others. Be advised, the festivals do not have identical lineups.

For more information: (480) 966-9920 or arizonainfo@countrythunder.com
Camping: Yes
Accommodations

■ **Blue Mist Motel**
40 S. Pinal Pkwy.
Florence, AZ 85232
(520) 868-5875

■ **Rancho Sonora Inn & RV Park**
9198 N. Hwy. 79
Florence, AZ 85232
(520) 868-8000

COUNTRY THUNDER USA (WISCONSIN)

Mid-July
Twin Lakes, Wisconsin
www.countrythunder.com
Admission: $$$

The sister festival to Country Thunder Arizona features an equally star-studded lineup (but not the same headliners) and equally large crowds, ample camping, and food and crafts booths galore.

For more information: (262) 279-6960 or
wisconsininfo@countrythunder.com
Camping: Yes
Accommodations

■ **Hut Motel**
108 N. Lake Ave.
Twin Lakes, WI 53181
(262) 877-2466

■ **Lakeview Motel**
131 S. Lake Ave.
Twin Lakes, WI 53181
(262) 877-3043

COUNTRY WESTERN JAMBOREE

First weekend in April
Dickinson, North Dakota
Admission: $

This is a very local competition that takes place on the grounds of Dickinson University in North Dakota. You will not encounter any familiar names here but you will undoubtedly witness a level of authenticity and ingenuousness often lost at larger festivals.

For more information: (701) 483-2185
Camping: Yes
Accommodations

■ **AmericInn**
229 15th St. W.
Dickinson, ND 58601
(701) 225-1400 or (800) 634-3444

■ **Best Western Badlands Inn**
71 W. Museum Dr.
Dickinson, ND 58601
(701) 225-9510 or (800) 285-1122

CREETOWN COUNTRY MUSIC FESTIVAL

September
Creetown, Scotland
www.creetown-countrymusic-festival.com
Admission: $$

Spend a few early autumn days in southwestern Scotland with performers such as Edward Warwick, the Dez Walters Band, and Sarah Jory. Four venues, sideshows, shopping, a beautiful countryside, and a fast-draw competition are only some of the attractions of this weekend festival.

Artist Submissions
The Jesse James Booking Agency
6 Silver St.
Creetown, Newton Stewart, DG8 7HN
United Kingdom
(44) 01671-820-281

For more information: jim.mcdowall@btinternet.com or enquiries@ellangowan.co.uk

Camping: Yes. There are tent and rough camping available at Creetown Caravan Park.

Accommodations

■ **Creetown Caravan Park**
Silver Street
Creetown
Newton Stewart DG8 7DQ
United Kingdom
(44) 01671-820-264
enquiries@creetown-caravans.co.uk

■ **Bobbin Guest House**
36 High St.
Gatehouse of Fleet
Castle Douglas, Kirkcudbrightshire DG7 2HP
United Kingdom
(44) 01557-814-229

■ **Ellangowan Hotel**
St. John Street, Creetown
Wigtownshire DG8 7JF
United Kingdom
(44) 01671-820-201
enquiries@ellangowan.co.uk

CROPREDY FESTIVAL

August
Cropredy, Oxfordshire, United Kingdom
Admission: $–$$

The Cropredy Festival was first organized in the late 1970s after the passing of beloved English folksinger Sandy Denny. Denny was once the main voice of the quintessential English folk-rock band, Fairport Convention. A farewell event for the band and fans was set up in Cropredy after Denny's passing, and it was so well received that one has been held every year since. Over the course of a weekend in early August, almost 20,000 people come to hear a selection of like-minded British folk artists, typically followed by a finale show featuring Fairport Convention and an assortment of their remaining members. Acclaimed guitarist Richard Thompson regularly takes part in the event, as do former Fairports Iain Matthews, Dave Swarbrick, Simon Nicol, and Ashley Hutchings.

Camping: Yes

Accommodations

■ **Heritage Eastgate Hotel**
High St.
Oxford OX1 4BE
United Kingdom
(44) 870-400-8201

■ **Red Lion**
Hart St.
Henley-on-Thames RG9 2AR
United Kingdom
(44) 01491-572161

♪ DANDENONG COUNTRY MUSIC MUSTER

Two days in March
Victoria, Australia
Admission: $$

This two-day Australian festival will entertain you with great country music from the likes of Rodney Vincent, Leanda O'Brien, and the Corporate Cowboys while helping you to be a better person (really!). Proceeds of the 2003 festival will go to Kids in Crisis, a branch of the Windmere fundraising organization dedicated to helping children in need. As if that weren't enough to get you there, the Muster offers such bonuses as a whip-cracking show and a Walkup Country Stage where you can sing your heart out to everyone in attendance.

For more information: (03) 9794-8966 or info@dandenongcountrymusic.com

Camping: Yes

Accommodations

■ **Dandenong Motel**
147 Princes Hwy.
Dandenong VIC 3175
Australia
(03) 9794 0599

■ **Willow Lodge Village**
Frankston-Dandenong Rd.
Dandenong South VIC 3175
Australia
(03) 9706 5433

■ **Imperial Quality Inn**
124 Princes Hwy.
Dandenong VIC 3175
Australia
(03) 9706 8611

■ **Twin Bridge Tourist Park**
370 Frankston Rd.
Dandenong VIC 3175
Australia
(03) 9706 5492

♪ DANDENONG RANGES FOLK FESTIVAL

Early March
National Rhododendron Gardens, Olinda, Australia
www.drfolk.com.au
Admission: $$

Contemporary and traditional Australian folk is served with food and wine in the stunning Dandenong Mountain Range in Olinda, Australia. There is also a massive rhododendron garden on the grounds. There are no American acts—the talent is strictly Australian.

Artist Submissions
www.drfolk.com.au/forms/RFFPerformersApplication2002.rtf
For more information: (61) 3-9754-1408 or mail@drfolk.com.au
Camping: Yes
Accommodations
■ **Loft in the Mill**
1-3 Harold St., corner of Mt. Dandenong Tourist Rd.
Olinda, VIC 3788
Australia
(61) 3-9751-1700

DARRINGTON BLUEGRASS FESTIVAL

Late July
Darrington, Washington
www.glacierview.net/bluegrass
Admission: $$

Top-flight bluegrass acts including IIIrd Tyme Out, Lost Highway, and the Knott Brothers are regular performers at this outdoor event, held on a campground in Darrington, Washington. Considering this festival takes place in the Pacific Northwest, the phrase "Dry Camping Available" may be a bit misleading, but the shows, food booths, and rampant open jamming at campsites occur rain or shine and folks make the best of it. An open mic is available to aspiring musicians, performers, and songwriters.
Artist submissions: Sandra Brahm: (360) 653-7472
For more information: (360) 436-1006 or diana@glacierview.net
Camping: Yes
Accommodations
■ **Stagecoach Inn**
1100 Seeman St.
Darrington, WA 98241
(360) 436-1776

DELAWARE VALLEY BLUEGRASS FESTIVAL

Labor Day weekend
Woodstown, New Jersey
www.brandywinefriends.org/dvbgf
Admission: $$

Past guests at the Delaware Valley Bluegrass Festival have included country diva Patty Loveless as well as the Dry Branch Fire Squad. Critically acclaimed bluegrass institution Del McCoury has performed practically every year since the festival was founded more than 30 years ago.

For more information: (302) 475-3454 or bfotm@dca.net

Camping: Yes

Accommodations

■ **Victorian Rose Farm**
947 Rt. 40
Woodstown, NJ 08098
(856) 769-4600

■ **Wellesley Inn**
New Jersey Turnpike & US Hwy. No. 2
Penns Grove, NJ 08069
(856) 299-3800

■ **Friendship Motor Inn**
605 Pennsville Auburn Rd.
Penns Grove, NJ 08069
(856) 299-3700

♪ DENTON BLUEGRASS FESTIVAL

Five days in June
Davie County, North Carolina
Admission: $–$$

The Denton Bluegrass Festival has been operating in the Advance, North Carolina, area for 20 years, and it recently made the Forest Lake Preserve its permanent home. Four days of jamming, performing, and recreation occur in the Thousand Trails camping facility, with music from noon until midnight each night and a roster of talent that has in the past included IIIrd Tyme Out, the Seldom Scene, and Rhonda Vincent, among a slew of regional acts.

For more information: Milton Harkey, P.O. Box 7661, Asheville, NC 28802-7661 or (828) 275-8650

Camping: Yes

Accommodations

■ **Comfort Inn**
1500 Yadkinville Rd.
Mocksville, NC 27028
(800) 852-0035 or (336) 751-7310

■ **Comfort Suites**
1620 Cotton Grove Rd.
Lexington, NC 27292
(336) 357-2333

■ **Royal 8 Motel**
402 National Blvd.
Lexington, NC 27292
(336) 248-5111

DOC WATSON MUSIC FEST

Mid-July
Sugar Grove, North Carolina
www.covecreek.net/docfest.htm
Admission: $

Held in honor of American flat-pick guitar treasure Doc Watson, the Doc Watson Music Fest is an outdoor event held in high summer, with a collection of well-known and not-so-well-known players paying tribute to the man and the far-reaching influence he has had on country music.

For more information: (828) 297-2200
Camping: No
Accommodations

■ **Holbrook Motel**
6626 W. US Hwy. 421
Wilkesboro, NC 28697
(910) 973-3693

■ **Lowe's Motel**
1201 Curtis Bridge Rd.
Wilkesboro, NC 28697
(336) 838-4186

DOOR COUNTY FOLK FESTIVAL

Fourth of July weekend
Ephraim, Wisconsin
www.jordan-webb.net/dcff
Admission: $$–$$$

Taking place every year from the Thursday after Independence Day through the weekend, the Door County Festival is a small but enjoyable event held in the Wisconsin vacation area known as "the Cape Cod of the Midwest." Sixteen dance workshops are offered in addition to the instrumental workshops that give students the opportunity to perform as a band at the Saturday concert. The village also holds parties each night of the festival in venues around town. The performing musicians are of the regional variety and the focus is on the area's largely Balkan descent, featuring folk music and religious services.

Artist Submissions
Paul Collins: (773) 463-2288 or (773) 506-8222
info@dcff.net
Gerhard Bernhard: (920) 854-2986
gerhard@concertcruises.com

For more information: (773) 463-2288 or dcff@jordan-webb.net
Camping: Yes
Accommodations
Package reservations made directly through the festival come with a weekend pass to the event.

▪ **Village Green Lodge**
P.O. Box 21
Ephraim, WI 54211
(920) 854-2515

▪ **Bay Breeze Resort**
P.O. Box 530
Ephraim, WI 54211
(920) 854-9066

▪ **Eagle Harbor Inn**
9914 Water St.
Ephraim, WI 54211
(920) 854-2121

♪ EAGLEWOOD FOLK FESTIVAL

Late August
Pefferlaw, Ontario, Canada
www.eaglewoodfolk.com
Admission: $–$$

The weekend before Labor Day each year serves as the date for this two-day showcase of local Canadian talent. The festival is held on the grounds of the Pefferlaw Resort in Ontario. Past performers have included Brent Titcomb and Katherine Wheatley.

Artist Submissions
Doug McArthur
9715 Morning Glory Rd.
P.O. Box 256
Pefferlaw ON L0E 1N0
Canada
dugimac@sympatico.ca
For more information: (705) 437-1634 or eaglewd@ils.net
Camping: Yes. On-site.
Accommodations

▪ **Colony Hotel Toronto**
89 Chestnut St.
Toronto, ON M5G 1R1
Canada
(800) 387-8687 or (416) 977-0707

▪ **Courtyard Downtown Toronto**
475 Yonge St.
Toronto, ON M4Y 1X7
Canada
(800) 847-5075 or (416) 924-0611

EDMONTON FOLK MUSIC FESTIVAL

Early August
Edmonton, Alberta, Canada
www.efmf.ab.ca
Admission: $$–$$$

This giant festival features multiple stages and more than 100 performers ranging from the legendary to the local. And of course there are tons of food vendors, crafts and workshops galore, and activities for children. New Orleans R&B icon Irma Thomas, Texas blues big shot Clarence "Gatemouth" Brown, retro rockers Big Sandy & his Fly-Rite Boys, and the Indigo Girls are just a few of the many excellent artists you can catch at this bustling event held on a hillside just outside of the city of Edmonton.

Artist Submissions
Deadline January 31; send demo to:
Edmonton Folk Music Festival
c/o Artist Submissions
Box 4130
Edmonton, AB T6E 4T2
Canada
For more information: (780) 429-1899 or postmaster@efmf.ab.ca or tickets@efmf.ab.ca
Camping: No
Accommodations
Edmonton Tourism
(800) 463-4667

EQUIBLUES: COUNTRY & WESTERN FESTIVAL

Mid-August
Saint-Agrève, France
www.equiblues.com
Admission: $$

Taking place in a French town famous for its food and beautiful landscape, Equiblues is almost more American than America itself, with its on-site rodeo, innumerable contests (bull riding and calf tying among them), and workshops galore. Eight years old and going strong, this festival attracts a fairly large crowd, due in part to appearances by queen of Americana Rosie Flores and the critically acclaimed contemporary country singer Jacob Lyda.

For more information: (33) 04-75-30-25-43 or (33) 06-70-71-79-48 or equiblues@equiblues.com

Camping: Yes

Accommodations

■ **L'Arrache**
La Gare
Saint-Agrève 07320
Ardèche, France
(33) 04-7530-1012

■ **Domain De Rilhac**
Rilhac
Saint-Agrève 07320
Ardèche, France
(33) 04-7530-2020

FALCON RIDGE FOLK FESTIVAL

Late July

Hillsdale, New York

www.falconridgefolk.com

Admission: $$–$$$

This family-friendly event takes place amid the calming green meadows of Long Hill Farm at the edge of the Berkshires in east-central New York. Performances, workshops, and dancing happen on four different stages. Past performers have included Odetta, Shawn Colvin, Tom Paxton, and a host of lesser-known regional acts.

Artist Submissions

Anne Saunders, Artistic Director: (860) 364-2138 or anne@falconridgefolk.com

For more information: (860) 364-0366 or info@falconridgefolk.com

Camping: Yes. On-site.

Accommodations

■ **Aubergine Cor**
Rt. 22 & Rt. 23
Hillsdale, NY 12529
(518) 325-3412
www.aubergine.com

■ **Flickers B&B**
2789 Rt. 23
Hillsdale, NY 12529
(518) 325-6467
www.flickersbandb.com

■ **The Honored Guest**
20 Hunt Rd.
Hillsdale, NY 12529
(518) 325-9100
www.honoredguest.com

FAN FAIR

Three days in June
Nashville, Tennessee
www.fanfair.com
Admission: $$$

A festival in Music City is worth going to simply because it's in Nashville. Even if you don't see your favorite country stars on the stage, there's a good chance you'll bump into them in the crowd. Still, Fan Fair boasts some big-name talent: Trace Adkins, Brooks & Dunn, Toby Keith, Alan Jackson—the list of stars goes on and on. This is a massive event and a haven for autograph seekers; most of the performers hold signing sessions in booths scattered throughout the fairgrounds. Exact appearance times are not posted, however, so you may find yourself scrambling all over, but that's part of the fun. Besides the festival, Nashville is also home to the Grand Ole Opry and the Country Music Hall of Fame, so if you need a break from the bustle of the Fan Fair, you have an entire country music mecca to explore.

For more information: (866) 326-3247
Camping: No
Accommodations
■ **Nashville Convention & Visitors Bureau**
(800) 657-6910

FARMFEST

Early August
Johannesburg, Michigan
www.farmhousemusic.org/farmfest
Admission: $$

The Johannesburg, Michigan, grassroots, not-for-profit arts and musical organization Farmhouse Productions stages this yearly festival in a clearing in the deep woods of northern Michigan. There are open jams and performances from touring folk, country, rock, and reggae bands (Eddie from Ohio, Reggae Jam, Maggie's Farm). Dancing, vendor booths, roving packs of fully made-up clowns, and the occasional traditional Irish music band are all to be expected.

Artist Submissions

Send demo packet to:

Farmhouse Music Organization

P.O. Box 525

Johannesburg, MI 49751

Be sure to follow the specific instructions given at the Web site.

For more information: (989) 786-3273 or info@farmhousemusic.org

Camping: Yes. On-site.

Accommodations

■ **Cedars Motel**
701 N. Center Ave.
Gaylord, MI 49735
(517) 732-4525

■ **Dixon Lake Motel**
2197 W. Dixon Lake Dr.
Gaylord, MI 49735
(517) 732-2802

■ **Chippewa Hotel**
26 Hayes Rd.
Gaylord, MI 49735
(517) 731-1216

♩ FERGUS SCOTTISH FESTIVAL

Early August

Fergus, Ontario, Canada

www.fergusscottishfestival.com

Admission: $–$$

Scottish culture is the theme of this late summer event, featuring bagpipe and drum performances and competitions, candle-lighting ceremonies, and discussions of Scottish heritage. You'll also find an invitational competition of "heavy events" in which men wearing kilts throw medium to extremely heavy objects (hammers, sticks, stones) for distance and gracefulness of flight. The competition is topped off with a brutal tug-of-war. There are Scotch tastings (sponsored by Dewar's), fiddling concerts, a Gathering of the Clans, and open Celtic jams.

For more information: (519) 787-0099 or info@fergusscottishfestival.com

Camping: Yes

Accommodations

■ **Groves Mill Inn Fergus**
170 St. David St. N.
Fergus, ON N1M 2L6
Canada
(519) 843-8871

■ **Best Western Emerald Inn**
106 Carden St.
Guelph, ON N1H 3A3
Canada
(519) 836-1331

■ **Highlander Inn**
280 Bridge St.
Fergus, ON N1M 1T6
Canada
(519) 843-3115

■ **Comfort Inn**
480 Silvercreek Pkwy.
Guelph, ON N1H 7R5
Canada
(519) 763-1900

♪ FESTIVAL INTERNATIONAL

April

Lafayette, Louisiana

www.festivalinternational.com/about.html#link1

Admission: $–$$

The Festival International in Lafayette, Louisiana, is a five-day marathon celebration of the diverse ethnic makeup of southern Louisiana, with a particular concentration on the heavy French influence, heritage, and history of the region. The music, dance, and foods of Hispanic, African, French, and Caribbean cultures are exhibited and enjoyed by festivalgoers who travel from all over the world to attend this eclectic affair. The list of performers includes the very biggest names of Louisiana's rich musical history playing alongside local talent and internationally recognized stars. Irma Thomas, Ladysmith Black Mambazo, Sonny Landreth, and Steve Riley & the Mamou Playboys have all appeared at past festivals.

For more information: (337) 232-8086 or lisa@festivalinternational.com

Camping: No

Accommodations

■ **Acadian Motel**
120 N. University Ave.
Lafayette, LA 70506
(318) 234-3268

■ **Bendel Executive Suites**
213 Bendel Rd.
Lafayette, LA 70506
(318) 261-0604

■ **Executive House Hotel**
115 Sycamore Dr.
Lafayette, LA 70506
(318) 988-1750

♪ FESTIVAL MEMOIRE ET RACINES

July
Joliette, Quebec, Canada
www.memoireracines.qc.ca
Admission: $

This Quebecois festival, held on the banks of the Outaragawesipi River in Joliette, specializes in the traditional music of the region (especially banjo music) but also incorporates plenty of themes and activities from the cultures of the world. Attend dance and instrumental workshops during the day, while taking a break from visiting the food and arts and crafts booths. Concerts begin in the evening, with past performers including the Brothers Brunet, Celtitude, and banjo virtuoso Guy Donis.

For more information: (450) 752-6798 or (888) 810-6798 or festival@memoireracines.qc.ca
Camping: No
Accommodations

■ **Motel Bonsoir**
120 Chemin du Club de Golf
Joliette, QC J6E 2B6
Canada
(514) 753-4258

■ **Chateau Joliette**
450 rue St. Thomas
Joliette, QC J6E 2C5
Canada
(450) 752-2525

♪ FESTIVAL OF AMERICAN FIDDLE TUNES

First weekend in June
Port Townsend, Washington
www.centrum.org
Admission: $$

Centrum, at historic Fort Worden State Park in the Victorian seaport of Port Townsend, Washington, hosts this festival each year, offering examples of all types of fiddle music from traditional American styles to Eastern

European and jazz styles as well as dancing, food vendors, and arts and crafts booths.

For more information: (360) 385-5320

Camping: No

Accommodations

■ **Aladdin Motor Inn**
2333 Washington St.
Port Townsend, WA 98368
(360) 385-3747

■ **Valley View Motel**
162 Hwy. 20
Port Townsend, WA 98368
(360) 385-1666 or (800) 280-1666

■ **Port Townsend Inn**
2020 Washington St.
Port Townsend, WA 98368
(360) 385-2211 or (800) 216-4985

♪ FESTIVAL OF FRIENDS

Early August
Hamilton, Ontario, Canada
www.creativearts.on.ca/viewsection.php/6
Admission: $$

This celebration of Canadian arts features exclusively Canadian musicians, a homegrown aerial act called High Strung, Canada-themed arts and crafts, and Canadian foods. Concerts take place on four stages on the grounds of Gage Park in Hamilton, Ontario.

Artist Submissions
108 James St. N.
Hamilton, ON L8R 2K7
Canada

For more information: (905) 777-9777 or info@creativearts.on.ca

Camping: No

Accommodations

■ **City Motor Motel**
1620 Main St.
Hamilton, ON L8K 1E8
Canada
(905) 549-1371

■ **Days Inn**
1187 Upper James
Hamilton, ON L8K 1C2
Canada
(905) 575-9666

FESTIVAL OF THE BLUEGRASS

Early June
Lexington, Kentucky
www.festivalofthebluegrass.com
Admission: $

Kentucky Horse Park annually hosts this summer weekend festival that features bluegrass and bluegrass only. Kentucky is, after all, the land of the Blue Grass, so this should come as no surprise. Fans of the pure American art will find themselves in paradise when attending this medium-sized, fully authentic event. There are plenty of activities for the kids, workshops for both young and old, and performers ranging from fairly well known (Dry Branch Fire Squad, IIIrd Tyme Out, Rhoda Vincent) to somewhat obscure (Kentucky Blue, Karl Schifflet & Big Country, Wildfire).

For more information: (859) 846-4995 or jean@festivalofthebluegrass.com
Camping: Yes. Call (859) 254-7628 or e-mail camping@festivalofthebluegrass.com

Accommodations

■ **Keenelodge Motor Inn**
5556 Versailles Pike
Lexington, KY 40506
(606) 254-6699

■ **Bryan Station Inn**
273 E. New Circle Rd.
Lexington, KY 40506
(606) 299-4162

■ **American Inn**
826 E. New Circle Rd.
Lexington, KY 40506
(606) 231-5890

FIESTA TROPICALE

Late February
Hollywood, Florida
www.fiestatropicale.com
Admission: $

This is a full-on Mardi Gras celebration including music, food, a parade, and dancing in the streets of this sunny south Florida town. Fiesta Tropicale actually started in 1935 and included a street circus, but the celebration was discontinued when its founder died in 1967. Thirty years later, in 1997, a community-based group revived the festival and it's going strong again today. Past performers have included C. J. Chenier and the Red Hot Louisiana Band, Steve Riley and the Mamou Playboys, and New Orleans bluesman John Mooney.

For more information: (954) 926-3377 or Info@MardiGrasFiesta.com

Camping: No

Accommodations

■ **Ramada Hollywood**
1160 N. Vermont Ave.
Hollywood, CA 90029
(954) 927-3341

FINGER LAKES GRASSROOTS FESTIVAL

One weekend in late July
Trumansburg, New York
www.grassrootsfest.org
Admission: $$

Across four stages on as many nights, the Finger Lakes Grassroots Festival builds a small community in upstate New York. The acts here are always numerous and eclectic—ranging from funk to zydeco, with plenty of time for folk, roots, and world music. Since the festival's inception in 1991, artists such as 10,000 Maniacs, King Sunny Ade, NRBQ, and Burning Spear have performed. For those not camping on-site (camping spots sell out quickly), shuttle buses help get people to their hotel and back.

Artist Submissions

Artists should fill out the application on the Web site and mail it to:
GrassRoots Bands
P.O. Box 941
Trumansburg, NY 14886

For more information: grassroots@grassrootsfest.org

Camping: Yes

Accommodations

■ **Comfort Inn**
356 Elmira Rd.
Ithaca, NY 14850
(607) 272-0100

■ **The Archway**
7020 Searsburg Rd.
Trumansburg, NY 14886
(800) 387-6175

FINNEGAN'S WAKE MUSIC FESTIVAL

Early September
Summit, New York
www.nymusicfestival.com
Admission: $

This festival is a relaxing weekend of folk, blues, lite jazz, bluegrass, and traditional Celtic music by the banks of Summit Lake in Summit, New York. Featuring primarily local musicians, with a handful of Irish imports, the Finnegan's Wake Music Festival offers a focus on Irish music but incorporates all manner of acoustic music. The campground is connected to the festival and attendance includes a moderately sized, faithful crowd. Food is available, along with the festival staple of workshops and crafts sales.

For more information: (518) 287-1271 or bidwell@midtel.net
Camping: Yes. On-site.
Accommodations
■ **Lake View House**
P.O. Box 94
Summit, NY 12175
(518) 287-1356

FLAT ROCK MUSIC FESTIVAL

September
Flat Rock, North Carolina
www.flatrockmusicfestival.com
Admission: $$–$$$

If you ever needed an excuse to visit the beautiful mountains of western North Carolina, this is it. Enjoy diverse musical performances while making time for contra dancing, midnight jams, tons of music workshops, swimming, boating, open mic night, and the Hank Williams Songwriter Competition. Musical acts include Trout Fishing in America, Steady Rollin Bob Margolin, Rev. Billy C. Wirtz, and Snake Oil Medicine Show. Portions of the event's proceeds go to the Environment and Conservation Organization and to Camp Merry Times, a free camp for children with cancer and their families.

Artist Submissions
FRMF
Attention: Charlie Tucker
P.O. Box 1322
Flat Rock, NC 27831
(828) 692-2005
info@flatrockmusicfestival.com
For more information: (828) 692-2005 or info@flatrockmusicfestival.com
Camping: Yes
Accommodations

■ **Highland Lake Inn**
Highland Lake Rd.
P.O. Box 1026
Flat Rock, NC 28731
(800) 635-5101 or (828) 693-6812

■ **Holiday Inn Express**
111 Commercial Blvd.
Flat Rock, NC 28731
(828) 698-8899

■ **The Waverly Inn**
783 N. Main St.
Hendersonville, NC 28792
(800) 537-8195

♪ FLORIDA FOLK FESTIVAL

Late May
White Springs, Florida
www.dep.state.fl.us/parks/folkfest/index.asp
Admission: $

Florida's melting pot of bluegrass, country, folk, Latin, and Caribbean music is on display at this weekend-long festival held on the banks of the Suwanee River. A state fiddle contest, more than 200 concerts a day on multiple stages, storytelling for the kids, and dancing for everybody are all featured at this giant, longstanding (51 years and counting) event.
For more information: (850) 488-1484
Camping: Yes
Accommodations

■ **Colonial House Inn**
3151 Country Rd. 136
White Springs, FL 32096
(904) 963-2401

■ **U.S. Inn**
State Rd. 136 & IH 75
White Springs, FL 32096
(904) 397-2155

■ **Scottish Inn**
2969 County Rd. 136
White Springs, FL 32096
(904) 963-2501

FOGGY HOLLOW BLUEGRASS GATHERIN'

First week in June
Wellington, Alabama
www.foggyhollow.com
Admission: $

Held on the Foggy Hollow Farm in Wellington, Alabama, this laid-back and family-friendly festival has seen the likes of IIIrd Tyme Out and Continental Divide perform in the past. Foggy Hollow Farm house band Foggy Hollow also performs here regularly. Frequent, spontaneous jams crop up throughout the weekend, and people camp right on the grounds of the farm.

Artist Submissions
Foggy Hollow Farm
439 Ross Lake Rd.
Wellington, AL 36279
For more information: (256) 492-3700 or (256) 492-9080 or gwagency@cybrtyme.com
Camping: Yes
Accommodations
www.touralabama.org/index-FL.htm

FOLK ON THE ROCKS MUSIC FESTIVAL

Mid-July
Yellowknife, Canada
www.folkontherocks.com
Admission: $$

The Folk on the Rocks Music Festival is a large outdoor event that takes place in a beautiful valley in secluded Yellowknife, Canada. A dozen or so bands perform on a single stage over the course of three days, with workshops, kids games, and food booths aplenty. All styles of folk and world music are represented, with a smattering of good old rock 'n' roll thrown in for good measure. The roster is made up entirely of Canadian musicians.

Artist Submissions

The selection committee asks that you do not provide a link to your Web site or send in printed material without an accompanying CD. From September 1 to January 15 only, send CD and small press kit to:

Folk on the Rocks Music Festival

Attention: Artistic Director

Box 326

Yellowknife, NT X1A 2N3

Canada

selections@folkontherocks.com

For more information: (867) 920-7806 or fotr@ssimicro.com

Camping: Yes

Accommodations: www.canadianhotelguide.com/northwestterritory

♪ FOLK PROJECT SPRING FESTIVAL

Mid-May and mid-October

Sussex County, New Jersey

www.folkproject.org

Admission: $

The Northern New Jersey Folk Project holds two festivals a year, one in the spring and one in the fall. Both feature local talent playing on an outdoor stage, along with camping and boating in the lake adjacent to the Sussex County YMCA camp. Skits, square dancing, and educational workshops are also offered.

For more information: (609) 426-9064 or FestReg@FolkProject.org

Camping: Yes

Accommodations

■ **Fountain Square Inn**

82 Fountain Square

Sussex, NJ 07461

(973) 875-4198

■ **Rolling Hills Motel**

127 Rt. 23

Sussex, NJ 07461

(201) 875-1270

■ **High Point Motor Lodge**

1328 State Rt. 23

Sussex, NJ 07461

(732) 702-1860

♪ FOLKMOOT USA: NORTH CAROLINA INTERNATIONAL FOLK FESTIVAL

Two weeks in July
Waynesville, North Carolina
www.folkmoot.com
Admission: $$

This two-week event showcases many varieties of folk music, food, dance, and art from around the world against the jaw-dropping backdrop of the Great Smoky Mountains National Park. Performers come from as far afield as Eastern Europe and Tahiti to share the wonder and beauty of their respective cultures. Over the years this festival has seen more than 185 groups from almost 100 different countries perform.

For more information: (828) 452-2997 or (877) FOLK-USA or folkmoot@pobox.com

Camping: Yes

Accommodations

■ **Boyd Mountain Log Cabins**
R.R. 2, Box 167
Waynesville, NC 28786
(828) 926-1575

■ **Brookmont Motor Inn**
1401 N. Main St.
Waynesville, NC 28786
(704) 456-6094

♪ FOLKWOODS FESTIVAL

Early August
Philips van Lenneppark, Eindhoven, Netherlands
www.folkwoods.com
Admission: $

This outdoor festival is held during the summer months in the Netherlands, featuring indigenous folk musicians, puppet shows, and open jamming, so be sure to bring an instrument. Concerts take place inside a giant circus tent, and camping is available on the grounds.

Artist Submissions
Coöperatieve Vereniging U.A. Folkwoods
Kanaaldijk Zuid 7c
5611 VA, Eindhoven
Netherlands

For more information: (31) 040-243-2294 or info@folkwoods.com
Camping: Yes. On-site.
Accommodations: http://eindhoven.netherlands.allwebhotels.com

FRENCH QUARTER FESTIVAL

Mid-April
New Orleans, Louisiana
www.frenchquarterfestival.org
Admission: *FREE*

The French Quarter Festival covers all forms of New Orleans music: Dixieland jazz, Cajun, zydeco, New Orleans blues, and R&B, to name just a few. It celebrates its 20-year anniversary in 2003. No less than 14 stages are set up throughout the bustling French Quarter, and unsigned local musicians are given an opportunity to perform. Food and drink are plentiful—after all, this is New Orleans!—and if there's one place in America that knows how throw a party, it's the French Quarter. Be sure to bring your drinking cap.

Artist Submissions

August through November, send press kit (CD, press release, photo) to:
FQFI
100 Conti St.
New Orleans, LA 70130
For more information: Sandra Dartus (504) 522-5730 or info@frenchquarterfestival.org
Camping: No
Accommodations

■ **Chateau Hotel**
1001 Rue Chartres
New Orleans, LA 70116
(504) 524-9636

■ **Historic French Market Inn**
501 Rue Decatur
New Orleans, LA 70130
(888) 487-1543

FRIZZELL COUNTRY MUSIC FESTIVAL

One day in October
Pawnee, Oklahoma
www.frizzellfestival.com
Admission: $

A one-day tribute to the country music legend Lefty Frizzell features continuous live music throughout the afternoon and on into the evening. A selection of local country bands plays originals, country standards, and covers of Lefty's best songs. Food and arts and crafts booths are set up near the main stage.

For more information: (888) 917-5575
Camping: Yes
Accommodations

■ **Pawnee Antique Inn**
807 7th St.
Pawnee, OK 74058
(918) 762-3222

■ **Pecan Grove Motel**
611 4th St.
Pawnee, OK 74058
(918) 762-3061

FROSTBITE MUSIC FESTIVAL

Mid-February
Whitehorse, Yukon, Canada
www.frostbitefest.ca
Admission: $$

With more than 50 acts performing on five stages strategically placed throughout the fairgrounds in Whitehorse, Yukon, the Frostbite Music Festival promises a little something for everybody. In 2002, folksingers Kate and Anna McGarrigle performed alongside Deep Soul legends Dan Penn and Spooner Oldham. Musicians from Canada, the United States, and beyond perform over three days, with workshops, food booths, and arts and crafts in abundance.

For more information: frostbite@polarcom.com
Camping: Yes
Accommodations

■ **Westmark Whitehorse Hotel**
2nd Ave. & Wood St.
Box 4250
Whitehorse, YT Y1A 3T3
Canada
(867) 668-4700 or (800) 544-0970

■ **Yukon Inn**
4220 4th Ave.
Whitehorse, YT Y1A 1K1
Canada
(867) 667-2527

GALSTON COUNTRY MUSIC FESTIVAL

Early September
Sydney, Australia
www.galstonfestival.com
Admission: $

Held the second weekend of every September, the Galston Country Music Festival is a celebration of Australia's burgeoning country music scene, featuring such local favorites as Bullamakanka Bush Band, Carter and Carter, and Wayne Law. The festival is situated in an outlying rural part of Sydney and proceeds go to a number of charities.

For more information: (61) 02-9653-2483 or tpage@ozE-mail.com.au
Camping: Yes
Accommodations
■ Carlton Crest Hotel
169 179 Thomas St.
Sydney 2000
Australia
(61) 02-9281-6888

GAMBLE ROGERS FOLK FESTIVAL

Early May
St. Augustine, Florida
www.gamblefest.com
Admission: $$

More than 30 musicians—John Stewart, the Waybacks, and Clyde Walker among them— perform on multiple stages during this two-day festival held in classy St. Augustine, Florida. Storytelling, contra dancing, and square dancing are also featured.

For more information: (904) 794-0222 or downsd@mail-grms.stjohns.k12.fl.us
Camping: Yes. Contact Anastasia State Recreation Area at (904) 461-2033.
Accommodations

■ Florida Motel
253 San Marco Ave.
St. Augustine, FL 32084
(904) 824-2348

■ Seabreeze Motel
208 Anastasia Blvd.
St. Augustine, FL 32080
(904) 829-8122

■ **A-1-A Court**
825 Anastasia Blvd.
St. Augustine, FL 32080
(904) 824-2834

GENERAL SAM HOUSTON FOLK FESTIVAL

Mid-April
Huntsville, Texas
www.shsu.edu/~smm_www/FolkFest
Admission: $

This festival, sponsored by the General Sam Houston Museum Society, is a celebration of nineteenth century Texas featuring many musicians and old-time themed activities. History buffs take note: reenactments, tomahawk-throwing contests, and the firing of ancient cannons are all part of the fun. You can even become an honorary Ranger of the Texas Republic. Past performers include Sweet Song String Band, Eddie & Martha Adcock, and lauded Texan songwriter Steven Fromholz.

For more information: (936) 294-1832 or mmcmanus100@yahoo.com

Camping: No

Accommodations

■ **Baker Motel**
865 S. Sam Houston Ave.
Huntsville, TX 77340
(409) 295-3761

■ **Lakinta Inn**
1407 Interstate 45
Huntsville, TX 77340
(409) 295-6454

■ **Rodeway Inn**
3211 Interstate 34
Huntsville, TX 77340
(409) 295-7595

GETTYSBURG BLUEGRASS FESTIVAL

End of August
Gettysburg, Pennsylvania
www.gettysburgbluegrass.com/index2.cfm
Admission $–$$$

The Gettysburg Bluegrass Festival has been running for the past 25 years at Granite Hill Campground, just five miles from historic Gettysburg. A host of local country, folk, and bluegrass bands perform alongside national acts during this four-day gathering. In addition to almost continuous music, a number of workshops are held every year, focusing on arts and crafts.

For more information: (717) 642-8749 or gburggrass@aol.com

Camping: Yes

Accommodations

■ **College Motel**
345 Carlisle St.
Gettysburg, PA 17325
(717) 334-6731

■ **Colton Motel**
232 Steinwehr Ave.
Gettysburg, PA 17325
(717) 334-5514

■ **Colonial Motel**
157 Carlisle St.
Gettysburg, PA 17325
(717) 334-3126

♪ GOOD OLD FASHIONED BLUEGRASS FESTIVAL

Second weekend in July
Bolado Park, California
www.scbs.org/gofhomepage.htm
Admission: $$–$$$

As the name suggests, this is a laid-back, simple festival with plenty of talent (Stoney Mountain Ramblers and the Earl Brothers have appeared in the past). The easygoing atmosphere encourages between-set jamming with performers and audiences alike. If you're looking for an unpretentious, highly musical good time, with all the trappings of a giant festival and none of the overcrowded hassle, this gathering, held just outside Gilroy, California (the garlic capital of the world) is an excellent destination.

For more information: (831) 479-GOFI or fiddler@best.com

Camping: Yes

Accommodations

■ **Inn Of Gilroy**
360 Leavesley Rd.
Gilroy, CA 95020
(408) 848-1467

■ **Leavesley Inn**
8430 Murray Ave.
Gilroy, CA 95020
(800) 624-8225

■ **Forest Park Inn**
375 Leavesley Rd.
Gilroy, CA 95020
(408) 848-5144

GRAVES MOUNTAIN BLUEGRASS FESTIVAL

First weekend in June
Syria, Virginia
www.gravesmountain.com/bluegrass.htm
Admission: $$–$$$

J. D. Crowe & the New South and the Del McCoury Band are regulars at this three-day festival, held at the foot of the Blue Ridge Mountains in Syria, Virginia. The shows are put on at Grave's Mountain Lodge, a secluded, family-operated resort.

For more information: (540) 923-4231 or bluegrass@gravesmountain.com
Camping: No
Accommodations
■ **Graves' Mountain Lodge**
Route 670
Syria, VA 22743
(540) 923-4231

GREAT LAKES FOLK FESTIVAL

Early August
East Lansing, Michigan
www.greatlakesfolkfest.net
Admission: $

Now that the traveling treasure known as the National Folk Festival has moved from East Lansing, Michigan, to Bangor, Maine, for a three-year stint in that city, the University of Michigan has begun hosting its own yearly festival. You'll find plenty of local musicians, food, and crafts vendors and family-friendly activities at the Great Lakes Folk Festival. The event takes place in downtown East Lansing, and a number of local venues open their doors to host concerts.

Artist Submissions
Patrick Power
Great Lakes Folk Festival
Michigan State University Museum
West Circle Dr.
East Lansing, MI 48824
(517) 432-GLFF
glffbooking@museum.msu.edu

For more information: pr@museum.msu.edu
Camping: No
Accommodations

■ Travel Lodge East Lansing
2736 E. Grand River Ave.
East Lansing, MI 48823
(517) 337-1621

■ Willow Lakes Motel
7113 E. M 78
East Lansing, MI 48823
(517) 339-9021

GREAT RIVER FOLK FESTIVAL

Late August
La Crosse, Wisconsin
www.viterbo.edu/personalpages/faculty/rruppel/fest.html
Admission: $

Traditional folk musicians and contemporary singer-songwriters gather on the La Crosse campus of the University of Wisconsin, along with artists and square dance callers, but you'll also enjoy appearances by such acoustic music stars as John McCutcheon, Vance Gilbert, and Katy Moffatt. Workshops showcasing the hammered dulcimer and other traditional instruments are offered.

For more information: (608) 784-3033 or grff@juno.com
Camping: No
Accommodations

■ Bluff View Inn
3715 Mormon Coulee Rd.
La Crosse, WI 54601
(608) 788-0600

■ Brookstone Inn
1830 Rose St.
La Crosse, WI 54601
(608) 781-1400

■ Exel Inn of La Crosse
2150 Rose St.
La Crosse, WI 54601
(608) 781-0400

GREY FOX BLUEGRASS FESTIVAL

Mid-July
Ancramdale, New York
www.greyfoxbluegrass.com/gf_tickets.cfm
Admission: $$

Hosted by members of the Dry Branch Fire Squad, the Grey Fox Bluegrass Festival has been held on Rothvoss Farm, overlooking the beautiful Berkshire Mountains, for the past 26 years. You will find a lineup that includes many of the biggest names in bluegrass and a fun, communal atmosphere marked by contests and workshops.

For more information: GreyFoxOffice@aol.com or burdette@endor.com

Camping: Yes

Accommodations

■ **Blue Spruce Inn & Suites**

3093 Route 9

Valatie, NY 12184

(518) 758-9711

GUILDTOWN BLUEGRASS FESTIVAL

Early August

Guildtown, Perthshire, Scotland

www.ednet.co.uk/~russell/guild.htm

Admission: $$

The sounds of live bluegrass ring through the streets of Guildtown every August, as bands come from all over the United Kingdom not just to play but also to learn more about the music they love. Informal jams dominate the local pub scene, and camping is provided downtown, close to all the action.

For more information: (131) 333-5009 or john@jsheldon.freeserve.co.uk

Camping: Yes

Accommodations

■ **Anglers Inn**

Main Rd.

Guildtown

Perth, Perthshire PH2 6BS

United Kingdom

(44) 182-164-0329

■ **Newmiln Country House Hotel**

Newmiln Country Estate

Guildtown

Perth, Perthshire PH2 6AE

United Kingdom

(44) 173-855-2364

HANK SNOW TRIBUTE

Mid-August

Bridgewater, Nova Scotia, Canada

www.hanksnow.com
Admission: $$$

Beautiful Bridgewater, Nova Scotia, provides a picturesque backdrop for this annual event commemorating the music of native son and country great Hank Snow. Snow is best remembered for the honky-tonk ballads "Yellow Roses" and "(Now and Then There's) A Fool Such as I." Local musicians vie for various awards ("Sounds Like Hank," "Guitar Pickin'") while festivalgoers have the chance to win for best dressed. The whole thing takes place in the Hank Snow Country Music Centre, which is home to a large collection of Hank Snow memorabilia as well as the Nova Scotia Country Music Hall of Fame, complete with a giant music library and museum. This is a must for die-hard Hank Snow fans, but any fan of the classic pop country period of the 1950s and '60s will want to check this one out.

For more information: (902) 354-4675 or info@hanksnow.com

Camping: No

Accommodations

■ **Comfort Inn Bridgewater**
49 North St.
Bridgewater, NS B47 2V7
Canada
(866) 665-9330

♩) HAVELOCK COUNTRY MUSIC FESTIVAL

Mid-August
Havelock, Ontario, Canada
www.havelockjamboree.com
Admission: $$$

This Canadian festival promises to be a destination for families and partiers alike, proudly declaring, "This is as close as you'll get to Nashville in Ontario!" A separate, "partier" campground is set apart from the others and labeled with the warning (or the assurance, depending on your point of view), "no sleeping available." Lesser-known country acts make up the schedule of performers, but headliner Colin Raye has appeared here in the past. You can look forward to food vendors, plentiful camping, and open jam sessions.

For more information: (705) 778-3353 or info@havelockjamboree.com

Camping: Yes

Accommodations

■ **Elijah House B&B**
1450 Webster Rd.
Norwood, ON KDL 2V0
Canada
(705) 639-1355

■ **Comfort Inn**
1209 Landsdowne St.
Peterborough, ON K9J 7M2
Canada
(705) 740-7000

■ **Rush Point Cottages**
R.R. #4
Havelock, ON KDL 1Z0
Canada
(705) 778-3101

♪ HERITAGE CRAFT & OLDE TIME MUSIC FESTIVAL

Mid-June

Coshocton, Ohio

www.roscoevillage.com/festivals.cfm?content=oldetimemusic

Admission: $

Bluegrass and old-time fiddle music fills the air in the quaint downtown area of Coshocton, Ohio, during this two-day event held in early summer each year. There is also an art show and sale; guitar, fiddle, dulcimer, and banjo workshops; and a traditional flat-picking guitar contest open to guitar players of all ages.

For more information: (800) 877-1830

Camping: No

Accommodations

■ **Three Rivers Motel**
310 S. Whitewoman St.
Coshocton, OH 43812
(740) 622-3873

■ **Linwood by the River Motel**
20020 State Route 16
Coshocton, OH 43812
(740) 622-1004

■ **Downtown Motel**
723 Main St.
Coshocton, OH 43812
(740) 622-6607

♪ HIAWATHA TRADITIONAL MUSIC FESTIVAL

Mid-July
Marquette, Michigan
www.portup.com/~hiawatha/festival.html
Admission: $$

Regional bluegrass and folk acts such as True Blue, Tangerine Trousers, Greg Boerner, and Lousiana-based Cajun band La Feufollet have all appeared at the Hiawatha Festival. The event takes place on a wooded campground in Marquette, on Michigan's Upper Peninsula. In addition to the workshops and crafts shows, this festival is proactive about getting teenagers involved and provides a "Teen Zone" area. But supervisors still keep an eye on them because we all know what teenagers do in the woods without many adults around—they start fires, which can be dangerous. The Friday night of the festival features a rollicking barn dance.

Artist Submissions
Hiawatha Music Co-op
P.O. Box 414
Marquette, MI 49855
For more information: (906) 226-8575 or hiawatha@portup.com
Camping: Yes. On-site.
Accommodations

■ **Bavarian Inn**
2782 US Hwy. 41 W.
Marquette, MI 49855
(906) 226-2314

■ **Brentwood Motor Inn**
2603 US Hwy. 41 W.
Marquette, MI 49855
(906) 228-7494

■ **Birchmont Hotel**
2090 US Hwy. 41 S.
Marquette, MI 49855
(954) 745-2132

♪ HILLSIDE FESTIVAL

Late July
Guelph, Ontario, Canada
www.hillside.on.ca
Admission: $$

The Hillside Festival showcases local Canadian talent, with the majority of the acts coming from within the Grand River Conservation Area in Ontario.

The festival itself takes place on Guelph Lake Island, with concerts running from early afternoon into the night and educational workshops in the arts and musical performance offered over the course of a July weekend each year. There is a stage devoted strictly to spoken word performers: poets, authors, and songwriters. Past performers include critical fave indie songstress Neko Case, Fed Eaglesmith, Martin Sexton, and Richard Buckner.

Artist Submissions

Deadline March 1; send press kit (with photo) and demo to:

Artistic Committee, Hillside Festival Office

123 Woolwich St.

Guelph, ON N1H 3V1

Canada

For more information: 519-763-6396 or Hillside@hillside.on.ca

Camping: Yes. Call (866) ONT-CAMP.

Accommodations

■ **Super 8 Guelph**

281 Woodlawn Road W.

Guelph, ON N1H 7K7

Canada

(519) 836-5850

■ **Days Inn Guelph**

785 Gordon St.

Guelph, ON N1G 1Y8

Canada

(519) 822-9112

♪ HILTON BEACH SUMMER FESTIVAL

Fourth Saturday of July

Hilton Beach, Ontario, Canada

www.hiltonbeach.com/events/summerfestival.html

Admission: *FREE*

This free festival is held on the shores of Hilton Beach in Ontario, with an amusement park right next door to the festival grounds. The event includes a car show, arts and crafts booths, and performers from the town itself, primarily regulars from a local coffee shop, the Lost Loon Coffee House.

For more information: (705) 246-2242 or info@hiltonbeach.com.

Camping: Yes. Contact Busy Beaver Campground at (705) 246-2636.

Accommodations

■ **Hilton Beach Trailer Park and Cottages**

P.O. Box 145

Hilton Beach, ON P0R 1G0

Canada

(705) 246-2586

♪ HODAG COUNTRY FESTIVAL

Mid-July
Rhinelander, Wisconsin
www.hodag.com
Admission: $$

This massive four-day festival held in the northeastern part of Wisconsin features major headliners (Garth Brooks, Trisha Yearwood) on the main stage, plenty of lesser-known names on smaller stages, and opportunities for folks to join in karaoke. Also, each year a band contest is held, as well as a "clean campsite" contest, the winner of which wins free admission to the next year's festival.

Artist Submissions

If you or your band are from the Rhinelander area and are interested in competing in the band contest, you have to contact your local radio stations in order to apply.

For more information: (715) 369-1300 or hcf@hodag.com
Camping: Yes
Accommodations

■ **AmericInn**
638 W. Kemp St.
Rhinelander, WI 54501
(715) 369-9600

■ **Super 8 Rhinelander**
667 W. Kemp St.
Rhinelander, WI 54501
(715) 369-5880

■ **Comfort Inn Rhinelander**
1490 Lincoln St.
Rhinelander, WI 54501
(715) 369-1100

♪ HOKONUI COUNTRY MUSIC FESTIVAL

Mid-February
Dolamore Park, Gore, New Zealand
www.goldguitars.co.nz/hokonui_festival.htm
Admission: $

For more than 10 years, Gore, New Zealand, has hosted this two-day festival, which attracts talent from Australia and New Zealand. Raffles, crafts shows, food, and wine are offered along with live country music beginning in the afternoon and stretching into late in the evening.

For more information: (03) 418-0803 or marilynhugh@xtra.co.nz

Camping: No

Accommodations: www.purenz.com

HOME COUNTY FOLK FESTIVAL

Mid-July
London, Ontario, Canada
www.homecounty.ca
Admission: $

Home County Folk Festival celebrates the arts and crafts and contemporary folk music of North America, with a concentration on Canadian culture. The three-day event is marked by innumerable workshops on everything from brass forgery to textiles to painting with watercolors. Performers are almost all unsigned, regional acts selected by festival organizers.

Artist Submissions

Use on-line form or send demo and press kit to:
Artistic Director, Home County Folk Festival
c/o Community Resource Centre
388 Dundas St.
London, ON N6B1V7
Canada

For more information: (519) 432-4310

Camping: No

Accommodations

■ **Travelodge London South**
800 Exeter Rd.
London, ON N6E 1L5
Canada
(519) 681-1200

■ **Days Inn London**
1100 Wellington Rd. S.
London, ON N6E 1M2
Canada
(519) 681-1240

■ **Four Points Hotel London**
1150 Wellington Rd. S.
London, ON N6E 1M3
Canada
(519) 681-0600

♪ICA FOLK FESTIVAL

June–July
Victoria, British Columbia, Canada
www.icafolkfest.com
Admission: $$

Each year, the ICA Folk Festival attracts more than 150,000 people to Vancouver for this 10-day event celebrating cultures and folk styles from around the world. The entire city becomes one big festival. You'll find kiosks and booths housing more than 60 artists selling and exhibiting their crafts, dance ensembles from as far away as Eastern Europe, drumming groups, and concerts on multiple stages and in venues all over the island, featuring an array of Canadian, American, and international artists.

Artist Submissions
Deadline December 15
Small press kit and demo to:
Tracy Summers, Artistic Producer
930 Balmoral Rd.
Victoria, BC V8T 1A8
Canada
(250) 388-4728
For more information: folkfest@icavictoria.org
Camping: No
Accommodations

■ **Days Inn Victoria Waterway**
123 Gorge Rd. E.
Victoria, BC V9A 1L1
Canada
(250) 386-1422

■ **Holiday Inn Victoria**
3020 Blanshard St.
Victoria, BC V8T 5B5
Canada
(250) 382-4400

♪INDEPENDENT MUSICFEST

Three days in June
Nashville, Tennessee
http://nashvillemusicfest.com
Admission: $$

The Independent MusicFest takes place over three days and features all kinds of music, from country to jazz to rock to hip-hop. The festival is a large networking event that offers innumerable concerts by local and regional acts looking to secure record deals in Music City. Though the emphasis is on the music industry itself, all the trappings of a regular festival are included, which means booths, booths, booths, and workshops.

For more information: (615) 316-9850 or office@nashvillemusicfest.net

Camping: No

Accommodations

■ **Nashville Area Chamber of Commerce**

211 Commerce St., Suite 100

Nashville, TN 37201

(615) 743-3000

ISLANDS FOLK FESTIVAL

Late July

Duncan, British Columbia, Canada

www.folkfest.bc.ca/IFFhomepage.html

Admission: $

With five regular performance stages, one hybrid open jam/children's stage, and an easygoing attitude, the Islands Folk Festival has become a favorite spot for up-and-coming performers and festival junkies alike. Countless Vancouver musicians got their start here, and acclaimed headliners make the trip faithfully each year. Past performers include Fred Eaglesmith, Buffy Sainte-Marie, Willie P. Bennett, and Canadian festival staple Valdy. Celtic groups, worldbeat bands, and dance troupes also regularly appear.

Artist Submissions

Deadline February 28; send small press kit and demo to:

Brent Hutchinson, artistic coordinator

The Islands Folk Festival

P.O. Box 802

Duncan, British Columbia V9L 3Y1

Canada

For more information: (250) 748-3975 or information@folkfest.bc.ca

Camping: No

Accommodations

■ **Duncan Days Inn**

5325 Trans Canada Hwy.

Duncan, BC V9L 3X5

Canada

(250) 748-0661

♪ JAMBOREE IN THE HILLS

Mid-July
Morristown, Ohio
www.jamboreeinthehills.com
Admission: $$$

Jamboree in the Hills draws a good thousand people each year during its mid-summer weekend festival, billed as "the Superbowl of Country Music." A mixture of big-name talent and regional acts make up the near-continuous live music schedule in the blazing sun of Morristown, Ohio. Be sure to bring some sort of shade or canopy to keep yourself and your loved ones from frying like bacon. Past performers include Brad Paisley, George Jones, Joe Diffie, and SheDaisy.

For more information: (800) 624-5456
Camping: Yes
Accommodations

■ **Plaza Motel**
52509 National Rd. E.
Saint Clairsville, OH 43950
(740) 695-3378

■ **Red Roof Inn**
I-70 & Mall Rd.
Saint Clairsville, OH 43950
(800) THE-ROOF or (740) 695-4057

■ **Days Inn West**
52601 Holiday Dr.
Saint Clairsville, OH 43950
(800) 325-2525 or (740) 695-0100

♪ JENNY BROOK BLUEGRASS FESTIVAL

Late June
Weston, Vermont
www.jennybrookfestival.com
Admission: $$

Acts such as Big Country Bluegrass, Continental Divide, and the Gibson Brothers are sure to draw a crowd to the Jenny Brook Bluegrass Festival. Fans' appetites will be satisfied by greasy, tasty fairgrounds-style food, and massages are available for those who dance a little too hard. The special house band, the Seth Sawyer Band, will prove that the promoters of this event can play "Foggy Mountain Breakdown" just as well as any of the acts they book.

For more information: (802) 463-9330 or Candi@JennyBrookFestival.com

Camping: Yes

Accommodations

■ **Horseshoe Acres Campground**
1978 Weston-Andover Rd.
Chester, VT 05143
(802) 875-2960

JOHN DENVER CELEBRATION

Mid-October

Salida, Colorado

Admission: $$

This mountaintop gathering requires reservations and attracts about 200 people each year, so be sure to contact the organizers early to ensure you get a spot. You should also be sure that you're a big fan of the folk music icon this event is named after. A number of John Denver Memorial Awards are handed out over the course of the weekend, and there is a massive sign erected in lights on the side of the mountain that can be seen for miles—a heart with the letters "J" and "D" inside it. An array of lesser-known musicians from across the country perform Denver's songs for the crowd throughout the weekend.

Artist Submissions: christinesmith@amigo.net

For more information: (719) 942-9620 or christinesmith@amigo.net

Camping: Yes. On-site.

Accommodations

■ **Apple Grove Motel**
129 W. Rainbow Blvd.
Salida, CO 81201
(719) 539-4722

■ **Budget Lodge**
1146 E. US Hwy. 50
Salida, CO 81201
(719) 539-6695

■ **Aspen Leaf Lodge**
7350 W. US Hwy. 50
Salida, CO 81201
(719) 539-6733

CHRISTINE SMITH, *organizer of the John Denver Celebration in Salida, Colorado, answers our questions about the nature of her festival, what inspires her as an organizer, and the ups and downs of organizing a festival of this kind.*

Can you give a quick description of what goes on each year at the John Denver Celebration? Is it continuous music on a stage or is it a more informal camping-meets-music experience? What sort of bands do you have?

The Annual John Denver Celebration is a two-day event celebrating the music and message of John Denver. It takes place the first weekend of October in the beautiful mountain community of Salida. The main event is on Saturday and features performers (musicians, singers, bands) from across the country sharing their renditions of JD's music. We also feature guest speakers who explore the lessons to be learned from the messages in his music and the example he gave as a humanitarian and environmentalist.

All the music on Saturday is performed on stage with professional sound and lighting. The event has a preplanned schedule and performance order of nearly continuous music interspersed with occasional talks. Guests are seated and are free to enjoy wine, beer, and mixed drinks from the cash bar and a professionally catered, all-you-care-to-eat meal on Saturday as they listen to the musical performances and lectures. The John Denver Memorial Peace Prize is also awarded each year to an individual who has exemplified the love John Denver sang of and committed his life to. The prize is given to someone who has brought peace to their fellow man or Earth's environment and creatures.

On Sunday, guests interact by sharing their memories about how John's music touched and influenced their lives. More music is enjoyed, and specially selected film footage of John Denver is shown.

Also, on Friday, Saturday, and Sunday nights, the spectacular "John Denver Mountain" is lit. This beautiful tribute to John Denver features his initials ("JD") inside a large red heart on the side of a mountain. The J is over 40 feet long and 25 feet wide and, when lit, can be seen for miles around.

● ● ● ● ● ● ● ● ● ● ●

What inspired you to organize the festival?

Following John Denver's death, I wrote a tribute that was donated to several magazines worldwide, and later I wrote the book, *A Mountain in the Wind: An Exploration of the Spirituality of John Denver*. I received thousands of letters and e-mails from people around the world sharing poignant stories of how his music had touched their lives, and I saw that many others grieved his death as I had. I realized that it was important for all of us to have a place to come to where we could remember his music and his significance with others who felt the same way about him. I realized that people needed a place where they could learn more about him and about how they can be part of continuing his legacy and working toward the things he believed. I want people to fully realize and remember his musical significance (his body of work is far greater than most realize) and his commitment to creating a world of peace for the human family. He lived the life he sang of, and the celebration commemorates that.

What is it about the music of John Denver that inspires you to keep doing this?

John's music is powerful. His songs can inspire, motivate, encourage, and comfort. John was unafraid to bare his soul—whether expressing joy or sorrow—and his songs reflect the feelings, thoughts, and experiences we've all had. Whether he is singing of new love, lost love, despair for the state of the planet, or the joys and beauty of the natural world, he enunciates truth in a way the perceptive listener can understand and appreciate. His music can help you emerge from the depths of depression or it can bring you a deeper appreciation for the true joys of life: friends, family, the Earth. Or it can motivate and inspire you to get involved in humanitarian and environmental causes. But to me, the most important message derived from John's music is a message of unconditional love. As John so beautifully sings in "Wandering Soul," "Love is the answer, love is the way." His music is a celebration of life, and his message is that life is worth living despite the pain, and love is always the answer.

What is the hardest part of organizing a festival?

The hardest part is the actual nuts and bolts work of managing an annual event that is so important to so many people. The behind-the-scenes work starts liter-

● ● ● ● ● ● ● ● ● ● ●

ally right after the event ends each year. As soon as one is over, the work of organizing, auditioning, publicizing, financing, and obtaining sponsors begins again. We have to keep track of reservations, make menu and catering decisions, communicate with all the guests, and send them pre-programs with maps, places, and times, and write and print the Celebration Program (complete with bios of all performers and speakers and the weekend schedule of activities). And the amount of work that precedes the event during the week leading up to it is incredible! Lighting, sound system checks, stage and venue setup, responding to media requests for interviews—it's a lot of hard work.

Is it worth it?

Yes! It *is* worth it. To me, it is of great importance that the John Denver Celebration honor John as he deserves. I put my entire heart into making it the best it can be each year. John deserves that.

How much chance does an unknown act have of performing in some capacity at your festival? And how do you select performers?

Unknown acts (whether individual singers or bands) have an excellent chance of being selected to perform. We've found, on average, about half our performers selected in a given year are relatively unknown acts and the other half are professionals.

If a performer is interested, she should contact us and send in a demo. We base our decision first and foremost on quality—not whether the musician is known or unknown. I am pleased to present an opportunity for musicians to share their music with an audience of people from all around the world. I give our performers a chance to share who they are through their comments, performances, bios, and CDs.

Do any of the proceeds from the festival go to charity or a cause?

Proceeds from the event go directly to finance it. It is a self-sustaining event; ticket sales and other earnings go toward the considerable expense it takes to present this festival.

We do, however, occasionally offer John Denver memorabilia, and all proceeds from those sales go to Dreams of Freedom, Inc. Dreams of Freedom is a charity that brings JD's music and videos to thousands of incarcerated men and women across the United States, along with hygiene items and a newsletter of inmates' prose, poetry, and artwork.

We also encourage support for several charities doing humanitarian or environmental work. We provide brochures (and occasional guest speakers) from the National Arbor Day Foundation, the World Federalist Association, the International Center for Tropical Ecology (ICTE), Citizens United for Alternatives to the Death Penalty (CUADP), and Amnesty International's anti-death penalty programs.

JOHNSTOWN FOLKFEST

Labor Day weekend
Johnstown, Pennsylvania
www.jaha.org/folkfest/index.htm
Admission: *FREE*

This free celebration of traditional American music takes place during Labor Day weekend in the old coal mining town and immigration port of Johnstown, Pennsylvania. Gospel, blues, Cajun, zydeco, Appalachian folk —you name it, bands and musicians are playing it live on stages set up all over the festivities' five-block radius. Each year, a number of international groups broaden attendees' musical horizons with folk music from Ireland, the Ukraine, and the Middle East (among other locales). Guided tours of the historic downtown district are offered all weekend. Past performers include gospel acts Fairfield Four and Dixie Hummingbirds; blues legends Clarence Gatemouth Brown and Cephas & Wiggins; and country acts such as J. D. Crowe & the New South and Sleepy LaBeef.

For more information: info@jaha.org
Camping: No
Accommodations

■ **Sleep Inn**
453 Theatre Dr.
Johnstown, PA 15904
(814) 262-9292

■ **Comfort Inn**
455 Theatre Dr.
Johnstown, PA 15904
(814) 266-3678

■ **Econo Lodge**
430 Napoleon Pl.
Johnstown, PA 15901
(814) 536-1114

JULIAN BLUEGRASS FESTIVAL

Mid-September
Julian, California
www.julianbluegrassfestival.com
Admission: $$

Founded in 1970, this Southern California festival takes place just outside of San Diego and features a dozen small-time bluegrass acts from the region, including Bluegrass Redliners, Cliff Wagner and the Old #7, and the Witcher Brothers. Raffles, open jams, and food vendors round out the activities.

For more information: (760) 726-8380 or mzbeez@home.com

Camping: Yes. Contact K. Q. Ranch Camping Resort (RV and tent camping available) at (760) 765-2244 or (866) 217-8111.

Accommodations
■ **Julian Hotel**
2032 Main St.
Julian, CA 92036
(760) 765-0201

KENT STATE FOLK FESTIVAL

November
Kent, Ohio
www.kentstatefolkfestival.org
Admission: $–$$

Held over the course of two weekends in November each year, the Kent State Folk Festival boasts probably the biggest names of any of the folk festivals, with Bob Dylan and Roger McGuinn of the Byrds in attendance in 2003. Guerrilla concerts in cafés, bars, and bookstores all over town help bring the whole community into the festivities, and a variety of fun and instructional workshops are offered on the second Saturday of the festival.

For more information: (330) 672-3114 or info@kentstatefolkfestival.org

Camping: Yes

Accommodations

■ **Alden Inn**
4386 State Rte. 43
Kent, OH 44240
(330) 678-9927

■ **Inn of Kent**
303 E. Main St.
Kent, OH 44240
(330) 673-3411

■ **Eastwood Motor Inn**
2296 State Rte. 59
Kent, OH 44240
(330) 678-1111

KERRVILLE FOLK FESTIVAL

May–June
Kerrville, Texas
www.kerrville-music.com
Admission: $$$

This 18-day festival starts every year on the Thursday before Memorial Day. It features more than 100 artists performing throughout the weekends, with workshops and educational classes during the days between performances. Past festivals have featured the likes of Nanci Griffith, Raye Wylie Hubbard, and Sara Hickman.

For more information: (830) 257-3600 or info@kerrville-music.com

Camping: Yes. RV camping is available on-site.

Accommodations

■ **Y.O. Ranch & Resort Center**
2033 Sidney Baker
Kerrville, TX 78028
(830) 257-4440

KIHAUS FOLK MUSIC FESTIVAL

Early July
Rääkkylä, Finland
www.kihaus.fi
Admission: $

This Finnish festival celebrates the mysteries of the woods and lake that sit beside the festival grounds. The majority of the musicians come from

Finland, but don't be surprised to see some folks from abroad performing. The musical focus is on folk styles and the rich mythology of the region. Veteran players of the old styles offer tips to interested parties during the workshops and open jams held throughout the weekend.

Artist Submissions

Sari Kaasinen, artistic director

(358) 50-5640-930

sari.kaasinen@kihaus.fi

For more information: (358) 13-661-230 or (358) 13-661-233 or kihaus@kihaus.fi

Camping: Yes

Accommodations: Nearest are in Kitee or Joensuu; www.finland-helsinki-hotels.com

 ## LARAMIE PEAK BLUEGRASS FESTIVAL

Labor Day weekend

Douglas, Wyoming

www.laramiepeakbluegrass.com

Admission: $–$$

Rain or shine, this outdoor festival takes place each year on the Laramie Peak Campground, in Douglas, Wyoming, about three hours north of Denver, Colorado. The Laramie Peak Bluegrass Festival features two days of live music on multiple stages, numerous food and crafts vendors, and lots of fireside picking. The roster of musicians is strictly regional, with no nationally known artists but plenty of authentic, down-home talent.

For more information: (307) 358-3909 or sweih@coffey.com

Camping: Yes. RV and tent camping available on a first come, first served basis.

Accommodations

▪ **Super 8 Motel Douglas**
314 Russell Ave.
I-25 Exit 140
Douglas, WY 82633
(866) 836-9330

▪ **Best Western Douglas Inn**
1450 Riverbend Dr.
Douglas, WY 82633
(866) 836-9330

♪ LEICESTERSHIRE'S COUNTRY MUSIC FESTIVAL

First weekend in August
Sapcote, Leicester, United Kingdom
www.royscmf.co.uk
Admission: $$$

Europe's top country bands play great music for three days at Leicestershire's Country Music Festival while you enjoy comfortable camping and plenty of extras. Food, clothes, jewelry, drinks, and more food are all readily available at the festival's many stalls, so have fun and shop to the sounds of the John Gill Band, Talon, Lazy Dog, and many more.

For more information: Roy Ellis, (44) 01455-272410 or sean@royscmf.co.uk
Camping: Yes
Accommodations

■ Joyce and Bob O'Brien
Willowmead Bed & Breakfast
36 Stoney Stanton Rd.
Sapcote, Leicestershire
United Kingdom
(44) 01455-273545
willowmead@lineone.net

■ Mill-on-the-Soar Hotel
Sutton Hill Farm Coventry Road
Leicester, Leicestershire LE9 4JU
United Kingdom
(44) 01455-282419

♪ LEIGH FOLK FESTIVAL

Late June
Leigh, Essex, United Kingdom
www.essexfolknews.co.uk/leighfolkfestival/index.htm
Admission: FREE

The Leigh Folk Festival is a free festival of dance, crafts, and music held in the town that gives this event its name. This is one of England's oldest and largest festivals. It runs for two days during summer, rain or shine, and offers both national and international folk music acts, lots of food, and tons of vendors.

For more information: (44) 01702-390454 or john@essexfolknews.co.uk
Camping: Yes, provided free.

Accommodations

■ **The Grand Hotel**
The Broadway
Leigh-on-Sea, Essex SS9 1PJ
United Kingdom
(44) 01702-710768

■ **Cobham Lodge Hotel**
2 Cobham Rd.
Westcliff-on-Sea, Essex
United Kingdom
(44) 01702-332377 or
(44) 01702-346438

■ **Erismere Hotel**
24/32 Pembury Rd.
Westcliff-on-Sea, Essex
United Kingdom
(44) 01702-349025

♪ LION'S HEAD BLUEGRASS & COUNTRY MUSIC FESTIVAL

One day in August
Lion's Head, Ontario, Canada
www.geocities.com/thayes.geo/cmf.html
Admission: $

Canadian musicians gather at the Lion's Head Arena in Lion's Head, Ontario, for an afternoon-into-evening series of concerts on a single stage surrounded by a plethora of foods from around the world. Vendors sell musical instruments and handmade crafts. The roster is made up of strictly regional acts, and the action takes place on the beautiful Bruce Peninsula, a stretch of earth that pokes out into Lake Huron.

For more information: thayes@amtelecom.net
Camping: Yes
Accommodations

■ **Lion's Head Bed & Breakfast**
5239 River Rd.
Niagara Falls, ON L2E3G9
Canada
(905) 374-1681

■ **The 45th Parallel**
21 Main St., Lion's Head
Niagara Falls, ON L2E3G9
Canada
(519) 793-3529

■ **The Bees Knees**
23 Main St., Lions Head
Niagara Falls, ON L2E3G9
Canada
(519) 793-3733

■ **Lion's Head Beach Motel**
1 McNeil St., Lion's Head
Niagara Falls, ON L2E3G9
Canada
(519) 793-3155

■ **Harvest Moon B&B**
3927 Hwy. 6, Lion's Head
Niagara Falls, ON L2E3G9
Canada
(519) 592-5742

LIVE OAK MUSIC FESTIVAL

Mid-June
Santa Barbara, California
www.liveoakfest.org
Admission: $$–$$$

Several thousand people camp out in Santa Ynez Valley each year to attend this three-day event that offers an eclectic program of 20 bands playing a wide spectrum of genres, from traditional American folk and bluegrass to jazz, gospel, world, and classical music. Kids are included in storytelling, arts and crafts workshops, and scavenger hunts. The mission of this festival is to broaden people's musical horizons, and bands almost never appear at Live Oak Music Festival two years in a row. Former Byrd and Burrito Brother Chris Hillman has performed, as have Robert Earl Keene and the fantastic New Orleans street parade crew Wild Magnolias.

Artist Submissions
Include a brief description of your musical style, Web site address, number in your band, and the area from which you will need to travel to reach the festival.
mwaddell@kcbx.org

For more information: (805) 781-3020 or leslieellen@thegrid.net
Camping: Yes, on-site.
Accommodations

■ **Marina Beach Motel**
21 Bath St.
Santa Barbara, CA 93101
(805) 963-9311

■ **Ala Mar Motel**
102 W. Cabrillo Blvd.
Santa Barbara, CA 93101
(805) 962-9208

■ **22 E. Victoria St. Ltd**
24 E. Victoria St.
Santa Barbara, CA 93101
(805) 966-7361

♪ LOWELL FOLK FESTIVAL

Late July
Lowell, Massachusetts
www.lowellfolkfestival.org/home.htm
Admission: FREE

Lowell, Massachusetts, has a rich tradition of New England maritime arts and crafts such as decoy carving and model shipbuilding and was one of the country's largest manufacturing centers during the early twentieth century. All this history makes it an excellent place to celebrate the many facets of Americana that make up a good folk festival. You'll find tons of activities for both grownups and kids, food and vendor booths, and concerts given by a wide selection of local, national, and international talent. Blues singer Shemekia Copeland, Bob French's Original Tuxedo Jazz Band, and cattle rancher/country star Wylie and the Wild West have all appeared at this, the largest free festival in the United States.

Artist submissions
Send press kit and demo to:
Lowell Folk Festival
c/o Special Events Coordinator
Lowell National Historical Park
67 Kirk St.
Lowell, MA 01852
For more information: (978) 970-5000 or ambrosino@nps.gov
Camping: No
Accommodations

■ **The Barnes House**
30 Huntington St.
Lowell, MA 01852
(978) 453-9763

■ **Motel 6**
95 Main St.
Tewksbury, MA 01876
(978) 851-8677

■ **Courtyard by Marriott**
30 Industrial Ave.
Lowell, MA 01852
(978) 458-7575 or (800) 321-2211

♪ LUNENBURG FOLK HARBOUR FESTIVAL

Early August
Lunenburg, Nova Scotia, Canada

www.folkharbour.com
Admission: $$–$$$

The coastal town of Lunenburg, Nova Scotia, serves as the setting for this small festival, offering four stages strategically placed throughout the town and on the wharf. Fiddlers and accordionists perform on the pier with a forest of yacht sails as a backdrop, and small bands take the stage on a gazebo in the town square. The Opera House features more concerts, and a large circus tent is set up on a hill overlooking the whole beautiful panorama. The roster of musicians is strictly regional. Workshops and dance exhibitions are featured as well.

Artist Submissions
Lunenburg Folk Harbour Society
P.O. Box 655
Lunenburg, NS B0J 2C0
Canada
info@folkharbour.com
For more information: (902) 634-3180 or info@folkharbour.com
Camping: Yes. Call (902) 634-3180.
Accommodations

■ **Bluenose Lodge**
10 Falkland St.
Lunenburg, NS B0J 2C0
Canada
(902) 634-8851
bluenose@fox.nstn.ca

■ **Commander's Inn**
56 Victoria Rd.
Lunenburg, NS B0J 2C0
Canada
(902) 634-3151

■ **Boscawen Inn**
150 Cumberland St.
Lunenburg, NS B0J 2C0
Canada
(902) 634-3325
boscawen@ns.sympatico.ca

■ **Dockside Suites**
84 Montague St.
Lunenburg, NS B0J 2C0
Canada
(902) 634-3005
dockside@docksider.ns.ca

MANITOWISH WATERS BLUEGRASS FESTIVAL: MIDSUMMER IN THE NORTHWOODS

Last weekend of July
Manitowish Waters, Wisconsin
www.onemorebluegrassshow.com
Admission: $$

North Wisconsin is home to this yearly event, which has, in the past, attracted such bluegrass hotshots as Bill Monroe, Ralph Stanley, and the father of Wisconsin bluegrass, Bill Jorgenson. Raffles, arts and crafts, food vendors, and other concessions are all part of the experience. There is also a water ski show and a parade through town.

For more information: (715) 543-2166 or jerryf@gotnet.net

Camping: Yes

Accommodations

■ **Aberdeen Lodge**
25 Twin Pines Rd.
Manitowish Waters, WI 54545
(715) 543-8700

■ **Timberline Inn**
72 Ilg Rd.
Manitowish Waters, WI 54545
(715) 543-8080

■ **Pea Patch Motel & Saloon**
145 County Rd. W.
Manitowish Waters, WI 54545
(715) 543-2455

■ **Wilderness Inn**
HC 2 Box 880
Presque Isle, WI 54557
(715) 543-8375

♪ MAPLE CITY BLUEGRASS FESTIVAL

Late June
Norwalk, Ohio
Admission: $

This three-day summer festival is held indoors and features regional acts playing traditional bluegrass. Elder statesman Ralph Stanley, the Country Gentlemen, and James King have all appeared at recent festivals. Food vendors and arts and crafts booths are available as well.

For more information: (419) 588-3503 or BGShow@accnorwalk.com

Camping: No

Accommodations

■ **Dreamland Motel**
704 US Hwy. 20 E.
Norwalk, OH 44857
(419) 668-5159

■ **Norwalk Inn**
283 Benedict Ave.
Norwalk, OH 44857
(419) 668-8255

♪ MARDI GRAS IN MAY

Early May
Branson, Missouri

www.cajunzydecofestival.com

Admission: $$

Branson, Missouri, is known as the live music capital of the world, due to the fact that there are more than 30 venues in the city, with shows scheduled seven days a week. In early May each year, Branson salutes Cajun and zydeco music with a three-day festival held, within city limits, on the Ramada Inn festival grounds. Cajun food is served, crawfish-eating contests are staged, and the alternately ebullient and tragic sounds of Louisiana fill the air.

For more information: (866) 556-3378

Camping: No

Accommodations

■ **Dogwood Inn**
1420 W. 76 Country Blvd.
Branson, MO 65616
(417) 334-5101

■ **Ramada Inn**
1700 W. Hwy. 76
Branson, MO 65616
(877) 334-2364

MARIPOSA FOLK FESTIVAL

Early July

Orillia, Ontario, Canada

www.mariposafolkfestival.com/index.html

Admission: $–$$

Tudhope Park in Orillia, Ontario, hosts this annual event, which gathers together a broad spectrum of folk and country-folk talent. From big stars (Steve Earle) to promising newcomers (L.A. singer-songwriter Lynn Miles), the roster normally features a heavy Canadian slant with a handful of American and international acts thrown in. In 2002 British mime Jude Parry stunned the crowd with a convincing portrayal of a woman hopelessly trapped inside a cage.

For more information: (705) 326-9809 or office@mariposafolkfestival.com

Camping: Yes. Contact Hammock Harbour at (705) 326-7885.

Accommodations

■ **Couchiching Inn**
440 Couchiching Pt. Rd.
Orillia, ON L3V 6P8
Canada
(705) 325-6505
info@couchichinginn.on.ca

■ **Eagle Inn**
493 Laclie St.
Orillia, ON L3V 4R2
Canada
(705) 329-0983

■ **Econo Lodge**
265 Memorial Ave.
Orillia, ON L3V 5X8
Canada
(705) 326-3554

■ **Highwayman Inn & Conference Centre, Orillia**
201 Woodside Dr.
Orillia, ON L3V 6T4
Canada
(705) 326-7343

MARITIME FIDDLE FESTIVAL

Mid-July
Dartmouth, Nova Scotia, Canada
www3.ns.sympatico.ca/marfiddlefest/Home.htm
Admission: $

For more than 50 years, the tight-knit community of Dartmouth, Nova Scotia, has been holding yearly fiddle contests. The tradition started in a local man's kitchen way back when, and, over time, the long weekend of music and dance has grown into an event cherished by both the locals and the many folks who come in from all over Nova Scotia and Canada to participate in, experience, and perpetuate this cultural exhibition. Recently, the organizers added a square dancing contest and an award for "Best Jig." The contests are divided into groups by age and leave no one out; awards are given to the best fiddlers and dancers under the age of 12 as well as folks in their 60s. Friday night is devoted to a fiddle jam session, and the competitions begin on Saturday.

Artist Submissions
Maritime Fiddle Festival
P.O. Box 3037, Dartmouth East
Dartmouth, NS B2W 4Y3
Canada
For more information: (902) 435-4892 or (902) 435-1052 or marfiddlefest@ns.sympatico.ca
Camping: No
Accommodations

■ **Keddy's Dartmouth Inn**
9 Braemar Dr.
Dartmouth, NS B2Y 3H6
Canada
(902) 469-0331

■ **Ramada Plaza Hotel**
  Dartmouth/Halifax
240 Brownlow Ave.
Dartmouth, NS B3B 1X6
Canada
(888) 298-2054 or (902) 468-8888

MELFEST

End of May
White Lake, North Carolina
www.melfestbluegrass.com
Admission: $

A dozen or so local bluegrass bands perform on a small stage in Melwood Music Park in the quaint resort town of White Lake, North Carolina. Within walking distance of the stage is White Lake itself, a beautiful, thousand-acre body of water with soft sandy beaches, ideal for cooling off between sets, jams, and dances in the hot summer weather.

For more information: jrmelvin@intrstar.net
Camping: Yes. Camp Clearwater is adjacent to the festival.
Accommodations

■ **Crystal Beach Motel**
RR 2, Box 414
White Lakes, NC 28337
(919) 862-3660

■ **Melwood Court**
1994 White Lake Dr.
White Lake, NC 28337
(910) 862-2416

MERLEFEST

Last weekend in April
Wilkesboro, North Carolina
www.merlefest.org
Admission: $$–$$$

This community college event brings big-name talent to the town of Wilkesboro, North Carolina. Merlefest honors the legacy of Merle Watson and his father, Doc Watson. Emmylou Harris, Bruce Hornsby, and Belá Fleck & the Flecktones are among some of the notable names that have graced this premier festival of Americana music, crafts, and food. Wilkesboro is located in northwestern North Carolina, 80 miles from Charlotte, 45 miles from Winston-Salem.

Artist Submissions
Claire Armbruster, (336) 838-6130 or clairearmbruster@hotmail.com
For more information: Kathy Gray, (336) 838-6133 or grayk@wilkes.cc.nc.us
Camping: Yes

Accommodations

■ **Old Traphill Mill Inn & Resort**
452 Traphill Mill Rd.
Traphill, NC 28685
(336) 957-3713

■ **The Holiday Inn Express**
1700 Winkler St.
Wilksboro, NC 28679
(877) 4-WILKES

■ **Addison Inn**
1842 Winkler St.
Wilkesboro, NC 28697
(336) 838-1000

■ **Hampton Inn-Wilkesboro**
1700 Winkler St.
Wilksboro, NC 28679
(800) HAMPTON

MERRITT MOUNTAIN MUSIC FESTIVAL

Mid-July
Merritt, British Columbia, Canada
www.mountainfest.com
Admission: $$$

Merritt Mountain, British Columbia, is a resort town featuring a massive amusement park and raceway. It's also home to the annual Mountainfest, one of Canada's largest music festivals. Just about every big name in new country has appeared here—from Alan Jackson and Martina McBride to Clint Black, George Strait, LeAnn Rimes, and the Great One himself, Jerry Lee Lewis. This is a giant, corporate-sponsored event.

For more information: (604) 525-3330 or info@mountainfest.com
Camping: Yes. RV camping and parking is available.

Accommodations

■ **Quilchena Hotel**
P.O. Box 1
Quilchena, BC V0E 2R0
Canada
(250) 378-2611
info@quilchena.com

■ **Merritt Motor Inn**
3561 Voght St.
Merritt, BC V1K 1C5
Canada
(800) 668-9244

■ **Merritt Lodge Motel**
2751 Nicola Ave.
Merritt, BC V1K 1B8
Canada
(250) 378-0424

♪ MICHAEL MARTIN MURPHEY'S WESTFEST

Summer
Location changes each year; usually in Colorado
www.westfest.net
Admission: $$–$$$

This roving festival has been a favorite destination for country music lovers for the past 16 years. Its location changes every year as the promoters search for a permanent home. We weren't going to include roving festivals in this guide, but the Westfest is such an extravaganza—with its rodeo competitions, booths galore, and list of performers that has included country music staples such as Lynn Anderson, the Texas Playboys, and 1970s country rock kings Poco—that we had to include it. Be sure to call the very friendly folks at the front office or check the Web site for details of where they are holding the next event. Proceeds from the festival go to various charities; in 2002, it was held in historical Red River, New Mexico, benefiting the Wildlands Fire Prevention and Relief Campaign for Forest Fire Prevention and Aid. Here's hoping Mr. Murphey & Co. find a permanent spot for their yearly gathering.

For more information: (505) 758-1873
Camping: Yes

♪ MID WINTER CELTIC FESTIVAL

One day in February
Regina, Saskatchewan, Canada
www.gpfn.sk.ca/culture/arts/celtic
Admission: $

Irish fiddle playing and dances are the emphasis of this Regina event, held in a handful of venues and pubs located within the city limits. Although the official events all take place on Saturday, the festival is traditionally kicked off on Friday night with a rowdy "Pub Night" at the local tavern. Saturday is devoted to workshops during the day and a series of concerts given by regional and Irish acts at the Regina Center for the Performing Arts.

For more information: iainmacd@sk.sympatico.ca
Camping: No

Accommodations

■ **Delta Regina Hotel**
1919 Saskatchewan Dr.
Regina, SK S4P 4H2
Canada
(800) 268-1133 or (306) 525-5255

■ **Regina Travelodge Hotel**
4177 Albert St. S.
Regina, SK S4S 3R6
Canada
(306) 586-3443

■ **Super 8 Motel Regina**
2730 Victoria Ave.
Regina, SK S4N 6M5
Canada
(306) 789-8833

♪ MIDLAND DULCIMER FESTIVAL

Late August
Midland, Michigan
www.dulcimers.com/fmsm/festival.htm
Admission: $$

Midland City Fairgrounds hosts this annual celebration of dulcimer music, offering workshops that cover everything from playing the instrument to building one of your own. This is a small event and plenty of people come just to hang out and jam with the dulcimer players.

For more information: (989) 662-2191 or loperme@aol.com or skaryd@dulcimers.com

Camping: Yes

Accommodations

■ **Ashman Court**
111 W. Main St.
Midland, MI 48640
(517) 839-0500

■ **Plaza Suites**
5217 Bay City Rd.
Midland, MI 48640
(517) 496-0100

■ **Fairview Inn**
2200 W. Wackerly St.
Midland, MI 48640
(517) 631-0070

♪ MILDURA COUNTRY MUSIC FESTIVAL

September–October
Mildura, Victoria, Australia

www.milduracountrymusic.com.au

Admission: $

The Australian town of Mildura in Victoria, Australia, offers itself up for the purposes of this marathon festival, featuring up to 800 hours of music performed in multiple venues over the course of 10 days. The roster of musicians is made up entirely of indigenous, independent artists. The good news is that the Australian country music scene is teeming with talent and would undoubtedly come as a breath of fresh air to those overloaded with American-style pop country.

For more information: (61) 800-039-043

Camping: Yes

Accommodations

■ **Wentworth Central Motor Inn**

41 Adams St.

Wentworth, NSW 2648

Australia

(61) 800-337-030

MILL RACE FESTIVAL OF TRADITIONAL FOLK MUSIC

One day in August

Cambridge, Ontario, Canada

www.millracefolksociety.com

Admission: *FREE*

Recognizing Cambridge's origins as a Scottish settlement back in the 1800s, the Mill Race Festival tends to lean in a somewhat Celtic direction. But the festival organizers are always sure to include at least a few artists and musicians from outside the Celtic universe, in their ongoing effort to have various cultures represented in some way at each year's event. Concerts occur all over the city, in coffee shops, pubs, bookstores, and on outdoor stages set up amid international food booths and an arts and crafts bazaar.

Artist Submissions

Brad McEwen, Artistic Director

P.O. Box 22148

Galt Centre Postal Outlet

Cambridge, ON N1R 8E3

Canada

For more information: (519) 621-7135 or mill_race@yahoo.com

Camping: No

Accommodations

- **Holiday Inn Cambridge**
200 Holiday Inn Dr.
Cambridge, ON N3C 1Z4
Canada
(519) 658-4601

- **Days Inn Cambridge**
650 Hespeler Rd.
Cambridge, ON N1R 6J8
Canada
(519) 622-1070

MIRAMICHI FOLK SONG FESTIVAL

Four days in August
Miramichi, New Brunswick, Canada
www.mibc.nb.ca/folksong
Admission: $$

This five-day festival held in New Brunswick, Canada, has been going for almost 50 years, offering live concerts each night and workshops concerning Canadian and Celtic folk styles during the day. Irish tenor Jimmy Carton appeared in 2002.

For more information: (506) 623-2150 or bb2@nb.sympatico.ca
Camping: No
Accommodations: www.canadianhotelguide.com/newbrunswick

MIRANDE COUNTRY MUSIC FESTIVAL

Mid-July
Mirande, Gascony, France
www.country-musique.com
Admission: $$

The largest country music festival held in Europe, Mirande's festival offers visitors an opportunity to see French people wearing cowboy hats and pointy boots. In fact, the entire town of Mirande assumes an American theme and more than a hundred country music artists perform on multiple stages to crowds of more than 100,000 annually. In the past Jerry Lee Lewis has appeared alongside Narvel Felts and the questionable country icon, 1980s TV star Larry Hagman. This festival will be nothing short of a blast for Americans, and for European country fans, it's one of few opportunities to see authentic American groups perform live.

For more information: (33) 05-6266-6810 or countrymusicmirande@wanadoo.fr
Camping: Yes

Accommodations
■ **Office du Tourisme**
(33) 05-6266-6810
bienvenue@ot-mirande.com

♪ MOUNT HELENA MUSIC FESTIVAL

Mid-June
Helena, Montana
www.downtownhelena.com/musicfest2003.htm
Admission: $

Twenty-five rock, country, and blues bands perform on four stages at this large Montana festival taking place over a June weekend in state capitol Mount Helena. You can also expect arts and crafts booths and a farmers market. The talent is mainly local, with such bands as the Levitators, Scott Ellison, and Sonny Rhodes performing.

Artist Submissions
Press kit and demo to:
Jim McHugh
Downtown Helena
225 Cruse Ave., Suite B
Helena, MT 59601
For more information: (406) 447-1535 or jmchugh@mt.net
Camping: No
Accommodations
■ **Aladdin Motor Inn**
2101 11th Ave.
Helena, MT 59601
(406) 443-2300
■ **Barrister Bed & Breakfast**
416 N. Ewing St.
Helena, MT 59601
(406) 443-7330

■ **Appleton Inn Bed & Breakfast**
1999 Euclid Ave.
Helena, MT 59601
(406) 449-7492

♪ MR. B'S BLUEGRASS FESTIVAL

Two days in June
Warren Farm, Ladysmith, Virginia

www.bluegrassville.com/events.dir/mrb/june2003.htm
Admission: $$–$$$

Seminal bluegrass duo Jim & Jesse are slated to appear at this two-day out-door gathering in Ladysmith, Virginia, situated in central Virginia, approximately 40 miles from Richmond. The rest of the weekend's roster is just as impressive, with big names IIIrd Tyme Out and Doctor Ralph Stanley on the bill. Local sleeping arrangements are in short supply, so your best bet may be to rough it—camping is $8 per night or free with the cost of a three-day pass. The festival is held on Warren Farm in Ladysmith, just off Route 1 and amid the verdant beauty of the Shenandoah Valley. An excellent place to stop on your way through the state.

For more information: (804) 449-6350
Camping: Yes
Accommodations
■ **Carmel Church Days Inn Kings Dominion**
P.O. Box 70
Ruther Glen, VA 22546
(804) 448-2011

MUSIC IN THE VINEYARD: THE FESTIVAL

Labor Day weekend
Morgan Hill, California
www.napafest.com
Admission: $$

This one-day festival of music, food, and wine is held on the grounds of the vaunted Guglielmo Winery in California's gorgeous Napa Valley. Hawaiian slack-key guitar masters Ledward Kaapana and Cyril Pahinui have performed alongside singer-songwriter Katy Moffatt, with local bands and musicians rounding out the bill.

For more information: (408) 358-3505 or tobynita@earthlink.net
Camping: No
Accommodations

■ **Executive Inn Suites**
16505 Condit Rd.
Morgan Hill, CA 95037
(408) 778-0404

■ **Holiday Motel**
16210 Monterey St.
Morgan Hill, CA 95037
(408) 779-2666

■ **Morgan Hill Inn**
16250 Monterey St.
Morgan Hill, CA 95037
(408) 779-1900

NACOGDOCHES RED RIVER RADIO AMERICANA MUSIC FESTIVAL

Labor Day weekend
Nacogdoches, Texas
www.redriverradio.com/americana.html
Admission: $

Held for the first time in 2002, this Labor Day weekend event takes place in the oldest town in Texas—Nacogdoches, a Spanish settlement founded in the 1700s. The one-day event features live music from 11:00 A.M. until some time after 9:00 P.M., in addition to songwriting and guitar workshops and an old-fashioned medicine show. There's also lots of stuff for the kids—temporary tattoos, face-painting, clowns, and a "misting station" to cool down in. Past performers include singer-songwriter Guy Clarke, Austin alternative country band the Gourds, and up-and-coming local new country act the Gillette Brothers.

Artist Submissions
Deadline is the end of January each year
Nacogdoches Convention and Visitors Bureau
200 E. Main
Nacogdoches, TX 75961
For more information: (888) 564-7351 or info@visitnacogdoches.org
Camping: Yes
Accommodations

■ **Caraban Motor Hotel**
6906 North St.
Nacogdoches, TX 75961
(409) 560-3531

■ **Continental Inn**
2728 North St.
Nacogdoches, TX 75961
(409) 564-3726

■ **The Fredonia Hotel & Convention Center**
200 N. Fredonia St.
Nacogdoches, TX 75961
(409) 564-1234

NATIONAL COUNTRY MUSIC FESTIVAL

Second weekend in August
Ainsworth, Nebraska
www.loc.gov/bicentennial/propage/NE/ne_s_hagel2.html
Admission: $

Taking place in the official country music capital of Nebraska, Ainsworth's festival is more of a town fair than a traditional music festival. Instead of bands performing on stage, the weekend-long event is made up of contests, games, and various music-related activities including a "band scramble" in which bands are assembled arbitrarily from members of the audience and given almost no time to rehearse their performance. The festival is a celebration of the town of Ainsworth itself more than anything.

Camping: Yes

Accommodations

■ **Ainsworth Inn Bed & Breakfast**
400 N. Main St.
Ainsworth, NE 69210
(402) 387-0454

■ **Skinner's Motor Court**
215 S. Mai St.
Ainsworth, NE 69210
(402) 387-2021

■ **Remington Arms Hotel**
E. Hwy. 20
Ainsworth, NE 69210
(402) 387-2220

NATIONAL FOLK FESTIVAL

August
Various traveling locations
www.nationalfolkfestival.com
Admission: $

National Folk Festival is a 40-year old traveling event that sets up residence in a different city every three years. The main objectives of the festival are to bring the sounds of Americana to as many new ears as possible and to jump-start new festivals in the areas where the organizers set up shop. All manner of American and world music is represented, from zydeco to rock, from jazz to old-timey country songs. Authentic renditions are the order of the day—Beausoleil and Boozoo Chavis have appeared at past festivals, alongside Doc Watson, Johnny Copeland, and South African vocal group Mahotello Queens. Check the Web site or call the number provided for details on where the festival will be located this year.

For more information: (207) 992-2630 or info@nationalfolkfestival.com

NEW HAVEN FOLK FESTIVAL

Mid-September
Edgerton Park, New Haven, Connecticut
www.ctfolk.com
Admission: $$

Connecticut's largest festival features 16-plus hours of regional and national performance; artists such as Tom Rush, Vance Gilbert, and Eddie from Ohio have all appeared in years past. During the festival each year, the city of New Haven hosts the Sacco & Vanzetti Songwriting Competition to observe the unjust execution of two Italian American progressives in 1927 and award a prize for the best song written on the subject of what true American liberty means. There is no smoking allowed anywhere at this festival.

Artist Submissions
New Haven Folk Festival
39 Goodrich St.
Hamden, CT 06517
For more information: (203) 624-3559 or (877) 9-CTFOLK or info@ctfolk.com
Camping: No
Accommodations

■ **Atlantic Motel**
45 Pond Lily Ave.
New Haven, CT 06515-1109
(203) 387-2518

■ **Inn at Chapel West**
1201 Chapel St.
New Haven, CT 06515
(860) 777-1201

■ **Hotel Duncan**
1151 Chapel St., No. 100
New Haven, CT 06515
(203) 787-1273

NEW JERSEY FOLK FESTIVAL

One day in April
New Brunswick, New Jersey
http://njfolkfest.rutgers.edu/home.htm
Admission: FREE

Organized and run by students at nearby Rutgers University, the New Jersey Folk Festival takes place on the campus of Douglass College. Admission is free. A collection of regional bands and singer-songwriters perform throughout the day, on the grounds of the Eagleton Institute.

For more information: (732) 932-5775 or njff@rci.rutgers.edu

Camping: No

Accommodations

■ **Brunswick Hotel**
10 Livingston Ave.
New Brunswick, NJ 08901
(908) 214-1717

NEWFOUNDLAND AND LABRADOR FOLK FESTIVAL

Early August
St. John's, Newfoundland, Canada
www.sjfac.nf.net
Admission: $$

A small crowd gathers underneath a large tent set up in a tree-lined meadow in St. John's for the Newfoundland and Labrador Folk Festival. Here they listen to live folk music, listen in on and participate in discussions on the roots of Newfoundland's folk song heritage, and learn about the instruments, dance, and singing styles of their region. Respected local musicians give workshops and concerts, and elder statespeople are often called upon to speak before the crowd, imparting their own knowledge and experience with folk music.

For more information: (709) 576-8508 or (709) 722-2863 or jhewson@nfld.com or bridget@sjfac.nf.net

Camping: No

Accommodations

■ **Delta St. John's**
120 New Gower St.
St. John's, NF A1C 6K4
Canada
(709) 739-6404 or (800) 563-3838

■ **Hotel St. John's**
102 Kenmount Rd.
St. John's, NF A1B 3R2
Canada
(709) 722-9330

NORFOLK ISLAND COUNTRY MUSIC FESTIVAL

Five days in May
Norfolk Island, New Zealand
www.norfolk.nu/other/lothercm.htm
Admission: $

Australian and New Zealander country acts perform and compete for the Trans-Tasman Entertainer of the Year Award at this five-day festival held on beautiful and exotic Norfolk Island off the coast of New Zealand. The last night of the festival features a casual but spirited dance where headliners from the past week perform in an informal setting.

Camping: Yes
Accommodations: http://nz.wheretostay.net/

NORTH COUNTRY FAIR

Late June
Joussard, Alberta, Canada
www.northcountryfair.ab.ca
Admission: $

More than 40 groups, ranging from jazz fusion acts to truly exotic world musicians to straight-up rock and jam bands deliver one show after another over the course of a June weekend every year in Joussard, Alberta, on Lesser Slave Lake. An overall vibe of pleasant spaciness and sonic innovation is the defining characteristic of the North Country Fair, as it attracts a select, somewhat alternative crowd. The emphasis is on talent rather than star power here, so don't let the absence of any major-label artists deter you from attending or applying for an opportunity to perform.

Artist Submissions

NCF Artistic Team

6604 106 St.

Edmonton, AB T6H 5E8

Canada

carolwea@shaw.ca

For more information: (780) 988-3258 or ncf@northcountryfair.ab.ca

Camping: Yes

Accommodations

■ **Super 8 Slave Lake**

1240 14 Avenue SW

Slave Lake, AB T0G 2A0

Canada

(800) 800-8000

NORTH COUNTRY JAMBOREE

Mid-August

Sudbury, Ontario, Canada

www.angelfire.com/nt/northcountry

Admission: $$

In the past, the North Country Jamboree has featured such major names as George Jones and Ricky Scaggs, but the last couple years have seen a bit of a drop-off in star power. Don't let that discourage you from attending, though—independent country musicians can often be as entertaining as any star, and with more than 100 acres of free camping, this festival could just as easily serve as a getaway vacation as a musical excursion.

Artist Submissions

Miami Sound Entertainment

Rob Roussel: (705) 969-9488

Ron Pinard: (705) 693-7895

For more information: (705) 522-9614 or miamisounds@sympatico.ca

Camping: Yes

Accommodations

■ **Best Western Sudbury**

151 Larch St.

Sudbury, ON P3E 1C3

Canada

(800) 387-0697

NORTHERN LIGHTS FESTIVAL BORÉAL

Early July
Sudbury, Ontario, Canada
www.nlfb.on.ca
Admission: $

A two-day gathering situated on the shores of Ramsey Lake in Sudbury, Ontario, the Northern Lights Festival Boréal celebrates the rich diversity of northern Ontario with live music, dance, handcrafted arts, food, and story-telling. Concerts are given in the Bell Park Amphitheater. Musical acts are almost exclusively Canadian, playing a variety of folk and world styles.

Artist Submissions

NLFB Office
Bureau De Festival
P.O. Box 1236, Stn. B
Sudbury, ON P3E 4S7
Canada

For more information: (705) 674-5512 or info@nlfb.on.ca
Camping: Yes
Accommodations

- Best Western Downtown Sudbury
  Centreville
  151 Larch St.
  Sudbury, ON P3E 1C3
  Canada
  (800) 387-0697

- Days Inn Sudbury
  117 Elm St.
  Sudbury, ON P3C 1T3
  Canada
  (705) 674-7517

NORTHWEST FIDDLEFEST

Mid-March
Smithers, British Columbia, Canada
www.bvfms.org/nwfiddlefest
Admission: $$–$$$

Smithers, British Columbia, hosts this four-day event, offering instructional classes in the art of Canadian fiddle styles as well as a number of concerts by local musicians. Registrants from out of town are put up in the homes of locals who will also be attending the festival. A day-care center is provided for families. This makes for a friendly, fun, and educational weekend.

Artist Submissions: On-line application only

For more information: 6whites@uniserve.com
Camping: Yes
Accommodations: Food and lodging provided with registration

NORTHWEST FOLKLIFE FESTIVAL

One day in May
Seattle, Washington
www.nwfolklife.org
Admission: *FREE*

The heritage of the Northwest is celebrated at this Seattle festival, with a focus on Native American culture. Thousands of regional, national, and international artists contribute performances, folklore exhibits, dance routines, and food, in a large sector of the festival called the International Food Village.

Artist Submissions
Northwest Folklife
158 Thomas St., Ste. 32
Seattle, WA 98109
For more information: (206) 684-7300 or folklife@nwfolklife.org
Camping: No
Accommodations

■ **Camlin Hotel**
1619 Ninth Ave.
Seattle, WA 98101
(206) 682-0100

■ **The Comfort Suites Downtown**
  Seattle Center
601 Roy St.
Seattle, WA 98109
(206) 282-2600

■ **Mediterranean Inn on Queen Anne**
425 Queen Anne Ave. N
Seattle, WA 98109
(206) 428-4700 or (866) 525-4700

■ **The Hampton Inn & Suites**
700 5th Ave. N
Seattle, WA 98109
(206) 282-7700

NORTHWEST STRING SUMMIT

End of June
North Plains, Oregon
www.stringsummit.com
Admission: $$$

Yonder Mountain String Band, David Grisman, Hot Rize, and Kelly Joe Phelps have all appeared at the Northwest String Summit in the recent past. Jam rockers and hippies favor this weekend festival full of camping and the kind of folk music that made David Crosby a star. Food is plentiful, as are the crafts vendors and informal, fireside jam sessions.

For more information: (503) 230-1978 or ryan@segueproductions.com

Camping: Yes, on-site and included in price of admission.

Accommodations

■ **Candlewood Suites**
3133 NE Shute Rd.
Hillsboro, OR 97124
(503) 681-2121

■ **Dunes Motel**
452 SE 10th Ave.
Hillsboro, OR 97124
(503) 648-8991

■ **Park Dunes Motel**
622 SE 10th Ave.
Hillsboro, OR 97124
(503) 640-4791

O*A*T*S BLUEGRASS FESTIVAL

First week in June
Benton, Pennsylvania
http://oatsfestival.com
Admission: $–$$$

Come to the four-day O*A*T*S festival ready for some serious field-picking. Roving packs of musicians spend almost the entire weekend playing and looking for folks to play with, but when your fingertips get sore, you can just sit back and enjoy quality acts such as Charlie Waller & the Country Gentlemen, the James King Band, and Bob Paisley & Southern Grass. Concerts take place at the Benton Rodeo Grounds in Benton, Pennsylvania, outdoors under the stars, which is what the name of the festival means —Out Under the Stars, except for that damned letter *A*. O*A*T*S is traditionally kicked off with a pig roast the night before the first day's activities.

Artist Submissions

Trish Lundberg, (215) 328-9767 or trish@oatsfestival.com or write to:
Eye-Yee, Inc.
OATS Festival
100 Hastings Ave.
Wallingford, PA 19086

For more information: Info@oatsfestival.com

Camping: No

Accommodations

■ **Outpost Inn**
Route 29
Hunlock Creek, PA 18621
(717) 477-2126

■ **Hotel Iola Inc.**
P.O. Box 390
Millville, PA 18746
(717) 458-6496

■ **Tuscarora Motor Inn**
RR 4, Box 142
Mifflintown, PA 17059
(717) 436-2127

♪ O'CAROLAN HARP FESTIVAL

Early August
County Roscommon, Ireland
www.harp.net
Admission: $

Irish stars the Chieftains, Sean Keane, and Dervish are regular performers at this festival held to honor the memory of Irish harp master Turlough O'Carolan. Workshops on the playing and construction of harps are offered in addition to séisun jams and Irish Céilís dances. A harp competition, with a £2000 first prize and £500 senior first prize, is open to all.

Artist Submissions
Also for harp contest entry:
Brid McMorrow
Keadue, Co.
Roscommon, Ireland
(353) 078-47221

For more information: (353) 078-47204 or ocarolan@eircom.net

Camping: No

Accommodations

■ **Riversdale House**
64 Knockvicar
Boyle, Ireland
(353) 796-7012

■ **Royal House**
Bridge St.
Boyle, Ireland
(353) 796-2016

♪ OKLAHOMA INTERNATIONAL BLUEGRASS FESTIVAL

First weekend in October
Guthrie, Oklahoma
www.oibf.com
Admission: $$

Musicians from around the world perform at this celebration, which is packed with workshops and food vendors and sprawls throughout the downtown sector of beautiful Guthrie, Oklahoma. Over the course of its six-year existence, the festival has grown in popularity, garnering an American Bus Association Award for one of the Top 100 Events in 2001. This is an excellent festival to attend if you are interested in more than just American bluegrass bands, as acts from as far away as Japan have performed here in the past. A variety of food vendors and a crafts market are spread out among the six stages. There is also a battle of the bands held for musicians under the age of 18, with an entry form posted on the OIBF Web site. Camping is available in an area adjacent to the festivities.

For more information: (877) 203-1206 or (405) 282-4446 or office@oibf.com
Camping: Yes
Accommodations

■ **Best Western Motel**
I-35 exit 157
(405) 282-8831
has RV Park

■ **Interstate Motel**
2115 E. Oklahoma Ave.
Guthrie, OK 73044
(405) 282-7700

■ **Town House Motel**
223 E. Oklahoma Ave.
Guthrie, OK 73044
(405) 260-2400

♪ OLD SONGS FESTIVAL

Late June
Altamont, New York
www.oldsongs.org/festival/index.html
Admission: $

This inclusive festival offers workshops on songs of social justice, murder ballads, and hobo songs in addition to Italian, Irish, and African traditional dance events and jam sessions. The bill is comprised of a series of somewhat obscure regional acts, but you may have heard of Tom Paxton, No Strings Attached, and Beppe Gambetta. Still, this is a laid-back, informative, and progressive-thinking festival.

For more information: (518) 765-2815 or oldsongs@oldsongs.org

Camping: No

Accommodations

■ **Denny's Motel**
RR 3, Box 137
Altamont, NY 12009
(518) 456-4430

♪ OLD TOWN TEMECULA BLUEGRASS FESTIVAL

March
Temecula, California
www.temeculacalifornia.com/Bluegrass_Festival/bluegrass_festival.html
Admission: FREE

The whole town of Temecula comes out for the bluegrass festival, which features a handful of local bands playing the traditional music of the mountains. Workshops for the kids, crafts shows, and horse-drawn carriage rides are offered.

For more information: (909) 587-6504 or Melsads@aol.com

Camping: Yes, on-site.

Accommodations

■ **Butterfield Inn**
28718 Front St.
Temecula, CA 92590
(909) 676-4833

■ **Palomar Hotel**
28522 Front St.
Temecula, CA 92590
(909) 676-6503

■ **Loma Vista Bed & Breakfast**
33350 La Serena Way
Temecula, CA 92590
(909) 676-7047

♪ OLD-TIME WEEK

One week in August or October
Elkins, West Virginia

www.augustaheritage.com/octotw.html
Admission: $$$

While there are informal performances and plenty of open jamming at Old-Time Week, the main focus of this festival is education. Taking place on campus at Davis & Elkins College in Elkins, West Virginia, Old-Time Week offers workshops instructing students in the traditional instruments of West Virginian old-timey music. Banjo, dulcimer, and fiddle lessons are given over the course of a full week with beginner, intermediate, and advanced classes available. (In 2002 tuition was $355.) The finale is the Fiddler's Reunion, a free-admission festival that attracts the region's elderly players who jam with the students and perform for the crowd. This is an excellent opportunity for musicians interested in folk music to learn from and play with masters of the art.

Artist Submissions: Check Web site
For more information: (304) 637-1209 or (800) 624-3157 ext. 1209 or augusta@augustaheritage.com
Camping: No
Accommodations
■ **On-campus housing available.**
See www.augustaheritage.com/reginfo.html

■ **Graceland Inn & Conference Center**
100 Campus Dr.
Elkins, WV 26241
(304) 637-1600 or (800) 624-3157

■ **The Kerr House Bed & Breakfast**
519 Davie Ave.
Statesville, NC 28677
(704) 881-0957 or (877) 308-0353
thekerrhouse@abts.net

OREGON BLUEGRASS & COWBOY MUSIC FESTIVAL

Mid-August
Odell, Oregon
Admission: $$$

Four days of music with a barbecue cook-off, cowboy shows, raffles, wine-tasting, and a crafts fair right near the Oregon-Washington border. Regional bluegrass acts share the main stage with seasoned cowboy singers, delivering live performances as well as instructional workshops regarding the instruments they use and the roots of the music they play.

For more information: (503) 261-9887 or dlspeakertrainer@msn.com
Camping: Yes, on-site.

Accommodations

■ **Inn At The Dalles**
3550 SE Frontage Rd.
The Dalles, OR 97058
(503) 296-1167

■ **Huntley Inn**
2500 W. 6th St.
The Dalles, OR 97058
(503) 296-1191

♪ OREGON JAMBOREE

First weekend in August
Sweet Home, Oregon
www.oregonjamboree.com
Admission: $$$

A big-budget, star-studded two-day festival of country music, designed much the same way a large rock festival would be. Festivalgoers mill around a campground area, with stages situated throughout, and a large open space in front of the main stage. Food and crafts vendors offer their wares, and the crowd is sprayed down with hoses if it gets too hot. Past festivals have featured Martina McBride, Keith Urban, and Montgomery Gentry.

Artist Submissions
Oregon Jamboree
P.O. Box 430
Sweet Home, OR 97386
(541) 367-8800
info@oregonjamboree.com
For more information: (541) 367-8909 or jamman@oregonjamboree.com
Camping: Yes, on-site.

Accommodations

■ **Phoenix Inn Suites**
3410 Spicer Rd. SE
Albany, OR 97321
(541) 926-5696 or (888) 889-0208

■ **Santiam River Resort B&B**
27945 Santiam Hwy.
Sweet Home, OR 97386
(541) 367-4837
srr@relax-here.com
www.relax-here.com

■ **La Quinta Inn & Suites**
251 Airport Rd. SE
Albany, OR 97321
(800) 531-5900 or (541) 928-0921

♪ OSSIPEE VALLEY BLUEGRASS FESTIVAL

Late July
Cornish, Maine
www.ossipeevalley.com
Admission: $$

Just outside of Cornish, Maine, near the meeting of the Ossippee and Little Rivers, the Ossipee Valley Bluegrass festival offers two days and three nights of entertainment. Regional acts favoring nearby Canada make up the roster of talent, while an open stage provides a place for first-timers and nonprofessionals to perform. Potential artists are OK'd for open stage performance on a first come, first served basis, so be sure to submit your material to the address provided below sooner rather than later.

Artist Submissions
OVBA
P.O. Box 593
Cornish, ME 04020
(207) 625-8656
ossipeebluegrass@yahoo.com
www.ossipeevalley.com
For more information: (207) 625-8656 or ossipeebluegrass@yahoo.com
Camping: Yes
Accommodations
■ Midway Motel
712 S. Hiram Rd.
Cornish, ME 04020
(207) 625-8835

♪ PARK CITY BLUEGRASS FESTIVAL

Early May
Park City, Kansas
www.parkcitybluegrass.com
Admission: $-$$

Held at the Park City Indoor Pavilion, this three-day festival features the usual suspects of the bluegrass festival circuit, along with big names J. D. Crowe and the New South, Continental Divide, and Larry Stephenson. Arts and crafts booths, lots of food choices, and widespread informal jamming fill up the time between sets on the main stage.

Artist Submissions

Park City Festivals, Inc.

6110 N. Hydraulic

Park City, KS 67219

For more information: (316) 691-8178 or (316) 838-1909 or mail@parkcitybluegrass.com

Camping: Yes. For reservations call (316) 755-7328.

Accommodations

■ **Super 8**

6075 Air Cap Dr.

Wichita, KS 67219

(316) 744-2071

■ **Best Western**

915 E. 53rd St. N.

Wichita, KS 67219

(316) 832-9387

■ **Days Inn**

901 E. 53rd St. N.

Wichita, KS 67219

(316) 832-1131

■ **Comfort Inn**

990 Connolly Ct.

Wichita, KS 67219

(316) 744-7711

PEMI VALLEY BLUEGRASS FESTIVAL

First weekend in August

West Campton, New Hampshire

www.pemivalleybluegrass.com

Admission: $$

New Hampshire's White Mountains set a gorgeous backdrop for this three-day party at the Branch Brook Campground. Branch Brook Campground also happens to be the home of Pie Guy Pies, a homemade pie retailer offering absolutely delicious whole pies. Order the pie of your choice a week in advance of your arrival and you will be treated to one of New Hampshire's best-kept secrets. And when you're done eating maybe you'll want to check out the performers plucking homespun bluegrass on a single, easy-to-see stage. Attend one of the many bluegrass-related workshops held throughout the weekend, or do a little square dancing (an annual occurrence at the Recreation Hall on Saturday night). Past festivals have featured the music of the Gibson Brothers, Skip Gorman, Gopher Broke, and the Barney family, among others.

For more information: (603) 726-3471 or russue@pemivalleybluegrass.com
Camping: Yes. Contact the Branch Brook Campground at (603) 726-7001.
Accommodations

■ **Colonel Spencer Inn**
3 Colonel Spencer Rd.
Campton, NH 03223
(603) 536-3438
alan_m_hill@hotmail.com

■ **The Crowes' in Campton Village**
1 Mad River Rd.
Campton, NH 03223
(603) 726-5555
info@thecrowesincampton.com

■ **Mountain Fare Inn**
#5 Old Waterville Rd.
Campton, NH 03223
(603) 726-4283
mtnfareinn@cyberportal.net

♪ PHILADELPHIA FOLK FESTIVAL

Two days in August
Old Pool Farm, Philadelphia, Pennsylvania
www.folkfest.org
Admission: $$

Storytelling, traditional cowboy songs, and special appearances by distinguished acts such as legendary Texan band the Flatlanders (Joe Ely, Jimmie Dale Gilmore, Butch Hancock) as well as Tuvan throat singers from Tibet make this 42-years-old-and-counting festival a much loved event in Philadelphia.
Artist Submissions: info@folkfest.org
Camping: Yes, on-site.
For more information: (215) 242-0150 or (800) 556-FOLK (3655) or
info@folkfest.org
Accommodations

■ **Alexander Inn**
304 S. 12th St.
Philadelphia, PA 19102
(215) 923-3535

■ **Apollo Hotel**
1918 Arch St.
Philadelphia, PA 19103
(215) 567-8925

■ **Aramark Corp**
1101 Market St. #45
Philadelphia, PA 19107
(215) 238-3000

PICKATHON MUSIC FESTIVAL

One day in September
North Plains, Oregon
www.pickathon.com
Admission: $$

The proceeds from Pickathon Music Festival benefit community radio station KBOO in Portland, Oregon. Concerts take place on the grounds of a place called Horning's Hideout, just outside the city. Festivalgoers are encouraged to bring instruments along to join in the many jams that sprout up all around the festival. A host of semiobscure acts play everything from bluegrass to Cajun music and traditional Irish music to roots rock. Friday night of the festival traditionally features a surprise guest artist followed by old-fashioned square dancing.

For more information: info@folkfest.org or festival@teleport.com

Camping: Yes, on-site.

Accommodations

■ **Candlewood Suites**
3133 Northeast Shute Rd.
Hillsboro, OR 97124
(503) 681-2121

■ **Phoenix Inn**
14797 NW Jewell Ln.
Portland, OR 97229
(503) 614-8400

PORTERFIELD COUNTRY MUSIC FESTIVAL

Mid-June
Marinette, Wisconsin
www.countrymusicfestival.com
Admission: $$–$$$

Held on a giant stretch of campground dotted with streets named Tammy Wynette Drive and Pam Tillis Road, the Porterfield Festival is a country music lovers' dream. This massive country music festival features many top name acts such as Suzy Boggus and Colin Raye, but you might also make a no-name discovery. There are tons of food vendors as well as all the merchandise one could want situated throughout the grounds during the three-day affair. The main stages are reserved for big-name acts and up and comers, while there are a number of bars with smaller names and regional acts on the bill. It is not recommended to anyone looking for an intimate weekend, however, as literally thousands attend each year.

For more information: (920) 834-2465 (evenings) or pcf@cybrzn.com
Camping: Yes
Accommodations
■ **Best Western Riverfront Inn**
1821 Riverside Ave.
Marinette, WI 54143
(715) 732-1000

PORTSMOUTH MARITIME FOLK FESTIVAL

Late September
Portsmouth, New Hampshire
http://home.earthlink.net/~pcontrastano/folk_horizons/pmff.htm
Admission: *FREE*

The Portsmouth Maritime Folk Festival is a nautically themed festival of the maritime arts held in Portsmouth, New Hampshire, a major New England port and former whaling village. Model ship building, wood carving, presentations on historical figures such as seaman John Paul Jones, and instrumental workshops for both beginners and intermediate players are just a few of the activities offered. Past performers include Roy Clinging, sea shanty specialists the NexTradition, and maritime traditionalist Mary Malloy.
For more information: plc@folkhorizons.org
Camping: No
Accommodations

■ **Anchorage Inn**
417 Woodbury Ave.
Portsmouth, NH 03801
(603) 431-8111

■ **Bow Street Inn**
121 Bow St.
Portsmouth, NH 03801
(603) 431-7760

■ **Bickford's Family Restaurant**
I-95 Portsmouth Traffic Circle
Portsmouth, NH 03801
(603) 436-6640

PREDDYFEST BLUEGRASS FESTIVAL

Early August
Franklin County, North Carolina

www.preddyfest.com

Admission: $–$$

Held on the banks of the Tar River in Franklin County, North Carolina, the PreddyFest Bluegrass Festival is a family-oriented celebration of the traditional folk and country music of the region. A festival in North Carolina is worth going to if only for the barbecue, but you can also expect authentic local bluegrass bands and family harmony acts to perform. This festival was founded in 1997 and is growing fast. Past festivals have included appearances by Grand Ole Opry banjo regular Mike Snider, traditional bluegrass band Steep Canyon Rangers, and the James King Band.

For more information: (919) 494-7471 or bluegrass@preddyfest.com

Camping: Yes, on-site.

Accommodations

■ **Burrell's Motel**
3108 S. Georgia Rd.
Franklin, NC 28734
(704) 524-2444

■ **Colonial Inn**
Hwy. 441-23 S.
Franklin, NC 28734
(704) 524-6600

■ **Carolina Motel**
625 Georgia Hwy.
Franklin, NC 28734
(828) 524-3380

♪ PUCKERAMA: A WHISTLING FESTIVAL

October

Tulsa, Oklahoma

www.thewhistler.com/puckerama.htm

Admission: FREE–$

In the words of the organizers themselves, Puckerama "aims to encourage awareness of the musical art of whistling through education, training, and fellowship of artists." A celebration of putting your lips together and blowing, this good-natured event offers several performances and workshops, all dedicated to whistling. If you fancy yourself a strong whistler, are simply a fan, or are just curious, Tulsa is a destination that should definitely be on your agenda come October.

For more information: info@puckerama.com

Camping: No

Accommodations

■ **Ramada Inn**
17 W. 7th St.
Tulsa, OK 74119
(888) 298-2054

■ **Doubletree Hotel**
616 W. Seventh St.
Tulsa, OK 74127-8983
(918) 587-8000

♪ RED MULE BLUEGRASS FESTIVAL

Three days in May
Relief, Kentucky
Admission: $$

J. D. Crow and New South, Doctor Ralph Stanley, and the Osborne Brothers have appeared at past incarnations of this spring weekend festival. A host of lesser-known regional acts fill out the roster of events with workshops, and the spectacular barbecue of the region provides sustenance for the crowd. Camping and concerts occur on the grounds of Patoker Music Park in Relief, Kentucky.

For more information: (606) 886-2990 or (606) 266-1991 or donfromky@webtv.net

Camping: Yes

Accommodations

■ **Stamper Motel**
323 Main St.
West Liberty, KY 41472
(606) 743-3054

♪ RIVERBEND BLUEGRASS FESTIVAL

October
Ocilla, Georgia
www.riverbendbluegrass.com
Admission: $

This modest, friendly festival occurs in late October with a handful of both regional and national acts filling out the bill and performing on the porch of a cabin in the woods, rain or shine. Open jamming and instructional workshops fill in the spaces between sets. Past performers include Rhoda Vincent, Larry Stephenson, and house favorite, the Riverbend Bluegrass Band.

For more information: (229) 468-4120 or (229) 468-5581 or mattp@alltel.net or veniece@alltel.net

Camping: Yes

Accommodations

■ **Country Hearth Inn**
125 Stuart Way
Fitzgerald, GA 31750
(229) 409-9911

■ **Jameson Inn**
111 Bull Run Rd.
Fitzgerald, GA 31750
(229) 424-9500

■ **Holiday Inn Express**
265 Ocilla Hwy.
Fitzgerald, GA 31750
(229) 423-5151

♩ RIVERLAND COUNTRY MUSIC FESTIVAL

Ten days in June
Barmera, South Australia, Australia
www.riverlandcountrymusic.com
Admission: $

This giant Australian festival takes over the entire Riverland region with hundreds of acts performing in innumerable venues. The festival takes in a carnival atmosphere as the 10-day stretch takes its toll on hardcore partiers. Performers are exclusively from Australia and New Zealand. Square, contra, and barn dancing are all regular occurrences, as are informal jams and workshops. A number of state-sponsored music awards are given out during the course of the event.

For more information: (61) 08-8588-1030 or rcmcfest@riverland.net.au

Camping: Yes

Accommodations

■ **Barmera Travel Centre**
Barwell Ave.
Barmera, SA 5345
Australia
(61) 08-8582-1655

■ **Loxton Tourist and Travel Centre**
East Terrace
Loxton, SA 5333
Australia
(61) 08-8584-7919

■ **Berri Tourist and Travel Centre**
24 Vaughan Tce.
Berri, SA 5343
Australia
(61) 08-8582-1655

■ **Renmark Information Centre**
Murray Ave.
Renmark, SA 5341
Australia
(61) 08-8586-6704

ROCKY MOUNTAIN FOLKS FESTIVAL

Mid-August
Lyons, Colorado
www.planetbluegrass.com
Admission: $$–$$$

Also known as the RockyGrass Folks Festival, this event provides an excellent opportunity for interested people to learn more about bluegrass music. You can also learn how to play it, learn how to build its traditional instruments, and think about where the genre is headed. The festival offers an "academy" to young and old fans alike featuring serious bluegrass "ambassadors" helping with instruction and sharing their know-how. Del McCoury himself has served as an ambassador in the past, along with such bluegrass luminaries as Missy Raines, Dr. Banjo, Dennis Caplinger, and Sandy Munro. In addition to the expected festival goings-on (concerts, food vendors, informal jams), each year RockyGrass holds a songwriter competition with a cash prize and an opportunity for the winner to play on the main stage. The event takes place on the Planet Bluegrass Ranch, with plenty of camping, within the town limits of Lyon, Colorado.

For more information: (800) 624-2422 or planet@bluegrass.com

Camping: Yes, on-site.

Accommodations

■ **Super 8 Longmont**
2446 Main St.
Longmont, CO 80501
(303) 772-8106

■ **Stone Mountain Lodge**
18055 North St. Vrain Dr.
Lyons, CO 80540
(800) 282-5612

■ **Westwood Inn**
1550 Main St.
Longmont, CO 80501
(303) 776-2185

ROLLO BAY FIDDLE FESTIVAL

Late July
Rollo Bay, Prince Edward Island, Canada
http://RolloBayFiddleFest.com
Admission: $

The Rollo Bay Fiddle Festival is approaching 30 seasons of business, and over the years the organizers have learned that to throw a good festival you don't need 100 bands from all over, booths upon booths, and people selling $16 hot dogs. All you need is a stage, some good music, and a place for folks to sit. This Prince Edward Island institution is the sort of festival that will take you back 100 years—and you will be thankful for the trip. A single, simple stage on the porch of a beautiful, unadorned house bears witness to the delightful talents of up-and-coming Canadian folksingers each year, with J. P. Cormier, Natalie MacMaster, and Carl MacKenzie topping the list. Rollo Bay Fiddle Festival recently added a Saturday night Ceilidh—a traditional Celtic barn dance/jam session.

For more information: (902) 687-2584 or Info@RolloBayFiddleFest.com

Camping: Yes. RV and rough camping are available on-site.

Accommodations

■ **Delta Prince Edward**
18 Queen St.
P.O. Box 2170
Charlottetown, PE C1A 8B9
Canada
(902) 566-2222

SADDLEWORTH FOLK FESTIVAL

Three days in July
Uppermill, United Kingdom
www.safra.org.uk
Admission: $$–$$$

Held on the edge of the Pennines, a region better known as England's somber, spectacular moors, the Saddleworth Folk Festival offers lots of room for camping. There's a nearly continuous roster of local and national musicians (no big names) and a plethora of workshops, sing-a-longs, and open jams, which are known in Ireland and England as *seisiuns* (pronounced "sessions").

For more information: (44) 01457-870391 or info@safra.org.uk

Camping: Yes, on-site.

Accommodations

■ **Egerton House Hotel**
Blackburn Road, Egerton
Bolton, Lancashire BL7 9PL
United Kingdom
(44) 01204-307171

■ **Millstone Hotel**
Church St., Mellor
Blackburn, Lancashire BB2 7JR
United Kingdom
(44) 01254-813333

SAN FRANCISCO BLUEGRASS FESTIVAL

Ten days in February
San Francisco, California
www.sfbluegrass.org
Admission: $–$$$

The San Francisco Bluegrass Festival takes place in a half a dozen venues spread across the Bay Area. You'll visit nightclubs and coffeehouses in the city itself, but the festival will also take you all the way out to Sweetwater, a bastion of Americana music located in Mill Valley, just a short ride over the Golden Gate Bridge. In operation since 2000, the festival has nearly outgrown its modest beginnings; the 2002 festival featured the likes of the Del McCoury Band and the Laurel Canyon. The majority of the roster is still made up of local acts, however, so this festival has not yet become too big for more discerning bluegrass fans to attend.

For more information: barbara@sfbluegrass.org
Camping: No
Accommodations: http://bayarea.citysearch.com

SANTA FE THIRSTY EAR FESTIVAL

Labor Day weekend
Santa Fe, New Mexico
www.thirstyearfestival.com
Admission: $$–$$$

With artists such as Pinetop Perkins, Doc Watson, Odetta, Joan Baez, and Ramblin' Jack Elliott appearing at various recent festivals, the Santa Fe Thirsty Ear fest certainly lives up to its reputation as New Mexico's best roots music festival. An area downtown is cordoned off for the Labor Day weekend event. You'll find multiple stages, a beer garden, ethnic foods from all over, and booth after booth of desert-bound hippies selling all kinds of handmade crafts and trinkets.

Artist Submissions
P.O. Box 29600
Santa Fe, NM 87592
For more information: (505) 473-5723 or info@thirstyearmagazine.com
Camping: No

Accommodations

■ **Adobe Abode B & B Inn**
202 Chapelle St.
Santa Fe, NM 87501
(505) 983-3133

■ **Alexander's Inn**
529 E. Palace Ave.
Santa Fe, NM 87501
(505) 986-1431

SANTA FE TRAILS BLUEGRASS FESTIVALS

Mid-May
Bonner Springs, Kansas
Admission: $

The Santa Fe Trails Bluegrass Festival is part of a three-day extravaganza called Americana Weekend, held in Bonner Springs, Kansas. A kite festival, a barbecue cook-off, and an arts and crafts fair coincide with the happy chaos of more than 20 performers appearing on five stages. Acts range from strict bluegrass to Irish folk and country—in other words, all manner of acoustic music.

For more information: (913) 722-9300 or info@santafetrails.org
Camping: Yes
Accommodations

■ **Day's Inn Lenexa**
9630 Rosehill Rd.
Shawnee Mission, KS 66215
(913) 492-7200

■ **Comfort Inn**
234 N. 78th St.
Kansas City, KS 66112
(913) 299-5505

■ **Hampton Inn of Shawnee**
16555 Midland Dr.
Shawnee Mission, KS 66217
(913) 248-1900

SAVANNAH FOLK MUSIC FESTIVAL

Mid-October
Savannah, Georgia
www.savannahfolk.org/festival.html
Admission: $$

The beautiful city of Savannah, Georgia, sets a wonderful backdrop for this two-day festival featuring concerts, booths, and an evening of square and contra dancing called by local favorite Ralph Blizard and the New Southern

Ramblers. Performances during the festival are given by other regional acts, specializing in hammered dulcimer, old-time harmony, and pure, white-bearded mountain music.

Camping: No

Accommodations

■ **Baymont Inn & Suites**
Savannah, GA
(912) 927-7660
(a discount may available for festivalgoers)

SAWLOG & STRINGS BLUEGRASS FESTIVAL

August

Jetmore, Kansas

http://sawlog.org

Admission: $

Follow US 283 through the blistering heat of the Kansas summer until you arrive at the cool, tree-shaded oasis of Sawlog Creek. The Housmans, Homestead, John LeBoeuf, and many more talented acts will serenade you as you partake in all that the Sawlog & Strings festival has to offer. Multiple workshops, family activities, and a mysterious "big surprise" are sure to keep you entertained throughout the weekend.

Artist Submissions: sawlog54@hotmail.com

For more information: ron@sawlog.org

Camping: Yes

Accommodations

■ **Bel Air Motel**
2000 E. Wyatt Earp Blvd.
Dodge City, KS 67801
(620) 227-7155

■ **Boot Hill Bed & Breakfast**
603 W. Spruce St.
Dodge City, KS 67801
(620) 225-7600

■ **Super 8**
1708 W. Wyatt Earp Blvd.
Dodge City, KS 67801
(800) 843-1991

■ **Holiday Inn Express**
2320 W. Wyatt Earp Blvd.
Dodge City, KS 67801
(620) 227-5000

■ **Silver Spur Best Western**
1510 W. Wyatt Earp Blvd.
Dodge City, KS 67801
(620) 227-2125

SEA MUSIC FESTIVAL

Early June
Mystic, Connecticut
www.mysticseaport.org
Admission: $

More than 60 performers from America and Europe sing, strum, and tell stories from the decks of tall ships and in venues around the old whaling city of Mystic, Connecticut. Pub sing-alongs and contra dances are held at nearby taverns and dance halls. Past performers include the Clancy Brothers, Matapat, Magpie, and Cindy Kallet.

For more information: (888) 9-SEAPORT
Camping: No
Accommodations

■ **Harbour Inn & Cottages**
15 Edgemont St.
Mystic, CT 06355
(860) 572-9253

■ **Inn at Mystic**
Intersection of Rt. 1 & Rt. 27
Mystic, CT 06355
(860) 536-9604

■ **Old Mystic Motor Lodge**
251 Greenmanville
Mystic, CT 06355
(860) 536-9666

SEATTLE BANJO FESTIVAL

Two days in April
Seattle, Washington
http://seattlebanjoclub.com
Admission: FREE

The Seattle Banjo Club spreads the bluegrass gospel with this yearly event, offering lots of jams and workshops, even going so far as to provide banjos for first-timers interested in learning the art. In 2002, Banjo Man Johnny Baier headlined, along with the Sidemen Quartet Kitsap and the Banjo Band. The Seattle Banjo Club also uses the weekend as an opportunity to showcase the talents of its members, who perform and give workshops throughout the event.

For more information: (206) 24-BANJO or festival@seattlebanjoclub.com
Camping: No

Accommodations

■ **Eastlake Inn**
2215 Eastlake Ave. E.
Seattle, WA 98102
(206) 322-7726

■ **A-1 Motel**
4450 Green Lake Way N.
Seattle, WA 98103
(206) 632-3733

♪ SHADY GROVE BLUEGRASS MUSIC FESTIVAL

Second weekend in August
Nanton, Alberta, Canada
www.melmusic.com/sgrove
Admission: $$

Held on the grounds of the Broadway Farm in Alberta, Canada, the Shady Grove Festival is a three-day gathering where you can experience nearly continuous bluegrass music, participate in informal jams, or maybe perform on an open stage. You can also learn how to play traditional bluegrass instruments such as the banjo, mandolin, or fiddle at one of the many musically themed workshops offered throughout the weekend. Past festivals have featured such artists as Lost Highway and the Dirty Hat Band in addition to more regional acts. All in all, this is a laid-back and well-paced weekend.

For more information: (403) 652-5550 or sgrove@melmusic.com
Camping: Yes

Accommodations

■ **Foothills Motel**
67 8 Ave. SE
High River, AB T1V 1E8
Canada
(403) 652-1395

■ **High River Motor Hotel**
P.O. Box 5584
High River, AB T1V 1E8
Canada
(403) 652-4339

■ **Heritage Inn**
1104 11 Ave. SE
High River, AB T1V 1E8
Canada
(403) 652-3834 or (888) 888-4374

■ **Victorian Dreams**
4440 Macleod Trail SW
High River, AB T1V 1E8
Canada
(403) 601-2340

♪ SHENANDOAH VALLEY MUSIC FESTIVAL

May to September
Orkney Springs, Virginia

www.musicfest.org

Admission: $–$$

The stunning Shenandoah Valley houses this summer-long festival that features big band, jazz, classical music, rock, and old-time folk music. Concerts are held in an open-air pavilion on the grounds of a historic mineral springs spa and resort hotel. Contemporary folk singer-songwriter Christine Lavin headlined the most recent Shenandoah Festival.

For more information: (540) 459-3396 or (800) 459-3396 or svmf@shentel.net

Camping: No

Accommodations

■ **The Hill at Bryce**
1382 Resort Dr.
Basye, VA 22810
(800) 307-3938
http://home.rica.net/thehill

■ **Inn at Narrow Passage**
P.O. Box 608
Route 11 S.
Woodstock, VA 22664
(800) 459-8002
innkeeper@innatnarrowpassage.com

■ **Hotel Strasburg**
213 S. Holliday St.
Strasburg, VA 22657
(800) 348-8327
thehotel@shentel.net

♪ SIOUX RIVER FOLK FESTIVAL

First weekend in August

Newton Hills State Park, South Dakota

www.fotm.org/festival

Admission: $

The Sioux River Folk Festival features both traditional and contemporary folk music performed in the desolate but beautiful badlands of South Dakota. Past performers include Brand New Old Time String Band, Buffalo Gals, and the Red Willow Band.

For more information: (605) 987-2582 or info@fotm.org

Camping: No

Accommodations

■ **Gateway Motel**
4400 W. Custer Ln.
Sioux Falls, SD 57106
(605) 987-2692

SISTERS FOLK FESTIVAL

Early September
Sisters, Oregon
www.sistersfolkfestival.com
Admission: $$

The Sisters Folk Festival promises the sort of no-nonsense old-time country and bluegrass music that true fans of the form will travel across the country to experience and participate in. Shows take place on a single stage in the grass lawn in the center of town, regularly featuring bluegrass stalwarts such as Chris Smither and the Nashville Bluegrass Band alongside local acts. Plenty of workshops are offered in addition to a songwriting competition. It seems like every year a new songwriter appears at this festival and goes on to national acclaim.

For more information: info@sistersfolkfestival.com
Camping: No
Accommodations

■ **Rags to Walker B & B Guest Ranch**
17045 Farthing Ln
Sisters, OR 97759
(800) 422-5622 or (541) 548-7000

■ **Sisters Motor Lodge**
550 W. Cascade
McKenzie Hwy.
Sisters, OR 97759
(541) 549-2551

■ **Sisters KOA**
67667 Hwy. 20
Bend, OR 97701
(541) 549-3021

SLEEPLESS NIGHTS

January
San Francisco, California
Admission: $

The Sleepless Nights music festival was first organized in 2000, and the idea behind it was to gather a group of like-minded musicians to perform in honor of the late country-rock pioneer Gram Parsons. Each successive year, the event gathers momentum and regularly features a variety of takes on the Parsons oeuvre. A selection of Bay Area and national performers can be expected to perform; folks such as Chuck Prophet and Dave Gleason will typically be featured on the bill.

Camping: No
Accommodations

■ **Phoenix Hotel**
601 Eddy St.
San Francisco, CA 94109
(800) 248-9466

■ **The Red Victorian**
1665 Haight St.
San Francisco, CA 94117
(415) 864-1978

ERIC SHEA *is a Bay Area musician who plays dirty rock 'n' roll with the band Mover and has organized the Sleepless Nights music festival for the past several years. He is also a big fan of skateboarding and designer cats and is, along with Homer Simpson, one of the few champions of the lite-rock sounds of the band Bread.*

How do festival crowds differ from your average concert crowds?

It really depends what kind of festival you're talking about. If you're talking about the CMJ festival, it really doesn't differ much from concert crowds. But if you're talking about the kind of outdoorsy, take-your-shirt-off festival, then I think those crowds tend to be mostly festival enthusiasts. You know, they're more into hanging out and eating food on a stick or juggling a stick between two other sticks. Concert crowds tend to be more enthusiastic about the actual music they paid to experience live.

Do you enjoy playing festivals?

I enjoy playing the Cosmic American Music Festival because it's in Joshua Tree, California, and all these rock 'n' roll kooks come out of the woodwork to dig what's going on. But as far as CMJ, South by Southwest (SXSW), or North by Northwest (NXNW) are concerned, I'd rather attend those festivals than play them. Once you've gone for a few years, it's easy to become suspicious of these festivals because many of them promise young bands that their music will be heard by top industry executives or whatever. But the truth is that A&R people don't really attend music conferences to sign bands. They attend these happenings to party and network. Most

. . . .

of the bands who buzz hard at industry festivals already have some kind of deal pending and are looking for overseas licensing or something else.

What festivals have you played at?

I've played the Cosmic American Music Festival, Sleepless Nights, NXNW, SXSW, and Nadine's Wild Weekend.

Is it hard getting booked into a festival? What hardships (if any) have you encountered?

It's much too easy getting booked into a music industry festival. These days, they just want your registration money. The only hardships I have encountered as an artist at these things is getting my band to actually agree to play SXSW or NXNW. The guys I play with are smart guys and they know that these kinds of festivals don't really exist to break unsigned talent. These kinds of festivals exist to line the pockets of certain industry heads.

What is your funniest and/or worst festival experience?

The worst festival experience was the last Nadine's Wild Weekend that we played. It was at this yuppie venue in North Beach, California, above the now defunct Mabuhay Gardens. The whole thing was totally unorganized. The sound guy didn't have any monitors working, and we had six singers in the band at this point. When it was our turn to take the stage, our gear had been sabotaged. Strings were cut on every one of our guitars, tubes in our amps were smashed, and wires were pulled. We had to borrow some band's cheapo Guitar Center equipment, we couldn't hear ourselves sing, and all the promised A&R attendees were nowhere to be seen.

Do you have any gripes regarding the current state of music festivals?

Music festivals, for the most part, are pretty fun. You can camp at some of them and have a really great time, even if you're not all that into the music. But industry festivals prey on the hopes and dreams of young local bands to make a buck. Kids think they're going to be playing at the same festival as Ryan Adams or the Strokes, whereas the reality for these young bands is more like showing up at Thanksgiving dinner and being assigned to sit at the kids' table.

. . . .

What purpose do music festivals serve in the current musical climate?

The same purpose music serves in the current musical climate—to make money.

What tips do you have for unestablished bands trying to get on the bill?

Don't believe the hype (or the brochure). Spend your money on your recordings and your own tour. If you are a baby band, focus on recording and delivering a solid product—something uncompromised and true to your art. Play your hometown enough to garner fans, but don't wear out your welcome. Play outside your hometown with other bands. Network with the bands you respect and exchange gigs with them, then find a band who does better than you and try and set up a tour with them. Soon enough you will be the band that younger bands want to tour with. Above all, be respectful and true to the music and those who inspire you.

SNOWSHOE BLUEGRASS FESTIVAL

June/July
Snowshoe, West Virginia
http://snowshoemtn.com
Admission: $$

Billing itself as "West Virginia's highest festival," this three-day series of country, bluegrass, and blues shows is held atop Snowshoe Mountain, approximately 5,000 feet above sea level. Food and beverages are in abundance but the main attraction is the high-profile roster of musicians, which in recent years has included the Del McCoury Band, Dr. Ralph Stanley, and Lost & Found.

For more information: (877) 441-4FUN or info@snowshoemtn.com
Camping: Yes, on-site.
Accommodations

■ **Overlook Village**
P.O. Box 324
Slatyfork, WV 26291
(304) 572-2290

■ **Snowshoe Mountain Inn**
P.O. Box 10
Snowshoe, WV 26209
(304) 572-2900

♪ SOUTH COUNTRY FAIR

Third weekend in July
Fort MacLeod, Alberta, Canada
www.scfair.ab.ca
Admission: $

With a roster of musicians that covers practically every genre of music imaginable and a laundry list of activities for kids, the South Country Fair is the sort of event entire families can attend and enjoy. There is something for everyone—poetry slam, wellness booths, face painting, independent films shown after the sun goes down, clowns, puppet shows, and storytelling. An exhaustive amount of attention is paid to putting this 16-year-old festival together each year, and the beauty of the Alberta prairie in summertime can be considered yet another attraction.

Artist Submissions

Deadline is end of February every year; send press kit and demo to:
South Country Fair
attn: Maureen Chambers, A.D.
P.O. Box 1251
Fort MacLeod, AB T0L 0Z0
Canada

For more information: (403) 553-3070 or asparagus@scfair.ab.ca

Camping: Yes. Provided on a first come, first served basis at Fish and Game Park, Lyndon Road.

Accommodations

■ **Holiday Inn MacLeod**
4206 MacLeod Trail SE
Calgary, AB T2G 2R7
Canada
(800) 661-1889

■ **Calgary MacLeod Trail Travelodge Hotel**
9206 MacLeod Trail S.
Calgary, AB T2J 0P5
Canada
(403) 253-7070

♪ SPRING COUNTRY MUSIC AND RHODODENDRON FESTIVAL

Ten days in May
Hiawassee, Georgia
www.georgia-mountain-fair.com/rhodie.html
Admission: $$

There are only two performers a year at the Spring County Festival but that's because the real star of the show is the Georgia Mountain Rhododendron Garden, the largest garden of its kind in the Southeast. Roughly 3,000 plants line a mile-long trail that runs alongside the coast of Lake Chatuge. In 2002, country stars Colin Raye and Lee Greenwood appeared, in a reserved-seating theater housed within the Georgia Mountain Fairgrounds, where the garden is located. An exhaustive arts and crafts fair takes place in the hours leading up to show time.

For more information: (706) 896-4191 or gamtfair@alltel.net

Camping: Yes

Accommodations

■ **Boundary Waters Resort & Marina**
528 Sunnyside Rd.
Hiawassee, GA 30546
(800) 323-3562 or (706) 896-2530

■ **Mull's Motel**
213 N. Main St.
Hiawassee, GA 30546
(706) 896-4195

■ **Lake Chatuge Lodge**
653 US Hwy. 76
Hiawassee, GA 30546
(800) 613-4349 or (706) 896-5253

STAN ROGERS FOLK MUSIC FESTIVAL

Late June
Canso, Nova Scotia, Canada
www.stanfest.com
Admission: $$–$$$

Local legend Stan Rogers influenced the entire region of Nova Scotia's Northwestern Shore with an enduring folk song tradition. His passing in 1983 inspired fans and colleagues to create this yearly event where folk musicians from all over Canada and the United States can come together to play, pay respects, and have a good time. Martin Sexton, the Waybacks, the Waifs, and Big Bill Morganfield have all appeared on one of the eight stages set up on the festival grounds.

Artist Submissions

Between September and January, send press kit and demo to:

Troy Greencorn, Artistic Director
P.O. Box 46
Canso, NS B0H 1H0
Canada
info@stanfest.com
For more information: (888) 554-7826 or info@stanfest.com
Camping: Yes, on-site.
Accommodations

■ **Pine Resort Hotel**
103 Shore Rd., Box 70
Digby, NS B0V 1A0
Canada
(902) 245-2511 or (800) 667-4637

■ **Fairview Inn Bridgewater**
25 Queen St.
Bridgewater, NS B4V 1P1
Canada
(902) 423-1102 or (800) SALTSEA

♪ STRICTLY BLUEGRASS

Early October
San Francisco, California
www.strictlybluegrass.com
Admission: FREE

This free event takes place in Golden Gate Park at the Speedway Meadows. There are two main stages on either side of the meadow that cater to all types of roots-based music, with a heavy slant toward bluegrass. The event began in 2001 and has since made a claim for itself as one of the most well organized, warmly received events in the park's great history. The crowds are friendly and energetic, peacefully relaxing on blankets with food, drink, and children at arm's length. Those with the inclination to dance do so in the middle thoroughfare, or up front by the stage. Kiosks up the hill provide festival-goers with free, well-designed posters and T-shirts. A great sound system allows you to hear music by folks such as Steve Earle, Hazel Dickens, and Alison Krauss wafting through the air. Hearing Emmylou Harris sing "Pancho & Lefty" as the sun goes down is an experience not often rivaled. The side stage provides a rockier alternative with artists such as Chuck Prophet delivering a fine blend of country, rock, and soul. All in all, this is a great event that should serve as a lesson to anyone hoping to conduct a free outdoor festival.

For more information: info@strictlybluegrass.com

Camping: No

Accommodations

■ **Phoenix Hotel**
601 Eddy St.
San Francisco, CA 94109
(800) 248-9466

■ **The Red Victorian**
1665 Haight St.
San Francisco, CA 94117
(415) 864-1978

STRINGBENDERS BLUEGRASS FESTIVAL

Two days in September
Fort Defiance Park, Iowa
www.stringbenders.com
Admission: $

Talented but lesser-known bluegrass bands from all over the United States come out to play at this two-day festival, held in lovely and historic Fort Defiance Park in Iowa. The park is very close to Iowa's Great Lakes Region and features plenty of camping, scenic hikes, and historical investigation.

For more information: (618) 764-2632 or caldwellsigns@earthlink.net

Camping: Yes

Accommodations

■ **Cozy Grove Motel**
1704 Central Ave.
Estherville, IA 51334
(712) 362-5831

■ **Villa Motel**
1202 2nd Ave. S
Estherville, IA 51334
(712) 362-2688

SUMMERFOLK MUSIC AND CRAFTS FESTIVAL

Mid-August
Owen Sound, Ontario, Canada
www.summerfolk.org
Admission: $$$

A favorite both with the musicians who perform there and the festivalgoers who watch them, the Summerfolk Music and Crafts Festival is a friendly, fun-filled weekend of camping, crafts, and music on Owen Sound in North Ontario. Kelso Beach Park is transformed into a winding village of stages, tents, and booths, and—rain or shine—more than 100 acts from Canada and the United States play from early afternoon well into the night. The roster of talent isn't always made up of the biggest names, but former Men at Work singer Colin Hay and acoustically minded cult favorite Trout Fishing in America have appeared at past festivals.

Artist Submissions

Georgian Bay Folk Society

P.O. Box 521

Owen Sound, ON N4K 5R1

Canada

For more information: (519) 371-2995 or gbfs@log.on.ca

Camping: Yes. Contact the Owen Sound KOA at (519) 371-1331.

Accommodations

■ **Owen Sound Motor Inn**

485 9th Ave.

East Owen Sound, ON N4K 3E2

Canada

(519) 371-3011

■ **Travellers Motel and Restaurant**

740 9th Ave.

East Owen Sound, ON N4K 3E2

Canada

(519) 376-2680

■ **Springmount Motel**

718010 Hwy. #6

North Owen Sound, ON N4K 5N7

Canada

(519) 376-5841

■ **Diamond Motor Inn**

713 9th Ave.

East Owen Sound, ON N4K 3E6

Canada

(519) 371-2011

SUWANEE SPRINGFEST

March

Live Oak, Florida

www.magmusic.com/suwannee.htm

Admission: $$$

Taking place on the grounds of the Spirit of the Suwannee Music Park (located between Jacksonville and Tallahassee, about 30 minutes south of the Georgia state line), the Suwanee Springfest features a star-studded lineup of folk and country musicians. Past performers includethe great Earl Scruggs, the Nitty Gritty Dirt Band, and acclaimed folksinger Jim Lauderdale. Non-professional musicians are invited to join in a songwriting competition.

For more information: (904) 249-7990 or Comments@magmusic.com

Camping: Yes

Accommodations

■ **Parker Motel**
966 Ohio Ave. N.
Live Oak, FL 32060
(904) 362-2790

■ **Villager Lodge**
P.O. Box 4345
Live Oak, FL 32060
(904) 658-5200

■ **Scottish Inn**
827 Howard St. W.
Live Oak, FL 32060
(904) 362-7828

TAKOMA PARK FOLK FESTIVAL

End of September
Silver Spring, Maryland
www.tpff.org
Admission: *FREE*

Seven stages (one just for kids), innumerable booths selling everything from baked goods to the handiwork of local artists, and a selection of homegrown folk talents and world musicians from as far afield as Africa and Ukraine make this one-day event held in and around the Takoma Park Middle School an excellent way to spend a Saturday afternoon in early fall. International dance workshops and exhibitions are featured in addition to all the music and foods of the world offered at this event.

For more information: (301) 589-3717 or info@tpff.org
Camping: No
Accommodations

■ **Choice Hotels International Inc.**
10750 Columbia Pike
Silver Spring, MD 20901
(301) 979-5000

■ **Silver Spring Motel**
7927 Georgia Ave.
Silver Spring, MD 20901
(301) 587-3200

■ **Manor Care Health Svc**
2501 Musgrove Rd.
Silver Spring, MD 20901
(301) 890-5552

TALKEETNA BLUEGRASS FESTIVAL

Early August
Talkeetna, Alaska

www.mosquitonet.com/~bluegrass

Admission: $

Dirty Ernie's Talkeetna Bluegrass Festival is a rowdy, biker-run and biker-attended party in the woods of Alaska. Over the years Ernie's various festivals have become something of a legend as folks tend to have a very good time at them. Held in the middle of the woods, with no official law to speak of, you are free to do what you please, although there is plenty of festival-provided security, known as Karma Control, to ensure things don't get out of hand. This is one of those Alaskan festivals that people speak of with multiple superlatives and in tones of semi-astonishment. Past performers have included the Cleary Brothers, Yukon Rider, and the Mo Better Blues band. Not for the kiddies.

Artist Submissions: Rick and Cora Moses, (907) 746-6461

For more information: (907) 495-6718 (Olive) or (907) 488-1372 (Ernie or Gia) or bluegrass@mosquitonet.com

Camping: Yes. Camping only; no other accommodations available.

TELLURIDE BLUEGRASS FESTIVAL

Late June

Telluride, Colorado

www.planetbluegrass.com

Admission: $$$

Nestled in a valley of the San Juan Mountains, the Telluride Bluegrass Festival boasts adventurous lineups and devoted festivalgoers who have been making the pilgrimage here for the past 30 years. You can catch such big names as Hot Rize, Mary Chapin Carpenter, Dave Grisman, and String Cheese Incident. It's not strictly bluegrass, but the focus is certainly on acoustic music.

For more information: (800) 823-0848 or planet@bluegrass.com

Camping: Yes

Accommodations

■ **The Inn at Lost Creek**
119 Lost Creek Ln.
Telluride, CO 81435
(888) 601-5678

■ **Wyndham Mountain Lodge**
457 Mountain Village Blvd.
Telluride, CO 81435
(800) 789-2220

■ **The Hotel Telluride**
199 North Cornet St.
Telluride, CO 81435
(970) 369-1188

♪ TELSTRA COUNTRY MUSIC FESTIVAL

Mid-January
Tamworth, Australia
www.tamworth.nsw.gov.au/tcc/cmf
Admission: $$

A ten-day event that emphasizes the country music talents of Australia's own cowboy singers. The city of Tamworth turns into a giant Australian-style party, with live music, tons of food booths, and folks selling pretty much everything under the sun.

Artist Submissions
Australian Country Music Foundation (ACMF)
93 Brisbane St., Tamworth 2340
Australia
(61) 02-6766-9696
info@acmf.org.au

Camping: Yes

Accommodations

■ **Powerhouse Boutique Motor Inn**
Armidale Rd.
Tamworth 2340
Australia
(61) 02-6766-7000

■ **Roydons Motel**
Corner New England Hwy.
  & Church St.
Tamworth 2340
Australia
(61) 02-6765-7355

■ **Quest Tamworth**
327 Armidale Rd.
Tamworth 2340
Australia
(61) 02-6761-2366

■ **Southgate Inn Hotel/Motel**
Corner Kathleen & Kent Sts.
South Tamworth 2340
Australia
(61) 02-6765-7999

♪ TENTERDEN FOLK FESTIVAL

Two days in October
Weald of Kent, Kent, United Kingdom
www.folkspots.btinternet.co.uk/trust/tfdt1.htm#top
Admission: $$

More than 50 local and national personalities from all over the United Kingdom perform at this weekend event, held every year in the Weald of Kent.

Tons of booths, a long roster of dancing "sides," magic shows, and church services are featured. The town is ancient, with many historical buildings and the cozy pubs the English countryside is famous for.

For more information: (44) 01580-763572 or web@Folkspots.btinternet.co.uk

Camping: No

Accommodations

■ **The Vine Inn**
76 High St.
Tenterden, Kent TN30 6BD
United Kingdom
(44) 01580-762922

■ **The White Lion Hotel**
57 High St.
Tenterden, Kent TN30 6BD
United Kingdom
(44) 01580-765077

■ **The William Caxton**
26 High St.
Tenterden, Kent TN30 6BD
United Kingdom
(44) 01580-763142

THOMAS POINT BEACH BLUEGRASS FESTIVAL

Labor Day weekend
Brunswick, Maine
www.thomaspointbeach.com/bluegrass.html
Admission: $$$

This four-day festival features some of the bigger names in bluegrass (in the past stars such as Del McCoury and Doc Watson have appeared) and is held at the Thomas Point Campground on the beautiful Brunswick Maine coast. Raffles, fireworks displays, food vendors, and a resort holiday feeling permeate this festival. You can look forward to continuous music for up to and over 12 hours each day.

For more information: (207) 725-6009 or summer@thomaspointbeach.com

Camping: Yes. Call (877) TPB-4321.

Accommodations

■ **Captain Daniel Stone Inn**
10 Water St.
Brunswick, ME 04011
(877) 573-5151 or (207) 725-9898

■ **Comfort Inn Brunswick**
199 Pleasant St.
Brunswick, ME 04011
(800) 228-5150 or (207) 729-1129

■ **Econo Lodge Brunswick**
215 Pleasant St.
Brunswick, ME 04011
(207) 729-9991

TIDEWATER TRADITIONAL ARTS FESTIVAL

October
Hampton, Virginia
www.tffm.org
Admission: $

The Tidewater Friends of Folk Music hosts a summer season of concerts and workshops intended to promote and preserve both American and world folk musics. Half a dozen venues in the Virginia Beach area hold concerts throughout the summer, with the official festival occupying three days during October and featuring mostly local talent.

Artist Submissions: booking@tffm.org
For more information: (757) 626-FOLK (3655) or tffm@tffm.org
Camping: No
Accommodations

■ **Arrow Inn**
7 Semple Farm Rd.
Hampton, VA 23666
(757) 865-0300

■ **Candlewood Hotel**
401 Butler Farm Rd.
Hampton, VA 23663
(757) 766-8976

■ **Buckroe Motel**
1512 E. Pembroke Ave.
Hampton, VA 23663
(757) 722-7611

TINTO FOLK FESTIVAL

Autumn
South Lanarkshire, Scotland
Admission: $$

Held in a giant Victorian house in Lanarkshire, Scotland, the Tinto Folk Festival offers a broad variety of folk musics, with a focus on the rich heritage of Scottish folk but also featuring blues, Brazilian jazz, and contemporary rock, among other genres. The whole town opens its doors as local merchants join in with food and craft booths. Dance, instrumental, and songwriting workshops are available.

For more information: (44) 01555-840028 or guy@tinto-folk-festival.com

Camping: Yes

Accommodations: www.visitscotland.com

TOPANGA BANJO FIDDLE CONTEST AND FOLK FESTIVAL

One day in May

Agoura Hills, California

www.topangabanjofiddle.org

Admission: $

Operating since 1961, the Topanga Banjo Fiddle Contest and Folk Festival is a fun-loving event held in the Santa Monica Hills. The festival features workshops, competitions, and performances by a collection of homegrown and national talent. Taj Mahal, Dan Crary, Frank Hamilton, and banjoist extraordinaire Steve Martin have all made appearances here.

Artist Submissions

To enter as a contestant, fill out the on-line registration form or call Joy Felt at (818) 382-4819 or e-mail registrar@topangabanjofiddle.org.

For more information: (818) 382-4819 or info@topangabanjofiddle.org

Camping: No

Accommodations

■ **Bayside Hotel**
2001 Ocean Ave.
Santa Monica, CA 90405
(310) 396-6000

■ **Goodnite Inn**
26557 Agoura Rd.
Calabasas, CA 91302
(818) 880-6000

■ **Village Inn**
1425 E. Thousand Oaks Blvd.
Thousand Oaks, CA 91366
(805) 496-0102

TOTTENHAM BLUEGRASS FESTIVAL

Late June

Tottenham, Ontario, Canada

www.tottenhambluegrass.ca

Admission: $$–$$$

A natural amphitheater on the grounds of the Tottenham Conservation Area in Ontario overlooks a small lake and features a single stage. This is where a dozen or so Canadian bluegrass acts perform live for the Tottenham Bluegrass Festival. A workshop is given on Saturday evening, and Sunday offers an early afternoon Gospel Hour. Food, crafts vendors, and activities for kids such as hay rides and clowns are also featured.

For more information: (888) BLUGRAS or (905) 936-4100 or cofac@idirect.com

Camping: Yes. Rough camping available on-site.

Accommodations

■ **Eaglescroft Bed & Breakfast**

6325 2nd Line

Tottenham, ON L0G 1W0

Canada

(905) 936-2964

♪ TOYOTA NATIONAL COUNTRY MUSIC MUSTER

August

Gympie, Australia

www.muster.com.au

Admission: $$

Yes, the emphasis is on country music, but the Toyota National Country Music Muster is ready and willing to incorporate rock, swing, and blues into the mix. This festival should appeal to a broad range of music fans. For six days and nights Amamoor Creek State Forest Park, located about two hours outside of Brisbane, is turned over to the festival: cafés, bars, tents, booths, and stages are set up—practically an entire town is constructed for the purpose of providing continuous live music, dance, and other performing arts to the giant crowds that attend each year. Acts from Australia, Europe, and the United States participate, and recent festivals have featured the rockin' swing of the Amazing Rhythm Aces, the jam rock band Southbound, Andy Baylor's Cajun Combo, and Australia's own Sensitive Cowpersons.

Artist Submissions: See Web site for details on the Muster Talent Search.

For more information: (61) 07-5482-2099 or info@muster.com.au

Camping: Yes, on-site.

Accommodations: For info on where to stay, call the Toyota National Country Music Muster directly at (61) 07-5482-2099.

TROUT FOREST MUSIC FESTIVAL

Mid-August
Ear Falls, Ontario, Canada
www.troutfest.com/frameset.htm
Admission: $–$$

Held in Ear Falls, Ontario, the Trout Forest Music Festival is a good-natured weekend of live music, with a section of the grounds set aside for local artists and crafters to sell their wares, a "family zone" for folks with small children, and a healthy lineup of local and regional Canadian acts playing all manner of country styles, from true hillbilly to modern pop country. In addition to hosting the Trout Forest Music Festival each year, secluded and scenic Ear Falls in northwest Ontario is known as the Bald Eagle capital of North America, so birdwatchers take note.

For more information: (866) TROUT-33 or (807) 222-2404 or trout@sunsetcountry.com
Camping: Yes, on-site.
Accommodations

■ **Northland Motor Hotel**
Hwy. 105 N.
Ear Falls, ON P0V 1T0
Canada
(807) 222-3050

■ **Trillium Motor Hotel**
40 Hwy. 105 N.
Ear Falls, ON P0V 1T0
Canada
(807) 222-3126

TUCSON BLUEGRASS FESTIVAL

Late October
Tucson, Arizona
http://home.att.net/~fertilepickens/Tucson.html
Admission: $

One of the big pluses with this festival is that it offers campsites in full view of the performance stage. Karl Shiflett & Big Country Show, the Schankman Twins, Perfect Strangers, the Lester Brothers, the Blade Runners, Crucial County, and the Burnett Family Band have all performed at past festivals.

For more information: (520) 296-1231 or basslady@worldnet.att.net

Camping: Yes. RV and tent camping on-site.

Accommodations

- Casa Tierra Adobe B&B
11155 W. Calle Tima
Tucson, AZ 85743
(520) 578-3058

- Adobe Rose Inn
940 N. Olsen Ave.
Tucson, AZ 85743
(520) 318-4644

♪ TURTLE HILL FOLK FESTIVAL

Two days in September
Honeoye Falls, New York
www.goldenlink.org/html/fest.html
Admission: $-$$

Contra dancing, folk music performers, and campfire singing are the order of the day at this Honeoye Falls event. Local musicians and artists gather in the woods to play songs together and lead children in activities such as finger-painting and drawing. This is a small, local festival perfect for families with small children who like camping.

For more information: (585) 234-5044 or glfestival@goldenlink.org

Camping: Yes, free and on-site.

Accommodations

- 490 Motel
360 Mount Read Blvd.
Rochester, NY 14611
(716) 235-1139

- Aloha Motel
2729 Monroe Ave.
Rochester, NY 14618
(716) 473-0310

- Bed & Breakfast at Dartmouth
215 Dartmouth St.
Rochester, NY 14618
(716) 271-7872

♪ UPTON RIVERSIDE FOLK FESTIVAL

Summer
Upton, Worcester, United Kingdom
www.upton.uk.net
Admission: $$

Upton Riverside Folk Festival is a small town festival in the English countryside featuring local acts such as Bob & Gil Berry, Cuckoo Oak, and the

Harry Browns. The festival is held every year around May Day, so maypole dancing is a tradition, as are dance contests and singing rounds in the local pubs. Perhaps the biggest reason to attend this festival, however, is the legend surrounding the town it's held in, Upton. The town is said to be haunted by a 350-year-old dead cat with one eye, a peg leg, and a talent for playing the fiddle. Thomas Bound's Cat can be heard thumping around in the night, and even his fiddle playing can sometimes be heard on the wind. The cat's owner is also a frequently spotted phantom, but he just rides around on a horse.

Artist Submissions

Verna Connolly

51 Chescombe Rd.

Yatton, Bristol BS19 4EU

United Kingdom

(44) 19348-32643

For more information: (44) 12807-01112

Camping: No

VANCOUVER FOLK MUSIC FESTIVAL

Late July

Vancouver, British Columbia, Canada

www.thefestival.bc.ca

Admission: $$

An eclectic collection of more than 50 artists appears at the Vancouver Folk Music Festival each year. The music runs the gamut of folk, jazz, world, and rock, with an emphasis on the underground before the mainstream, which will be a refreshing change for the more discriminating music fan. This is a highly organized event, and its planners do their best to truly broaden people's horizons with their workshops and selected artists. Out-there guitarist Eugene Chadbourne has appeared here, along with singer-songwriter Dan Bern and South African rhythm and vocal group Amampondo.

Artist Submissions

This festival has a million rules regarding submissions, including a form you need to download and fill out in order to be considered. So you may want to check the Web site's artist submissions page before doing the following:

Send band Web site URL to ad@thefestival.bc.ca before sending a press kit. The festival's art director can then decide if he wants to know more about you and check your site on his own time. If you don't have a Web site, send press kit with bio, photo, and demo to:

Dugg Simpson, Artistic Director

The Vancouver Folk Music Festival

916 Broadway West #381

Vancouver, BC V5Z 1K7

Canada

Regardless of the somewhat involved submission process, the festival treats its artists well, throwing two parties before and after the event for them and their friends and helping in whatever way they can to make sure everyone has a good experience.

For more information: (604) 602-9798 or info@thefestival.bc.ca

Camping: Yes

Accommodations: http://vancouver.com

♪ VILJANDI FOLK MUSIC FESTIVAL

End of July

Viljandi, Estonia

www.folk.ee

Admission: $$–$$$

This massive festival, held over a summer weekend in the mid-sized town of Viljandi, Estonia, offers more than 100 artists, primarily from Eastern Europe, playing an array of styles, from traditional Estonian folk to modern rock. The ancient Estonian instrument, the *kannel*, is a focal point of the goings-on, with workshops teaching folks how to play and also to build the dulcimer-like stringed instrument.

For more information: folk@folk.ee

Camping: Yes

Accommodations

■ **Hostel Oma Kodu**

Väike t. 6

Viljandi EE-71008

Estonia

(372) 0-43-55-755 or (372) 0-43-55-751

omakodu@omakodu.ee

www.omakodu.ee

■ **Hotell Centrum**

Tallinna tn.24

Viljandi EE-71008

Estonia

(372) 0-43-51-100

centrum@matti.ee

www.centrum.ee

■ **Huntaugu kodumajutus B&B**
A. Irve 3-1
Viljandi 71010
Estonia
(372) 0-43-38-506 or (372) 0-55-530-092
www.hot.ee/huntaugu

♪ WALNUT VALLEY FESTIVAL

Late September
Winfield, Kansas
http://wvfest.com/index.html
Admission: $$$

A jamboree in the truest sense of the word, the Walnut Valley Festival is an excellent festival to attend if you want to perform as well as soak up the music. There are many opportunities for the amateur musician: there's both a walk-on stage and festival-sanctioned "Parking Lot Pickin'" expected to go on all night each night. The well-organized, well-attended WVFest features continuous music on six stages and innumerable acts.

For more information: (620) 221-3250 or hq@wvfest.com
Camping: Yes, on-site.
Accommodations

■ **Wellington Motor Lodge**
1311 E. 16
Wellington, KS 67152
(620) 326-2266

■ **Steak House Motel**
1311 E. 16
Wellington, KS 67152
(620) 326-2266

■ **Sunshine Inn**
1001 E. 16th St.
Wellington, KS 67152
(620) 326-8944

♪ WARWICK FOLK FESTIVAL

Late July
Warwick, United Kingdom
www.warkfolk.demon.co.uk/thisyear.htm
Admission: $$

Held during the last weekend of July each year, the Warwick Festival offers open jams, dancing, storytelling, games for the kids, and arts, crafts, and food booths. June Tabor, Nancy Kerr, and legendary Scottish fiddler Brian McNeill have all performed here recently. The town of Warwick, deep in the English countryside, has a number of castles dating back to medieval times for the curious to explore.

Artist Submissions

Dick Dixon

P.O. Box 429

Coventry CV5 6ZS

United Kingdom

(44) 0-24-7667-8738

dixon@warkfolk.demon.co.uk

For more information: (44) 0-1926-614932 or dixon@warkfolk.demon.co.uk or WFFBoxOffice@aol.com (for tickets only)

Camping: Yes.

Accommodations

■ **Le Meridien Warwick**

Chesford Bridge, Kenilworth

Warwick, Warwickshire CV8 2LD

United Kingdom

(44) 0-1926-859331

WEST VIRGINIA STATE FOLK FESTIVAL

Three days in June

Glennville, West Virginia

http://etc4u.com/folkfest

Admission: $

The West Virginia State Folk Festival celebrates the history and arts and crafts of the Appalachian region as well as its music. Craftspeople from across the state come to ply their wares and join in the fun. Each county selects a handful of local women over the age of 70 to be the Belles of the Festival: they dress in the garb of the early twentieth century and are given special honors during the three-day affair.

For more information: folkfest@etc4u.com

Camping: No

Accommodations
- **Conrad Motel**
100 Conrad Ct.
Glenville, WV 26351
(304) 462-7316

♪ WHITE RIVER FOLK FESTIVAL

Two days in June
Fishers, Indiana
www.whiteriverfolkfestival.org
Admission: $$

This outdoor summer festival on the prairie features national and regional folk musicians performing on three stages amid a host of hands-on workshops and activities. You can learn new skills such as beginning dulcimer, blacksmithing, pottery, and textiles; one workshop even teaches kids how to make an instrument they can take home. Past performers include gospel pioneers Blind Boys of Alabama, folksinger Christine Lavin, Aengus Finnan, and the Gordon Bonham Blues Band.

Artist Submissions
Conner Prairie
13400 Allisonville Rd.
Fishers, IN 46038
For more information: (317) 776-6000 or info@connerprairie.org
Camping: No
Accommodations
- **Frederick-Talbott Inn**
13805 Allisonville Rd.
Fishers, IN 46038
(317) 578-3600

♪ WILL MCLEAN MUSIC FESTIVAL

March
Dade City, Florida
www.willmclean.com
Admission: $

Dade City celebrates its local singers and songwriters over the course of this spring weekend. The festival is named for Will McLean, a Florida native who performed folk music for more than 60 years, a distinction that has garnered him the title "Father of Florida Folk."

For more information: (352) 465-7208 or mlonghill@aol.com

Camping: Yes

Accommodations

■ **Azalea House Bed & Breakfast**
37719 Meridian Ave.
Dade City, FL 33525
(352) 523-1773

■ **Rainbow Fountain Motel**
16210 N. Hwy. 301
Dade City, FL 33525
(352) 567-3427

■ **Pasco Motel**
18051 US Hwy. 301
Dade City, FL 33525
(352) 567-6220

WINGS AND STRINGS AMERICANA MUSIC FESTIVAL

Early November
Polk City, Florida
www.wingsandstrings.com
Admission: $$

A full-on camping experience is in store for folks attending the Wings and Strings festival. Held in a tent surrounded by more than 150 acres of wilderness and camping areas, this four-day event is an excellent place for families. Youth programs are offered between performances of all kinds of American folk music, from Cajun and zydeco to contemporary pop country and the high-lonesome sound of bluegrass.

For more information: (863) 984-8445 or (888) 305-1208 or wingsandstrings@aol.com

Camping: Yes, on-site.

Accommodations

■ **Hi-Way Motel**
1364 SW Hwy. 17
Arcadia, FL 34266
(863) 494-5455

■ **Oaks Motel**
2559 SW Hwy. 17
Arcadia, FL 34266
(863) 494-2020

■ **Desoto Motel**
1021 N. Brevard Ave.
Arcadia, FL 34266
(863) 494-2992

■ **Magnolia House**
500 W. Oak St.
Arcadia, FL 34266
(863) 494-4299

WINNIPEG FOLK FESTIVAL

Four days in July
Winnipeg, Manitoba, Canada
www.wpgfolkfest.mb.ca
Admission: $$$

A cherished tradition for the past 30 years, the Winnepeg Folk Festival is a family-friendly gathering at beautiful Birds Hill Park in Winnipeg, Manitoba. There is near-continuous music from Friday evening through Sunday night, with past performers including the likes of Silly Wizard, Annie Gallup, and Queen Ida.

Artist Submissions

E-mail your Web site address to fenton@winnipegfolkfestival.ca or send press kit and demo to:

Rick Fenton, Artistic Director
Winnipeg Folk Festival
203-211 Bannatyne Ave.
Winnipeg, MB R3B 3P2
Canada

For more information: (204) 231-0096 or info@winnipegfolkfestival.ca
Camping: Yes, on-site.

Accommodations

■ **Canada Inns Garden City**
144 Frasers Grove
Winnipeg, MB R2V 3C8
Canada
(204) 633-0024

■ **Niakwa Inn**
20 Alpine Ave.
Winnipeg, MB R2M 0Y5K
Canada
(204) 255-6000

■ **Quality Inn**
635 Pembina Hwy.
Winnipeg, MB R2M 0Y5K
Canada
(204) 453-8247

■ **Super 8 Motel**
3760 Portage Ave.
Winnipeg, MB R3K 1A1
Canada
(204) 831-9800

♪ WINSTOCK COUNTRY MUSIC & CAMPING FESTIVAL

Early June
Winsted, Minnesota
www.winstockfestival.com
Admission: $$$

Some of the biggest stars in country music, including George Jones and Jo Dee Messina, are regularly scheduled to appear at this two-day event. Camping on the grounds is encouraged, and festivalgoers are encouraged to bring their own lawn chairs. This is a fairly large festival, so you can expect resort-like amenities to be available, but, as is often the case with festivals of this size, lines can be long and available space at a premium.

For more information: (888) 946-7865 or winstock@winstockfestival.com
Camping: Yes, on-site.
Accommodations
■ Winsted Motel
461 6th St. N
Winsted, MN 55395
(320) 485-4441

♪ WINTERGRASS BLUEGRASS FESTIVAL

Three days in February
Tacoma, Washington
www.wintergrass.com
Admission: $$–$$$

Founded in 1994, the Wintergrass Bluegrass Festival is a three-day affair featuring both a star-studded lineup and lots of informal jamming in the lobby of the Sheraton Tacoma Hotel. If you're looking to see some of the bigger names and older legends of the genre, this classy but down-to-earth showcase is just the place. In the past luminaries such as Hazel Dickens, Blue Highway, and the Osborne Brothers have performed.

For more information: (253) 428-8056 or patrice@wintergrass.com
Camping: No
Accommodations

■ Blue Spruce Motel
12715 Pacific Ave. S
Tacoma, WA 98444
(253) 531-6111

■ Colonial Motel
12117 Pacific Hwy.
Tacoma, WA 98499
(253) 589-3261

■ **La Quinta Inns Tacoma**
1425 E. 27th St.
Tacoma, WA 98421
(253) 383-0146

WINTERHAWK

August
Hillsdale, New York
www.winterhawk2000.com/index.html
Admission: $$

Although the main focus of the festival is always bluegrass, Winterhawk offers performances that span a wide range of American roots music, from Cajun and zydeco to Southern gospel and contemporary country. In operation for over 20 years, and recently moved from the famed Rothvoss Farm in New York to its present location, the festival offers rough camping on-site and many hotel and motels nearby. Vendors from all over bring an array of food, crafts, and merchandise to the festival. (This last statement may be interpreted to mean that you will encounter a number of entrepreneurial hippies.)

Artist Submissions
Winterhawk
attn: Artistic Director
74 Modley Rd.
Sharon, CT 06069
(860) 364-9396
anne@winterhawk2000.com

For more information: (860) 364-0366 or anne@winterhawk2000.com

Camping: Yes

Accommodations

■ **Coffing-Bostwick B&B**
98 Division St.
Great Barrington, MA 01230
(413) 528-4511
www.gmeadows.com

■ **Greenmeadows**
117 Division St.
Great Barrington, MA 01230
(413) 528-3897

■ **Monument Mountain Motel**
Stockbridge Rd
Great Barrington, MA 01230
(413) 528-3272
www.MonumentMountainMotel.com

♪ WOODFORD FOLK FESTIVAL

December–January
Woodford, Australia
http://woodfordfolkfestival.com/festival/index.html
Admission: $$$

The Woodford Folk Festival, an enormous celebration of the arts, features dance and instrument workshops in addition to a roster of more than 100 performers, practitioners, and personalities. The musical range covers everything from aboriginal Australian arts to imported folk music from around the world.

Of particular interest is the "Fire Event," the festival's closing ceremony. An enormous bonfire is built, and everyone participates: festivalgoers, performers, volunteers, and, well, giant puppets. Fireworks are set off and the fire burns throughout the night, much like the last day of Burning Man. (However, America's desert freak-out probably got the idea from Woodford.) Many people leave personal bits of emotional, spiritual, and physical baggage in the fire, in the form of drawings, letters, and mementos. The end result is a very powerful sort of spiritual cleansing.

Between 12,000 and 15,000 people attend Woodford each year—some to grow, some to hear music, and some to just party. Whatever your reason for going, the experience will not be easily forgotten. Daycare is available at limited times during the festival.

For more information: (61) 7-5496-1066 or qff@woodfordfolkfestival.com
Camping: Yes, on-site.

Accommodations

■ **Hunting Lodge Estate**
703 Mt. Kilcoy Rd.
Mt. Kilcoy, Qld 4515
Australia
(61) 7-5498-1243
huntinglodgeestate@bigpond.com
www.huntinglodgeestate.com.au

■ **Beachmere Motel**
30 Biggs Ave.
Beachmere, Qld 4510
Australia
(61) 7-5496-8577

■ **Chateau Cedarton**
2 Cedarton Rd.
Cedarton, Qld
Australia
(61) 7-549-617
chcedarton@eisa.net.au
www.babs.com.au/cedarton

■ **Stanley Hotel**
46 Mary St.
Kilcoy, Qld 4515
Australia
(61) 7-5497-1037

♪ WOODLAND VETERANS DAY BLUEGRASS FESTIVAL

Veterans Day weekend in November
Woodland, California
Admission: $

Held on the Yolo County Fairgrounds in Woodland, California, this two-day affair focuses on local talent; however, there will also be a couple big name headliners. There are plenty of events geared for children, and a "Band Scramble" hastily assembles groups who then have one hour to come up with a song and a skit. Plenty of RV camping is available.

For more information: (530) 749-9504 or fidle3@lanset.net

Camping: Yes

Accommodations

■ **Best Western Shadow Inn**
584 N. East St.
Woodland, CA 95776
(800) 669-1253

■ **Valley Oaks Inn**
600 N. East St.
Woodland, CA 95776
(800) 525-3330

♪ WOODLANDS COUNTRY MUSIC FESTIVAL

Two days in August
Long Sault, Ontario, Canada
www.stlawrenceparks.com/woodfest.htm
Admission: $

This extremely kid-friendly festival has everything—great music, a Saturday pancake breakfast, a "Frontier Town," shopping, and charity-supporting concession stands. The 2002 lineup featured performances by Jodi Hankshaw, Fenced In, Doc Walker, and more. Be sure to stick around for Sunday afternoon's Country Gospel Celebration.

For more information: (800) 437-2233 or (613) 543-4328

Camping: Yes

Accommodations

■ **Glengarry Park**
20800 South Service Rd.
Lancaster, ON K0C 1N0
Canada
(613) 347-2595

♪ WOODY GUTHRIE FOLK FESTIVAL

Mid-June
Tulsa, Oklahoma
www.woodyguthrie.com
Admission: $$

The nonprofit Woody Guthrie Coalition organizes this yearly event and has brought in performers such as Pete Seeger, Luke Reed, and the Red Dirt Rangers in the past. The weekend is rounded out with a Sunday morning gospel service and songwriters' competition. The whole event takes place at Cain's Ballroom in downtown Tulsa, Oklahoma.

Artist Submissions

Send press kit and demo to:

Bill McCloud

P.O. Box 45

Pryor, OK 74362

For more information: DMSJones@swbell.net

Camping: Yes. Call (918) 623-1050 for prepaid reservations only.

Accommodations

■ **OK Motor Lodge**
605 S. Woody Guthrie St.
Okemah, OK 74859
(918) 623-2200

■ **Circle G Motel**
1508 W. Columbia St.
Okemah, OK 74859
(918) 623-0537

■ **Colonial Motel**
608 E. Main St.
Henryetta, OK 74437
(918) 652-7100

■ **Old Corral Motel**
1002 W. Main St.
Henryetta, OK 74437
(918) 652-4237

4

ELECTRONIC

♪ ANGELICA FESTIVAL

May
Bologna, Italy
www.aaa-angelica.com
Admission: $$

For more than a decade the Angelica Festival has been considered one of the best experimental music festivals in Italy. A combination of jazz innovation and electronic spontaneity runs through the event. Many acts regularly give exclusive performances, providing attendees with once-in-a-lifetime musical experiences. Past performers have included sonic innovators such as Jim O'Rourke and Eyvind Kang. Angelica's success as a purveyor of contemporary sounds has led it to enter the realm of independent record labels, distributing music in keeping with the original spirit of the festival.

Artist Submissions
Angelica
Via Gandusio 10
40128 Bologna
Italy
For more information: info@aaa-angelica.com
Camping: No

Accommodations

■ **Hotel San Donato**
Via Zamboni, 16
Bologna 40126
Italy
(39) 0-5123-5395

■ **Best Western Hotel Maggiore**
Via Emilia Ponente 62/3
Bologna I-40133
Italy
(39) 0-5138-1634

ANNUAL ACTIVATING THE MEDIUM FESTIVAL

February
San Francisco, California
www.23five.org/atm
Admission: $

This festival has taken place in San Francisco's Museum of Modern Art for the past five years. This is where avant-garde, electronic sound sculptors are given a chance to perform their works live. Submissions are accepted, and invited performers come from all over the United States, as well as Germany and Japan, to present sets that the word *cerebral* was basically invented to describe.

Artist Submissions
23five Incorporated
c/o Activating the Medium
P.O. Box 460951
San Francisco, CA 94146-0951
For more information: (415) 285-6003 or auscultare@aol.com
Camping: No
Accommodations

■ **Phoenix Hotel**
601 Eddy St.
San Francisco, CA 94109
(800) 248-9466

■ **Hotel Bijou**
111 Mason St.
San Francisco, CA 94102
(800) 771-1022

ARS ELECTRONICA FESTIVAL

September
Linz, Austria

www.aec.at/festival
Admission: $$–$$$

The Ars Electronica Festival in Austria has been on the vanguard of electronic music, technology, and art since it began in 1979. The festival organizers schedule events that attempt to define the current state of electronic music and media while also setting their sights on what's still to come. You can expect many a discussion on the impact the information age has had on current sounds. You can also expect a dizzying array of performers in the hip-hop, techno, house, experimental, and electronic classical music realms.

For more information: (43) 732-72-72-0 or info@prixars.orf.at
Camping: No
Accommodations

■ **Austria Trend Hotel Schillerpark**
Rainerstrasse 2-4
Linz A-4020
Austria
(43) 732-6950

■ **Dom Hotel**
Baumbachstrasse 17
Linz
Austria
(43) 732-778-441

♪ AVANTO HELSINKI MEDIA ART FESTIVAL

Third week in November
Helsinki, Finland
www.avantofestival.com
Admission: $–$$

The Avanto Helsinki Media Art Festival presents a mixture of film and audio productions that belong on the experimental side of the electronic music scene. Many of the events seek to pay tribute to Finland's forefathers of experimental film and electronic music, and soundtracks are often presented live as accompaniments to the films. But the music is not limited to studied composition. At night events sprawl out into the clubs where festivalgoers and club kids can hear minimalist techno from the likes of Pan Sonic in a proper, dance-oriented setting.

For more information: info@avantofestival.com
Camping: No

Accommodations

■ **Lord Hotel**
Lönnrotinkatu 29
00180 Helsinki
Finland
(358) 961-5815
sales@lordhotel.fi
www.lordhotel.fi

■ **Palace Hotel**
Eteläranta 10
00130 Helsinki
Finland
(358) 913-4561
sales@palacehotel.fi
www.palacehotel.fi

CEAIT ELECTRONIC MUSIC FESTIVAL

Mid-January
Valencia, California
http://music.calarts.edu/ceait03
Admission: $

This event, organized by the Center for Experiments in Art, Information, and Technology (CEAIT) at the California Institute of the Arts, started back in 1998. This student-run event regularly showcases recent innovations in electronic music in addition to presenting audio installations and compositions. This is a great way for burgeoning electronic composers to get their music heard.

Artist Submissions
California Institute of the Arts
CEAIT Festival
School of Music
24700 McBean Parkway
Valencia, CA 91355

Camping: No

Accommodations

■ **Hyatt Valencia**
24500 Town Center Dr.
Valencia, CA 91355
(661) 799-1234

■ **Best Western**
27413 Wayne Mills Pl.
Valencia, CA 91355
(800) 944-7446

CREAMFIELDS FESTIVAL

Summer
Liverpool, United Kingdom

www.cream.co.uk

Admission: $$–$$$

The Creamfields event is one of the most eagerly anticipated electronic music festivals in all of the United Kingdom. Not only does Creamfields stage various events throughout England, they also organize shows in Ireland, Australia, South America, and the United States. This single-day event first began in 1998 and now regularly features an array of top dance acts and a wide range of skilled DJs. After the sun sets the party really kicks in as thousands of regular clubgoers brave muddy fields and portable toilets in order to hear some of the best electronic performances of the year. The Liverpool event takes place in an abandoned airfield and draws crowds of up to 30,000 people. Acts such as Underworld, Faithless, and Richie Hawtin have performed in the past.

For more information: (44) 0-7976-163528 or info@cream.co.uk

Camping: No

Accommodations

■ **The Herculaneum Bridge**
28-30 Herculaneum Rd.
Riverside, Liverpool L8 4TY
United Kingdom
(44) 0151-727-6211
or (44) 0151-727-4316
www.herculaneum-bridge.co.uk

■ **Derby Lodge Hotel**
Roby Road
Huyton, Liverpool L36 4HD
United Kingdom
(44) 0151-443-0932

♪ CYBERSONICA

June

London, United Kingdom

http://cybersonica.org

Admission: $$

A wide selection of DJs and visual artists take over London's Institute of Contemporary Art in June to present film screenings and other interactive media events. For three days an international array of artists and designers descend upon the ICA hoping to catch a glimpse of some of the more advanced elements of modern audio/visual art. You can expect to hear from musicians such as DJ Spooky and Pole, two electronic artists whose music goes far beyond the realm of the club scene.

For more information: (44) 0207-930-3647 or tickets@ica.org.uk

Camping: No

Accommodations

■ **Best Western Shaftesbury London
  Hotel**
165-73 Shaftesbury Ave.
London W1D 6EX
United Kingdom
(44) 0207-871-6000

■ **Regent Palace Hotel**
1 Glasshouse St.
London W1B 5DN
United Kingdom
(44) 870-400-8703

♪ DETROIT ELECTRONIC MUSIC FESTIVAL

Third week in May
Hart Plaza, Detroit, Michigan
Admission: $$$

Many would argue that electronic music as we know it today would not exist were it not for Detroit. It was there that people such as Derrick May and Juan Atkins used their limited technology to create music that held on to disco's beat but mechanized it, giving birth to a new type of funk. It's fitting then that Detroit's Electronic Music Festival would know how to throw the best party. This three-day event presents a barrage of electronic innovators and legends, from dub pioneer the Mad Professor to house legend Frankie Bones to drum 'n' bass figureheads such as DJ Krust.

For more information: (313) 392-9200 or info@popculturemedia.com

Camping: No

Accommodations

■ **Courtyard Detroit Downtown**
333 E. Jefferson
Detroit, MI 48226
(313) 222-7700

■ **Ramada Inn Downtown**
400 Bagley Ave.
Detroit, MI 48226
(888) 298-2054

♪ FESTIVAL OF ELECTRONIC MUSIC K.O.M.P.

Mid-June
Kwidzyn, Poland
http://komp-festival.net
Admission: FREE

This free festival in northern Poland aims to bring the sweeping electronic sounds of artists such as Vangelis and Jean-Michel Jarre to the masses. Some science fiction fans in Kwidzyn founded the K.O.M.P. Festival as a way to get these artists' epic sounds and their requisite elaborate light shows into town. So far, all efforts have been successful.

For more information: (48) 0-503-065-040 or mrqs@komp-festival.net

Camping: No

Accommodations

■ **Bialy Dwor Restaurant & Hotel**
Kwidzyn 36a (Podzamcze)
82-500 Kwidzyn
Poland
(48) 55-275-7710

FUTURESONIC

November
Manchester, United Kingdom
www.futuresonic.com
Admission: $$–$$$

Manchester's Futuresonic is a forward-looking event that emphasizes the fields of electronic, dance, and hip-hop music. These shows rival those of any electronic music festival anywhere and earn high marks for innovation. Studied avant-garde installations and dance-floor-filling beats intertwine here, making this event perfect for both the chin-strokers and the rump-shakers. Expect to see artists such as Mouse on Mars, the sound sculptors :zoviet*france:, and the hip-hop experimentalists El-P and Aesop Rock.

For more information: (44) 0-161-881-2345 or info@futuresonic.com

Camping: No

Accommodations

■ **Ibis Portland Street**
96 Portland St.
Manchester MI 4GY
United Kingdom
(44) 161-234-0600

■ **Castlefield Hotel**
Liverpool Rd.
Castlefield, Manchester M3 4JR
United Kingdom
(44) 0-161-832-7073

INTERNATIONAL FESTIVAL OF SOUND AND EXPERIMENTAL MUSIC

April
Sheffield, United Kingdom
www.maxis.org.uk
Admission: $$

The International Festival of Sound and Experimental Music, held at the University of Leeds, takes on some of the most challenging aspects of electronic composition around. Artists hoping to perform music at this festival should submit their entries to the review committee by the January preceding the event in April. The 2002 program was dedicated to "Innovative, Alternative, and Cross-Disciplinary Approaches in Sound." Certainly, this event is a far cry from the barefoot-on-the-grass, Frisbee-tossing festivals, but attendance should be mandatory for anyone interested in avant-garde composition and improvisation.

Artist Submissions: submit@maxis.org
For more information: scott@maxis.org.uk
Camping: No
Accommodations

■ **Merrion Thistle Hotel**
17 Wade Ln.
Merrion Centre
Leeds L52 8NH
United Kingdom
(44) 113-243-9191

■ **Aragon Hotel**
250 Stainbeck Ln.
Meanwood, Leeds LS7 2PS
United Kingdom
(44) 113-275-9306

KONEISTO FESTIVAL FOR ELECTRONIC MUSIC

July
Helsinki, Finland
www.koneisto.com
Admission: $$–$$$

The Koneisto Festival represents Finland's first foray into the world of electronic music festivals. A celebration of the many facets of this wide-ranging genre, Koneisto books a heavy selection of Finnish artists but doesn't neglect the rest of the world. Fans have an opportunity to hear a variety of music (house, drum 'n' bass, more experimental works) in nine different venues that range from a main arena with thousands of people to intimate rooms with only a few dozen. The open-air proceedings at Hietsu Beach provide a breathtaking distraction from the club environments.

For more information: (358) 40-700-3202 or koneisto@koneisto.com

Camping: No

Accommodations

■ **Lord Hotel**
Lönnrotinkatu 29
00180 Helsinki
Finland
(358) 9-615-815
sales@lordhotel.fi
www.lordhotel.fi

■ **Palace Hotel**
Eteläranta 10
00130 Helsinki
Finland
(358) 9-134-561
sales@palacehotel.fi
www.palacehotel.fi

LOVEPARADE

Mid-July
Berlin, Germany
www.loveparade.net
Admission: FREE

Berlin's annual Loveparade just might be one of the largest music-related gatherings in the world. Every July since 1989, people from all over the world have gathered here to dance for world peace. The event began as a political demonstration, organized by the youth of Germany and aimed at the Powers That Be, with the intention of expressing a desire for peace and love. They've certainly made that desire clear. In 1997, the event drew over one million people—clearly, the Loveparade is no longer just a gathering for peace-loving electronic music fans, but a centrally located global celebration that cannot be ignored.

For more information: infopool@loveparade.net

Camping: No

Accommodations

■ **Hotel California**
Kurfuerstendamm 35
Berlin 10719
Germany
(49) 30-88-01-20

■ **Hotel Tiergarten**
Alt Moabit 89
Berlin 10559
Germany
(49) 30-39-98-96-00

NATURE ONE

Early August
Hunsrück, Germany
www.nature-one.de
Admission: $$–$$$

Nature One is a four-day event that covers virtually all types of electronic music. Multiple tents and stages host representatives from clubs all across Europe. The open-air dance area, where thousands get together under the stars and move to the pulsating sounds of house, techno, and trance music, is one of the more popular parts of the festival. A camping village is set up for those seeking to escape for more than one evening. Past performers have included Paul Van Dyk, Chicks On Speed, and trance innovator Timo Maas.
For more information: (49) 0-261-85-230 or info@nature-one.de
Camping: Yes
Accommodations

■ **Hotel Zum Rehberg**
Muhlenweg 1
Kastellaun, Rhineland-Palatinate
  56288
Germany
(49) 6762-1331

■ **Kessler Hotel**
Brückenstrasse 23
Rhineland
Trier, Rhineland-Palatinate 54290
Germany
(49) 0-651-97-81-70

SAMOTHRAKI DANCE FESTIVAL

August
Samothraki Island, Greece
www.samothrakidancefestival.com
Admission: $$

This four-day extravaganza celebrates all aspects of electronic and dance music. More than one hundred acts, including both live musicians and DJs, perform their sets on three different stages on this island in the middle of the Aegean Sea. Camping is both available and highly encouraged as a way to experience the true beauty of the dense, green environment.
For more information: info@samothrakidancefestival.com
Camping: Yes

Accommodations
- **Kaviros Hotel**
68002 Loutra Samothrakis
Samothraki Island
Greece
(30) 05510-98277

SAN FRANCISCO ELECTRONIC MUSIC FESTIVAL

End of June
San Francisco, California
www.sfemf.org
Admission: $

This grassroots event, which began in 1999, is a weeklong exploration of electronic sound that has grown each year in both attendance and length. Working in conjunction with local galleries and nonprofit arts organizations, the San Francisco Electronic Music Festival (SFEMF) presents challenging installations and demonstrations of electronic innovation. Artists from around the globe come to perform and to join in on panel discussions. Anyone who thinks electronic music is about nothing more than the infinite beat should definitely spend some time at the SFEMF.

For more information: info@sfemf.org
Camping: No
Accommodations

- **Phoenix Hotel**
601 Eddy St.
San Francisco, CA 94109
(800) 248-9466

- **The Red Victorian**
1665 Haight St.
San Francisco, CA 94117
(415) 864-1978

SOLSTICE MUSIC FESTIVAL

July
Yamanashi, Japan
www.solstice23.com
Admission: $$$

Japan's Solstice Music Festival is a huge celebration of electronic trance music that's eagerly anticipated all year. The festival takes place in the Motosu

Highlands, right at the base of Mt. Fuji. Artists from around the globe fly in for the event, but the international lineup relies most heavily upon artists and DJs from Japan. Anyone unfamiliar with the genre's minimalist repetition and attention to detail will quickly get a history lesson here. The performances zigzag in style, but keen ears will be able to hear the genre's evolution from its harder, colder beginnings to its more recent lush, smooth rhythms. More than 10,000 people were in attendance at the most recent event, so come prepared for large crowds and be ready to camp.

For more information: info@solstice23.com

Camping: Yes

♪ SONAR

Mid-June
Barcelona, Spain
www.sonar.es
Admission: $$–$$$

A haven for electronic music fans for the past decade, Barcelona's Sonar festival is one of Spain's most creative and elaborate festivals. A mixture of live performances and DJs, the music here combines feel-good dance beats with studied, experimental works—basically, it's two different festivals (Sonar by Day and Sonar by Night) that run concurrently. Film and video presentations provide interactive entertainment, and new software innovations are showcased for the technologically minded. In addition, local museums help organize music-related installations. Musically, the acts range from the synth-pop of Pet Shop Boys to the techno innovations of Jeff Mills and Carl Cox. The 2002 festival also saw indie rock stalwarts Yo La Tengo on the bill. But with a city as beautiful as Barcelona, the musical happenings and technological wonders can only enhance your time spent here.

For more information: sonar@sonar.es

Camping: No

Accommodations

■ **Hotel Turin**
Pintor Fortuny 9
Barcelona 08001
Spain
(34) 93-302-4812

■ **Hotel Moderno**
Hospital, 11
Barcelona, Spain 08001
(34) 93-301-4154

STREET PARADE

October
Zurich, Switzerland
www.street-parade.ch
Admission: $$

Expect nothing less than a few hundred thousand partygoers when the Street Parade takes over Zurich in October. For more than a decade, the Street Parade has provided house and techno fans with one of the largest celebrations in Switzerland. Thirty floats (or "love mobiles") equipped with sound systems make their way around the shores of Lake Zurich, providing a constant source of inspiration for partygoers.

For more information: (41) 1-882-1614 or stefan@streetparade.ch
Camping: No
Accommodations

■ **Haus Zum Kindli**
Pfalzgasse 1
Zurich CH-8001
Switzerland
(41) 1-211-5917

■ **Hotel Zurichberg**
21 Orellistrasse
Zurich CH-8044
Switzerland
(41) 1-268-3535

WINTER MUSIC CONFERENCE

End of March
Miami Beach, Florida
www.wintermusicconference.com
Admission: $$$

The end of March usually heralds the arrival of the Winter Music Conference in Miami Beach. This industry-heavy event is attended by thousands of artists and DJs, label heads, promoters, and fans all hoping to make the right connection—and to hear the sounds that will most certainly dominate the clubs that year. It's also where retailers show off their top-of-the-line technology, while the trade show covers everything from magazines to clothes to energy drinks. This five-day event runs nonstop at the Radisson Deauville Resort and manages to fill just about every minute of the day with parties in clubs, at poolside, and even in the local Denny's restaurant. Previous performers have included innovative talents such as Afrika Bambataa, Photek, Warren G, Goldie, and Kruder & Dorfmeister.

For more information: (954) 563-4444 or info@WinterMusicConference.com

Camping: No

Accommodations

■ **Radisson Deauville Resort**
6701 Collins Ave.
Miami Beach, FL 33141
(305) 865-8511
sales@radissondeauville.com

■ **The Marlin**
1200 Collins Ave.
Miami Beach, FL 33139
(305) 604-5063
reservations@islandoutpost.com

♪ WORLD ELECTRONIC MUSIC FESTIVAL

Early August
Bobcaygeon, Ontario, Canada
www.wemf.com
Admission: $$$

Thousands of dance music fans flock to the town of Bobcaygeon every year for one of North America's biggest electronic music festivals. DJs from all over Canada, the United States, and the United Kingdom perform crowd-pleasing sets that keep people dancing long into the night. The DJs mix things up with a combination of house, techno, and trance, then save the mellow beats for the more peaceful moments. Vendors ensure that everyone is well fed, and the waterslide and skate park provide ample diversion for partygoers.

For more information: (416) 631-8821 or info@wemf.com

Camping: Yes

Accommodations

■ **Bobcaygeon Inn**
31 Main St., P.O. Box 669
Bobcaygeon, ON K0M 1A0
Canada
(705) 738-5433
info@bobcaygeoninn.com

■ **Bond Place Hotel**
65 Dundas St. E.
Toronto, ON M5B 2G8
Canada
(800) 268-9390

JAZZ

5

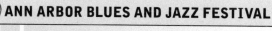

ANN ARBOR BLUES AND JAZZ FESTIVAL

Mid-September
Ann Arbor, Michigan
www.a2.blues.jazzfest.org
Admission: $$–$$$

Ann Arbor contributes to the world of jazz festivals by booking some of the most creative, critically acclaimed acts around and presenting them in a setting that should appeal to both jazz hounds and families hungry for activities. Eddie Palmieri, the Dirty Dozen Brass Band, and the Sun Ra Arkestra have all provided entertainment in the past. It's widely believed that Sun Ra's explosive, transcendent performances here in the early seventies are responsible for generating the following that the late conductor maintains to this day. It's safe to say you never know what kind of historical moments you might witness at this festival.

For more information: info@jazzfest.org

Camping: No

Accommodations

■ **Artful Lodger**
1547 Washtenaw
Ann Arbor, MI 48104
(734) 769-0653

■ **Quality Inn & Suites**
3750 Washtenaw
Ann Arbor, MI 48104
(734) 971-2000

ART TATUM JAZZ HERITAGE FESTIVAL

June
Toledo, Ohio
http://toledojazzsociety.org/TATUM/TATUM.html
Admission: $

For many music lovers, jazz at the piano begins and ends with Art Tatum, the brilliant pianist whose techniques and innovations are now part of any self-respecting jazz piano player's education. The man's genius is recognized annually in Toledo, Ohio (his birthplace), at the Art Tatum Jazz Heritage Festival. This outdoor festival features many excellent performers from the more traditional schools of jazz while also providing festivalgoers a relaxed, fun atmosphere.

Artist Submissions
The Toledo Jazz Society
406 Adams St.
Toledo, OH 43604
For more information: toledojazz@toledojazzsociety.org
Camping: No
Accommodations

■ **Radisson Hotel Toledo**
101 N. Summit St.
Toledo, OH 43604
(419) 241-3000

■ **Days Inn**
1800 Miami St.
At I-75, Exit 199
Toledo, OH 43605
(419) 666-5120

ASIAN AMERICAN JAZZ FESTIVAL

September–October
San Francisco, California
www.asianimprov.com
Admission: $$

The Asian American Jazz Festival is San Francisco's longest running jazz festival. The event gathers more supporters each year and features sister events in Chicago, Pennsylvania, San Jose, and Los Angeles. In addition to bringing together a tremendous amount of talent from all over the globe, the festival works hard for community development. Performances in a variety of venues range from traditional Chinese music to abstract bop improvisations.
For more information: contact@asianimprov.com

Camping: No
Accommodations

■ **Radisson Miyako**
1625 Post St.
San Francisco, CA 94115
(415) 922-3200
info@miyakohotel.com
www.miyakohotel.com

■ **Best Western**
1800 Sutter St.
San Francisco, CA 94115
(415) 921-4000

ATLANTA JAZZ FESTIVAL

May
Atlanta, Georgia
www.atlantafestivals.com
Admission: FREE

Atlanta's annual jazz festival has more than a quarter century of history behind it and makes for one of the better ways to spend a Memorial Day weekend in the South. More than one hundred artists perform at this free festival, which draws in about 150,000 attendees. The majority of the performances take place during the day in parks around the city, and a few ticketed events take place at night as well. Past performers Abbey Lincoln, Bebel Gilberto, and Joshua Redman are prime examples of this festival's diversity.

For more information: (404) 817-6851
Camping: No
Accommodations

■ **Wyndham Midtown Atlanta**
125 10th St.
Atlanta, GA 30309
(800) WYNDHAM

■ **Atlanta Downtown Travelodge**
311 Courtland St. NE
Atlanta, GA 30303
(800) 578-7878

ATLANTA JAZZ PARTY

April
Atlanta, Georgia
www.atlantajazzparty.com
Admission: $$–$$$

The Atlanta Jazz Party, nearly fifteen years old already, has distinguished itself as one of Georgia's key jazz festivals, especially for fans of traditional jazz.

The celebration takes place in the Westin Atlanta North Hotel's relaxed, wide-open Grand Ballroom. The organizers usually book a large group of performers from Atlanta and the surrounding areas who then perform several traditional jazz sets (in the West Coast style, in New Orleans combos, and so on) during the three-day festival. The ever popular musical brunches can be included as part of your ticket package if you plan ahead.

For more information: atleeobc@aol.com

Camping: No

Accommodations

- **Westin Atlanta North at Perimeter Center**
7 Concourse Pkwy.
Atlanta, GA 30328
(770) 395-3900

- **Atlanta Downtown Travelodge**
311 Courtland St. NE
Atlanta, GA 30303
(800) 578-7878

♪ ATLANTIC JAZZ FESTIVAL

July

Halifax, Nova Scotia, Canada

www.jazzeast.com/festival2003

Admission: $$

Halifax's Atlantic Jazz Festival has been going strong since 1986. For nine days, it offers up a wide selection of music in venues throughout the city. The events primarily take place on three main stages, but an assortment of clubs host additional shows as well. The Atlantic Jazz Festival is known for booking a variety of acts from around the world in all sorts of genres, so leave your blinders at home and come prepared for anything. Charlie Hunter and Oscar Lopez represent just a few of the kinds of artists you can expect to see here.

For more information: (800) 567-5277 or general@jazzeast.com

Camping: No

Accommodations

- **The Westin Hotel**
1181 Hollis St.
Halifax, NS B3H 2P6
Canada
(877) 9-WESTIN
www.westin.ns.ca

- **Waverly Inn**
1266 Barrington St.
Halifax, NS B3J 1Y5
Canada
(902) 423-9346

BERLIN JAZZ FESTIVAL

Early November
Berlin, Germany
www.berlinerfestspiele.de
Admission: $$

Berlin's annual jazz festival is not one to be taken lightly. Each year the organizers choose a festival director who puts together a thematic program (occasionally highlighting a specific country or region), so it's not uncommon to find boogie-woogie artists rubbing elbows with members of the European avant-garde. Solo artists are often given special attention; Max Roach, Roy Hargrove, Ken Vandermark, and Peter Brotzman have all appeared here as featured performers.

For more information: kartenbuero@berlinerfestspiele.de
Camping: No
Accommodations

■ **Hotel California**
Kurfuerstendamm 35
Berlin 10719
Germany
(49) 30-88-01-20

■ **Hotel Tiergarten**
Alt Moabit 89
Berlin 10559
Germany
(49) 30-39-98-96-00

BIG BEAR LAKE'S FESTIVAL OF JAZZ

September
Big Bear Lake, California
www.bigbearjazzfest.com
Admissions: $$–$$$

Big Bear Lake, a beautiful resort area, is located just a few hours outside Los Angeles, and for the last few years it's played host to the Big Bear Lake Festival of Jazz. More than 100 musicians will perform here, and all the monetary proceeds will go to youth-oriented jazz programs and scholarships.

For more information: (909) 866-5538 or jazz@bigbear.net
Camping: No
Accommodations

■ **Northwoods Resort**
40650 Village Dr.
Big Bear Lake, CA 92315
(800) 866-3121

■ **Honey Bear Lodge**
40994 Pennsylvania Ave.
Big Bear Lake, CA 92315
(800) 628-8714

BOSTON GLOBE JAZZ & BLUES FESTIVAL

June
Boston, Massachusetts
www.boston.com/jazzfestival
Admission: _FREE_–$$

This lively, weeklong event, which is comprised of both free and ticketed events, has been hosted by the city's oldest newspaper, the *Boston Globe*, for more than 30 years. The events are spread out around Boston and Cambridge, giving attendees a chance to explore the area's lovely parks and intimate clubs. In the past this festival has seen greats such as Dizzy Gillespie and Sonny Rollins take the stage, and you can still expect to hear a wide variety of wonderful, seasoned performances including everything from the avant leanings of the Art Ensemble of Chicago to the smooth grooves of the Rippingtons.

For more information: (617) 929-3460

Camping: No

Accommodations

■ **Seaport Hotel**
One Seaport Ln.
Boston, MA 02210
(877) SEAPORT
www.seaporthotel.com

■ **Copley Square Hotel**
47 Huntington Ave.
Boston, MA 02116
(800) 225-7062
www.copleysquarehotel.com

BUDDY DEFRANCO JAZZ FESTIVAL

Late April
Missoula, Montana
www.umt.edu/defrancojazz
Admission: $$–$$$

Buddy DeFranco is one of the most well respected clarinetists in all of jazz. Early in his career, he spent time on the stage with Gene Krupa and Count Basie and recorded with Art Blakey. Now he lends his name to this education-based festival at the University of Montana, which aims to foster jazz interest through small performances and critiques. Up-and-coming soloists are given the chance to shine away from the competitive spotlight.

For more information: lrboyd@selway.umt.edu

Camping: No

Accommodations

■ **Best Western**
5280 Grant Creek Rd.
Missoula, MT 59808
(888) 543-0700

■ **Red Lion Motel**
700 W. Broadway
Missoula, MT 59802
(800) 733-5466

♪ CACTUS JAZZ & BLUES FESTIVAL

September
San Angelo, Texas
www.sanangeloarts.com
Admission: $$

Early September heralds the arrival of the Cactus Jazz & Blues Festival in San Angelo, Texas. A wide assortment of traditional and Latin jazz flourishes on the stages at the Cactus Hotel. The historic hotel was once the tallest building on the San Angelo skyline but has since been eclipsed by the dormitory buildings at Angelo State University. However, its old world architecture still makes it among the most unique sites in town.

For more information: sacac@wcc.net
Camping: No

Accommodations

■ **Best Western Hotel**
3017 W. Loop 306
San Angelo, TX 76904
(915) 223-1273

■ **Holiday Inn Convention Center**
441 Rio Concho Dr.
San Angelo, TX 76903
(915) 658-2828

♪ CANCUN JAZZ FESTIVAL

May
Cancun, Mexico
www.specialeventhotels.com/cancun_jazz_festival.html
Admission: $$

Cancun becomes a haven for American tourists in May when they flock there to celebrate Memorial Day weekend. But, for those interested in more than just a beachfront getaway, they can absorb the fine festival programming at the Cancun Jazz Festival. For approximately a decade this festival has provided all manner of engaging jazz-related activities, which encompass music, film, and education. The wide range of music generally includes the best contemporary soloists and other notables in flamenco and Latin jazz.

For more information: vivamexicoencancun@hotmail.com

Camping: No

Accommodations

■ **Hyatt Regency Cancun**
Blvd Kukulcan km 8.5
P.O. Box 1201
77500 Cancun
Quintana Roo, Mexico
(52) 998-883-1234
hyattreg@hyattregencycancun.com.mx

♩ CAPE MAY JAZZ FESTIVAL

April and November
Cape May, New Jersey
www.capemayjazz.com
Admission: $–$$

The Cape May Jazz Festival began in 1994 and has grown exponentially since then. This festival not only programs some great entertainment but also provides educational outreach programs for students and lively panel discussions with performers and jazz scholars. The biannual festivities are usually dedicated to one specific jazz legend; Dizzy Gillespie, Louis Armstrong, and Miles Davis have all been past honorees. You can experience acts such as Chuck Mangione, Herbie Mann, and the incredible piano of McCoy Tyner in a variety of small venues that participate in the festival.

Camping: No

Accommodations

■ **Atlas Inn**	■ **The Blue Amber Motel**
1035 Beach Ave.	605 Madison Ave.
Cape May, NJ 08204	Cape May, NJ 08204
(888) 285-2746	(800) 371-8266
www.atlasinn.com	www.blueambermotel.com

♩ CARAMOOR JAZZ FESTIVAL

August
Katonah, New York

www.caramoor.org
Admission: $$$

Caramoor is the name of Walter and Lucie Rosen's beautiful estate in Westchester County, New York. The estate was built for public use so that people from all over the world could experience the aesthetic pleasures of their home and expansive grounds. Courtyards and theaters provide both the audience and the musicians with stately, lavish surroundings. Several concerts are held throughout the year with two days dedicated solely to the art of jazz.

For more information: Carolyn@caramoor.org
Camping: No
Accommodations

■ **The Castle at Tarrytown**
400 Benedict Ave.
Tarrytown, NY 10591
(914) 631-1980
www.castleattarrytown.com

■ **Westchester Marriott Hotel**
670 White Plains Rd.
Tarrytown, NY 10528
(914) 631-2200
www.marriotthotels.com

♪ CATALINA ISLAND JAZZTRAX FESTIVAL

October
Avalon, California
http://jazztrax.com/jazz/catalina.html
Admission: $$$

Catalina Island, located just twenty-five miles off of the coast of Los Angeles, offers a quick respite for folks tired of big city congestion. The island's Jazztrax Festival allows attendees to choose from three different weekend lineups throughout the month of October. Smooth jazz artists such as Acoustic Alchemy and Strunz & Farah perform to enthusiastic crowds at the Avalon Casino Ballroom.

For more information: jazztrax@jazztrax.com
Camping: No
Accommodations

■ **Catalina Island Inn**
125 Metropole Ave.
P.O. Box 467
Avalon, CA 90704
(800) 246-8134
www.catalinaislandinn.com

■ **Catherine Hotel**
708 Crescent Ave.
Avalon, CA 90704
(310) 510-0170
www.bdaservices.com/catherine

♪ CENTRAL PA JAZZ FESTIVAL

Mid-June
Harrisburg, Pennsylvania
www.pajazz.org
Admission: $

The Central Pennsylvania Friends of Jazz (CPFJ) Society first organized this summer festival more than two decades ago. Since then that small group has swelled to more than one thousand members who are enthusiastic about the history and the future of jazz, and year after year their summer jazz festival brings out the best in both the community and the performers. Dexter Gordon, Art Blakey, and Milt Jackson have all performed at past CPFJ events—a good indication this festival will continue to head in the right direction.

Artist Submissions
CPFJ
P.O. Box 10738
Harrisburg, PA 17105
For more information: (717) 540-1010
Camping: No
Accommodations

■ **Harrisburg Hilton**
One N. Second St.
Harrisburg, PA 17101
(717) 233-6000
www.visithhc.com/hhilton.html

■ **Super 8 Harrisburg North**
4125 N. Front St.
(I-81 Exit 22)
Harrisburg, PA 17110
(800) 800-8000

♪ CENTRUM JAZZ PORT TOWNSEND

July
Port Townsend, Washington
www.centrum.org/events/jazz.html
Admission: $$

Summertime brings jazz to Washington's Olympic Peninsula, and historic Port Townsend makes the most of its facilities when this festival comes to town. A multitude of venues throughout the city host scattered events, but the bulk of the performances take place at McCurdy Pavillion in Fort Worden State Park. Look for contemporary, mainstream jazz favorites such as pianists Kenny Barron and Dave Frishberg to appear here.

For more information: (800) 733-3608 or gregg@centrum.org

Camping: No

Accommodations

■ **Palace Hotel**
1004 Water St.
Port Townsend, WA 98368
(800) 962-0741

■ **Tides Inn**
1807 Water St.
Port Townsend, WA 98368
(800) 822-8696

♪ CHARLIE PARKER JAZZ FESTIVAL

August
New York, New York
www.charlieparkerjazzfestival.org
Admission: FREE

For two days in August, New York City pays tribute to Charlie Parker, prob-ably the greatest saxophonist who ever lived. The first of two main events takes place downtown in the East Village at Tompkins Square Park. Bird once lived near this park in an apartment at 151 Avenue B; the spot is currently marked by a plaque. The second half of the festival occurs uptown at Mar-cus Garvey Park, one of the oldest public areas in Manhattan and an impor-tant landmark in Harlem for the past 150 years. Both events are free and regularly feature acts such as Little Jimmy Scott, Hank Jones, and Greg Osby. These performers are there to enable festivalgoers to hear just how much the music of Charlie Parker continues to resonate with musicians even today.

For more information: sturvey@charlieparkerjazzfestival.org

Camping: No

Accommodations

■ **Sheraton Russell Hotel**
45 Park Ave.
New York, NY 10016

■ **Hotel 17**
225 E. 17th St.
New York, NY 10003
(212) 475-2845
hotel17@worldnet.att.net

♪ CHELTENHAM INTERNATIONAL JAZZ FESTIVAL

May
Cheltenham, United Kingdom

www.cheltenhamfestivals.co.uk

Admission: $$

According to local history, an increase in development began in Cheltenham in the seventeenth century after its residents observed some pigeons flocking to a nearby spring. After diving in this somewhat mysterious water, the people were convinced it contained some sort of healing power. From then on, the townspeople, with hopes of economic benefit, sought to attract the well to do and prosperous to their town.

While it's doubtful that locals will urge you to hop into the healing spring waters upon your arrival in Cheltenham, they certainly have managed to put together a festival that's hard to resist. The jazz fest began in 1996 and has quickly become one of the most well-received and well-attended festivals in Cheltenham. Contemporary innovators such as Brad Mehldau and English Dixieland pioneer Humphrey Lyttelton have been featured there in the past.

For more information: JaneEg@Cheltenham.gov.uk

Camping: No

■ **Stretton Lodge**
Western Road, Cheltenham
Gloucestershire GL50 3RN
United Kingdom
(44) 0-1242-570771
info@strettonlodge.co.uk
www.strettonlodge.co.uk

■ **The Carlton Hotel**
Parabola Road
Cheltenham GL50 3AQ
United Kingdom
(44) 0-1242-226487
enquiries@thecarltonhotel.co.uk
www.thecarltonhotel.co.uk

CHICAGO JAZZ FESTIVAL

August/September

Chicago, Illinois

www.ci.chi.il.us/SpecialEvents

Admission: FREE

The entire spectrum of jazz comes alive on three stages during this Labor Day weekend celebration. The festival is free and has seen attendance rates go well over 300,000 people—not bad for an event that started out as a small tribute to Duke Ellington. The wine and food are plentiful here, and music by respected artists such as Ahmad Jamal, Chucho Valdez, and Wayne Shorter flows freely.

Camping: No

Accommodations

■ **City Suites Hotel**
933 W. Belmont
Chicago, IL 60657
(800) 248-9108

■ **Chicago Marriott Downtown**
540 N. Michigan Ave.
Chicago, IL 60611
(312) 836-0100

♪ CITY OF LIGHTS JAZZ FESTIVAL

April
Las Vegas, Nevada
www.mspjazz.com
Admission: $$

The Las Vegas City of Lights Jazz Festival, now closing in on its first decade of existence, is a one-day event that provides a fun and relaxed outdoor atmosphere where you can enjoy smooth jazz acts such as Lee Ritenour, Chuck Mangione, and the Yellowjackets. The festival has been known to draw a few thousand folks and takes place in the newly renovated skateboarder mecca Desert Breeze Park, a short drive away from the Las Vegas main drag.

For more information: (800) 777-8342

Camping: No

Accommodations

■ **Palms Hotel**
4321 W. Flamingo Rd.
Las Vegas, NV 89103
(866) 725-6773
info@palms.com
www.thepalmslasvegas.com

■ **The Orleans**
4500 W. Tropicana Ave.
Las Vegas, NV 89103
(800) 675-3267
orleansinfo@coastcasinos.net
www.orleanscasino.com

♪ CLEARWATER JAZZ HOLIDAY

October
Clearwater, Florida
www.clearwaterjazz.com
Admission: *FREE*

Over the course of its two-decade history, the Clearwater Jazz Festival in Clearwater, Florida, has accrued a list of past performers that reads like the index of a jazz history book. Despite its early small-town stigma, this festival now enjoys international prestige and can pride itself on being one of the top draws in the Tampa Bay area. More than 100,000 people usually attend this four-day event to enjoy the jazz as well as the stunning views and warm evenings on the beach. Dizzy Gillespie, Stan Getz, Nancy Wilson, and Tito Puente have all made it down to Clearwater in years past, as should anyone with even a passing interest in jazz.

For more information: clearjazz@aol.com

Camping: No

Accommodations

■ **Comfort Inn North**
27988 US 19 N.
Clearwater, FL 33761
(800) 228-5150

■ **Econo Lodge Central**
21252 US 19 N.
Clearwater, FL 33765
(727) 799-1569

♪ CLIFFORD BROWN JAZZ FESTIVAL

June

Wilmington, Delaware

www.ci.wilmington.de.us/events.htm

Admission: $

Famed trumpeter Clifford Brown was born in Wilmington, Delaware, in 1930. During his tragically brief life span (he died in an auto accident in 1955), Brown's warm tone set the standard for all subsequent hard bop players. In the fifteen years since the riverfront city of Wilmington began honoring its hometown legend, this festival has showcased some of the nation's finest talent. Nicholas Payton, Joshua Redman, and Dianne Reeves have all performed here in the past.

For more information: (888) 328-5887

Camping: No

Accommodations

■ **Hotel Du Pont**
11th and Market Streets
Wilmington, DE 19801
(800) 441-9019
hotel.dupont@usa.dupont.com
www.dupont.com/hotel

■ **Courtyard Wilmington Delaware**
1102 West St.
Wilmington, DE 19801
(800) 321-2211

COLORADO SPRINGS JAZZ FESTIVAL

Fourth of July weekend
Colorado Springs, Colorado
www.coloradospringsjazzfestival.com
Admission: $

If you're seeking the ultimate in all-American celebrations, then spending Independence Day at the Air Force Academy in Colorado must be given due consideration. Still in its infancy, the Colorado Springs Jazz Festival drew more than 20,000 people to its first get-together. Revelers enjoyed a wide array of local performers and internationally known acts such as Cuban pianist Miguel Romero.

Artist Submissions: Judy@coloradospringsjazzfestival.com
For more information: info@coloradospringsjazzfestival.com
Camping: No
Accommodations

■ **Hilton Garden Inn**
1810 Briargate Pkwy.
Colorado Springs, CO 80920
(719) 598-6866
www.coloradosprings.gardeninn.com

■ **The Hampton Inn North**
7245 Commerce Center Dr.
Colorado Springs, CO 80919
(719) 593-9700
www.hampton-inn.com

COPENHAGEN JAZZ FESTIVAL

July
Copenhagen, Denmark
www.jazzfestival.dk
Admission: $$–$$$

Copenhagen's large annual jazz festival gathers together some of the biggest names in European and international jazz and, for a number of days, creates an event that understands and respects both the traditional aspects and future possibilities of the genre. You can visit several dozen venues around the city to hear not only jazz, but also electronic, Dixieland, and world music. It's not uncommon to take in performances from the likes of John Scofield, Joe Lovano, and Dave Holland. Each year the organizers identify current themes in jazz and then work to present a program that will represent these themes. This concern for the legacy of the music certainly elevates the Copenhagen Jazz Festival to one of the more interesting events around.

For more information: info@jazzfestival.dk

Camping: Yes. Contact Copenhagen City Camp at info@citycamp.dk or go to www.citycamp.dk.

Accommodations

■ **Hotel Kong Arthur**
Nørre Søgade 11
DK 1370
Copenhagen K
Denmark
(45) 33-11-12-12
hotel@kongarthur.dk
www.kongarthur.dk

■ **Absalon Hotel**
Helgolandsgade 15
DK-1653
Copenhagen V
Denmark
(45) 33-24-22-11
www.absalon-hotel.dk

DISCOVER JAZZ FESTIVAL

June
Burlington, Vermont
www.discoverjazz.com
Admission: $$

The Burlington Discover Jazz Festival takes place downtown, not too far from Lake Champlain. It seems the entire city gets caught up in the six-day celebration, throwing street parties and offering cruises on the "great sixth lake." And as for the music, listening to it can often be a transcendent experience. New jazz giants such as Greg Osby and David S. Ware need only take the stage to remind the audience that jazz is far from dead. The festival also arranges a "Meet the Artist" seminar where interested patrons can enter into a dialogue with noted performers about the current state of jazz. Overall, this is an excellent festival for serious jazz fans that provides enough variety to also entertain first timers or fun-seeking families.

Artist Submissions
Burlington Discover Jazz Festival
Attention: Booking
230 College St.
Burlington, VT 05401

For more information: info@discoverjazz.com

Camping: No

Accommodations

■ **Hawthorn Suites**
401 Dorset St.
S. Burlington, VT 05403
(866) 337-1616
www.hawthornsuitesburlington.com

■ **The Inn at Essex**
70 Essex Way
Essex, VT 05452
(800) 727-4295
innfo@innatessex.com
www.innatessex.com

EARSHOT JAZZ FESTIVAL

October/November
Seattle, Washington
www.earshot.org
Admission: $$–$$$

Seattle's Earshot Jazz Festival lasts a little more than two weeks every year and definitely makes the most of that time. Educational events and film screenings complement the succession of live shows programmed throughout the Seattle area. This festival is one of the most respected in its field due to the Earshot Jazz organization's dedication to bringing current but submainstream acts together with highly respected veterans. The Art Ensemble of Chicago, Greg Osby, Tin Hat Trio, and John Zorn are just a few of the diverse performers who've appeared at this festival in recent years.

For more information: (206) 547-9787
Camping: No
Accommodations

■ **Camlin Hotel**
1619 9th Ave.
Seattle WA, 98101
(800) 663-1144
www.camlinhotel.com

■ **Hotel Vintage Park**
1100 5th Ave.
Seattle, WA 98101
(800) 624-4433

EDGEFEST

First week in October
Ann Arbor, Michigan
www.kerrytown.com/concerthouse/edgefest
Admission: $$–$$$

Ann Arbor's Edgefest has been bringing avant-garde and chamber jazz from all over the world to Michigan for the past six years. Three different venues, all within walking distance of each other, provide homes for the fest's challenging lineup, which in 2002 featured the superb free improvisation of Roscoe Mitchell as well as the soulful, uncompromising saxophone of Tim Berne. Free educational sessions are offered in the afternoons during the three-day event; here you can be part of small group performances that are followed by an artist critique.

For more information: kch@kerrytown.com

Camping: No

Accommodations

■ **Courtyard Ann Arbor**
3205 Boardwalk
Ann Arbor, MI 48108
(734) 995-5900
www.courtyard.com

■ **Hampton Inn Ann Arbor—North**
2300 Green Rd.
Ann Arbor, MI 48105
(734) 996-4444
aan@fhginc.com
www.hamptoninnannarbor.com

♪ ELKHART JAZZ FESTIVAL

June

Elkhart, Indiana

www.elkhartjazzfestival.com

Admission: $$$

Every summer in June, the relatively small town of Elkhart, Indiana (pop. 43,000), hosts its own jazz festival. Attendance rates have skyrocketed in the 15 years since its inception; you can blame it on the dedicated organizers and volunteers or blame it on the years of stellar lineups. In any case, this family-friendly festival remains the one to beat in Indiana.

Artist Submissions

Elkhart Centre
227 S. Main St.
Elkhart, IN 46516

Camping: No

Accommodations

■ **Best Western Inn & Suites**
3326 Cassopolis St.
Elkhart, IN 46514
(800) 611-8262

■ **Sleep Inn**
220 Caravan Dr.
Elkhart, IN 46514
(219) 206-8290

EQUINOX MUSIC FESTIVAL

September
Boston, Massachusetts
www.jcmcsite.com/home/index.htm
Admission: FREE–$$

Although Boston's Equinox Music Festival is only two years old, the event's crowning moment—the John Coltrane Memorial Concert—has been going strong for a quarter of a century. This memorial concert is the oldest annual tribute in the world dedicated to John Coltrane, and the festival itself has somewhat sprung up around it. Past musical participants have included artists such as Pharoah Sanders and Yusef Lateef. In addition to presenting this historic concert, the festival provides other free concerts and media-related panel discussions.

For more information: info@jcmcsite.com
Camping: No
Accommodations

■ **Seaport Hotel**
One Seaport Ln.
Boston, MA 02210
(877) SEAPORT
www.seaporthotel.com

■ **Copley Square Hotel**
47 Huntington Ave.
Boston, MA 02116
(800) 225-7062
www.copleysquarehotel.com

ESTORIL JAZZ ON A SUMMER DAY

July
Estoril, Portugal
www.projazz.pt
Admission: $$

Serious jazz musicians from all over the globe come to Portugal every year for this weeklong event, and performers of all stripes, from trad jazz bands to bebop soloists, find representation. The coastal town of Estoril, just minutes away from the capital city of Lisbon, has welcomed greats such as Sonny Rollins, Charlie Haden, and Abbey Lincoln to its various bars and auditoriums in years past.

For more information: projazz@mail.eunet.pt
Camping: No

Accommodations

■ **Hotel Palacio**
Rua do Parque 2765
Estoril 2769-504
Portugal
(351) 21-464-80-00
palacioestoril@mail.telepac

■ **Hotel Apartamento Club Do Lago**
Avenida do Lago Monte Estoril
2765 Estoril
Portugal
(351) 21-467-18-70
clublago@net.sapo.pt

♪ FAIRFAX JAZZ FESTIVAL

End of September
Fairfax, California
www.fairfaxjazz.homestead.com
Admission: $–$$

The small town of Fairfax does its part to keep the history of jazz alive with its yearly festival. Typically, the weather in Northern California stays pretty warm into late September, so you can put aside any fears you might have that you'll be spending a chilly autumn day outdoors. In the past the festival has booked a broad range of acts that span nearly the entire history of jazz music. All venues, both indoor and out, are centrally located, so you can feel free to walk from one event to the next.

For more information: (415) 331-9999 or mollyvil@aol.com
Camping: No
Accommodations

■ **Fairfax Inn**
15 Broadway
Fairfax, CA 94930
(415) 455-8702

■ **Fairfax Motel**
Hwy. 321 N.
Fairfax, CA 29827
(803) 632-3533

♪ FANO JAZZ BY THE SEA

July
Fano, Italy
www.fanojazzclub.org/fanojazzbythesea.htm
Admission: FREE

This Italian festival enjoys the distinction of being able to present a jazz program that faces the Adriatic Sea. When it began in 1991, the event lasted more than three weeks and brought together a stellar mixture of jazz and blues.

More recently, the organizers have compressed the event into less than a week, while also making sure that tickets remain free. Plenty of space is allotted for Italian musicians, but a large number of well-known players such as McCoy Tyner, Greg Osby, and Ruth Brown generally turn out as well.

For more information: info@fanojazzclub.org

Camping: No

Accommodations

■ **Hotel Paradise**
V.le Adriatico, 126-61032
Fano (PS)-Italy
(39) 0-721-802-503
info@hotel-paradise.it
www.hotel-paradise.it

■ **Hotel Marina**
Viale Adriatico, 15, I-61032
Fano (PU) Italy
(39) 0-721-803-157
info@alexhotels.it

FILLMORE STREET JAZZ FESTIVAL

July

San Francisco, California

www.hartmannstudios.com/Fillmore.html

Admission: FREE-$

During its annual jazz festival, San Francisco's famed Fillmore district becomes a haven for jazz aficionados—and locals and tourists and anyone else who happens to wander by. The Fillmore Street area has changed a lot since its halcyon days as the city's hotbed of jazz activity and now features more upscale shops than music haunts. However, recent developments have seen the city refocusing its energies and emphasizing the area's historical and musical significance. This is great news for the festival and should only add to the already vibrant atmosphere. For two summer days in the city, you can submerse yourself in the great selection of jazz, soul, blues, and Latin music while enjoying some of the best food you're going to find anywhere in the state.

For more information: (800) 731-0003

Camping: No

Accommodations

■ **Phoenix Hotel**
601 Eddy St.
San Francisco, CA 94109
(800) 248-9466

■ **Hotel Bijou**
111 Mason St.
San Francisco, CA 94102
(800) 771-1022

♪ FORD DETROIT INTERNATIONAL JAZZ FESTIVAL

August/September
Detroit, Michigan
www.detroitjazzfest.com
Admission: FREE

Thanks in part to the sponsorship of the Ford Motor Company, this Motor City event bills itself as the largest free jazz festival in North America. For more than two decades, the Ford Detroit International Jazz Festival has brought many top names together on four diverse stages during Labor Day weekend. You can expect to see jazz/soul legends such as Lonnie Smith, Roy Ayers, and Mavis Staples among dozens of other regional and international performers.

For more information: info@musichall.org

Camping: No

Accommodations

■ **The Milner Hotel**
1538 Centre St.
Detroit, MI 48226
(877) MILNERS
milnerht@ix.netcom.com

■ **Ambassador Hotel**
1020 Washington Blvd.
Detroit, MI 48226
(313) 887-7000

♪ FREIHOFER'S JAZZ FESTIVAL

End of June
Saratoga Springs, New York
www.spac.org/calender/freihofer.html
Admission: $$–$$$

Every year, the benevolent organizers at the Saratoga Performing Arts Center put together one of the most popular festivals in upstate New York. Freihofer's Jazz Festival takes place during the peak of the summer heat, so you're virtually guaranteed a hot and humid experience. But this rarely dissuades the several thousand folks who flock there to hear a variety acts ranging from the Manhattan Transfer to the hardest working ex-con in show business, Mr. James Brown.

For more information: elinehan@spac.org

Camping: No

Accommodations

■ **Sheraton Saratoga Springs Hotel**
534 Broadway
Saratoga Springs, NY 12866
(518) 584-4000
www.starwood.com/sheraton

■ **Gideon Putnam Hotel and Conference Center**
24 Gideon Putnam Rd.
Saratoga Springs, NY 12866
(800) 732-1560
info-gideon@xanterra.com
www.gideonputnam.com

♪ GENE HARRIS JAZZ FESTIVAL

Early April
Boise, Idaho
Admission: $$

The Gene Harris Jazz Festival celebrates the soul-infused piano style of its namesake, Gene Harris. When Harris passed away in 2000, he left a legacy of five decades of strong recordings. His funky sides for Blue Note from the early seventies represent perhaps his best work, but all his recordings maintain a level of confident excellence. He retired to Boise in the late seventies and became beloved by the city, which honored him by throwing the first Gene Harris Jazz Festival in 1998. The festival not only provides evenings filled with big band and contemporary jazz, but also aims to foster the talents of student performers through clinics and competitions.

For more information: bpeters@boisestate.edu

Camping: No

Accommodations

■ **The Grove Hotel**
245 South Capitol Blvd.
Boise, ID 83702
(208) 333-8000
grovesales@westcoasthotels.com

■ **Doubletree Hotel**
1800 Fairview Ave.
Boise, ID 83702
(208) 344-7691

♪ GENUINE JAZZ

June
Breckenridge, Colorado
www.genuinejazz.com
Admission: FREE

Set at the foot of the Rocky Mountains, this picturesque festival has been going strong for the past 18 years. All aspects of jazz find representation here during the performances that fill up the days and nights. Several local clubs participate in the event by providing reasonably priced ticketed events in the evenings. The bulk of the rest of the festival is free, but be sure to bring enough money for concessions. Neither animals nor coolers are allowed, so plan accordingly.

For more information: (888) 355-6235

Camping: No

Accommodations

■ **The Village At Breckenridge**
535 South Park Ave.
P.O. Box 8329
Breckenridge, CO 80424
(888) 355-6235
www.villageatbreckenridge.com

■ **Breckinridge Wayside Inn**
165 Tiger Rd.
Breckenridge, CO 80424
(970) 453-5540
wayside@colorado.net
www.summitnet.com/wayside

GLENDALE KIWANIS JAZZ FESTIVAL

June

Glendale, California

www.glendalekiwanisjazz.org

Admission: $$

The good people at the Glendale Kiwanis Club have been organizing this festival in southern California for three years now. The friendly atmosphere provides a great way for families and friends to get together and enjoy some traditional jazz—the fest serves up some mighty fine Dixieland and ragtime with a side of zydeco thrown in occasionally. In order to further the feeling of homeyness, festival organizers provide two meals during the day for guests; the most recent was a full-blown creole feast.

For more information: jazz@vnla.com

Camping: No

Accommodations

■ **Days Inn Glendale**
600 N. Pacific
Glendale, CA 91203
(818) 956-0202

■ **Rodeway Inn Regalodge**
200 W. Colorado St.
Glendale, CA 91204
(818) 246-7331

♪ GREAT CONNECTICUT JAZZFEST

July
Guilford, Connecticut
www.ctjazz.org
Admission: $$

This Connecticut festival has been going strong since its inception in the mid-eighties. The Guilford Fairgrounds provides a temporary home along the Connecticut shoreline for fans of big band and Dixieland. The festival also provides a Jazz Camp for kids where they can learn more about these traditional jazz sounds while sharpening their own musical talent.

For more information: ct.traditional.jazz@snet.net

Camping: No

Accommodations

■ **New Haven Hotel**
229 George St.
New Haven, CT 06510
(203) 498-3100

■ **Regal Inn**
1605 Whalley Ave.
New Haven, CT 06515
(203) 389-9504

♪ GREATER HARTFORD FESTIVAL OF JAZZ

July
Hartford, Connecticut
www.jazzhartford.org
Admission: FREE

Founded in 1991, the Greater Hartford Festival of Jazz is one of the largest jazz festivals in the New England area. About 50,000 people show up over a three-day period for this free event that aims to celebrate a true American art form. If a little bit of education sneaks in along with it, then that's fine, too. Past festivals have been dedicated to greats such as Miles Davis and John Coltrane and have featured performances by John Scofield, Yusel Lateef, and McCoy Tyner.

Camping: No

Accommodations

■ **Hilton Hartford**
315 Trumbull St.
Hartford, CT 0610
(860) 728-5151

■ **Capitol Hill Ramada Inn**
440 Asylum St.
Hartford, CT 061033
(888) 298-2054

GUELPH JAZZ FESTIVAL

September
Guelph, Ontario, Canada
www.guelphjazzfestival.com
Admission: $$

Ontario's Guelph Festival has been pushing boundaries within the jazz world since its inception a decade ago. The Guelph Festival not only manages to present high profile, critically acclaimed artists in a warm setting, but also works to combine jazz with different media—be it photography, opera, or dance. Through informative discussions and a multitude of versatile performers, this festival presents a fuller picture of this great music and embodies the true spirit of jazz in the process.

For more information: jazzfest@uoguelph.ca
Camping: No
Accommodations

■ **Days Inn**
785 Gordon St.
Guelph, ON N1G 1Y8
Canada
(519) 822-9112

■ **Super 8 Motel**
281 Woodlawn Road West
Guelph, ON N1H 7K7
Canada
(519) 836-5850

HARVEST JAZZ & BLUES FESTIVAL

Mid-September
Fredericton, New Brunswick, Canada
www.harvestjazzblues.nb.ca
Admission: FREE–$$

The Harvest Jazz & Blues Festival offers more than 100 shows on 26 stages over the course of five days, making every effort to satisfy all your musical needs from acoustic to zydeco. The organizers utilize their dozen years of experience to make sure that both families and single travelers leave feeling sated. Most of the events here are free (or at least reasonably priced) so you can feel free to either quaff a few cold ones or enjoy a decent outdoor meal. A subset of the festival entitled Kidsfest gives the wee ones a chance to hear music just for them and to do everything from painting themselves up like clowns to making their own instruments.

For more information: harvest@brunnet.net

Camping: No

Accommodations

■ **Roadside Motel**
3005 Woodstock Rd.
Route 102
Fredericton, NB E3C 1R2
Canada
(506) 450-2080

■ **Ramada Hotel**
480 Riverside Dr.
Fredericton, NB E3B5E3
Canada
(888) 298-2054

♪ HAWAII INTERNATIONAL JAZZFEST

July
Honolulu, Hawaii
http://hawaiijazz.com
Admission: $$

For jazz fans looking for an exotic locale in which to experience live music or for jazz neophytes looking for an excuse to go to Hawaii—the Hawaii International Jazzfest solves all problems. The first half of the event takes place on the island of Oahu, while the latter half takes place on Maui. In addition to favorites such as flutist Herbie Mann and saxophonist Eric Marienthal, you can expect to hear an array of traditional Hawaiian music placed in a jazz context.

For more information: AEWjazz1@aol.com

Camping: No

Accommodations

■ **Marriott Waikiki**
2552 Kalakaua Ave.
Honolulu, Oahu, HI 96815
(808) 922-6611

■ **Waikiki Parc Hotel**
2233 Helumoa Rd.
Honolulu, Oahu, HI 96815
(800) 422-0450

♪ INDY JAZZ FEST

Mid-June
Indianapolis, Indiana
Admission: $–$$

Since its inauguration into the world of jazz festivals in 1999, the Indianapolis Jazz Festival has brought in the kinds of crowds most festivals rarely see in their entire life spans. Several stages are set up in downtown Indianapolis, featuring lineups that touch on jazz, soul, funk, and rock. In addition to the professional performers, areas such as the Emerging Talent stage give school ensembles a chance to show off their up-and-coming talent.

Artist Submissions

Indy Jazz Fest, Inc.

938 Indiana Ave.

Indianapolis, IN 46202

For more information: info@indyjazzfest.org

Camping: No

Accommodations

■ **Radisson Hotel City Centre**
31 West Ohio St.
Indianapolis, IN 46204
(317) 635-2000
jblattert@remingtonhotels.com
www.radisson.com/indianapolisin
  _citycentre

■ **Canterbury Hotel**
123 South Illinois St.
Indianapolis, IN 46335
(317) 634-3000
info@canterburyhotel.com
www.canterburyhotel.com

INTERNATIONAL FESTIVAL MUSIQUE ACTUELLE

May

Victoriaville, Quebec, Canada

www.fimav.qc.ca

Admission: $$–$$$

This five-day event takes place in the welcoming, musically diverse environment of Victoriaville in southern Quebec. It's the type of event that fosters an interest in jazz through presenting some of the leading figures in avant-garde and experimental music. In the past this festival has brought Japanese noise groups such as Melt Banana and Merzbow together with well-regarded free jazz players such as Cecil Taylor and Fred Frith. Their dedication to jazz and other improvised music makes this one festival that no open-minded jazz fan should miss.

For more information: info@fimav.qc.ca

Camping: No
Accommodations

■ **Auberge Aquarelle**
640, boul. Bois-Francs Sud
Victoriaville, QC
Canada
(888) 357-5060
info@aubergeaquarelle.com
www.aubergeaquarelle.com

■ **Hotel Colibri**
19, Route 116
Victoriaville, QC
Canada
(800) 563-0533
www.hotelcolibri.com

♪ INTERNATIONAL ISTANBUL JAZZ FESTIVAL

July
Istanbul, Turkey
www.istfest.org
Admission: $$

For nearly ten years, the International Istanbul Jazz Festival has been providing an outlet for all types of musicians: hip-hop, world music, and electronic music are all part of the program. The festival's roots actually go back to 1984 when Chick Corea took the stage as part of the less musically specific Istanbul Festival. Unexpectedly, huge crowds gathered outside the venue, unable to gain access to the event. It was then that organizers knew Istanbul was ready for a jazz festival of its own. Oddly enough, Istanbul's jazz festival has turned into an event as diverse as the one it originally sought to replace. Acts such as Lou Reed and Dead Can Dance play along with artists such as Bobby McFerrin and the Manhattan Transfer.

For more information: press.pr@istfest-tr.org
Camping: No
Accommodations

■ **Best Western Hotel Spectra**
Sehit Mehmetpasa Yokusu No:2
Sultanahmet-Istanbul Turkey
(90) 212-516-3546
contact@hotelspectra.com

■ **Marmara Hotel**
Taksim Meydanı, Taksim 80090
Istanbul Turkey
(90) 212-251-4696
info@themarmaraistanbul.com
www.themarmara.com.tr

♪ IOWA CITY JAZZ FESTIVAL

July
Iowa City, Iowa
www.iowacityjazzfestival.com
Admission: *FREE*

The first weekend in July is when Iowa City generally shuts down its streets and begins its three-day testament to jazz music and outdoor hijinks. When the festival began in 1991, crowds peaked at just a few thousand; recent festivals have seen that number increase to an average of 25,000. The large crowds can be attributed to both the attractive price (free) and the typical quality of the lineup (Neville Brothers, Kenny Garrett, Joe Lovano). Workshops and underwriting from local businesses ensure that this event will help benefit younger jazz fans in addition to the town's economy.

Artist Submissions
Iowa City Jazz Festival
P.O. Box 10054
Iowa City, IA 52240
For more information: (319) 358-9346
Camping: No
Accommodations

■ **Sheraton Iowa City Hotel**
210 South Dubuque St.
Iowa City, IA 52240
(800) 848-1335

■ **Iowa House Hotel**
Madison St. at Jefferson St.
121 IMU
Iowa City, IA 52242
(319) 335-3513
iowahouse@uiowa.edu

♪ JAMAICA OCHO RIOS JAZZ FESTIVAL

June
Ocho Rios, Jamaica
www.ochoriosjazz.com
Admission: *FREE*–$$

This event began in 1991 with the hopes of exposing both locals and tourists to the history and sounds of Jamaican and Caribbean jazz. By combining a well-thought-out musical program with educational tools, the festival has more than achieved its goals. Concerts are staged all around this city on the north coast of the island while multimedia exhibits tell the story of Jamaican jazz. This family-focused event has seen artists such as Terrence Blanchard, the Platters, and king of the jazz bagpipe, Rufus Harley, make special appearances.

For more information: jazzinfo@ochoriosjazz.com

Camping: No

Accommodations

■ **Renaissance Jamaica Grande**
P.O. Box 100
Ocho Rios, St. Ann, Jamaica
(876) 974-2201
www.renaissancehotels.com

■ **Hibiscus Lodge**
Main St.
P.O. Box 52
Ocho Rios, St. Ann, Jamaica
(876) 974-2676

♪ JAZZ ASPEN SNOWMASS

June and August
Aspen, Colorado
www.jazzaspen.com/default.cfm
Admission: $$–$$$

Jazz Aspen Snowmass presents plenty of entertainment come summertime: one festival arrives at the beginning of the season and another traditionally falls on Labor Day weekend. Both events consistently deliver a mixed bag of funk, blues, and stellar vocal jazz. Wynton Marsalis, Crosby, Stills & Nash, and Ray Charles are typical examples of artists usually on the program. The event takes place in the Buttermilk Ski Area, which offers an outdoor, amphitheater-style setting. Buses are available for those who plan on imbibing the plentiful suds you'll find here and don't wish to drive to the festival grounds.

For more information: llasko@jazzaspen.com

Camping: No

Accommodations

■ **Aspen Square Hotel**
617 E. Cooper
Aspen, CO 81611
(800) 470-0530
info@aspensquarehotel.com

■ **The Inn at Aspen**
38750 Hwy. 82
Aspen, CO 81611
(800) 952-1515
innataspen@eastwestresorts.com
www.innataspen.com

♪ JAZZ IN MARCIAC

First two weeks in August
Marciac, France
www.marciac.com
Admission: $$–$$$

Jazz in Marciac is one of France's many great jazz festivals. It occurs annually, generally during the first two weeks of August. Thousands of fans eagerly await this event, which brings this quaint French village in the center of Gascogne into the jazz forefront. While French performers are given plenty of time on the stage, it is the more internationally known performers such as Wynton Marsalis and Bobby McFerrin that spark the adoration of the crowds. In fact, after an exhaustive, exhilarating performance given by Marsalis one year, the town erected a statue in his honor and named a wine after him. Some accommodations may be found in town, but travelers are advised that these spaces fill up fast. You should consider traveling in from one of the nearby villages such as the protectively titled town of Condom.

For more information: jim@marciac.com

Camping: No

Accommodations

■ **Hôtel Comtes de Pardiac**
Place de l'Hôtel de Ville
32230 Marciac
France
(33) 05-62-08-20-00
jacques.cazaban@hotel-
  comtespardiac.fr
www.hotel-comtespardiac.fr

■ **Logis Des Cordeliers**
Rue Des Cordeliers
Condom 32100
France
(33) 05-62-28-03-68
www.logisdescordeliers.com

♪ JAZZ IN THE VALLEY FESTIVAL

July
Ellensburg, Washington
www.jazzinthevalley.com
Admission: $

Washington's Jazz in the Valley Festival brings a number of jazz and blues fans into this luscious Cascade Mountain region. Local and national acts seek to entertain attendees at various venues around town, where a great selection of wines and cheeses are available for those seeking respite from the meat-on-a-stick tradition. Children are a priority here too; music-based activities will be provided for their amusement.

Artist Submissions

Jazz in the Valley

P.O. Box 214

Ellensburg, WA 98926

For more information: jazzinfo@jazzinthevalley.com

Camping: No

Accommodations

■ **Majestic Country Bed & Breakfast**

2830 Thorp Hwy. S.

Ellensburg, WA 98926

(509) 962-6605

majestic.country@home.com

■ **Harold's Motel**

601 N. Water St.

Ellensburg, WA 98926

(509) 925-4141

JAZZFEST INTERNATIONAL

June

Victoria, British Columbia, Canada

www.vicjazz.bc.ca/jazzfest

Admission: $$

Victoria's JazzFest International offers the chance to see famed jazz musicians such as Charlie Haden and Dave Brubeck perform to large, friendly crowds as well as the opportunity to explore more intimate club venues featuring performances from blues musicians, world beat practitioners, and every other kind of artist in between. Restaurant lounges and cafes also participate in the festival, providing attendees with a whole slew of entertainment options. Jazz workshops allow students to learn about music from those who know best—the artists themselves.

For more information: vicjazz@pacificcoast.net

Camping: No

Accommodations

■ **Hotel Grand Pacific**

463 Belleville St.

Victoria, BC V8V 1X3

Canada

(800) 663-7550

www.hotelgrandpacific.com

■ **Best Western Carlton Plaza**

642 Johnson St.

Victoria, BC V8W 1M6

Canada

(800) 663-7241

JAZZIN' THE CATSKILLS

July
Stamford, New York
www.newcenturyjazz.com
Admission: $$

Summer in the Catskill Mountains now seems even more inviting with the recent addition of Jazzin' the Catskills to the world of jazz festivals. A rain-or-shine weekend brought to you by the nonprofit organization New Century Jazz, this festival guarantees some excellent food and excellent music by artists such as saxophonist/flutist T. K. Blue and vocalist Lesette Wilson.

For more information: info@newcenturyjazz.com

Camping: No

Accommodations

■ **Belvedore Country Inn**
10 Academy St.
Stamford, NY 12167
(607) 652-6121

■ **Deer Run Resort**
Route 10
Stamford, NY 12167
(607) 652-2001

JVC JAZZ FESTIVAL

June
New York, New York
www.festivalproductions.net
Admission: *FREE*–$$

Always an eagerly awaited event, New York's JVC Jazz Festival has been packing houses for 30 years. The most well-known and highly attended events take place at Carnegie Hall, while other theaters, clubs, and smaller venues also participate. Past lineups have seen performers such as Brad Mehldau, Lauryn Hill, and João Gilberto wow audiences The critically acclaimed artists booked for this event year after year guarantee the jazz festival season's most eclectic and satisfying lineup.

Camping: No

Accommodations

■ **Empire Hotel**
44 W. 63rd St.
New York, NY 10023
(212) 265-7400

■ **Wellington Hotel**
871 7th Ave.
New York, NY 10019
(800) 652-1212

JVC JAZZ FESTIVAL NEWPORT

August
Newport, Rhode Island
www.festivalproductions.net
Admission: $$–$$$

The Newport Jazz Festival began back in 1954 under the sponsorship of pianist George Wein. The festival was one of the first to provide an outdoor arena for an all-jazz program. In the years since, the festival has grown to be one of the most well-known jazz events in the United States, as well as becoming a part of one of the most far-reaching international jazz programs in the world. The festival relocated to New York City in 1972 and in 1986 was renamed the JVC Jazz Festival (part of the JVC International Jazz Festival Program). The event returned to Newport in 1991 where it remains to this day.

Basically, you can name just about any notable jazz performer born in the twentieth century and chances are they've performed at Newport. Most famously, Duke Ellington performed a set here in 1956 that caused a near ecstatic riot and resulted in a career comeback for him. This event was captured in the film *Jazz on a Summer's Day*, which is usually regarded as one of the best live documents of jazz ever filmed.

Camping: No
Accommodations

■ **Hotel Viking**
One Bellevue Ave.
Newport, RI 02840
(800) 556-7126
www.hotelviking.com

■ **Mill Street Inn**
75 Mill St.
Newport, RI 02840
(800) 392-1316
www.millstreetinn.com

KINCARDINE SUMMER MUSIC FESTIVAL

August
Kincardine, Ontario, Canada
www.ksmf.ca
Admission: $–$$

A true combination of education and entertainment, this music festival takes place in the beautiful coastal area of Kincardine, Canada, bordering Lake

Huron. Part summer camp, part music festival, this event gives both children and adults a chance to learn the ins and outs of music performance. For two weeks, attendees can polish their skills in one of the camp's music programs and, at night, enjoy performances given by the dedicated staff members. Musicians of any and all ages are welcome to sign up for the festival camps. Accommodations for the younger attendees can be made on-site, while adults are more than welcome to stay in any of the surrounding hotels or bed-and-breakfasts. This event is a great for those who wish to learn about music in a noncompetitive and friendly atmosphere.

For more information: imills@tnt21.com

Camping: No

Accommodations

■ **Harbour Motor Inn**
249 Harbour St.
Kincardine, ON N2Z 2X3
Canada
(519) 396-3311

■ **Save Inn**
612 King St.
Kincardine, ON N2Z 2X3
Canada
(519) 396-5454

♪ LIONEL HAMPTON JAZZ FESTIVAL

End of February
Moscow, Idaho
www.jazz.uidaho.edu/default.htm
Admission: $$

The Lionel Hampton Jazz Festival is a top destination for young musicians looking to interact with some of their heroes. The event is held at the University of Idaho in the small town of Moscow and has been since its inception in 1967. The intervening years have seen the likes of Stan Getz, Dizzy Gillespie, and Sarah Vaughan take the stage. Competitions for performers at the college, high school, and elementary school levels take up a good portion of the four-day event while interactive clinics and standard performances account for the rest.

For more information: (208) 885-6765 or jazzinfo@uidaho.edu

Camping: No

Accommodations

■ **Hampton Inn**
185 Warbonnet Dr.
Moscow, ID 83843

■ **Best Western University Inn**
1516 Pullman Rd.
Moscow, ID 83843
(800) 325-8765

♪ LITCHFIELD JAZZ FESTIVAL

August
Litchfield, Connecticut
www.litchfieldjazzfest.com
Admission: $–$$

The afternoons and evenings are filled with the sounds of improvisation and celebration when the Litchfield Jazz Festival hits Connecticut in early August. Sonny Rollins, Dianne Schuur, and Kenny Rankin represent the kinds of performers showcased here regularly. Tickets are fairly priced for adults and free admission is available for children. There are many locally brewed ales on hand to enjoy while you're soaking up the music and perusing the wares of local arts and crafts dealers.

For more information: tiesler@litchfieldjazzfest.com
Camping: No
Accommodations

■ **Mohegan Sun Hotel**
1 Mohegan Sun Blvd.
Uncasville, CT 06382
(888) 777-7922
information@mohegansun.com
www.mohegansun.com

■ **Litchfield Inn**
432 Bantam Rd.
Litchfield, CT 06759
info@litchfieldinn.com
www.litchfieldinn.com

♪ LITCHFIELD JAZZ FESTIVAL AT SEA

January
www.jazzfestatsea.com
Admission: $$$

The Litchfield Jazz Festival at Sea premiered in 2003 in conjunction with the Litchfield Jazz Festival. This incredibly unique experience is comprised of seven nights of travel aboard a luxury cruise ship bound for the Caribbean.

You'll stop in Jamaica, Mexico, and Grand Cayman and enjoy performances along the way. In addition to the scheduled concerts, you can look forward to a reception with the musicians; you'll even have the chance to arrange for a private lesson, so bring your instrument. Vocalist Vanessa Rubin and trombonist Slide Hampton were some of the names along for the inaugural journey out to sea.

For more information: ddunbar@litchfieldjazzfest.com or www.thevoice-news.com/News/2002/1122/Arts_And_Amusements/A07.html

M & T SYRACUSE JAZZ FEST

June
Syracuse, New York
www.syracusejazzfest.com
Admission: FREE

Providing two decades of great free music from some of the world's greatest jazz talent is something worth boasting about, but the M & T Syracuse Jazz Fest keeps things simple. Anywhere between 5,000 and 20,000 people gather on lawn chairs, rain or shine, each day to take advantage of the music and concessions. This sort of low-key approach has seen the festival become an award-winning favorite over the years—that, and the lineup of artists such as Dr. John, Dizzy Gillespie, and the Sun Ra Arkestra, all of whom have passed by through the years.

Artist Submissions: fmalfitano@syracusejazzfest.com
For more information: info@syracusejazzfest.com
Camping: No
Accommodations

■ **Wyndham Hotel**
6301 Route 298
East Syracuse, NY 13057
(315) 432-0200

■ **Syracuse Sheraton**
801 University Ave.
Syracuse, NY 13210
(315) 475-3000
www.syracusesheraton.com

MAMMOTH LAKES JAZZ JUBILEE

Mid-July
Mammoth Lakes, California

www.mammothjazz.org

Admission: $$$

Whether you've come to dance or just lounge on the grass, the Mammoth Lakes Jazz Jubilee will provide the solutions you seek. The festival is split into two main areas with a grand total of ten venues where you can enjoy a wide variety of musical entertainment. Mammoth Lakes is a stunning resort area in the Sierra Mountains, so there are plenty of outdoor activities and natural wonders to explore independent of the festival-sponsored events. Musically, the Jubilee steers a traditional route, offering up feverish takes on Dixieland and ragtime.

For more information: info@mammothjazz.org

Camping: No

Accommodations

■ **Sierra Lodge**
3540 Main St.
P.O. Box 9228
Mammoth Lakes, CA 93546
(800) 356-5711
www.sierralodge.com

■ **Holiday Inn Hotel & Suites**
3236 Main St.
Mammoth Lakes, CA 93546
(760) 924-1234
www.mammothholidayinn.com

MANLY INTERNATIONAL JAZZ FESTIVAL

End of September

Sydney, New South Wales, Australia

www.manly.nsw.gov.au/minisites/main.asp?ms=27

Admission: $$

The Manly International Jazz Festival, Australia's longest running jazz fest, has a 25-year history of delivering stellar lineups that combine the best of local and national talent. Most of the concerts take place within walking distance of Manly Beach, so if you need a break, you're only minutes away from relaxing on one of the world's most beautiful beachfronts. And as for the music, the festival regularly offers up a varied menu of international jazz that encompasses both the contemporary and the traditional.

For more information: vic@manlycouncil.nsw.gov.au

Camping: No

Accommodations

■ **The Steyne Hotel**
75 The Corso
Manly, NSW 2095
Australia
(61) 2-9977-4977
stay@steynehotel.com.au
www.steynehotel.com.au

MARKHAM JAZZ FESTIVAL

August
Markham, Ontario, Canada
www.jazzfest.markham.on.ca
Admission: $–$$

The Markham Jazz Festival has been delivering a friendly, family-oriented festival in an array of settings for five years now. From large theatres to intimate cafes to local watering holes, Markham (just north of Toronto) provides enough diversity for everyone.

For more information: bebop@sympatico.ca
Camping: No
Accommodations

■ **Comfort Inn Northeast**
8330 Woodbine Ave.
Markham, ON L3R 2N8
Canada
(905) 477-6077

■ **Holiday Inn Hotel & Suites**
7095 Woodbine Ave.
Markham, ON L3R 1A3
Canada
(905) 474-0444

MARY LOU WILLIAMS WOMEN IN JAZZ FESTIVAL

May
Washington, DC
www.kennedy-center.org/womeninjazz
Admission: $–$$

Mary Lou Williams was one the true legends of jazz. Her stride piano techniques were on par with the likes of Duke Ellington, and she was also a talented arranger and songwriter who worked with big band greats such as

Benny Goodman and Tommy Dorsey. Over the years, she refused to stick to the traditional ways and flirted musically with members of the new school such as McCoy Tyner and Cecil Taylor. Her passing in 1981 was a great loss to the world of music. This festival commemorates her strong-willed legacy with a series of concerts from female artists such as Dianne Schuur, Shirley Horn, and Nnenna Freelon and with workshops on topics ranging from performance techniques to tips on booking your own shows. It's an empowering event, both for jazz fans and starry-eyed hopefuls looking to make it to the top.

For more information: (800) 444-1324

Camping: No

Accommodations

■ **Clarion Hampshire Hotel**
1310 New Hampshire Ave. NW
Washington, DC 20036
(202) 296-7600

■ **The George Washington University Inn**
824 New Hampshire Ave. NW
Washington, DC 20037
(800) 426-4455
www.gwuinn.com

MEDFORD JAZZ JUBILEE

October

Medford, Oregon

www.medfordjazz.org

Admission: $$–$$$

The largest town in southern Oregon, Medford welcomes the fall with three jazz-soaked days in October. The Jubilee provides eight stages for its performances, which focus on the traditional side of jazz, with an emphasis on Dixieland. The festival began in 1989 and prides itself on its dedication to youth programs and educational outlets.

For more information: info@medfordjazz.org

Camping: No

Accommodations

■ **Knight's Inn Motel**
500 N. Riverside
Medford, OR 97501
(800) 531-2655

■ **Reston Hotel**
2300 Crater Lake Hwy.
Medford, OR 97504
(800) 779-7829
www.restonhotel.com

♪ MEIHO JAZZ FESTIVAL

July
Meiho, Gifu, Japan
Admission: $$$

This single day event features some of the best-known names from the world of Japanese jazz and from the international spectrum of players as well. You can expect acclaimed saxophonists Sadao Watanabe and Jackie MacLean and trumpeter Terumasa Hino to perform blistering sets.

Camping: No
Accommodations
■ **Minshuku Sosuke**
1-64 Okamotocho Takayama
Gifu, Japan 506-0054
(81) 0-577-32-0818

♪ MELLON JAZZ FESTIVAL

June
Philadelphia, Pennsylvania
www.mellon.com/jazz
Admission: FREE–$$

In 2002, Philadelphia celebrated its seventeenth annual Mellon Jazz Festival. Year after year, a diverse set of performers (and an even more diverse crowd) descends upon the city, bringing together fans, aficionados, and artists. Musicians ranging from Tony Bennett to Chuck Mangione to John Scofield will typically perform in any given year. Concerts are normally geared around a theme—be it a tribute to past jazz legends or to people who have contributed greatly to the Philadelphia jazz scene. Local musicians are given equal billing to the big names, and stage time is usually allotted to youth groups, making this an event geared to all kinds of jazz fans.

For more information: (610) 667-3559
Camping: No
Accommodations

■ **Harrisburg Hilton**
One N. Second St.
Harrisburg, PA 17101-1601
(717) 233-6000
www.hilton.com

■ **Crowne Plaza Hotel**
23 S. Second St.
Harrisburg, PA 17101
(717) 234-5021

MOERS NEW MUSIC FESTIVAL

May
Moers, Germany
www.moers-festival.com
Admission: $$

The Moers New Music Festival has been a fixture in Germany for over thirty years. In that time crowds have seen electric performances from Anthony Braxton, Sun Ra, and Maceo Parker light up the stage. Moers has cultivated a celebration that draws from all the world's cultures over the years and now happily includes Latin jazz, Japanese theater, and African percussion in its four-day roster of events.

For more information: info@moers-music.com

Camping: Yes. Contact info@moers-music.com for exact details.

Artist Submissions

Moers Music Burkhard Hennen GmbH
P.O. Box 30 01 20
47426 Moers
Germany
(49) 0-28-41-77-41

Accommodations

■ Hotel Moers Van Der Valk
Krefelder Strasse 169
Moers, Germany
(49) 877-678-9330

MOLDE INTERNATIONAL JAZZ FESTIVAL

Mid-July
Molde, Norway
www.moldejazz.no
Admission: $$

A giant array of talent is the norm when it comes to evaluating the program at Norway's Molde International Jazz Festival. Top acts such as Paul Simon and guitarist John McLaughlin have made exclusive appearances here in the past, but considering the festival was first organized in 1961, those names just scratch the surface of the list of esteemed performers that have graced the stages here. The festival biannually commissions an artist to compose a piece of music unique to the festival, and the piece is then performed for the thousands of people in attendance. It's one of the many reasons this event is eagerly anticipated by the Norwegian jazz community, not to mention by jazz-loving travelers worldwide. If that's not enough, the city of Molde provides a coastal European setting against a mountainous Scandinavian backdrop.

For more information: post@moldejazz.no

Camping: Yes. A camping area is set up for attendees. Contact post@moldejazz.no for details.

Accommodations

■ **Quality Hotel Alexandra**
Storgaten 1-7
P.O. Box 23
Molde, Norway 6413

■ **Rica Hotel**
Storgata 8
6400 Molde, Norway
(47) 71-20-35-00
rica.hotel.molde@rica.no

MONTEREY JAZZ FESTIVAL

September
Monterey, California
www.montereyjazzfestival.org
Admission: $$–$$$

As the longest-running jazz festival in the world, the Monterey Jazz Festival has the kind of history and presence that most other festivals aspire to. Held in the stylish yet comfortable coastal town of Monterey, the sea air and small town hospitality provide a mellow backdrop for some of the liveliest performances in the jazz spectrum.

A main arena plays host to the event's high-profile performers. Here, over the years, legends such as Dizzy Gillespie and Dave Brubeck have performed invigorating live sets. The surrounding area is made up of small outdoor stages that provide entertainment from a variety of blues, swing, and bebop artists. This outdoor area is also where you will find all sorts of Cajun, Thai, and classic deep-fried festival foods along with clothing vendors selling everything from Indian saris to Miles Davis T-shirts. More intimate indoor venues allow performers to deliver personal sets that range from world music to avant-garde improvisation.

Be advised that the event can be costly: a $35 ticket will get you into the surrounding stages but won't cover your admission to the arena. Children between the ages of 2 and 14 are also required to have a slightly discounted ticket. But if cost isn't an issue, the Monterey Jazz Festival, with its amazing display of organization and musical variety, is an event that no self-respecting jazz fan should go without attending at least once in his or her life.

For more information: info@montereyjazzfestival.org

Camping: Yes. Camping is available in the surrounding areas. Contact Marina Dunes at (831) 384-6914 or the Laguna Seca Recreational Area at (831) 755-4899 for information.

Accommodations

■ **Hotel Pacific**
300 Pacific St.
Monterey, CA 93940
(800) 554-5542
reservations@innsofmonterey.com
www.hotelpacific.com

■ **The Monterey Hotel**
406 Alvarado St.
Monterey, CA 93940
(800) 727-0960
www.montereyhotel.com

♪ MONTREAL INTERNATIONAL JAZZ FESTIVAL

Year-round
Montreal, Quebec, Canada
http://montrealjazzfest.com
Admission: $$$

Montreal's approach to the jazz festival is far from typical. Instead of pouring all their efforts into a single weekend or several days, they concentrate on arranging reasonably priced events throughout the year. Individual tickets and concert packages are available for the traditional concert seasons: spring, winter, summer, and fall. These are top-scale events featuring folks such as Patricia Barber, Dee Dee Bridgewater, and Brazilian legend Caetano Veloso, so be sure to buy in advance.

For more information: commentaires_jazz@equipespectra.ca

Camping: No

Accommodations

447 St.-François Xavier
Montreal, QC H2Y 1Z5
Canada
(514) 844-1448

Hotel du Fort
1390 rue du Fort
Montreal, QC H3H 2R7
Canada
(514) 938-8333

MONTREUX JAZZ FESTIVAL

July
Montreux, Switzerland
www.montreuxjazz.com
Admission: $$–$$$

The Montreux Jazz Festival is nearing its fourth decade of jazz celebrations. It would be hard to calculate exactly how many acts and spectators have passed through this stunning environment known as the Swiss Riviera. It's also fair to wager that many a fledgling jazz career has been founded upon one of the performances witnessed on these stages. Montreux is probably one of the few places in the world where you can enjoy jazz music on a train. And did we mention the boat performances? Various traditional venues such as clubs, cafes, casinos, and auditoriums (including the wonderfully named Miles Davis Hall) also get into the act during this two-week stretch of live performances. You can expect to hear jazz and blues regulars such as Dr. John and Buddy Guy as well as radio heavyweights such as David Bowie and Paul Simon.

For more information: (41) 021-963-8282

Camping: No

Accommodations

■ **Hotel La Rouvenaz**
1 Rue du Marché
Montreux, Switzerland
(41) 021-963-2736

■ **Hotel Elite**
25 Avenue du Casino
Montreux, Switzerland
(41) 021-966-0303
hotel.elite@vtx.ch

MORRO BAY JAZZUARY FESTIVAL

January
Morro Bay, California
www.morro-bay.net/jazz
Admission: $$

Beautiful Morro Bay is a great location in southern California where you can continue your New Year's celebrations at the Morro Bay Jazzuary Festival. Count on three days of acts to represent the liveliest aspects of jazz: Dixieland, swing, and zydeco, to name a few. Four different venues participate in the festivities, and for all the variety-seekers, a free trolley car provides transportation between them all.

For more information: jazz@morro-bay.net

Camping: Yes, available in the nearby Morro Dunes. Call (805) 772-2722.

Accommodations

■ **Econo Lodge**
1100 Main St.
Morro Bay, CA 93442
(805) 772-5609

■ **Best Value Inn**
220 Beach St.
Morro Bay, CA 93442
(805) 772-3333

♪ MT. HOOD JAZZ FESTIVAL

August
Gresham, Oregon
www.mthoodjazz.com
Admission: $$

For more than twenty years, the Cascade Mountains in Gresham, Oregon, have served as the gathering place for an exuberant weekend of live jazz, good food, and good drink. Classical jazz, classic jazz, jazz classics, and eclectic, non-traditional jazz groups that are totally classic perform. Throughout the two-day event, local breweries and vineyards proudly show off their latest products. The grounds are perfect for camping and a recently improved 14-mile bike trail leads in and out of the park, an excellent perk for riding enthusiasts. Past events have included appearances by Kenny Barron, Stefon Harris, and critically acclaimed vocalist Nnenna Freelon.

Artist Submissions
Bill Royston
Mt. Hood Jazz Festival
P.O. Box 2043
Gresham, OR 97030
Royston@mthoodjazz.com

For more information: (503) 665-3827 or info@mthoodjazz.com

Camping: Yes

Accommodations

■ **Golden Knight Motel**
750 E. Powell Blvd.
Gresham, OR 97030
(503) 665-9127

■ **Gresham Suites**
24124 SE Stark St.
Gresham, OR 97030
(503) 465-1515

■ **Pony Soldier Inn**
1060 NE Cleveland Ave.
Gresham, OR 97030
(503) 665-1591

■ **Shilo Inn Hotel Gresham**
2752 NE Hogan Dr.
Gresham, OR 97030
(503) 907-1777

NEW ORLEANS JAZZ & HERITAGE FESTIVAL

April/May
New Orleans, Louisiana
www.nojazzfest.com
Admission: $$–$$$

It shouldn't take too much enticement from anyone to consider making a trip to bizarre and beautiful New Orleans. Day after day, the city is rife with parties, concerts, and a lively atmosphere that would bring the most avid partygoer to a standstill.

But the New Orleans Jazz & Heritage Festival has been gathering momentum over the years, and this weeklong celebration just might be the best time to experience life in the bayou. Music from all walks of life—big name rock bands, southern-style R&B, gospel, folk, hip-hop—comes together during this festival. It's the kind of event where you can follow up a performance by Hootie & The Blowfish with one by the great Dr. John. You can see The Band perform in all their rootsy glory and then explore the boogie-woogie stylings of the latest Professor Longhair protégé. The majority of events take place at the Heritage Fair at the Fairgrounds Race Course, but the always lively French Quarter is just ten minutes away.

Of course the food is on par with any of the acts you might see on the big stages. Crawfish étouffée, shrimp po'boys, alligator sausage, creole stuffed bread, gumbo, beignets, and red beans and rice will quickly have you rethinking your proposed diet.

Artist Submissions
New Orleans Jazz & Heritage Festival
attn: Music Production
336 Camp St., Ste. 250
New Orleans, LA 70130
(504) 410-4100
Camping: No

Accommodations

■ **Chateau Hotel**
1001 Rue Chartres
New Orleans, LA 70116
(504) 524-9636

■ **Historic French Market Inn**
501 Rue Decatur
New Orleans, LA 70130
(888) 487-1543

NEWPORT BEACH JAZZ FESTIVAL

May
Newport Beach, California
www.newportbeachjazzfestival.com
Admission: $$–$$$

The Newport Beach Jazz Festival recently relocated to a new venue that's more suited to loud music and able to accommodate thousands of visitors, so get ready to enjoy the great picnic weather and excellent music in a relaxing setting. Classic acts such as WAR and the Average White Band have performed in the past. There's parking at the venue itself, and the Double Tree Hotel offers its guests free transportation to the festival grounds.

For more information: nbjf@ritz-entertainment.com
Camping: No
Accommodations

■ **Double Tree Hotel**
90 Pacifica Ave.
Irvine, CA 92618
(949) 471-8888
www.doubletreeirvinespectrum.com

■ **Radisson Hotel**
4545 MacArthur Blvd.
Newport Beach, CA 92660
(949) 833-0570

NORTH SEA JAZZ FESTIVAL

Mid-July
The Hague, Netherlands
www.northseajazz.nl
Admission: $$–$$$

When it began in 1976, the North Sea Jazz Festival was a simple, three-day event featuring a few notable performers and welcoming only a few thousand locals and tourists. Now tens of thousands of people flock from all corners of the Earth to catch acts such as Wynton Marsalis, Tony Bennett,

and Herbie Hancock performing in open-air venues. Children are made especially welcome here; the festival's traditional "Gigs For Kids" gives the young
ones a chance to experience music at their own level.

For more information: (31) 152-14-8393 (fax)

Camping: No

Accommodations

■ **Parkhotel Den Haag**
Molenstraat 53
2513 BJ
The Hague

■ **Royal Dutch Lion Hotel**
Laan van Meerdervoort 108
2517 AS
The Hague

OLD PASADENA JAZZFEST

Mid-July
Pasadena, California
www.omegaevents.com/oldpasadena/index.html
Admission: $$

Old town Pasadena is the backdrop for this classic festival, which mixes up a
variety of performers and styles in a wonderfully intimate outdoor envi-
ronment. Local food vendors and restaurants provide a diverse mix of fla-
vors for jazz fans. The festival even sets up a temporary music shop to enable
visitors to meet some of the artists and purchase music. Pete Escovedo, The
Rippingtons, and quiet storm soul crooner Jeffery Osbourne have all per-
formed here in the past.

For more information: (818) 771-5544 or info@omegaevents.com

Camping: No

Accommodations

■ **Pasadena Hilton**
168 S. Los Robles Ave.
Pasadena, CA 91101
(626) 577-1000

■ **Econo Lodge**
2860 E. Colorado Blvd.
Pasadena, CA 91107
(626) 792-3700

OREGON FESTIVAL OF AMERICAN MUSIC

August
Eugene, Oregon

www.ofam.org

Admission: $$

Every year this Oregon-based festival masterfully pulls together thematically linked jazz events, all the while paying careful attention to ensure a variety of genres are represented. Advisor Dick Hyman has years of experience as solo recording artist and as the composer/arranger for Woody Allen's films. He brings a touch of perfection to the events, creating lineups that mix swing, classical, bebop, and American roots music. The 2002 festival was a tribute to the genius of George and Ira Gershwin, complete with film screenings and performances that showed the versatility of the brothers' music (with smooth and traditional jazz takes on the Gershwin oeuvre). You can be assured that the best has yet to come.

For more information: info@ofam.net

Camping: No

Accommodations

■ **Hilton Eugene and Conference Center**
66 E. 6th Ave.
Eugene, OR 97401
(541) 342-2000
www.eugene.hilton.com

■ **Valley River Inn**
1000 Valley River Way
Eugene, OR 97401
(800) 543-8266
www.valleyriverinn.com

PARK CITY JAZZ FESTIVAL

August

Park City, Utah

www.parkcityjazz.com

Admission: $$–$$$

The ski resort town of Park City welcomed 15,000 people to its most recent jazz festival. This well-attended event stretches out over three days in four different venues all around town. Just five years old, the Park City Jazz Festival specializes in booking some of the biggest names in smooth jazz and quiet storm-style soul: Natalie Cole, Al Jarreau, and Acoustic Alchemy have all been recent guests.

For more information: info@parkcityjazz.com

Camping: No

Accommodations

■ **Yarrow Resort Hotel**
1800 Park Ave.
Park City, UT 84060
(800) 927-7964
www.yarrowresort.com

■ **Best Western Landmark Inn**
6560 N. Landmark Dr.
Park City, UT 84098
(800) 548-8824
sales@bwlandmarkinn.com
www.bwlandmarkinn.com

♪ PLAYBOY JAZZ FESTIVAL

Mid-June
Los Angeles, California
www.playboy.com
Admission: $$–$$$

The Playboy Jazz Festival has been providing jazz entertainment to Southern California for almost a quarter of a century now. It's one of the best-known jazz festivals in the world, due in part to its consistently strong lineups—well, that and the bunny ears. Traditionally held at the Hollywood Bowl, the event gathers an assortment of jazz greats, mixes in some smoother elements, and adds a sprinkling of Latin and world acts to liven things up. Bill Cosby usually presides as emcee, which means even the breaks between acts are worth sticking around for. Grover Washington, Jr., Etta James, and Herbie Hancock represent just a fraction of the guests that this frequently sold-out event has gathered in the past.

Camping: No

Accommodations

■ **Holiday Inn Hollywood**
2005 N. Highland Ave.
Hollywood, CA 90068
(800) 645-5901

■ **Liberty Hotel**
1770 Orchid Ave.
Hollywood, CA 90028
(323) 962-1788
liberty@travelbase.com

♪ PUERTO RICO HEINEKEN JAZZ FESTIVAL

May
San Juan, Puerto Rico
www.prheinekenjazz.com
Admission: $$–$$$

The Puerto Rico Heineken Jazz Festival does its best to spotlight some of the biggest acts in the Latin jazz genre. Since its inception in 1991, this celebration has juxtaposed live performances from Chucho Valdes and Eddie Palimieri with more straightforward sets by the likes of George Benson and Al Jarreau. The festival began simply as a way for players on the island to get together but has since blossomed into an internationally known event.

For more information: (787) 277-9200

Camping: No

Accommodations

■ **Hyatt Dorado Beach**
Hwy. 693
Dorado, PR 646
(800) 233-1234
http://doradobeach.hyatt.com

■ **At Wind Chimes Inn**
1750 Ashford Ave.
San Juan 00911 PR
(800) 946-3244

RENO JAZZ FESTIVAL

Early May
Reno, Nevada
www.dce.unr.edu/jazz
Admission: $–$$

This festival is brought together by the people at the University of Nevada in Reno, which explains the emphasis placed on the educational aspects and advancement possibilities of jazz. Critiques follow many of the younger performers' shows, providing the musicians with feedback and tips. Individual tickets are available for the larger concerts, which in the past have featured artists such as Bobby Hutcherson and Nicholas Payton, and ticket packages are offered for those who want to experience all facets of this respected festival. Of course, getting to the festival in the first place is contingent upon whether or not you can pry yourself away from the nickel slots.

For more information: jazz@unr.edu

Camping: No

Accommodations

■ **Holiday Inn & Diamonds Casino**
1000 E. Sixth St.
Reno, NV 89512
(800) 648-4877

■ **Sands Regency Hotel Casino**
345 N. Arlington Ave.
Reno, NV 89501
(800) 648-3553
admin@sandsregency.com
www.sandsregency.com

RIMOUSKI FESTI JAZZ INTERNATIONAL

Labor Day weekend
Rimouski, Quebec, Canada
www.festijazzrimouski.com
Admission: $$–$$$

More than one hundred musicians can be expected to perform over a four-day period at the Rimouski Festi Jazz International Festival. All manner of clubs, cafes, and restaurants—not far from the St. Lawrence River—participate in the event, while the high profile showcases take place at the Georges-Beaulieu Auditorium. Wayne Shorter, Holly Cole, Dizzy Gillespie, and Spyro Gyra have all passed through Rimouski.

For more information: festijazz@globetrotter.qc.ca

Camping: No

Accommodations

■ **Hotel Rimouski**
225, boul. René-Lepage Est
Rimouski QC G5L 1P2
Canada
(800) 463-0755
hotelrim@hotelrimouski.com
www.hotelrimouski.com

■ **Hotel Gouverneur**
155, René-Lepage East Blvd.
Rimouski QC G5L 1P2
Canada
(888)·910-1111
www.gouverneur.com

ROYAL BANK GLASGOW JAZZ FESTIVAL

June/July
Glasgow, Scotland
www.jazzfest.co.uk
Admission: $$–$$$

The Royal Bank Jazz Festival takes place in the Merchant City area of Glasgow. Merchant City has been a mecca for artisans and traders since the seventeenth century, so it makes sense that it exists today as one the most lively shopping and entertainment districts in all of the United Kingdom. But the jazz festival has only been around for the past sixteen years, so it's a relative babe in the woods. Recent performers at this gathering have included artists who weave in and out of the jazz spectrum—ranging from McCoy Tyner to Isaac Hayes to jazz/electronic favorite, St. Germain.

For more information: glasgow@jazzfest.co.uk

Camping: No

Accommodations

■ **The Beardmore Hotel**
Beardmore Street, Clydebank
Glasgow G81 4SA Scotland
(44) 0-141-951-6000
beardmore.hotel@hci.co.uk
www.beardmore-hotel.co.uk

■ **City Inn**
Finnieston Quay
Glasgow G3 8HN Scotland
(44) 0-141-240-1002
glasgow@cityinn.com
www.cityinn.com

SAN DIEGO THANKSGIVING DIXIELAND FESTIVAL

November or December
San Diego, California
www.dixielandjazzfestival.org/jazzfest.html
Admission: $$$

What would Thanksgiving be without Dixieland? For most of us, it would just be another Thanksgiving—but in San Diego, the two go hand in hand. Held at the Town & Country Resort Center, this festival offers several indoor settings where you can enjoy a variety of early jazz sounds. Musicians come from everywhere—from New Orleans to Germany—to get together to create a hotbed of fiery soloing and improvisation. Straw hats not provided.

For more information: sandiegothanksgiving@dixielandjazzfestival.org
Camping: No
Accommodations
■ **Town & Country Resort Hotel**
500 Hotel Circle North
San Diego, CA 92108
(800) 772-8527
www.towncountry.com

SAN FRANCISCO JAZZ FESTIVAL

October–November
San Francisco, California
www.sfjazz.org
Admission: $$–$$$

The San Francisco Jazz Festival primarily stretches itself out over the months of October and November but also features a spring season, which means both tourists and locals have plenty of opportunities to experience some of the finest jazz festival programming around. The events are organized by the

San Francisco Jazz Organization, a nonprofit group devoted both to jazz education and to audience expansion. The festival has been a fixture in the city for the past 20 years and will undoubtedly continue on for the next 20. The 2002 festival was typically star-studded, featuring performances from Ornette Coleman, Yusef Lateef, and unsung guitar genius James "Blood" Ulmer. Rare appearances by great Brazilian vocalist Caetano Veloso and legendary country singer Merle Haggard were also scheduled into the program. You can look forward to checking out these shows in some of the most stunning venues in the city, from Grace Cathedral to the Masonic Auditorium to the Herbst Theatre. You most certainly will want to buy your tickets in advance.

For more information: mailbox@sfjazz.org

Camping: No

Accommodations

■ **Maxwell Hotel**
386 Geary St.
San Francisco, CA 94102
(888) 734-6299

■ **Hotel Triton**
42 Grant Ave.
San Francisco, CA 94108
(800) 800-1299

RANDALL KLINE *is the co-founder of the nonprofit organization SFJAZZ and the lead organizer of the San Francisco Jazz Festival. His contributions to the jazz scene in San Francisco are as valuable today as the famed North Beach haunts of the past once were. Here, he gives us a brief history of a life dedicated to jazz along with some words to the wise for young upstarts.*

Why did you choose to work in this field to begin with?

It kind of chose me. I was a music performance major at San Francisco State University. I wanted to be a jazz musician. I was a jazz lover. During my senior year, I got the idea that I could produce a series of jazz concerts that would help me pay my way through school. It turned out to be not such a great idea. Eventually, I ended up leaving school to repay my debts. I was seduced into the idea that I wanted to produce a concert. I thought it would be easy. You hire a band you love, you get them onstage—then you collect the kudos and the money. [laughter] I learned a lot. I took some off night acts and had them perform in my six concert series. It was an artistic success. A couple concerts paid their own way, the rest didn't. The ones that didn't put a lot of pressure on me. I had to learn how to do publicity. I had to learn how to do marketing. I had to learn ticket selling, poster design—I did everything. It was like when the Little Rascals put on a show—only slightly more professional. (I would like to think now, anyway.)

At what point did it become worth the effort?

It's always been worth it to a certain degree. I wouldn't have done it the second year if it hadn't been worth the effort. But it started changing character in the late eighties and early nineties. It started blossoming, and the idea of the San Francisco Jazz Organization started emerging. By 1990, we were running three events, but we had a big deficit. We couldn't figure it out: we were doing well, the shows were good and well attended, but our small staff was scrambling. We decided to throw all our eggs in one basket in 1992 and put together a huge festival that incorporated film, big concerts, and outdoor events. It was our tenth anniversary. We were starting to get some national press, the jazz magazines were writing about us. It was a big risk—and it worked. It was a watershed year for us and it also featured some of the best programming we've done. We did a solo Cecil Taylor show. We recreated Charles Mingus's *Epitaph*. We put Dizzy Gillespie together with a big band again.

What would you tell a potential organizer who is currently in the situation you were in twenty-one years ago?

Passion, passion, passion. Research, research, research. Having the passion is the easy part—doing the homework is the hard part. You have to figure out what you're going to do and how it's going to happen, and you have to be patient. You should be willing to change and learn from others. My credo is "look who's doing it right." *How* do they do it right? Someone spent many years and lots of effort learning how to do one thing really well. Can you apply that to how you want to do your thing? We used the Boston Symphony Orchestra (among others) as our model. This model works well for arts programming. We're still learning from that model. It's a more sophisticated application of good business for a cultural good.

SAN JOSE JAZZ FESTIVAL

August
San Jose, California
www.sanjosejazz.org
Admission: FREE

Organized by the San Jose Jazz Society, this event gathers some of the largest festival crowds in the south bay area. At last count more than 150,000 people enjoyed more than 90 different performances on nine major stages here. The main stage is located in San Jose's Cesar Chavez Plaza, right in the heart of the vibrant downtown area. The festival is also broadcast to more than one hundred different public radio affiliates, expanding the audience even farther. Best of all, this event is free. Because of the large array of musicians and stages, the San Jose Jazz Festival can include elements of Latin jazz, big band, blues, and world music without alienating any purists in the audience.

For more information: jazzmaster@sanjosejazz.org
Camping: No
Accommodations

■ **Wyndham Hotel San Jose**
1350 N. First St.
San Jose, CA 95112
(408) 453-6200
www.wyndham.com/SanJose

■ **Fairmont Hotel**
70 S. Market St.
San Jose, CA 95113
(408) 998-1900
sanjose@fairmont.com
www.fairmont.com

SAN SEBASTIAN JAZZ FESTIVAL

July
San Sebastian, Spain
www.jazzaldia.com
Admission: FREE–$$

San Sebastian's jazz festival, its history stretching back nearly 40 years, provides an excellent mixture of top acts performing in various halls, clubs, and cafés around the city. A large portion of the events are free, making it hard to pass up this blend of Spanish and American jazz if you're in the area. Funk greats such as James Brown and Maceo Parker are up on the bill alongside contemporary jazz greats such as Chick Corea and Elvin Jones. The jam session arranged by the festival and featuring some of the biggest names in Spanish jazz is guaranteed to be a major highlight.

For more information: jazzaldia.donostia@donostia.org

Camping: No

Accommodations

■ **Hotel Orly**

Plaza Zaragoza, 4

20007 San Sebastian

Spain

(34) 943-463-200

■ **Hotel Zaragoza Plaza**

Plaza Zaragoza 3

20 007 San Sebastian

Spain

(34) 943-452-103

www.hotelzaragozaplaza.com

♪ SANTA FE JAZZ & INTERNATIONAL MUSIC FESTIVAL

October

Santa Fe, New Mexico

www.santafejazzfestival.com

Admission: $–$$

The Santa Fe Jazz & International Music Festival is an ambitious 18-day festival with a solid lineup that relies heavily on the best in mainstream jazz multi-instrumentalists—with a wealth of Latin styles thrown in for good measure. First organized in 2000 by the Open Arts Foundation, the festival has already booked top players and innovators such as Bill Frisell, Patricia Barber, and pianist Geri Allen. In addition, thousands of local children have learned about jazz fundamentals thanks to this festival's commitment to educational workshops.

For more information: info@santafejazzfestival.com

Camping: No

Accommodations

■ **Hilton Santa Fe**

100 Sandoval St.

Santa Fe, NM 87501

(800) 336-3676

www.hiltonofsantafe.com

■ **Old Santa Fe Inn**

320 Galisteo St.

Santa Fe, NM 87501

(800) 745-9910

www.oldsantafeinn.com

♪ SASKTEL SASKATCHEWAN JAZZ FESTIVAL

June

Saskatoon, Saskatchewan, Canada

www.saskjazz.com/#sask

Admission: FREE–$$

Saskatchewan's annual jazz festival is a well-organized mixture of ticketed and free events likely to please a large majority of people. By mixing up jazz and blues favorites such as Oscar Lopez and Son Seals with younger funk and hip-hop acts such as Antibalas and The Herbaliser, the festival programmers are definitely making sure that the music is both excellent and eclectic.

For more information: jazz@sk.sympatico.ca

Camping: No

Accommodations

■ **Saskatoon Inn**
2002 Airport Dr.
Saskatoon, SK S7L 6M4
Canada
(306) 242-1440

■ **Imperial 400**
610 Idylwyld Dr. North
Saskatoon, SK S7L 0Z2
Canada
(306) 244-2901

♪ SATCHMO SUMMERFEST

August
New Orleans, Louisiana
www.satchmosummerfest.com
Admission: FREE–$

For most people, the New Orleans Jazz & Heritage Festival (see page 286) is the fest to set your schedule around when planning a visit to this beautiful, swampy town. While the relatively new Satchmo Summerfest may not pack the streets in quite the same manner, it is definitely worth your time. There is probably no better place to experience all things Louis Armstrong than in this town. The architecture and landscape provide the ultimate backdrop for listening to his music; a walk through the French Quarter finds almost every other store piping great tracks such as "St. Louis Blues" and "Ain't Misbehavin'" through the speakers. It is obvious that this festival is dear to the hearts of the locals.

Satchmo Summerfest is small and relatively intimate. Four stages are set up around the historic mint, providing a space for friends and families to get together and fan themselves in the scarce amounts of shade, happily eating their requisite helpings of red beans and rice. All bets are off once the music kicks in and as groups such as the New Birth Brass Band breathe new life into the sounds of early jazz, rediscovering the soul and downright funkiness of this music. Dancers young and old take to the grass and effortlessly swing and shake and sweat to the groove just as people always have and always will.

If it's a history lesson you're after, then getting a grasp on Satchmo himself is easy to do with the numerous lectures and panel discussions designed for experts to wax informatively on the man. Several tables are set up selling books that don't just trace the story of Louis Armstrong but survey the history of jazz and gospel as well.

For more information: info@frenchquarterfestivals.org

Camping: No

Accommodations

■ **Chateau Hotel**
1001 Rue Chartres
New Orleans, LA 70116
(504) 524-9636

■ **Historic French Market Inn**
501 Rue Decatur
New Orleans, LA 70130
(888) 487-1543

♪ SIOUX FALLS JAZZ AND BLUES FESTIVAL

July

Sioux Falls, South Dakota

http://jazzfestsiouxfalls.com

Admission: *FREE*

South Dakota's Sioux Falls Jazz and Blues Festival is a two-day event that takes place during the third weekend in July. Previous attendance rates have pushed the 70,000 mark, no doubt due to the free cost of admission. The outside setting provides the perfect atmosphere for enjoying the urban blues of Delbert McClinton, the zydeco of C. J. Chenier, or the swing of Lavay Smith & The Red Hot Skillet Lickers—to name just a few of the past performers. Organizers provide plenty of activities for the kids and ATMs for the adults. Also, heat is a given in those South Dakota summers, so be sure to leave the pets at home and bring some sort of festive outdoor hat.

For more information: (605) 335-6101

Camping: No

Accommodations

■ **Holiday Inn Downtown City Center**
100 W. 8th St.
Sioux Falls, SD 57104
(605) 339-2000

■ **Residence Inn**
4509 W. Empire Pl.
Sioux Falls, SD 57106
(605) 361-2202

SISTERS JAZZ FESTIVAL

Mid-September
Sisters, Oregon
www.sistersjazzfestival.com
Admissions: $$

The Sisters Jazz Festival brings together an eclectic lineup that features everything from high school jazz ensembles to stomping, New Orleans-style combos. Three different venues offer up a variety of backdrops in which to enjoy the performances. The extraordinarily scenic town of Sisters is located just east of the Cascade Mountains and offers some of the best natural environments in which to relax and enjoy the music.

For more information: (800) 549-1332 or jazz@sistersjazzfestival.com

Camping: No

Accommodations

■ **Best Western Ponderosa Lodge**
505 Hwy. 20 W.
P.O. Box 218
Sisters, OR 97759
(541) 549-1234

■ **Comfort Inn**
540 US 20 W.
Sisters, OR 97759
(541) 549-7829

SLEEPING GIANT SWING 'N' JAZZ JUBILEE

Mid-June
Helena, Montana
www.helenajazz.com
Admission: $$$

The title does not mislead: this Montana festival delivers a healthy dose of classic swing with plenty of sounds from the bayou. Held in the state capital of Helena, this friendly get-together offers plenty of opportunities to dance to raging hot ragtime and Dixieland music from a mixture of established acts and youth ensembles.

For more information: director@helenajazz.com

Camping: No

Accommodations

■ **Elkhorn Mountain Inn**
1 Jackson Creek Rd.
Montana City, MT 59634
(406) 442-6625

■ **Knight's Rest Inn**
1831 Euclid
Helena, MT 59601
(406) 442-6384

SNOWBIRD JAZZ AND BLUES FESTIVAL

Last weekend in July
Snowbird, Utah
www.snowbirdjazz.com/jazz&blues2.html
Admission: $$–$$$

The last weekend in July is typically when the Snowbird Jazz and Blues Festival takes a hold of the popular ski resort town of Snowbird, Utah. Fans come here both for the environment and to see artists such Koko Taylor and Sergio Mendes perform but are also treated to a wide variety of food and unique crafts. Travel package deals, featuring concert tickets and lodging, are available to those who are able to plan their trip in advance.

For more information: Call (801) 933-2110 for festival information. Call (800) 453-3000 for information on the travel package.

Camping: No
Accommodations
■ **Snowbird Ski and Summer Resort**
Little Cottonwood Canyon
Hwy. 210
Snowbird, UT 84092-9000
(800) 453-3000

ST. LUCIA JAZZ FESTIVAL

May
St. Lucia, West Indies
http://stluciajazz.org
Admission: $$

The island of St. Lucia is a democratic nation unto itself but can also be counted as a member of the British Commonwealth; as such, it's brimming with a vibrant mixture of English and Caribbean cultures. Each successive jazz festival held here finds itself invested with the truly unique spirit of the island. Both the main and side stages overflow with local and international talent ranging from new age to fusion to straightforward R&B. Gladys Knight, Pharoah Sanders, Herbie Hancock, and newcomer Angie Stone, all past performers, are prime examples of the sort of diversity you'll find here.

Camping: No

Accommodations

■ **Rex. St. Lucian**
P.O. Box 512, Reduit Beach
Castries, St. Lucia
(758) 452 8351
stlslu@rexresorts.net
www.rexcaribbean.com

■ **Cara Suites**
La Pansee
P.O. Box 1109
Castries, St. Lucia
(758) 452-4767
carasuiteslc@carahotels.com
www.carahotels.com/st_lucia.htm

♪ STOCKHOLM JAZZ FESTIVAL

Mid-July
Stockholm, Sweden
www.stockholmjazz.com
Admission: $$–$$$

The Stockholm Jazz Festival takes place on the island of Skeppsholmen, right in the center of Stockholm. Skeppsholmen is also the home of several museums so it makes perfect sense that this area provides a small refuge for those looking to indulge in the pleasures of the musical arts. More than 40 events are staged here with a heavy slant placed on Swedish acts, but with a few internationally renowned artists appearing as well. (Both Chaka Khan and John Scofield were recent performers.) The musical map is traversed several times over, as performances mix up jazz, blues, funk, soul, R&B, and other genres.

For more information: info@stockholmjazz.com

Camping: No

Accommodations

■ **Radisson SAS Strand Hotel**
Nybrokajen, 9
P.O. Box 16396 S-103 27 Stockholm
Sweden
(46) 850-66-4000
Sales.Strand.Stockholm@
 RadissonSAS.com
www.radissonsas.com

■ **Radisson SAS Royal Viking Hotel**
Vasagatan, 1
P.O. Box 234 S-101 24 Stockholm
Sweden
(46) 850-65-4000
Sales.Royal.Stockholm@
 RadissonSAS.com
www.radissonsas.com

♪ SUMMIT JAZZ

September
Denver, Colorado

www.summitjazz.org/sjw.html

Admission: $$

For three days in September, Colorado's Summit Jazz Foundation organizes an intimate jazz festival at the Hyatt Regency Tech Center in Denver. This event brings together fans of big band, swing, traditional jazz, and ragtime and provides a forum for educating people in the ways of collective improvisation.

For more information: summitjazz@compuserve.com

Camping: No

Accommodations

■ **Hyatt Regency Tech Center**
7800 E. Tufts Ave.
Denver, CO 80237
(303) 779-1234

■ **Loews Denver Hotel**
4150 E. Mississippi Ave.
Denver, CO 80246
(800) 235-6397

♪ SUNCOM JAZZ NORFOLK CONCERT

August

Norfolk, Virginia

www.festeventsva.org/festevents/jazz_Blues.htm

Admission: $$

Located at the waterfront park of Town Point, just minutes from popular shopping destination the MacArthur Center, the SunCom Jazz concert presents a fine forum for young and old alike to enjoy the best in contemporary jazz. The concert is a single-day event, but many local venues provide related entertainment in the days before and after.

For more information: festevents@festevents.org

Camping: No

Accommodations

■ **Norfolk Waterfront Marriott**
235 E. Main St.
Norfolk, VA 23510
(800) 228-9290
www.norfolkmarriott.com

■ **Best Western Center Inn**
One Best Square
Norfolk, VA 23502
(800) 237-5517

♪ SWING'N'DIXIE JAZZ JAMBOREE

Mid-October

Sun Valley, Idaho

http://sunvalleyjazz.com

Admission: $$–$$$

Spending five days in the scenic ski resort town of Sun Valley is a vacation in and of itself, but adding a traditional jazz festival to the agenda really sweetens the deal. Enjoy the music of the twenties and take your pick of any of the other events happening around town. A shuttle bus will soothe your transportation woes while big band sounds soothe the ears.

For more information: (208) 344-3768

Camping: Yes. RV Camping is available.

Accommodations

■ **Sun Valley Lodge**
Sun Valley Rd.
Sun Valley, ID 83353
(800) 786-8259

■ **Elkhorn Lodge**
100 Elkhorn Rd.
Sun Valley, ID 83354
(208) 622-4511

♩ TANGLEWOOD JAZZ FESTIVAL

August–September

Lenox, Massachusetts

www.bso.org

Admission: $$–$$$

Tanglewood is most commonly known as the home of the Boston Symphony Orchestra, but as the summer evenings turn to fall, the sounds of jazz begin to fill the air. Tanglewood, part of a family estate donated by Mary Aspinwall Tappan back in 1936, is located in the Berkshire Mountains in northwestern Massachusetts, one of the more luscious regions of the East Coast. Since the donation of the grounds, Tanglewood has become a cultural center for music appreciation. The jazz festival is comprised of various ticketed afternoon and evening events. Previous programs have welcomed artists such as Diana Krall, Dave Brubeck, and Jimmy McGriff.

For more information: customerService@bso.org

Camping: No

Accommodations

■ **Crowne Plaza Hotel**
One West St.
Pittsfield, MA 01201
(413) 499-2000
crplaza@berkshire.net

■ **Howard Johnson Express Inn**
462 Pittsfield Rd.
Lenox, MA 01240
(800) 446-4656

TELLURIDE JAZZ CELEBRATION

Early August
Telluride, Colorado
www.telluridejazz.com
Admission: $$–$$$

Combining thoughtful organization with an ideal location, the Telluride Jazz Celebration manages to create a unique festival that should appeal to both the performer and the audience member. An institution in Colorado since 1977, this festival treats folks to afternoons of natural splendor and evenings of high-altitude carousing. Telluride prides itself on a diverse lineup; past performers have included Jon Hendricks, Charlie Hunter, and Spyro Gyra.
For more information: Paul@telluridejazz.com
Camping: Yes. Call (970) 728-7009 or reserve a spot here: www.telluridejazz.com/ticket.html
Accommodations

■ **Wyndham Peaks Resort**
136 Country Club Dr.
Mountain Village
P.O. Box 2702
Telluride Mountain Village, CO 81435
(800) 789-2220
dcarey@wyndham.com
www.thepeaksresort.com

■ **The Ice House**
310 S. Fir
P.O. Box 2909
Telluride, CO 81435
(800) 544-3436
nfo@icehouselodge.com
www.icehouselodge.com

TIME IN JAZZ

August
Berchidda, Italy
www.timeinjazz.it
Admission: $$

Italy's Time in Jazz Festival celebrated its fifteenth anniversary in 2002. Each year, the festival ensures that jazz has a uniquely defined space in Europe. Time in Jazz encourages improvisation and multiculturalism, and it's not uncommon to see French, Dutch, Italian, and American performers all onstage together. Well-regarded flamenco artist Geraldo Nunez and pianist Uri Caine represent the caliber of artists booked here.

For more information: info@timeinjazz.it

Camping: No

Accommodations

■ **Sos Chelyos**
Via Umberto I 52
7022 Berchidda
Italy
(39) 079-704-921

■ **Nuovo Limbara**
Vicolo Coghinas 1
7022 Berchidda
Italy
(39) 079-704-165

TORONTO DOWNTOWN JAZZ FESTIVAL

June
Toronto, Ontario, Canada
www.tojazz.com
Admission: FREE–$$

Bringing quality jazz to Toronto since 1987, the Downtown Jazz Festival brings renowned headliners to the main stages in the evening while filling the days with free events featuring some extraordinary local and national talent. You'll be able to witness spellbinding vocal jazz, swampy New Orleans rhythms, and classic piano stylings in some of Toronto's best music venues. The history of the Downtown Jazz Festival has been a colorful one—Miles Davis, Sarah Vaughan, and Joshua Redman are just a few examples of the notable names from festivals past.

For more information: tdjs@torontojazz.com

Camping: No

Accommodations

■ **Toronto Colony Hotel**
89 Chestnut St.
Toronto, ON M5G 1R1
Canada
(800) 387-8687
www.colonyhoteltoronto.com

■ **Stratchcona Hotel**
60 York St.
At Wellington St.
Toronto, ON M5J 1S8
Canada
(800) 268-8304

TRI-C JAZZFEST CLEVELAND

April
Cleveland, Ohio

www.cleveland.com/jazzfest

Admission: :FREE:-$$

The organizers of Cleveland's JazzFest have more than 20 years of experience putting this event together. In that time some of jazz music's most sacred luminaries have graced the stage: Miles Davis, Ella Fitzgerald, and Sarah Vaughan are a few names you might recognize. Most of the well-known artists perform around the city in venues that require tickets, but there are also many free and child-friendly shows staged during the festival's run. Tri-C JazzFest Cleveland also reaches out to thousands of students every year through workshops and performances.

For more information: terri.pontremoli@tri-c.edu

Camping: No

Accommodations

■ **Hilton Garden Inn**
1100 Carnegie Ave.
Cleveland, OH 44115
(216) 658-6400

■ **Sheraton City Centre**
777 St. Clair Ave.
Cleveland, OH 44114
(800) 321-1090

ULRICHSBERGER KALEIDOPHON

May

Ulrichsberg, Austria

www.jazzatelier.at

Admission: $$

The roots of this Austrian festival stretch back almost 30 years, and, like most festivals, it was started by a small group of people with a serious passion for music and a desire to share that passion with others. The organization Jazzatelier Ulrichsberg was founded in 1973 with the intention of putting on the occasional jazz show. Since then the idea has grown to encompass several high profile concerts per year, art and media installations, and the Ulrichsberger Kaleidophon festival. All of the concert events take place inside a home purchased by the organizers. In the past, performers such as Sun Ra and Evan Parker have recorded live albums in this unique setting. The focus here in Ulrichsberg is on the outer limits of jazz—and beyond. Past performers have included Peter Brotzmann, Cecil Taylor, and the experimental electronics of Christian Fennesz.

For more information: afischer@jazzatelier.at

Camping: No

Accommodations

■ **Hotel Böhmerwaldhof**
Kirchengasse 4
A-4161 Ulrichsberg
Austria
(43) 07288-2218
boehmerwaldhof@netway.at
www.tiscover.com/boehmerwaldhof

■ **Pension Pfoser**
1 Ulrichsberg
Berdetschlag 39
Austria
(43) 07288-6559
info@pension-pfoser.com
www.pension-pfoser.com

♪ UNC/GREELEY JAZZ FESTIVAL

April

Greeley, Colorado

http://arts.unco.edu/uncjazz/festival/festival.html

Admission: $$

More than 300 acts come together each April for three days at the University of Northern Colorado. The UNC/Greeley Jazz Festival provides a forum for students of all ages and in the past has culminated with highly regarded performances from artists such as Bob Dorough and Bob Brookmeyer.

For more information: jazzstudies@arts.unco.edu

Camping: No

Accommodations

■ **Best Western**
701 Eighth St.
Greeley, CO 80631
(970) 353-8444

■ **Days Inn**
2467 West 29th St.
Greeley, CO 80631
(970) 330-6380

♪ VANCOUVER INTERNATIONAL JAZZ FESTIVAL

June–July

Vancouver, British Columbia, Canada

www.jazzvancouver.com

Admission: $$–$$$

This summertime event has brought many of the most prestigious figures in jazz music to the Vancouver area year after year. Dave Brubeck, Dianne Reeves, and the Buena Vista Social Club have all shared their talents at fine venues such as the Orpheum Theatre. Several other smaller venues host more intimate concerts. You can expect to hear any number of musical styles here, ranging from bebop to electronic, from ragtime to avant-garde noise. Several reasonably priced ticket packages are available, so it's best to phone ahead.

For more information: (888) GET-JAZZ or john@jazzvancouver.com

Camping: No

Accommodations

■ **Metropolitan Hotel**
645 Howe St.
Vancouver, BC V6C2Y9
Canada
(800) 667-2300
je@metropolitan.com
www.metropolitan.com/vanc

■ **Sylvia Hotel**
1154 Gilford St.
Vancouver, BC V6G 2P6
Canada
(604) 681-9321

♩ VERIZON MUSIC FESTIVAL NEW YORK

September
New York, New York
www.festivalproductions.net
Admission: FREE–$$

The Verizon Music Festival in New York is part of series of festivals put together by communications company Verizon. (Similar events take place in Florida, California, and Washington, D.C.) The New York version takes special care to include a variety of acts; large ticketed events, small club performances, and a free outdoor concert are all on the program. Though this is not strictly a jazz event, the organizers have brought in late night soul crooner Isaac Hayes and relative newcomer Oleta Adams to appear along with crowd pleasers such as the ever-entertaining Tony Bennett. A downtown program challenges audiences with noted performers such as Matthew Shipp who are sure to remind everyone what jazz is all about.

For more information: (212) 501-1390

Camping: No

Accommodations

■ **Wellington Hotel**
871 7th Ave.
New York, NY 10019
(800) 652-1212
www.wellingtonhotel.com

■ **Salisbury Hotel**
123 W. 57th St.
New York, NY 10019
(888) NYC-5757
www.nycsalisbury.com

VISION FESTIVAL

May–June
New York, New York
www.visionfestival.org
Admission: $–$$$

New York's Vision Festival has been bringing improvised music to the downtown area for seven years and has been gaining international recognition for these events organized throughout the months of May and June. With their commitment to providing a showcase for contemporary avant-garde performances from the likes of Peter Brotzmann, William Parker, and Matthew Shipp, the festival brings together the best in forward-thinking music, visual media, and dance.

For more information: info@visionfestival.org
Camping: No
Accommodations

■ **Holiday Inn**
138 Lafayette St.
New York, NY 10013
(212) 966-8898
http://holidayinn-nyc.com

■ **Chelsea Hotel**
222 W. 23rd St.
New York, NY 10011
(212) 243-3700
www.hotelchelsea.com

VITORIA-GASTEIZ JAZZ FESTIVAL

Mid-July
Vitoria-Gasteiz, Spain
www.jazzvitoria.com
Admission: $$–$$$

The Vitoria-Gasteiz Jazz Festival is the only Spanish festival acknowledged by the prestigious European Jazz Festival Organization. While that's not to say it's the only jazz festival worth checking out in Spain, it certainly means it's regarded as one of the best. Since 1977 this event has welcomed greats such as Muddy Waters, Ella Fitzgerald, and Jaco Pastorius to the stage. The blend of regional performers and current acts such as Wynton Marsalis and Joe Lovano is bound to make for a singular experience. The organizers also throw in some street performances and classic jazz festival staples such as a New Orleans-style marching band and a gospel brunch.

For more information: jazzvitoria@jazzvitoria.com

Camping: No
Accommodations

■ **Hotel General Alava**
Avda, Gasteiz 79 01009
Vitoria-Gasteiz
Spain
(34) 945-215-000
www.hga.info

■ **Hotel Barcelo Gasteiz**
Avda, Gasteiz, 45 01009
Vitoria-Gasteiz Álava
Spain
(34) 945-228-100
hotelbcgasteiz@barceloclavel.com
www.barcelo.com

WASHINGTON MUTUAL LONG ISLAND JAZZ FESTIVAL

August
Oyster Bay, New York
http://friendsofthearts.com/jazz/index.htm
Admission: $$

This festival takes place at the Planting Fields Arboretum State Historic Park on the north shore of Long Island. The beautiful outdoor environment provides the perfect setting for this event. Organized by the nonprofit group Friends of The Arts, the event gathers top acts such as Ray Charles and the Rippingtons and gets them to perform on the wonderfully landscaped grounds. If you need a break from the festivities, paths leading through the woodland areas will allow you to commune with nature.

For more information: info@friendsofthearts.com
Camping: No
Accommodations

■ **Long Island Marriott**
101 James Doolittle Blvd.
Uniondale, NY 11553
(516) 794-3800
www.marriott.com

■ **Executive Inn Woodbury**
8030 Jericho Turnpike
Woodbury, Long Island, NY 11797

WATERTOWN JAZZ FESTIVAL

July
Watertown, Tennessee
www.softek.net/glenn.martin/tennesse.htm
Admission: FREE

Frank Sinatra once sang about a town called Watertown. And while he probably never made it out to this particular jazz festival, the mythical town he
sang of couldn't have been that different from the Watertown here in Tennessee. It's a warm, friendly place that dedicates its public square for two
summer days of fine contemporary jazz. This free event takes place only 40
miles outside Nashville, so if you're in the area, you might want to think
about making a special trip.

Artist Submissions: GMartin@Softek.net

For more information: mccomb28@earthlink.net

Camping: No

Accommodations

■ **Watertown Bed and Breakfast**
116 Depot Ave.
Watertown, TN 37184
(615) 237-9999

WEST COAST JAZZ PARTY

Labor Day weekend
Irvine, California
www.westcoastjazzparty.com
Admission: $$–$$$

This Labor Day weekend event takes place in the Irvine Marriott in southern California. Catering to "right down the middle and straight ahead" jazz,
the event's organizers book well known performers for shows in the grand
ballroom, while a smattering of other events are set up just about as far from
the bar as they are from the pool. Smooth guitarist Henry Johnson and tenor
saxophonist Harry Allen have been known to entertain hotel guests and festival visitors. The Sunday brunch jazz cruise is usually a highlight of the
weekend.

For more information: (949) 759-5003

Camping: No

Accommodations

■ **Irvine Marriott**
18000 Von Karman Ave.
Irvine, CA 92612
(949) 553-0100
www.marriott.com

■ **Hyatt Regency Irvine**
17900 Jamboree Blvd.
Irvine, CA 92615
(949) 975 1234
www.irvine.hyatt.com

♪ WIGAN INTERNATIONAL JAZZ FESTIVAL

July
Wigan, United Kingdom
www.wiganjazzclub.co.uk
Admission: $–$$

The Wigan International Jazz Festival is organized by the Wigan Jazz Club, a committee dedicated to putting together shows throughout the year that culminate with July's main event. The emphasis here is often on local talent, particularly on the sounds of big band music, with Wigan's own Youth Jazz Orchestra performing for the people. Local pubs also sponsor afternoon events. The festival has also been known to book internationally respected artists such as pianist Shelly Berg and saxophone great Red Holloway.

Artist Submissions: ian.darrington@btinternet.com
For more information: wigan.jazz@virgin.net
Camping: No
Accommodations

■ **Wigan Oak Hotel**
Riverway, Wigan
Lancashire WN1 3SS
United Kingdom
(44) 01-942-826-888

■ **Quality Hotel**
Riverway, Wigan
Greater Manchester WN1 3SS
United Kingdom
(44) 01-942-826-888
admin@gb058.u-net.co
www.gb058.u-net.com

♪ WOLF TRAP JAZZ & BLUES FESTIVAL

June
Vienna, Virginia
www.wolf-trap.org
Admission: $$–$$$

The beautiful wooden stage here at Wolf Trap provides a unique context for enjoying live jazz in Virginia. A contemporary mixture of jazz and blues comes alive here during three summer days. You can expect to see the likes of classic jazz enthusiast Joshua Redman, old favorites Tower of Power, and heir apparent to the afro-funk throne Femi Kuti bring their distinctive rhythms to the proceedings.

For more information: wolftrap@wolftrap.org

Camping: No

Accommodations

■ Tysons Corner Marriott Hotel
8028 Leesburg Pike
Vienna, VA 22182
(703) 734-3200

■ Embassy Suites
Tyson's Corner
8517 Leesburg Pike
Vienna, VA 22182
(703) 883-0707

♪ ZIEGLER KETTLE MORAINE JAZZ FESTIVAL

September
West Bend, Wisconsin
www.kmjazz.com
Admission: $$

Southeastern Wisconsin becomes a hotbed of contemporary jazz activity in September thanks to the organizers at the West Bend Sunrise Rotary Club. A huge tent covers the stage where performers such as Chuck Mangione, Spyro Gyra, and Ramsey Lewis display their finely tuned chops. An excellent array of regional restaurateurs and artisans provide food and crafts while attendees rest in the shade near the banks of the Milwaukee River.

For more information: (877) 271-6903

Camping: No

Accommodations

■ West Bend Fanta Suite
2520 W. Washington St.
West Bend, WI 53095
(414) 338-0636

■ Country Inn & Suites West Bend
2000 Gateway Ct.
West Bend, WI 53095

ROCK, INDIE ROCK, PUNK, and HIP-HOP

♪ ADIRONDACK MOUNTAIN MUSIC FESTIVAL

June
Lyonsdale, New York
www.adirondackmountainmusic.com
Admission: $

The Adirondack Mountain Music Festival gathers acts that range from hip-hop to folk to jazz and presents them in a great scenic environment in upstate New York, just outside of Syracuse. Attendees are free to camp and relax by the lake or rush to the stages to enjoy artists like Mos Def, John Medeski, and outstanding reggae trio Culture. Undoubtedly, stylistic parameters will be pushed.

For more information: (802) 372-6142
Camping: Yes
Accommodations

- **Edge Hotel**
P.O. Box 375
Route 12
Lyons Falls, NY 13368
(315) 348-4211
email@theedgehotel.com
www.theedgehotel.com

- **Flat Rock Inn**
Flat Rock Rd.
Martinsburg, NY 13404
(315) 376-2332
gordon@northnet.org

AGAWAM SUMMERFEST

July–August
Agawam, Massachusetts
www.agawamcc.org
Admission: $

Organized by the Agawam Rotary Club, this rain-or-shine event is great for families and friends who wish to experience a great variety of music in the outdoors. Encompassing alternative country music, rock, swing, and African rhythms, this low-profile event provides a great opportunity for up-and-coming artists to be heard in a friendly environment.

Artist Submissions
Agawam Cultural Council
36 Main St.
Agawam, MA 01001
agawam@mass-culture.org

Camping: No

Accommodations

■ **Holiday Inn Springfield**
711 Dwight St.
Springfield, MA 01104
(866) 836-9330

■ **Radisson Hotel Springfield**
1 Bright Meadow Blvd.
Enfield, CT 06082
(860) 741-2211

ALL GOOD MUSIC FESTIVAL

May
Terra Alta, West Virginia
Admission: $$

The All Good Music Festival is a yearly grassroots affair that brings together thousands of people who arrive as strangers and leave as friends. The event's intimacy and emphasis on community over consumerism—plus skilled organization and production and an eclectic music sense that leans toward jam bands, roots, bluegrass, world music, and more—make it worth your time. Previous artists include John Scofield, Sam Bush, Moe, and the Grateful Dead tribute act, Dark Star Orchestra.

Camping: Yes

Accommodations
■ Alpine Lake Resort
RR 2 Box 99D2
Terra Alta, WV 26764
(304) 789-2481

ALL TOMORROW'S PARTIES

Various dates
Various locations
www.atpfestival.com
Admission: $$$

All Tomorrow's Parties began in the United Kingdom, but lately it has been popping up in the United States, in Los Angeles and New York. The event generally lasts three days and presents some of the best-known names in experimental music, while not forgetting key acts of the past and present in the realms of independent rock, jazz, hip-hop, and electronic music. The event debuted in 1999, organized by the Scottish group Belle & Sebastian. The idea was to have the band pick some of their favorite acts and build a festival around them. Each year since, a specific artist like Sonic Youth or Chicago's Tortoise has taken charge. *Simpsons'* creator Matt Groening curated the 2003 event in Los Angeles. Performers in past years have been all across the map—from the key underground sounds of Television and the Fall, to Boards of Canada and Aphex Twin, to the out-jazz sounds of Cecil Taylor. Needless to say, this is one of the more keenly anticipated events of the music festival year.
Camping: No

ALLEYFEST

June
Longview, Texas
www.alleyfest.org
Admission: $

AlleyFest encompasses three days of music in East Texas that runs from straightforward, hard-hitting blues to zydeco and beyond. It's a successful mix that has seen everyone from the Dixie Chicks to Leon Russell grace both stages.

For more information: casey@longviewpartnership.org

Camping: No

Accommodations

■ Comfort Suites
3307 N. 4th St.
Longview, TX 75605
(903) 663-4991

■ Best Western Inn
3119 Estes Pkwy.
Longview, TX 75602
(903) 758-0700

♪ AREA 51 SOUND TEST

April

Indian Springs, Nevada

www.area51soundtest.com

Admission: $$

The Area 51 Sound Test is put together yearly by the Las Vegas Jam Band Society, a southern Nevada organization dedicated to providing an outlet for jam musicians and their fans. The event takes place in Indian Springs (about a half-hour north of Las Vegas), long known as a hotbed for UFO sightings. The name "Area 51" is taken from the supposedly top-secret air force base that many a conspiracy theorist has located in these parts. Chances are, unless you find drum circles somewhat alien, your encounters here will be more pedestrian than extraterrestrial. The event focuses on regional acts and allows free camping for anyone attending all three days.

For more information: smokinjoemontana@aol.com

Camping: Yes

Accommodations

■ Indian Springs Hotel
372 Tonopah Hwy. 95
Indian Springs, NV 89018
(702) 384-7449

♪ ARVIKAFESTIVALEN

July

Arvika, Värmland, Sweden

www.galaxen.se/main.php

Admission: $$$

The Arvikafestivalen is more than a mouthful; it's Sweden's most popular annual festival. This event books high-profile acts from all over the United Kingdom and Europe to perform for happy-go-lucky revelers. As far as European festivals go, it's a relatively small affair with just more than 10,000 people attending the most recent event. You can usually expect a mixture of rougher, punk-rock acts mixed in with Swedish performers, alternative rock staples, and electronic performances. A dance area keeps music pumping 'til dawn for all the night owls. Primal Scream, Orbital, Motorhead, and the Cure have all been recent invitees to the main stage.

For more information: (46) 0-57-013-666 or festivalen@galaxen.se

Camping: No

Accommodations

■ **Best Western Elite**
Kungsgatan 22
Karlstad 652 24
Sweden
(46) 0-54-293-000

■ **Best Western Carlstad**
Tage Erlandergatan 10
Karlstad 65184
Sweden

♪ ATHFEST

June
Athens, Georgia
www.athfest.com
Admission: ⫶FREE⫶–$

Athens has long been an integral part of the college music scene. Acts such as REM and the B-52s gave birth to the genre in the early 1980s. More recent acts such as Olivia Tremor Control and Neutral Milk Hotel have proven that creativity and musicianship are in no short supply in this town. This annual event focuses on area talent, with a variety of signed and unsigned artists performing free afternoon and evening concerts. A "club crawl" is staged for those curious about nightlife in Athens, and a Kidsfest puts the focus on younger attendees. All in all, AthFest remains one of the best ways to explore both the city of Athens and the music it produces.

For more information: media@athfest.com

Camping: No

Accommodations

■ **Courtyard Athens Downtown**
166 N. Finley St.
Athens, GA 30601
(706) 369-7000

■ **Travelodge Downtown**
898 W. Broad St.
Athens, GA 30601
(706) 549-5400

BALÉLEC

May
Lausanne, Switzerland
www.balelec.ch
Admission: $–$$

The Swiss Balélec festival began in 1980 with very modest goals. Originally, it drew mainly college students and rarely had more than a thousand attendees, who came to see a variety of regional artists perform in a multitude of genres. But the word spread, and by 1998, almost 20,000 people were in attendance. The festival now books top rock acts from Europe and America like Therapy?, the Divine Comedy, the James Taylor Quartet, and Nada Surf.

Camping: No
Accommodations

■ **Hotel Elite Lausanne**
Avenue Sainte-Luce 1
Switzerland
(41) 21-320-2361
info@elite-lausanne.ch
www.elite-lausanne.ch

■ **Hotel Victoria Lausanne**
46, Avenue de la Gare
CH-1001 Lausanne
Switzerland
(41) 21-342-0202

BAYFEST

October
Mobile, Alabama
www.bayfest.com
Admission: $$

With eight years under its belt and more sure to come, BayFest attracts upward of 100,000 music fans to Alabama for three days in October. For a reasonable fee, you'll be treated to seven different stages that provide a musical forum to more than 100 acts. If you're planning to travel with a large group, discounted rates are available. (Hell's Angels, take heed!) Everyone from Creed to Lee Ann Womack has performed at this popular festival, so be prepared for some diversity.

For more information: info@bayfest.com

Camping: No

Accommodations

■ **Lafayette Plaza Hotel**
301 Government St.
Mobile, AL 36602
(800) 692-6662

■ **Adam's Mark**
64 S. Water St.
Mobile, AL 36602
(251) 438-4000 or (800) 444-ADAM

♩ BAYPOP

November
San Francisco, California
www.baypop.com
Admission: $

Baypop is slowly becoming San Francisco's key celebration of all things pop, past and present. The last few Baypop festivals have taken place in November; they generally invade several well-known venues in San Francisco and occasionally stretch out into Berkeley as well. Baypop keeps an ear tuned to the sounds of pure pop music and books groups such as the Beachwood Sparks and Call and Response—acts who have one foot in the great sounds of sixties pop and the other stepping forward into the twenty-first century. In addition to new acts, in 2002 Baypop hosted a rare live event featuring reunited psychedelic acts such as the Electric Prunes and the Chocolate Watchband.

Artist Submissions: don2@pobox.com

Camping: No

Accommodations

■ **Phoenix Hotel**
601 Eddy St.
San Francisco, CA 94109
(800) 248-9466

■ **Hotel Bijou**
111 Mason St.
San Francisco, CA 94102
(800) 771-1022

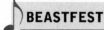

BEASTFEST

December
Oakland, California
www.beastfest.com
Admission: $

This nonprofit event celebrates the wealth of independent talent springing from the East Bay area of California. All facets of the arts are represented, from comedy to sculpture to, of course, live music—especially jazz, folk, experimental electronic, and independent-minded rock. Small club venues provide the backdrop for this growing event, which has been known to book more than 100 different acts over the course of its four-day run.

Artist Submissions
bEASTfest
P.O. Box 16158
Oakland, CA 94610
Camping: No
Accommodations

■ **Howard Johnson Express**
423 7th St.
Oakland, CA 94607
(800) 406-1411

■ **Hotel Ibiza**
10 Hegenberger Rd.
Oakland, CA 94621
info@hotelibiza.com

BIG DAY OUT

January–February
Australia and New Zealand
www.bigdayout.com
Admission: $$–$$$

Big Day Out is one of the largest festivals in Australia. This traveling circus of alternative music from established talent takes place at six different venues over six days. Recent events have featured the Foo Fighters, New Order, PJ Harvey, and Queens of the Stone Age. The festival began in the early 1990s and has become perhaps the premiere live event for alternative music in Australia and New Zealand.

For more information: info@bigdayout.com
Camping: No

♪ BIZARRE FESTIVAL

Mid-August
Weeze, Germany
www.bizarre.de
Admission: $$$

Germany's Bizarre Festival stages performances by some of the most influential alternative acts around. It began in 1987, just a few years before the alternative sound became mainstream. Thousands of people flocked to the very first event, which featured Iggy Pop and Siouxsie and the Banshees. By 1999, the Bizarre Festival had moved to an abandoned airport to ensure there would be enough room for everyone. Now one of the most highly anticipated European festivals, it pulls in acts such as Sonic Youth, Red Hot Chili Peppers, and the Chemical Brothers as headliners.

For more information: (49) 0-228-367-6767 or info@ccb-gmbh.de
Camping: Yes
Accommodations
■ **Mercure Hotel**
Stationsplein 29
6512 BA Nijmegen
Holland
(31) 0-24-323-8888

♪ BONNAROO MUSIC FESTIVAL

June
Manchester, Tennessee
www.bonnaroo.com
Admission: $$

A 500-acre farm in Manchester, Tennessee, is the setting for the annual Bonnaroo Music Festival. Camping, music, and peace go hand-in-hand at this event, which, in recent years, has seen more than 70,000 people set up camp during its three-day run. Bonnaroo caters to the jam band crowd and regularly invites artists such as Phil Lesh, Bob Weir, Trey Anastasio, and Galactic to perform uninterrupted free-form jams that go long into the night. Hip-hop artists such as Jurassic Five and Blackalicious have also been invited into the fray. Despite its size, it is known for being one of the cleaner, better-organized events. Blame it on the peace-loving, groove-centric music or on the laid-back inhabitants of Tennessee—either way, this event makes another Woodstock seem possible after all.

For more information: info@bonnaroo.com

Camping: Yes

Accommodations

■ **Knights Inn**
224 Express Way Dr.
Manchester, TN 37355
(931) 728-1001

■ **Hampton Inn**
I-24 & Hwy. 53 Exit #110
Manchester, TN 37355
(931) 728-3300

♪ BRECKENRIDGE MUSIC FESTIVAL

Year-round
Breckenridge, Colorado
www.breckenridgemusicfestival.com
Admission: $$

Located in the popular ski resort of Breckenridge, this festival combines a few dozen classical music events with about fifteen others that range from bluegrass to swing. Organized yearly in conjunction with the National Repertory Theatre and the Breckenridge Music Institute, it presents plenty of music-related educational opportunities for both kids and adults.

For more information: bmi-nro@breckenridgemusicfestival.net

Camping: No

Accommodations

■ **The Village at Breckenridge**
535 S. Park Ave.
Breckenridge, CO 80424
(970) 453-2000

■ **Breckenridge Wayside Inn**
165 Tiger Rd.
Breckenridge, CO 80424
(970) 453-5540
Wayside@colorado.net
www.summitnet.com/wayside

♪ BUMBERSHOOT

August–September
Seattle, Washington
www.bumbershoot.org
Admission: $$

Bumbershoot is not strictly a music festival; it celebrates all aspects of artistic expression from dance to poetry to the visual arts. Since 1970, Bumbershoot has made every Labor Day weekend in Seattle a haven for the eclectic and avant-garde. Artists such as James Brown, Emmylou Harris, Randy Newman, and even faux-rockers Spinal Tap have been known to take the stage here, and more recently, the Foo Fighters, Ben Harper, and Macy Gray have appeared as well. This is a great place to explore sculpture, film, books, and handcrafted clothing with the air of off-kilter experimentation that only a town like Seattle can provide.

For more information: info@onereel.org

Camping: No

Accommodations

■ **Sheraton Seattle**
1400 Sixth and Pike Sts.
Seattle, WA 98101
(206) 621-9000
sheraton.seattle@sheraton.com

■ **Best Western Pioneer Square Hotel**
77 Yesler Way
Seattle, WA 98104
(800) 800-5514
www.pioneersquare.com

♪ BURLINGTON'S SOUND OF MUSIC FESTIVAL

June

Burlington, Ontario, Canada

www.soundofmusic.on.ca

Admission: FREE

This four-day event takes place in Ontario and is known for its lively lineups of well-known and well-respected Canadian acts. Folk, rock, country, jazz, blues, and even music for kids is given stage time. Marching bands, floats, and much more come together on the first day for the Grand Festival Parade. The subsequent days are a cavalcade of music, art, and food, perfect both for families and for those feeling the need to let loose.

Artist Submissions

Entertainment Committee
Burlington's Sound of Music Festival
P.O. Box 85007
561 Brant St.
Burlington, ON L7R 4K3
Canada

For more information: linda@affirmative.com

Camping: No

Accommodations

■ **Travelodge Hotel Burlington-on-the-Lake**
2020 Lakeshore Rd.
Burlington, ON L7R 4G8
Canada
(905) 681-0762
travelodge@look.ca
www.travelodge.com

■ **Esquire Motel**
1110 Plains Rd. W.
Burlington, ON L7T 1H3
Canada
(905) 529-3915

♪ CANTERBURY FAYRE

August

Hernhill, Kent, United Kingdom

www.canterburyfayre.com

Admission: $$–$$$

The Canterbury Fayre takes place on the grounds of a Victorian mansion in the lush countryside that Kent is known for. Since the late 1960s, the scene in Canterbury has been associated with musical innovation and experimentation, with bands such as Soft Machine, Caravan, and Gong providing refreshing glimpses of post-psychedelic art rock. This particular festival began in 2000 and has been making a tremendous effort to welcome fans and performers of this music. The combination of classic art-rock acts such as Hawkwind and the Electric Prunes with innovators such as Porcupine Tree virtually guarantees that both old and new fans of this sub-genre will leave satisfied.

For more information: (44) 01-494-794-887

Camping: Yes, included in the ticket price.

Accommodations

■ **Holiday Inn Express**
Upper Harbledown
Canterbury, Kent CT2 9HX
United Kingdom
(44) 0800-434040

■ **Falstaff Hotel**
8-10 St. Dunstans St.
Canterbury, Kent CT2 8AF
United Kingdom
(44) 1227-462138

♪ CARLING WEEKEND/READING FESTIVAL

August
Reading and Leeds, United Kingdom
www.readingfestival.com
Admission: $$$

The Reading Festival typically takes place during the last Friday, Saturday, and Sunday of August and is one of the premier festivals in the world. You can expect to join upward of 50,000 people in camping, dancing, and enjoying various types of revelry throughout the weekend. Camping is not mandatory, although it is definitely key to the full experience.

Reading, which takes place in conjunction with Carling Festival in Leeds, is the longest-running festival in England, and its approach to organization and band lineup has influenced all major rock festivals in Europe and beyond. Reading originated in the early 1970s, with performances by AC/DC and Thin Lizzy blowing everyone's collective mind. The festival maintained a classic rock bent until the late 1980s, when the promoters at Mean Fiddler took over and decided to shake things up a bit. They put a youthful spin on the event, inviting the top acts championed by papers such as the NME and the now-defunct *Melody Maker*. New Order, Nirvana, Oasis, The Verve, and The Strokes have all performed here, and each year's roster reads like a "what's hot" list of musical acts. Reading is really more a rite of passage than a festival—and so it shall remain it for probably many years to come.

For more information: (44) 020-8963-0940
Camping: Yes
Accommodations

IN READING

■ **Travelodge Reading Central**
60 Oxford Rd.
Reading RG1 7LT
United Kingdom
(44) 0870-191-1710

■ **Quality Hotel**
654 Oxford Rd.
Reading RG30 IEH
United Kingdom
(44) 118-950-0541

IN LEEDS

■ **Golden Lion Hotel**
2 Lower Briggate
Leeds LS1 4AE
United Kingdom
(44) 1132-436454

■ **Cliff Lawn Hotel**
Cliff Road
Headingley, Leeds LS6 2ET
United Kingdom
(44) 0-113-278-5442

LINDA RYAN, *music industry mover and shaker, Gaelic football fan and festivalgoer extraordinaire, has attended the Reading Festival nearly a dozen times. We talked to her about why it's so fun to spend several days among drunken, mud-caked Europeans.*

What is the allure of attending a music festival as opposed to your basic rock show?

Part of the allure is totally immersing yourself in the event. For two to three days, twenty-four hours a day, you are living, eating, sleeping, and drinking rock 'n' roll. That's as close to being in a band as many people are going to get! And you're doing it with a bunch of like-minded people who are similar enough to be "safe," but different enough to seem new and exciting. It's a party for a few days. There's no thought of drinking and driving or getting up for work the next day. There's certainly no thought of doing laundry!

What do you look for in a music festival? Is it strictly a good lineup, is it a worthy cause, or is it the cheese fries?

If I'm going to spend the money to travel to a festival, buy tickets, and budget for food, T-shirts, and whatever else, then the lineup has to be worth all that. To a lesser extent, the logistics of the event also come into play. If it's not going to be relatively easy to get in and out, that might sway me not to go.

What is the biggest problem with festivals today?

The biggest problem with festivals today is the total lack of respect for the tens of thousands of other people you're there with. Setting things on fire, moshing so violently that you crush people, taking advantage of people who have perhaps partied a bit too much—it all contributes to an atmosphere of mistrust and anxiety, and that's not what these festivals are supposed to be about.

What have been some of the musical highlights of your festival-going experience?

• • • • • • • • • • •

Without a doubt, the highlight was the 1992 Reading Festival. Beastie Boys, Neil Young, Nirvana, Ride, the Charlatans, Public Enemy, Suede—oh my God! Whoever booked the festival that year deserves a Hall of Fame honor!

What is the strangest thing you've seen at a festival?

That would have to be the naked, mud-caked old men at Glastonbury. And I mean, old! Way too old to be running around naked, you know? And there were hundreds of them dancing around the Wicker Man! It made me seriously wish I were on drugs.

What place do you think a music festival has in today's musical climate?

Well, that's hard to say. The crowds seem to get worse and worse as time goes on—people getting raped, crushed, or injured in other ways is a far cry from the original spirit of these festivals. It still can be the single best experience a person has. But it can also be the single biggest nightmare, and that's a shame.

• • • • • • • • • • •

♪ CAVESTOMP

January
New York, New York
Admission: $$–$$$

For fans of sixties garage music, the annual Cavestomp festival at the Westbeth Theater in New York is akin to manna falling from heaven. Every year, the organizers put together legendary lineups that not only feature bands who maintain the spirit of that fuzz-drenched sound but also the original artists themselves. The event generally lasts about three days and in the past has seen artists such as the Troggs, the Monks, the Pretty Things, and the Standells take to the stage. The Cavestomp organizers also put together other limited engagements throughout the year.

For more information: cavestomper@aol.com
Camping: No

Accommodations

■ **Holiday Inn**
138 Lafayette St.
New York, NY 10013
(212) 966-8898
http://holidayinn-nyc.com

■ **Chelsea Hotel**
222 W. 23rd St.
New York, NY 10011
(212) 243-3700
www.hotelchelsea.com

♪ CEDAR MOUNTAIN FESTIVAL

Mid-September
Cedar City, Utah
www.cedarmountainfestival.com
Admission: $

The combination of music enthusiasts and dedicated craftspeople who flock to Cedar City makes this Mountain Festival a great family destination. This nonprofit organization sets out to teach both young and old alike the benefits of the arts through clinics and workshops. The two-day event provides a bounty of food and music among the beautiful foothills of southwestern Utah.

Artist Submissions
Cedar Mountain Festival
attn: Booking Director
P.O. Box 1163
Cedar City, UT 84721
(435) 463-7121
For more information: info@cedarmountainfestival.com
Camping: No
Accommodations

■ **Holiday Inn Cedar City**
1575 W. 200 N.
Cedar City, UT 84720
(435) 586-8888

■ **Cedar City Travelodge**
2555 Main St.
Cedar City, UT 84720
(435) 586-7435

♪ CHICAGO INDIEPOP FESTIVAL

Late May
Chicago, Illinois

http://homepage.interaccess.com/~aadam
Admission: $–$$

The Chicago Indiepop Festival takes place over four consecutive nights and gathers notable performers from the realm of indie pop. Those who long for the days of jangling guitars and sunshine melodies are sure to be pleased by the event's lineup. Past performers such as Archer Prewitt and the Apples in Stereo have brought an unlimited number of smiles and ironic T-shirts to venues such as Schubas and the Abbey Pub.

For more information: aadam@interaccess.com

Camping: No

Accommodations

■ **City Suites Hotel**
933 W. Belmont
Chicago, IL 60657
(800) 248-9108

■ **Chicago Marriott Downtown**
540 N. Michigan Ave.
Chicago, IL 60611
(312) 836-0100

♪ CLARKSVILLE RIVERFEST CELEBRATION

September
Clarksville, Tennessee
http://clarksvilleriverfest.com
Admission: $

Riverfest provides multiple stages that showcase an excellent variety of musical talent. But that's not all: dancers, comedians, even possible karaoke stars are given a chance to shine during the talent show, not to mention the art exhibits, wacky boat races, and battle-of-the-bands-type shows that also take place during the three-day event. Performers range from local talent to acclaimed country, soul, and rock acts. Recently, classic R&B hit-makers the Drifters and the Marvelettes have performed here.

For more information: jhuber@cityofclarksville.com

Camping: No

Accommodations

■ **Riverview Inn**
50 College St.
Clarksville, TN 37040
(931) 552-3331

■ **Wingate Inn**
251 Holiday Dr.
Clarksville, TN 37040
(931) 906-0606
www.wingateinns.com

CMJ MUSIC MARATHON

October–November
New York, New York
www.cmj.com/marathon
Admission: $$$

CMJ is one of the key band showcases in the United States for up-and-coming artists, and has been since its inception in the early 1980s. Year after year, known and unknown artists alike perform throughout the city to houses packed with industry representatives, A&R people, fellow musicians, and fans. Films, panels, and parties abound as well. Whether it's the latest buzz band from England or the newest Internet technology, CMJ helps to set the music standard. CMJ has presented legendary performances from acts such as REM, Red Hot Chili Peppers, Blur, Chemical Brothers, Eminem, and Aphex Twin.

For more information: marathon@cmj.com
Camping: No
Accommodations

■ **Hilton New York**
1335 Avenue of the Americas
New York, NY 10019
(800) 445-8667

■ **Holiday Inn**
138 Lafayette St.
New York, NY 10013
(800) HOLIDAY

COACHELLA VALLEY MUSIC AND ARTS FESTIVAL

April
Indio, California
www.goldenvoice.com/coachella
Admission: $$$

In the few years since its inception, the Coachella Valley Music and Arts Festival has established itself as one of the leaders in alternative music festivals in the United States. The eclectic lineups are reminiscent of the Lollapalooza events of the 1990s where weekend travelers can expect to hear high-profile hip-hop, alt-rock staples, and English bands-of-the-moment. The 2002 event saw The Strokes, The Vines, Oasis, Mos Def, Chemical Brothers, Belle & Sebastian, Foo Fighters, and countless others competing against the heat for attention. The dance tents keep people entertained after hours and the desert location makes camping a must.

Artist Submissions: art@goldenvoice.com

Camping: Yes. Camping is available at nearby Lake Cahuilla. Contact (800) 234-7275 for reservations.

Accommodations

■ **Best Western Date Tree**
81-909 Indio Blvd.
Indio, CA 92201
(760) 347-3421

■ **Royal Plaza Inn**
82-347 Hwy. 111
Indio, CA 92201
(760) 347-0911

♪ COMMON GROUND FESTIVAL

July
Lansing, Michigan
www.commongroundfest.com/index2.htm
Admission: $$$

This large, six-day event is a relative newcomer to Lansing, Michigan. It's only been around since 2000 but has quickly established itself as Michigan's premier festival. Several smaller stages keep the music going throughout the afternoons while the two main stages provide entertainment at night. With its mixture of classic rock, country, and R&B artists—notables such as Styx, the Doobie Brothers, Lee Ann Womack, and the Commodores have performed here—the event brings in roughly 50,000 people. Other bonuses include a skate park, Ferris wheel, assorted rides, and other attractions for the young ones.

For more information: comments@commongroundfest.com

Camping: No

Accommodations

■ **Sheraton Lansing Hotel**
925 S. Creyts Rd.
Lansing, MI 48917
(517) 323-7100
www.sheratonlansing.com

■ **Clarion Hotel**
3600 Dunckel Drive
Lansing, MI 48910
(517) 351-7600

♪ COSMIC AMERICAN MUSIC FESTIVAL (GRAM FEST)

October
Joshua Tree, California
Admission: $

This daylong event celebrates the life and music of the late Gram Parsons and usually takes place in the high desert of California. Often regarded as the father of alternative country music, Parsons was able to feed country music to artists such as the Byrds and the Rolling Stones with his rock-star lifestyle and down-home roots. Of course, he was simultaneously penning his own heart-wrenching ballads and country-rock barnstormers.

Parsons spent a lot of his spare time out in Joshua Tree and in 1973 overdosed in one of the area's hotels. After his funeral, road manager Phil Kaufman stole the casket and drove it out to Joshua Tree, where he burned it (supposedly up by Cap Rock). Parsons's cult status has grown exponentially since his passing, and this event is one of the year's highlights for his fans. You can expect to hear a variety of roots music, country picking, and power pop in the small local venues. Artists such as Lucinda Williams have dropped by in the past.

For more information: (760) 366-5414

Camping: Yes. Joshua Tree is a national park, with plenty of camping and backpacking.

Accommodations

■ **Joshua Tree Inn**
61259 Twenty-Nine Palms Hwy.
P.O. Box 1966
Joshua Tree, CA 92252
(760) 366-1188
www.joshuatreeinn.com

■ **Rosebud Ruby Star**
P.O. Box 1116
Joshua Tree, CA 92252
(760) 366-4676
sandy@rosebudrubystar.com
www.rosebudrubystar.com

CREEKSIDE JAMBOREE

May–June
Forksville, Pennsylvania
www.azpro.com
Admission: $$–$$$

Creekside Jamboree began its run in 1998 and immediately distinguished itself with its intimate surroundings and innovative lineups. Set in a lush wonderland of creeks, hiking trails, and swimming areas, the festival puts together elements of jazz, funk, electronica, bluegrass, and everything in between. Both vegetarians and meat-eaters will be pleased with the foods available, and tai chi classes are held twice daily for those seeking a little inner peace during the festival. Camping is included in the ticket price, so come prepared!

Artist Submissions

A-Z Productions

P.O. Box 3321

Williamsport, PA 17701

For more information: info@azpro.com

Camping: No

Accommodations

■ **Millview Motel**

Rte. 87 Box 1002

Forksville, PA 18616

(570) 924-3226

DAWSON CITY MUSIC FESTIVAL

July

Dawson City, Yukon Territory, Canada

www.dcmf.com/index2.html

Admission: $

A warmly welcomed event in the Yukon since 1979, the Dawson City Music Festival brings together a wide variety of Canadian favorites and up-and-coming hopefuls. In the past, the Crash Test Dummies, Jane Siberry, and Bruce Cockburn have wowed the crowds who come for a mixture of blues, folk, rock, and world music.

Artist Submissions

Dawson City Music Festival

Box 456

Dawson City, YT Y0B 1G0

Canada

For more information: dcmf@yknet.yk.ca

Camping: No

Accommodations

■ **Bombay Peggy's Inn**

P.O. Box 411

2nd Ave. & Princess St.

Dawson City, YT Y0B 1G0

Canada

(867) 993-6969

info@bombaypeggys.com

www.bombaypeggys.com

■ **Downtown Hotel**

Box 780

Corner of Second and Queen

Dawson City, YT Y0B 1G0

Canada

(867) 993-5346

downtown@yknet.yk.ca

www.downtown.yk.net

♪ DAY OF THE ACCORDION

June
San Francisco, California
www.thecannery.com/event/accordion.html
Admission: *FREE*

Not only is the accordion the official musical instrument of San Francisco, but the Day of the Accordion has been celebrated here every June since 1998. The event takes place on the courtyard stage of the scenic Cannery, right down by Fisherman's Wharf. It's a great area to explore, with countless shops and restaurants nearby and North Beach and Chinatown not too far off. The music here is resolutely accordion-based, so you can leave your harmonium at home.

For more information: info@thecannery.com

Camping: No

Accommodations

■ **Sheraton Fisherman's Wharf**
2500 Mason St.
San Francisco, CA 94133
(800) 325-3535
SheratonSF@meristar.com
www.sheratonatthewharf.com

■ **Canterbury San Francisco**
750 Sutter St.
San Francisco, CA 94109
(800) 528-1234

♪ DE STIJL FESTIVAL OF MUSIC

July
Minneapolis, Minnesota
Admission: $

This event began in 2002 and features a nonstop cavalcade of folk/noise/psychedelic experimental music. For nearly 14 hours more than 200 acts perform in the basement of an abandoned church. Some of the most respected names in underground music appear at this event, from the anarchic electro-rock of Wolf Eyes to the dark, musty folk of Six Organs of Admittance.

For more information: destijl@mindspring.com

Camping: No

Accommodations

■ **Best Western Downtown**
405 S. 8th St.
Minneapolis, MN 55454
(612) 370-1400

■ **Quality Inn & Suites**
41 N. 10th St.
Minneapolis, MN 55454
(612) 339-9311

CLINT SIMONSON *is a first-time organizer of the De Stijl Music Festival in Minneapolis. He runs De Stijl Records, a vinyl-only label that specializes in oddities and forgotten folk and psychedelic music.*

Why in the world would you want to start putting together your own music festival?

Minneapolis is a vacuous town, and things like this don't happen on their own. I like the concept of great musicians coming together, and it's a celebration of the work that I've put into the label.

What is it about the music that inspires you to keep doing this?

Well, I've only done one so far. But I intend to do another because I found the first to be satisfying.

What is the hardest part?

Nothing about it is easy. Finding the place, advertising, etc. are all difficult, but the hardest part is the stress of knowing that if you don't hit the break-even point at the door, you'll have people from California, Texas, New York, and Europe who want their guarantees filled, and it's coming out of your pocket!

Is it worth it?

Yeah, I think so.

Do any of the proceeds from the festival go to charity or a cause?

No, but it was not-for-profit. I hit the break-even point around one in the morning. I charged maybe ten more people because I forgot to budget in the soundman, and then I enjoyed the rest of the event. Latecomers got in free by default.

What advice would you give to potential festival organizers?

Have fun! And it might be wise to invest in a good doorman. I wish I'd hired someone who wouldn't have let anyone in for free, hot chick or no. Instead, I ran the door myself. I also think it's important to base your lineup on quality acts, rather than ones that you know will fill the hall or whatever. That's my two cents.

DETROIT SUMMER SMASH

June
Detroit, Michigan
Admission: $–$$

Classic pop songwriting skills are on display for three days straight when the Detroit Summer Smash hits the Motor City in June. Jam-packed with bands from the area and some of the best up-and-coming independent artists you can find, the Summer Smash consistently delivers eclectic showcases that range from avant-garde to pure pop. From the buzzing pop of Outrageous Cherry to the rustic crunch of My Morning Jacket, the Detroit Summer Smash offers plenty of solace for those summer nights.

Camping: No

Accommodations

■ **Days Inn Downtown Detroit**
3250 E. Jefferson
Detroit, MI 48207
(313) 568-2000

■ **Ramada Inn Downtown Detroit**
400 Bagley Ave.
Detroit, MI 48226
(888) 298-2054

E.A.R.T.H. AWARENESS FESTIVAL

April
Live Oak, Florida
www.earthawareness.org
Admission: $$

This festival, organized by Entertainers Against Ruining Their Home (E.A.R.T.H.), provides an entertaining forum for families who wish to educate their children about nature and the environment. Of course music is a high priority, plenty of it geared specifically for children. But parents need not fret, as they will be enjoying classic rock performances from acts such as Pat Travers and Badfinger. Artisans and food vendors are on hand to provide sustenance and shopping opportunities.

For more information: EarthFestival@bellsouth.net

Camping: No

Accommodations

■ **Clarion Hotel**
260 E. Merritt Island Causeway
  (S.R. 520)
Merritt Island, FL 32952
(800) 584-1482
sales@clarionspacecoast.com
www.clarionspacecoast.com

■ **Holiday Inn Express Hotel & Suites**
6694 US 129 N.
Live Oak, FL 32060
(386) 362-2600

ELVIS PRESLEY FESTIVAL

May–June
Tupelo, Mississippi
www.tupeloelvisfestival.com
Admission: $–$$

Located in the birthplace of the King, the Elvis Presley Festival sets aside a few summer days where Elvis-philes, music fans, and the curious can celebrate the man and the music that made him. Bluegrass, blues, country, and gospel music are a major part of the lineup, and performers such as B. B. King and Charlie Daniels do their best to pour their hearts and souls into each performance. In addition to the music, there are less traditional events to enjoy, such as the Elvis Look-Alike Pet Parade and the Recliner Races. All in all, a suitably quirky event that manages not to take itself too seriously.

For more information: debbie@tupeloelvisfestival.com

Camping: No

Accommodations

■ **Scottish Inn**
401 N. Gloster St.
Tupelo, MS 38801
(662) 842-1961

■ **All American Coliseum Motel**
767 E. Main St.
Tupelo, MS 38801
(662) 844-5610

ELVIS WEEK

August

Memphis, Tennessee

Admission: –$$

While some people spend their lives as if every week were Elvis Week, the folks here in Memphis have narrowed it down just a bit. This is the time to visit Graceland, see live music, and people watch. But if you can't make it down here, you can witness a live Webcast of the week's key events from home. Anyone lucky enough to make it here in the flesh would do right to check out the gospel brunch and live entertainment served up at Elvis Presley's Memphis—the only restaurant/bar to bear the King's name. Art contests, special tours, candlelight vigils, and dance parties are just some of the activities attendees will be privy to.

Camping: No

Accommodations

■ **Elvis Presley's Heartbreak Hotel**
3677 Elvis Presley Blvd.
Memphis, TN 38116
(877) 777-0606
www.elvis.com/epheartbreakhotel

■ **Holiday Inn Select Memphis—
   Downtown (Beale St.)**
160 Union Ave.
Memphis, TN 38103
(901) 525-5491
sales@holidayselect-downtown.com

FARMAPALOOZA

Mid-June

Black River Falls, Wisconsin

www.farmapalooza.com

Admission: $$–$$$

Farmapalooza is a three-day event organized in part by some freethinking Wisconsin students. The event began in 1998 after the founders came upon an area surrounding a small farmhouse that they thought would be perfect for a music festival and campsite. Although the festival has since moved on to larger grounds, the name remains. Farmapalooza is fast becoming one of the key festivals for both regional and nationally touring artists on the jam band circuit. Dark Star Orchestra, roots rockers Big Wu, and acclaimed singer-songwriter Willy Porter have all found themselves in this warm, hospitable environment.

For more information: farmapalooza@interlobate.com

Camping: Yes

Accommodations

■ **Holiday Inn Express**
Black River Falls
Intersection of I-94 & Hwy. 54 E.,
   Exit 116
W10170 Hwy. 54 E.
Black River Falls, WI 54615
(715) 284-0888

■ **Days Inn**
919 Hwy. 54 E.
Black River Falls, WI 54615
(715) 284-4333

FESTIVAL INTERNACIONAL DE BENICASSIM (FIB HEINEKEN)

August

Benicassim, Spain

www.fiberfib.com

Admission: $$–$$$

One of Spain's finest festivals, Benicassim offers three days of unique, critically acclaimed music and three nights of fabulous camping. Since 1995 the festival has booked some of most respected international music acts available, many of them hailing from the United Kingdom. Paul Weller, Radiohead, the Beta Band, the Stone Roses, and Black Rebel Motorcycle Club have all performed here. Lineups such as these have made Benicassim a key European destination for music fans.

For more information: englishinfo@fiberfib.com

Camping: Yes

Accommodations

■ **Trinimar**
Avda. Ferrandis Salvador, 184
12560 Benicassim
Spain
(34) 964-30-08-50

■ **Vista Allegre**
Avda. Barcelona, 71
12560 Benicassim
Spain
(34) 964-30-04-00

JOAN VICH MONTANER *is one of the organizers behind Spain's Benicassim Festival. Here, he explains how his love of the music has kept him coming back year after year, despite the occasional natural disaster.*

What was the inspiration behind the Benicassim Festival?

In 1995 there were no summer festivals at all in Spain. All the people who were starting the Spanish independent pop scene (bands, labels, fanzines, radio stations, and the crowd this scene was generating) needed a meeting point.

What has been the hardest part of putting this event together?

The first two years the festival ended up with economic losses. The third year, a very big storm (almost a small hurricane) tore down the light towers over the main stage while Scottish band Urusei Yatsura was playing. Fortunately there were no victims and no one got hurt. Surviving economic hardships and natural disasters has given the festival a strength that is now one of its characteristics. It takes a lot of hard work, passion, and confidence.

What is it about the music that inspires you to work for the festival?

I love music and everything surrounding it. Working in the music business makes you realize how fake all the glamour is that we usually stick to it. On the other hand it lets you meet a lot of people who share the same love for music. The atmosphere at the Benicassim festival is infused with this love for music.

Is it worth it?

Definitely. Every year I've said, "this is my last year working for the festival." And then every year after that I was back, happy to see everyone again. Not only

• • • • • • • • • • • •

because of the good atmosphere, but because we're getting paid better! As the festival grows, you feel like you're part of something important, helping make a little history.

What is the hardest part?

The superlong shifts! During the festival you can hardly sleep. You have to work over sixteen or seventeen hours in a row and can only take a few short stops for a sandwich. And the weather in southern Spain in August is very hot.

What are the three things you think set this festival apart from other festivals?

The weather: it's sunny, and we're by the beach. The atmosphere: you can tell that both the people working the shows and the crowd are there for the music. I haven't seen any violence in these eight years. The music: the lineup has always mixed some well-known acts with lots of great unknown names just waiting to be discovered by curious listeners. It's a very eclectic lineup, focused on independent pop, rock, and electronic music.

Which act do you think put on the best show?

The Jon Spencer Blues Explosion blew my mind in '98. The three of them were playing very close together in the middle of the main stage. The lights (mainly yellow and red) were focused on them, leaving the rest of the stage in darkness, so it seemed as if they were playing in a small club instead of on a big stage in front of 25,000 people. And they rocked.

Pizzicato Five put on a great show, too. It was so funny and cute, nobody cared she was lip-synching. Björk came with an eight-piece classical group, and she did one of the best shows in the festival's history. When she finished her set, all the people backstage were waiting for her instead of staying at the bar or swimming pool. They made a human corridor for her stretching all the way to her dressing room. They clapped the entire time in the most respectful manner I've ever seen.

What advice would you give to potential festival organizers?

Don't try to make it big the first time. Start slowly and then keep growing if circumstances allow you to. Keep an open mind, but don't lose the original idea you had. If you do, people will notice, and that will be the end.

• • • • • • • • • • • •

FESTIVAL OF THE HALF MOON

April
Amherst, Virginia
http://cliffordpark.com
Admission: $$$

This festival is held annually in Clifford Park, a 25-acre retreat in a tranquil region at the base of the glorious Blue Ridge Mountains. Combining a relaxed camping atmosphere with the free-spirited sounds of reggae, roots music, funk, and folk, this event caters to those seeking something outside the usual. Yoga, drum circles, glass blowing, and stargazing are some of the workshops you can explore when you make it out to this peaceful event.

For more information: clfrdpk@aol.com

Camping: Yes

Accommodations

■ **Blackberry Ridge Inn**
1770 Earley Farm Rd.
Amherst, VA 24521
(877) 724-7041
info@Blackberryridge.com
www.whitetailridge.com

■ **Dulwich Manor**
550 Richmond Hwy.
Amherst, VA 24521
(800) 571-9011
www.thedulwichmanor.com

FREEDOMFEST

April
Sweetwater, Tennessee
Admission: $$

Sweetwater's FreedomFest summons a collection of like-minded jam and funk bands that get together along with a few thousand of their newest, closest friends for this three-day, two-night event in April. Camping is included with the ticket price and the reasonable cost makes it more than worthwhile.

For more information: (423) 745-4029

Camping: Yes, included in the price of the ticket.

Accommodations

■ **Best Western Sweetwater**
1421 Murray's Chapel Rd.
Sweetwater, TN 37874
(800) 647-3529

■ **Comfort Inn Sweetwater**
731 S. Main St.
Sweetwater, TN 37874
(800) 228-5150

♪ FUJI ROCK FESTIVAL

Late July
Naeba, Niigata, Japan
www.fujirockfestival.com
Admission: $$$

One of the most popular music events in Japan, the Fuji Rock Festival takes place every year at the Naeba Ski Resort, about three hours outside of Tokyo. Some of the best-known names from the West in popular and underground rock, hip-hop, and electronica have performed here since the festival began in 1997. But plenty of stage time is also devoted to Japanese artists, to ensure that out-of-town visitors get a chance to hear some of the more popular eastern acts. It's no surprise, then, that this event—with its multiple stages and 100-acts roster—attracts about 80,000 people every year (not to mention the occasional monkey). Past performers have included the Red Hot Chili Peppers, Aphex Twin, System of a Down, Stereolab, and Eminem.

Camping: Yes
Accommodations
■ **Naeba Prince Hotel**
Mikuni, Yuzawa-machi
Minami-Uonuma-gun, Niigata 949-6292
Japan
(81) 257-89-2211

♪ GATHERING ON THE MOUNTAIN

August
Lake Harmony, Pennsylvania
Admission: $$

Gathering on the Mountain is one of the many excellent festivals that takes place at the Big Boulder Ski Area in the off-season. The organizers invite in a host of high-profile acts that cover the best in roots rock, reggae, world music, and jam bands. Banjo virtuoso Bela Fleck, seminal reggae act the Wailers, and the Band's very own Garth Hudson represent the diversity and excellence put forth at this event. Let the good vibes flow!

Camping: Yes. Camping is available at the nearby Fern Ridge Campgrounds.

Accommodations

■ **Ramada Inn**
P.O. Box 600
Rt. 940 & I-80
Pocono-Lake Harmony, PA
(570) 443-8471

■ **The Resort at Split Rock**
1 Lake Drive
P.O. Box 567
Lake Harmony, PA 18624

CONAN NEUTRON *is the guitarist and vocalist for the noise rock group Repli-cator. He's also more than a little peeved with the state of the modern music festival. Don't even get him started on Clear Channel.*

How do festival crowds differ from your average concert crowds?

Your average festival attendee is very different from your average concert attendee. Somebody at a festival might not even care about the bands or community, they may be there just because it's a gathering or because it's something to do or because it's a great place to go and letch upon members of the opposite sex.

A festival type crowd can bring out both the best and the worst in people. They're often tired, hungry, listless, burned-out, and cranky. The entire situation can be patently unpleasant if you ever take it too seriously. But people can also be in the mood to be open-minded and accommodating. The realization that there are so many people out there like you provides a great reason to abate the hate for a while.

On the whole I would say people are more willing to enter into a herd mind-set in a festival environment. In some ways this can actually be a good thing because it fosters a sense of community and camaraderie with utter strangers, but in other ways it's very dangerous because it can lead to downright boorish and embarrassing behavior.

Being in a festival crowd can also prove that you have nothing in common with someone other than musical taste.

Do you enjoy playing festivals?

Absolutely. A well-organized festival is a wonderful, wonderful thing. You get a sense of fulfillment there that you can't get anywhere else, along with a sense that you're part of a larger whole. A festival that's been put together well has great bands and great times and your music gets exposed to an entirely different audience. The event can take on an almost magical, superhuman aspect that puts everything in a better light. That's the good side.

The bad side involves planning more ridiculously bad than the worst, most unprofessional show you've ever played; bands that sound worse than they would on the most off night at a club; sound mixed worse than what the most inept, tone-deaf soundperson could manage; and a general feeling of "why are we even here?" that is soul-breakingingly depressing.

It all depends.

What festivals have you played?

The two most recent festivals that spring to mind are bEASTfest and the Noise-rock Picnic. Noiserock Picnic is an annual event that I organize, which celebrates bands and their local scenes that are definitely "rock"—not art noise—but that tend to be more abrasive than what your average indie rock fan is into.

We've talked for many years about being involved in the Mission Creek Festival and Noisepop, but for whatever reasons—be it scheduling on our end or the right bill just not being there—it has yet to happen.

Is it hard getting booked into a festival? What difficulties have you encountered?

Every festival, like every band and every venue, is completely different. Having said that, we try to be proactive about where we do and do not fit in musically. So the festivals we are interested in playing, generally speaking, are the ones that are appropriate for our kind of music. For example, we may be feminists, but we won't be playing something like Lilith Fair anytime soon.

It's important to remember, especially in the Bay Area, that there are a lot of bands out there, and a lot of them are just as great and just as deserving of a chance as you are. And maybe one of them has a member who's the brother-in-law of the organizer, who knows?

. . . .

However, you'll mostly find that there are just too many bands and not enough slots. Any festival that's worth a damn is going to run into this problem because the band-to-slot ratio is, generally, not going to be equal.

The only problem we've ever experienced personally with booking in a festival situation is that it's just not appropriate for us, in that year, under those circumstances. You have to take those kinds of things not as outright rejection, but as a learning experience.

What are your funniest and/or worst festival experiences?

I'm glad to say that I can't think of a really bad festival experience. We tend to be pretty choosy about what we will play because it reflects on the image of the band just as much as the festival. But I'd have to say the funniest experience at a festival would be our first year at bEASTfest.

We'd had a really good, high energy set that was well received and won over a number of new fans. So we really needed to finish things off on an even crazier note to top what we'd done the rest of the show. I was using a wireless system that night and spent the whole last song roaming through the audience. Eventually I got up on the bar and started walking across it. The antsy and presumably spun-out bartender didn't appreciate that too much and actually tried to chase me away. He was yelling the whole time, but the crowd loved it. It was that venue's last night hosting shows so we figured we had to give it, and the festival, a decent send-off.

Got any gripes regarding the current state of music festivals?

More than anything else, I'm disappointed by festival organizers' lack of adventurousness. The best festivals around are the ones where the organizers are willing to go out on a limb and try something untested or a little risky. Always going with the surefire and safe bets, just results in bland, eighth generation Lollapalooza rip-offs, which nobody needs.

What purpose do music festivals serve in the current musical climate?

Well, your music festival of today is a different beast than your music festival of the past. The concept of "music festival as social event" has been outmoded; more often than not, festivals are just presented as a collection of bands.

. . . .

The branding of festivals like Lollapalooza is a perfect example of how festival organizers use the marketing techniques of corporations to their own ends. What products do they create? Nothing. They create no products, but the brand is invaluable because the bands themselves lend their names to the festival.

The way I see it, a good festival will put on a bunch of *great* bands—bands that you maybe wouldn't expect to see in the same lineup—and will bring people together for the common purpose of seeing some really amazing music. Bringing people together for that purpose creates the sense of community that the shameless marketers and promoters of the world try to foist on people. But if people are putting together a festival for the express purpose of trying to create a brand and "move some units," then they might as well get backing from Clear Channel because they are just as bad as the big boys for sure.

This isn't to say that festivals should only be nonprofit entities or anticorporate crusaders. It's just that there are some festivals that are there to put on good music and some that are there to make money. That should be obvious to anybody with any sort of intelligence.

So, to answer your question: in the current musical climate, music festivals present the opportunity to see bands that the average showgoer may want to see, alongside bands that perhaps they were not aware of. When pulled off properly, this makes the people attending the show realize the power they hold as a member of a community, no matter how nebulous and fleeting it may be. And that's empowering. Without getting all hippie about it.

Build it, and they will come. Build it so it doesn't suck, and they'll stay.

What tips do you have for unestablished bands trying to get on the bill?

Well, I'd say one of the best ways to increase your chances is to be really, *really* great. It may sound like a snide answer, but it's true. As in, not just a "good" band —the world is full of those—but a "great" band. One that people will just lose it over. The best kind of marketing in the world is to have a product that just blows people away.

Another good idea is to have a recording that accurately represents what the band does. Festival organizers are busy people; you have to assume that they've never heard of your band, and then you have to give them a reason to give a damn. (If they won't know who you are, sending press clippings isn't a bad idea either.)

From what I understand, most festival organizers actually listen to everything. So the real question should be, "what's the best way to get them to really *notice* my CD?" My answer for that would be to make an interesting package.

Bookers and organizers have to wade through hundreds and hundreds of these things, many of which come with the same generic cover letter that doesn't take into account the pain of what it's like to organize one of these damned things. A genero-brand CD-R with the band's name on it isn't going to cut the mustard. If you have a legit release, I would say submit that so the bookers will have the artwork and full package to contend with. If you don't, and even if you do—seriously—never forget contact info, contact info, contact info! CDs have a way of getting "lost" (especially the good ones), and cases get lost too—put contact info on everything. There is no such thing as overdoing it. Seriously.

The most important things I can say to somebody unestablished who's trying to get on a bill is be understanding, organized, not too overly needy, and try to take the work off the organizer whenever possible. All these things are going to put you in a much better position. Don't wait for somebody to do it for you; do it yourself if you can.

In a perfect world, the band to play after yours would be:

In a perfect world? Not counting bands that aren't around anymore, I'd probably have to say Fugazi. That would be incredible because not only are they an amazing band, but their ethics and practices would also pretty much ensure that it would be the coolest festival ever.

GLASTONBURY FESTIVAL

June
Glastonbury, United Kingdom
www.glastonburyfestivals.co.uk
Admission: $$$

Glastonbury is probably the most influential festival in Europe and remains the role model for anyone planning a major outdoor music event. The event was founded by Michael Eavis in 1970 and has grown into a huge cultural happening for both the musicians and the fans. It takes place on 600 acres of Worthy Farm in scenic Pilton, about eight miles from Glastonbury proper. Originally, it was known as the Glastonbury Fayre and catered to the peace-loving, post-hippie, countercultural renaissance of the early 1970s. Acts like Hawkwind, Fairport Convention, Marc Bolan, and Traffic played elongated sets for legions of denim-clad folks.

By the 1980s, the event was known as the Glastonbury Festival and began to book the best in New Wave and alternative music. The Smiths, the Cure, and Echo and the Bunnymen surfaced as headlining acts. Attendance steadily increased over the years, with recent events nearly topping the 100,000 mark. In 1993, the Velvet Underground made an incredibly rare appearance. People who attend Glastonbury generally return with stories of the best performances they've ever seen, interspersed with mud-drenched revelry.

Rock is not the only focus here; there are stages devoted to electronic music, jazz, and film. The organization of the event itself has also made much progress since the mid-1990s, when the state of the portable bathrooms was almost as widely reported as the lineup (best described as "memorable"). More recently, acts such as Oasis, Radiohead, and Primal Scream have performed at this event, which shows no sign of dropping behind the festival pack.

For more information: infoman@glastonburyfestivals.co.uk

Camping: Yes

Accommodations

■ **George and Pilgrims Hotel**
1 High St.
Glastonbury BA6 9DP
United Kingdom
(44) 01458-831146

■ **Number 3 Hotel**
3 Magdalene St.
Glastonbury BA6 9EW
United Kingdom
(44) 01458-832129

♩ GRASS ROOTS MUSIC FESTIVAL

August
Fort Wayne, Indiana
www.grassrootsfestival.com
Admission: $$

Since 1996 Fort Wayne's Grass Roots Music Festival has provided a temporary home for fans of jam rock and the musicians who excel at this improvisational form. True to its name, the Grass Roots festival is run without corporate sponsorship and provides an outlet for bands that might not have a chance to be heard in a larger festival. The music is divided between an electric stage and an acoustic stage. This convenient arrangement allows festivalgoers to settle into the area that best suits them. Natural foods and homemade crafts will be on hand, and camping is available for ticket holders for a nominal extra charge.

For more information: (219) 420-4023

Camping: Yes

Accommodations

■ **Signature Inn Fort Wayne**
1734 W. Washington Center Rd.
Ft. Wayne, IN 46818
(219) 489-5554

■ **Fairfield Fort Wayne**
5710 Challenger Pkwy.
Ft. Wayne, IN 46818
(260) 489-0050
www.fairfieldinn.com

GRIZFEST

August

Tumbler Ridge, British Columbia, Canada

www.grizfest.com

Admission: $$

Grizfest began in 2002 with the hopes of bringing some top-notch regional rock entertainment to the Tumbler Ridge area. Tumbler Ridge is located about 500 miles from Vancouver and is prone to stormy weather, which got the festival off to an uneven start. Such disadvantages often breed resilience, however, and Grizfest's star will undoubtedly rise in the future. The festival runs concurrently with Grizzly Valley Days, a much longer day event that takes place in town and features a golf tournament, races, a carnival, and much more.

Artist Submissions

Grizfest
Box 98
Tumbler Ridge BC V0C 2W0
Canada

For more information: fest@grizfest.com

Camping: No camping on-site, but a few campsites are located not too far off the festival grounds. Call either Lion's Campground at (250) 242-4353 or Monkman RV Park at (250) 242-5717. Some tent sites might be available.

Accommodations

■ **Tumbler Ridge Inn**
Box 99
Tumbler Ridge BC VOC 2W0
Canada
(800) 663-3898
ehaley@pris.bc.ca

■ **Twilight Lodge**
Box 2145
Tumbler Ridge BC V0C 2W0
Canada
(250) 242-3383

♪ GUILFEST

End of July
Guildford, Surrey, United Kingdom
www.guilfest.co.uk
Admission: $$

Guilfest takes place at Stoke Park, in the south of England. The historic town of Guildford has provided a home for the festival since its inception in 1993. Originally a one-day event, Guilfest has now grown to three days of music and fun, with headlining performances from artists such as Van Morrison, James, Motorhead, and David Gray.

For more information: info@guilfest.co.uk

Camping: Yes

Accommodations

■ **Jarvis Hotel**
253 High St.
Surrey, Guildford GU1 3JG
United Kingdom
(44) 01483-564511

■ **Inn on the Lake**
Ockford Rd.
Guildford
United Kingdom
(44) 01483-419997

♪ HEALTH & HARMONY ARTS & MUSIC FESTIVAL

June
Santa Rosa, California
www.harmonyfestival.com
Admission: $–$$

The Health & Harmony Arts & Music Festival takes place just an hour or so north of San Francisco at the Sonoma County fairgrounds. Hundreds of booths and tables showcase the latest in organic foods and other health and ecologically minded products for about 20,000 visitors. Live music is performed on several stages, with another location reserved for a late night DJ party featuring some of the best techno DJs in the Bay Area on the decks. The live entertainment ranges from funk to ethnic folk and reggae. Added perks include panel discussions, belly dancing, and a surreal giant Uncle Sam and Statue of Liberty on stilts. Expect to come away from this event with something made of hemp.

For more information: (707) 575-9355 or info@harmonyfestival.com

Camping: No

Accommodations

■ **Flamingo Hotel**
2777 4th St.
Santa Rosa, CA 95401
(707) 545-8530

■ **Sandman Hotel**
3421 Cleveland Ave.
Santa Rosa, CA 95401
(707) 544-8570

♪ HIGH SIERRA MUSIC FESTIVAL

July
Quincy, California
www.hsmusic.net/hsmf
Admission: $$$

The High Sierra Music Festival takes place every Independence Day weekend in the northern California town of Quincy. Excellent camping facilities and the lush High Sierras make this ideal for a weekend getaway. The festival regularly books a selection of top-notch folk and roots acts and has welcomed Bela Fleck, Los Lobos, JJ Cale, and David Grisman in the past. Different tent-stages allow you to see a variety of acts in more intimate settings during the day, while some of the other stages provide an opportunity to stay up late into the evening. Add in the local foods, crafts, games, and activities for the children, and you've got your holiday weekend set.

For more information: mail@hsmusic.net

Camping: Yes. Camping is permitted on-site and is included in the ticket price. Lodging in the surrounding area is very limited, so plan on camping.

Accommodations

■ **Ranchito Motel**
2020 E. Main St.
Quincy, CA 95971
(530) 283-2265

■ **Spanish Creek Motel**
233 Crescent St.
Quincy, CA 95971
(530) 283-1200

HOMO A GO-GO

September
Olympia, Washington
www.homoagogo.com
Admission: $–$$

A spin-off on the popular Yo-Yo a Go-Go festival (see page 390), this four-day event is a celebration of independent music in Olympia with an emphasis on gay artists. All manner of artists and activists are invited to attend and bear witness to spoken-word performances, punk acts, hip-hop, folk, and more. The music is interspersed with workshops and film screenings. Expect to hear from performers such as Mirah, Tara Jane O' Neil, and the Gossip.

For more information: info@homoagogo.com

Camping: No

Accommodations

■ **Golden Gavel**
909 Capital Way
Olympia, WA 98501
(360) 352-8533

■ **Aladdin Motor Inn**
900 Capital Way
Olympia, WA 98501

JUBILEE JAM

May
Jackson, Mississippi
www.jubileejam.com
Admission: $–$$

Since its beginnings in 1987, Mississippi's Jubilee Jam has presented some of the true musical greats from the realms of rock, soul, blues, and beyond. From James Brown to John Prine, from Wilson Pickett to Bonnie Raitt, Jubilee Jam excels at putting together a three-day event that entertains a huge cross section of folks across five different stages. A wide variety of jewelry and sculpture is available to purchase, while magicians, clowns, and face painting will keep the children happy.

Artist Submissions

JAM
P.O. Box 23413
Jackson, MS 39225

Camping: No

Accommodations

■ **Crowne Plaza Hotel**
200 E. Amite St.
Jackson, MS 39201
(601) 969-5100
cp-jackson-dwntn@bristolhotels.com

■ **Edison Walthall Hotel**
225 E. Capital
Jackson, MS 39201
(800) 932-6161
www.edisonwalthallhotel.com

♪ KANSAS CITY SPIRIT FESTIVAL

August–September
Kansas City, Missouri
www.spiritfest.org/index2.html
Admission: $$

The Kansas City Spirit Festival's origins stretch back to 1984, when the city fathers decided they needed an event to promote town pride and history. Over the years, the festival has seen attendance swell, along with the number of stages and activities. Now more than three-dozen acres of land host regional and international acts, with stages organized by music genre—you'll find everything from classic rock to reggae to electronic music. Past performers have ranged from old favorites such as .38 Special to newer artists such as Better Than Ezra.

Artist Submissions
Attn: Program Committee
Kansas City Spirit Festival
2100 Grand, Suite 600
Kansas City, MO 64108
For more information: kcspirit@spiritfest.org
Camping: No
Accommodations

■ **Hyatt Regency Crown Center**
2345 McGee St.
Kansas City, MO 64108
(816) 421-1234

■ **Quarterage Hotel**
560 Westport Rd.
Kansas City, MO 64111
(816) 931-0001
info@quarteragehotel.com
www.quarteragehotel.com

♪ KONINGINNENPOP FESTIVAL

April
Santpoort-Zuid, Netherlands
www.koninginnenpop.nl
Admission: *FREE*

This free festival in the Netherlands mixes up any number of alternative, funk, and electronic artists. This single-day event is popular with bands touring their way through Europe, so you never know who might take the stage.

For more information: info@koninginnenpop.nl

Camping: No

Accommodations

■ **Bastion Hotel**
Vlietweg 20
Santpoort 2071 KW
Netherlands
(31) 23-538-7474

♪ LIVERPOOL SUMMER POPS

July
Liverpool, United Kingdom
www.liverpoolpops.com
Admission: $$–$$$

Over 50,000 people convene annually on the banks of the Mersey River for the Liverpool Summer Pops Festival. For nearly three weeks in July, tourists and locals mingle down by the docks in the Big Top Arena, where they witness performances by the likes of Bob Dylan, Tom Jones, and B. B. King.

For more information: (44) 08-707-460-000

Camping: No

Accommodations

■ **Aachen Hotel**
89-91 Mt. Pleasant
Liverpool L3 5TB
United Kingdom
(44) 01-517-093-477
enquiries@aachenhotel.co.uk
www.aachenhotel.co.uk

■ **Dolby Hotel**
36-42 Chaloner St.
Queens Dock
Liverpool, L3 4DE
United Kingdom
(44) 01-517-087-272
www.dolbyhotels.co.uk

LONG BEACH CHILI COOK-OFF

June
Long Beach, California
www.beachfest.com
Admission: $$

Formerly known as Beach Fest, this southern California event is one of the largest music- and food-based gatherings in the state. Don't let the name fool you; there's much more to this festival than stirring a pot of beans. For more than 20 years, people have come to Long Beach for this two-day party. Recent performers have included acts such as Booker T. & the MGs, Soul Asylum, and Michael Franti. This event is great way to experience excellent music and excellent food around the Long Beach marina.

Artist Submissions: Chris@mowalla.com
Camping: No
Accommodations

■ **Travelodge**
80 Atlantic Ave.
Long Beach, CA 90802
(562) 435-2471

■ **Vagabond Inn**
150 Alamitos Ave.
Long Beach, CA 90802
(562) 435-7621

MELTING POT JAM

June
Gardner, Massachusetts
www.meltingpotjam.com
Admission: $$

A grassroots event built around community, the central-Massachusetts-based Melting Pot Jam combines acoustic and electric performances from local groups to achieve the feeling of a camping trip with close friends. The festival is put together by fans of the music and is free from corporate impersonality because its existence relies solely on donations. Artists and attendees alike can enjoy themselves in this noncompetitive environment. Camping is included in part of the ticket price, but the event is only open to those 21 and older.

For more information: info@meltingpotjam.com
Camping: Yes

Accommodations

■ **Gardner Super 8**
22 Pearson Blvd.
Gardner, MA 01440
(800) 800-8000

■ **Colonial Bed & Breakfast**
625 Betty Spring Rd.
Gardner, MA 01440
(978) 630-2500

♪ METALFEST

July
Milwaukee, Wisconsin
www.metalfest.com
Admission: $$

This metal extravaganza is a hallowed occasion in Milwaukee: two days of up-and-coming acts mixed in with some of the best-known and most powerful metal bands on the planet. More than one hundred different acts perform, and artists such as the Misfits, Napalm Death, Gwar, and Testament provide plenty of fodder for concerned parents. For a few days, Milwaukee is *the* place to be for anyone interested in metal in the United States. The festival has become so popular that soon different cities around the nation will be playing host to their own variations on Metalfest.

For more information: rgmetalboy@webtv.net
Camping: No
Accommodations

■ **Ambassador Hotel**
2308 W. Wisconsin Ave.
Milwaukee, WI 53233
(414) 342-8400
reserve@ambasshotel.com
www.ambasshotel.com

■ **Howard Johnson Express**
176 W. Wisconsin Ave.
Milwaukee, WI 53203
(414) 271-4656

♪ MICHIGAN FEST

March
Wayne, Michigan
Admission: $$

This three-day event concentrates on the more intense, aggressive side of independent music and features a wide array of punk and college radio acts in a well-organized grassroots environment. Bands such as Karate, Sweep the Leg Johnny, Hot Snakes, and Death Cab for Cutie perform eagerly anticipated sets for swarms of underground music fans. The event began very low-key in the mid-1990s, but has since grown into an unexpectedly large event that now donates money to charities. The organizers are involved in all aspects of the event, from planning and booking to building the stages. Because the majority of music festivals featuring noncommercial, radio-oriented rock take place in major cities, Michigan Fest is warmly welcomed by the people in Wayne and its surrounding cities.

Camping: No

Accommodations

■ **Wayne's Red Apple Inn**
32711 Michigan Ave.
Wayne, MI 48184
(734) 722-4100

■ **Days Inn Downtown Detroit**
3250 E. Jefferson
Detroit, MI 48207
(313) 568-2000

MISSION CREEK MUSIC FESTIVAL

May
San Francisco, California
www.mcmf.org
Admission: $

This festival has been taking place in San Francisco since the late 1990s and generally features a variety of musicians and bands from the Bay Area with a smattering of out-of-towners. Intimate venues all across the city, from the luscious Café Du Nord to the more worn-in Bottom of the Hill, provide just a few of the stages where these consistently eclectic lineups are unleashed on the public. By incorporating punk rock, experimental sounds, Americana, garage rock, and assorted DJs, the Mission Creek Music Festival has become known for putting together the best in local talent.

For more information: jtray7@directvinternet.com

Camping: No

Accommodations

■ **Phoenix Hotel**
601 Eddy St.
San Francisco, CA 94109
(800) 248-9466

■ **Hotel Bijou**
111 Mason St.
San Francisco, CA 94102
(800) 771-1022

JEFF RAY, *organizer of the Mission Creek Music Festival in San Francisco, is also a founding member of local indie rock band Zmrzlina. Ray founded the festival in 1996 and can be seen every year running around town like a crazy man, trying to get everything just right. He usually does.*

How did the Mission Creek Music Festival get started?

The annual Mission Creek Music Festival started seven years ago at a venue called Starcleaners, which was a music collective in the Mission. Jennifer Shagwat ran the place. Bands such as Hickey, Fantasy, and 50 Million used to hang out and play there—it was really just a warehouse. The next year the festival moved over to the El Rio and turned into an all-day and night event. My band, Zmrzlina, used to help curate and produce it, and now I continue to act as executive curator and producer along with a few friends. The festival takes place all over town for a period of up to two weeks. It was named after the creeks and swamps that lie underneath the streets of SOMA and the Mission.

Why the hell would you want to organize a music festival?

Short Version: I like local music.

Long version: I like to fill in cultural voids. Maybe it is something missing in my own life, but I won't go there. During high school I used to set up shows in Fairfax, Virginia. I would try to bring down bands from D.C. such as Scream and Minor Threat to play our little community center in suburbia hell. Of course my band at the time, Seepage, would play as well. So, it was also a way to promote my band. I did the same sort of thing in college in Richmond. The Mission Creek Music Festival is a continuation of this desire to fill a cultural void. I also feel that the scene in the Bay Area could benefit from a local-centric music festival that spans different genres and venues.

What is it about the music that inspires you to keep doing this?

It is all about the music, right? I don't know. I love music. I like a lot of the local bands partly because it is the music I know best and partly because I feel the scene here in San Francisco is better than in most other cities. Some of the local musicians are genius at what they do and it inspires me in my own music. I hope it inspires the attendees of the festival as well.

What is the hardest part?

The hardest part? I don't like dealing with the money (or lack of money) aspect. I don't like working with bands who ask for huge guarantees I can't afford. I never like to tell a band that they did not make it into the festival, especially if they're my friends.

Is it worth it?

I guess it is worth it, in a sadomasochistic way. It takes a lot of time, it's never financially rewarding, and it's pretty stressful. Despite all that, I do enjoy sorting through the mountain of music and getting surprised by the talent we have in this area. There is a feel-good aspect to it as well when you're watching bands play together on a good night with a good lineup that seem to inspire and energize the night and the scene.

How much chance does an unknown act have of performing in some capacity at your festival?

There's a pretty good chance, but I have to say that "unknown" is a bit of a loaded description. It may not be a band that I have heard of, but the band may be popular in another local scene. Even if I don't like them or know them, if they have integrity or offer something interesting to the festival, or have contributed to their scene for a while, I use those as major factors when deciding who to include.

Do any of the proceeds from the festival go to charity or a cause?

In previous years all the money went to pay for expenses (I also pitched in some of my own money). This year we are working with a nonprofit organization, Soundsafe, and they are both helping finance the costs as well as keeping some or any of the gross to help pay for next year's festival. We are also having a benefit show for the San Francisco Late Night Coalition (SFLNC), a local music activist group that includes a crew of lawyers who help protect the nightlife and its music and venues. I might also try to put together a benefit show for our label guy and friend Brad Stark, the KUSF DJ. He's still recovering from a near death experience in a fire.

What are the three things you think set your festival apart from other festivals? More chaotic, more inclusive, more grassroots?

A. I think it is definitely more chaotic than other festivals, from the lineups to the organization (and lack thereof). The shows are sometimes pretty insane as well, like when you have the Extra Action Marching Band flag girls almost kicking the audience in the head.

B. I like to think that it is a pretty inclusive festival, in terms of the Bay Area music scene. It is in our mission statement that at least eighty percent of the bands are local. We are now trying to expand on the genres that we accept as well.

C. We're definitely grassroots. Just look at all the local businesses, venues, and radio stations that sponsor the festival and the friends and bandmates that volunteer and help put it together!

What is the strangest thing you've ever seen at your festival?

During a Virginia Dare set at the El Rio a few years ago, a pet rabbit on the loose came out to a drum mike and started singing. Well, it looked like it was singing. It was cute, yet bizarre, because it only went up to the mike when lead vocalist Mary O'Neil was singing. I also sort of enjoyed the time when Virgil Shaw got punched by a gay biker at the Eagle. The biker thought Virgil called him an old crow when he was just ordering a shot of Old Crow Whiskey. I guess it was weirdly funny.

Which act or acts stick out in your mind as providing the best performances at Mission Creek?

Black Dot Collective, Extra Action Marching Band, Craig Ventrusco, Crack W.A.R., Live Human, the Centimeters, Marcus Shelby, Court and Spark, Nate Denver—the list goes on. They were great mostly because I was surprised at how much integrity they had along with their performances. I especially enjoyed the noise show last year at Adobe Books, which was inspired by the Pubis Noir "pancake and noise" shows they used to have on Mission Street. It was a free show and we

• • • • • • • • • • •

served pancakes to the sounds of Big Techno Werewolf, Hans Gruel's Kranken-kabinet, among others.

What advice would you give to potential festival organizers?

Start organizing early. Let someone else help you. Don't let it destroy your mind.

What hopes do you have for the festival's future?

More of the same, but better, I guess. I am adding film and video nights this year. More of that in the future. More free shows. I would also like to experiment even more with eclectic lineups and venues; for example, I'd love to see Polyphonic Spree, The Coup, and Ledisi at Grace Cathedral, or an "Andrew W.K. Versus Anthony (of Gay Barbarians and E-Zee Tiger)" rock battle in the battlebot ring. I would also like to emulate the experiences I have had at European festivals or what I imagine the festivals in SF were like in the sixties. For example, I'd like to have three days and nights of camping and music in Golden Gate Park where we all can have a big love fest while being put to sleep by Sonny Smith and woken up at 6:00 A.M. by the diaphanous sounds of Fennesz and/or Wobbly. That sort of thing. Those hippies did something right.

• • • • • • • • • • •

MOBFEST

June
Chicago, Illinois
www.chicagomobfest.com
Admission: $$$

MOBfest is an industry showcase for Chicago area bands vying to be the next big thing. The participating venues are responsible for taking submissions from bands, with a focus on heavier, alternative music. For example, the popular nu metal group Disturbed is a MOB (Music Over Business) success story. Nonindustry folks are welcome to buy tickets, enjoy the shows, and sit in on the many music discussion panels. It's a great opportunity to see bands on their way up and to get a sense of how this aspect of the music industry functions.

For more information: info@mobfest.com

Camping: No

Accommodations

■ **City Suites Hotel**
933 W. Belmont
Chicago, IL 60657
(800) 248-9108

■ **Chicago Marriott Downtown**
540 N. Michigan Ave.
Chicago, IL 60611
(312) 836-0100

♪ MOONDANCE JAM

July

Walker, Minnesota

www.moondancejam.com

Admission: $$$

Moondance Jam was started back in 1992 when Walker, Minnesota, residents Bill and Kathy Bieloh were thinking of ways to promote their riding stables. Each year, the festival grew a little bit bigger, adding a list of internationally known performers to what was once just a few regional acts. The most recent events have welcomed more than 50,000 people to the grounds over a four-day period. Acts such as Styx, Kansas, and Pat Benatar rub shoulders with newer bands such as the Wallflowers and Blues Traveler. Ample campgrounds are available and often provide as much entertainment as the stages.

For more information: (877) MOONJAM

Camping: Yes

Accommodations

■ **Americinn**
Hwy. 371
Walker, MN 56484
(866) 836-9330

■ **Country Inn & Suites**
442 Walker Bay Blvd.
Walker, MN 56484

♪ MOTHER EARTH REVIVAL

April

Samsula, Florida

Admission: $

This festival places as much emphasis on education as it does on entertainment. Dedicated to ecology and a general awareness of nature, it brings together a diverse mixture of bands representing a great many genres, from funk to folk. Visitors can feel free to relax on the grass and enjoy the event for an afternoon or make a weekend of it.

For more information: cmrmusicmgmt@lycos.com

Camping: Yes

Accommodations

■ **Oceans Trillium Suites**
3405 S. Atlantic Ave.
New Smyrna Beach, FL 32116
(904) 428-9106

■ **Riverview Hotel**
103 Flagler Ave.
New Smyrna Beach, FL 32116
(904) 428-5858

♩ MUSIKFEST

August
Bethlehem, Pennsylvania
www.musikfest.org
Admission: *FREE*

Downtown Bethlehem becomes a cross section for all types of music, from classical to country, when Musikfest comes to town in August. For nearly two decades, the festival has brought together people from all over the globe to celebrate the power of music. During this 10-day period, you can choose from more than 1,000 free performances—that means hundreds of acts from just as many genres. Recent editions of Musikfest have seen more than a million people attend, so plan ahead!

Artist Submissions

Bethlehem Musikfest Association
Robin Zaremski, Director of Performing Arts
25. W Third St., Suite 300
Bethlehem, PA 18015
rzaremski@fest.org

Camping: No

Accommodations

■ **Radisson Hotel Bethlehem**
437 Main St.
Bethlehem, PA 18018
(610) 625-5000
rhi_beth@radisson.com

■ **Fairfield Inn**
2140 Motel Dr.
Bethlehem, PA 18018
(610) 867-8681

♪ NEMO MUSIC SHOWCASE AND CONFERENCE

April
Boston, Massachusetts
www.nemoboston.com
Admission: $$

NEMO is one of the key music showcases on the East Coast, presenting more than 250 artists over three days and winding things up with the Boston Music Awards. A mixture of live performances, trade shows, and panel discussions, this event should be required for anyone with more than a passing interest in the music industry. The artists who perform here are generally unsigned, but some past showcases have included concerts by Staind, Linkin Park, and De La Soul. Local Boston bands especially should look into submitting their demos to the organizers of this eagerly awaited event.

For more information: (781) 306-0441 or info@nemoboston.com
Camping: No
Accommodations

■ **Swissôtel Boston**
1 Ave. de Lafayette
Boston, MA 02111
(800) 621-9200
Emailus.boston@swissotel.com
www.swissotel.com

■ **Omni Parker House**
60 School St.
Boston, MA 02108
(800) 843-6664

♪ NEW ORLEANS HURRICANE FESTIVAL

September
New Orleans, Louisiana
Admission: $$

This single-day event is named after the infamous drink served throughout New Orleans. If made correctly, it can do a lot more damage than its deceptively sweet taste lets on; you'll have the opportunity to find out for yourself when September rolls around. In grand New Orleans style, this festival is a big party with almost 7,000 people hanging out and soaking up the heat and humidity right by the Mississippi River. Roots and jam-based artists such as Cowboy Mouth, Ratdog, Cracker, and the Old 97s made the 2002 event a highlight in a town where live music is almost mandatory every night of the year. The festival takes place in Riverview Park, not far from the Audubon Zoo.

For more information: (877) 669-2552

Camping: No

Accommodations

■ **Chateau Hotel**
1001 Rue Chartres
New Orleans, LA 70116
(504) 524-9636

■ **Historic French Market Inn**
501 Rue Decatur
New Orleans, LA 70130
(888) 487-1543

♪ NEW POP FESTIVAL

October

Baden-Baden, Stadttheater, Germany

www.swr3.de/fun/events/newpop

Admission: $$–$$$

Organized by the German radio station SWR3, the New Pop Festival books a huge variety of European and American acts across several stages. Thousands of fans come from the Baden-Baden area (and from all over Europe) to hear great music from a wide range of youth-oriented acts such as Sugar Ray and Uncle Kracker.

For more information: hithop@swr3.de

Camping: No

Accommodations

■ **Hotel Am Markt**
Marktplatz 18
Baden-Baden, Baden-
  Wurttemberg 76530
Germany
(49) 07221-27040

■ **Deutscher Kaiser**
Merkurstrasse 9
Baden-Baden, Baden-
  Wurttemberg D-76530
Germany
(49) 07221-2700

♪ NOISE POP

February

San Francisco, California

www.noisepop.com

Admission: $–$$$

With a history stretching back to 1993, San Francisco's Noise Pop festival is slowly becoming a Bay Area institution for indie rockers. The event generally stretches out over the course of a week, with shows in both the daytime and the evenings. All-access passes are available, or you can check out individual shows in stunning venues such as Bimbo's 365 Club or the Great American Music Hall. Local movie houses hold screenings of rarely seen music films. But the music is the best of all, ranging from the loud pop sounds of Flaming Lips and Guided by Voices to legends such as Big Star to the quieter British folk sounds of Gorky's Zygotic Mynci. Noise Pop is a great way to explore the current musical climate and to get lost in the great city of San Francisco. The organizers have also put together a similar event in Chicago.

Artist Submissions

Noise Pop Submissions

375 Alabama St., Suite 490

San Francisco, CA 94110

submit@noisepop.com

Camping: No

Accommodations

■ **Phoenix Hotel**

601 Eddy St.

San Francisco, CA 94109

(800) 248-9466

■ **Hotel Bijou**

111 Mason St.

San Francisco, CA 94102

(800) 771-1022

OAK RIDGE FEST

June

Scottown, Ohio

www.earthproductions.net/oakridge-fest.html

Admission: $

The Oak Ridge Festival began in 2001 with the premise that people should be able to gather and discuss ideas in an outdoor environment while some great music plays onstage. All efforts have been successful so far. A wide variety of regional jam bands has gathered there to provide the musical interludes in between heated bouts of self-expression. Consider it therapy in the beautiful natural backdrop of southern Ohio.

For more information: rdelong@earthproductions.net

Camping: Yes

Accommodations

▪ Comfort Inn & Suites
70 Private Rd. 302
South Point, OH 45680

OLYMPIA EXPERIMENTAL MUSIC FEST

Mid-June
Olympia, Washington
www.geocities.com/agentduckhugger/olyexpfest8.html
Admission: $

Since 1995, the Olympia Experimental Music Fest has summoned some of the more left-of-center practitioners of new and uncompromising music to perform at three different venues. Most of the acts hail from the Pacific Northwest. Noise, improvisation, and avant-jazz are well represented, although to pigeonhole any type of experimental music would do it a disservice. Let's just say that if the manipulation of sound intrigues you, there is no better place for you to be come June.

For more information: agentduckhugger@hotmail.com

Camping: No

Accommodations

▪ West Coast Olympia Hotel
2300 Evergreen Park Dr.
Olympia, WA 98502
(800) 325-4000
olympiasales@westcoasthotels.com

▪ Phoenix Inn Olympia
415 Capitol Way N.
Olympia, WA 98501
(360) 570-0555
phoenixinn@olywa.net

OPEN EYE FESTIVAL

May
Seaforth, Ontario, Canada
Admission: $$

The Open Eye Festival is a small weekend event focused on bringing like-minded folks together under the lovely Canadian skies. Featuring a musical lineup that combines jam rock with heavier alternative music, this event gets by more on its atmosphere than on the fame of its performers. It's a nice change of pace from the larger festivals, which can sometimes be the polar opposite. In addition to regional performances, cult films are screened and various daytime activities are arranged. You can be sure that drum circles will abound. Tent camping is encouraged.

For more information: openeyefestival@hotmail.com

Camping: Yes

Accommodations

■ **Brentwood on the Beach**
St. Joseph Shores 1, R.R. #2
Zurich, ON N0M 2T0
Canada
(519) 236-7137
beachbnb@hay.net
www.brentwoodonthebeach.com

■ **The Little Inn of Bayfield**
P.O. Box 100, Main St.
Bayfield, ON N0M 1G0
Canada
(519) 565-2611
innkeeper@littleinn.com
www.littleinn.com

♪ ORANGE TWIN MUSIC FESTIVAL

End of September
Athens, Georgia
www.orangetwin.com/fest.html
Admission: $

The Orange Twin Music Festival is organized by Athens's Orange Twin record label. Orange Twin releases some of the most interesting independent music around in addition to re-releasing lost classics and presenting odd field recordings. This eclecticism extends to the festival, where a variety of indie-pop acts such as Elf Power and Masters of the Hemisphere perform among fire jugglers and trapeze acts. Camping and hiking are available and encouraged. During the weekend, attendees can look forward to a communal dinner and breakfast.

For more information: orangetwin@yahoo.com

Camping: Yes

Accommodations

■ **Downtown Travelodge**
898 W. Broad St.
Athens, GA 30601
(706) 549-5400

POCONO CLASSIC ROCK BIKERS' RALLY

August
Lake Harmony, Pennsylvania
www.jackfrostbigboulder.com/classic-rock.asp
Admission: $$

This event takes place during the off-season at the Big Boulder ski area and provides a haven for motorcycle fanatics in August. The natural surroundings provide an easy, relaxed atmosphere for both musicians and bike fans. You can feel free to experience the chairlift views and get a breath of even fresher air. Food and drink are plentiful here, so don't pack a lunch. In the past, the lineups have been a who's who of FM radio, with performances by the Marshall Tucker Band, Bad Company, and Rick Derringer making their mark alongside tribute acts such as the Unforgettable Fire (U2) and the B-Streets (Bruce Springsteen).

Camping: Yes. Camping is available at the nearby Fern Ridge Campgrounds.

Accommodations

■ **Ramada Inn**
P.O. Box 600
Rt. 940 & I-80
Pocono-Lake Harmony, PA 18624
(570) 443-8471

■ **The Resort at Split Rock**
1Lake Drive
P.O. Box 567
Lake Harmony, PA 18624

POPKOMM

Mid-August
Cologne, Germany
www.popkomm.de
Admission: $$$

Popkomm began in 1989 and is one of the music industry's biggest trade shows in the world. While the trade aspect of Popkomm might not appeal to anyone outside the industry, the live performances from hundreds of acts certainly will. Popkomm works in conjunction with the Musikfest am Ring Festival—an event that draws in almost two million people for a three-day festival. The music ranges from the sunny pop of the Cardigans to the fist-pumping heavy metal of Manowar. The combination of the two events makes this one of the largest music gatherings you can find anywhere.

For more information: (49) 221-91655-0 or popkomm@musikkomm.de

Camping: No

Accommodations

■ **Flandrischer Hof**

Flandrische Strasse 3-5
Cologne, North Rhine-
  Westphalia 50674
Germany
(49) 221-25209-5

■ **Hotel Buchholz**

Kunibertsgasse 5
Cologne, North Rhine-
  Westphalia 50668
Germany
(49) 221-16083-0

♪ ROCK FEST

July

Cadott, Wisconsin

www.rock-fest.com

Admission: $$$

With a title like Rock Fest, you know what you're in for when you make the journey to Cadott, Wisconsin: rock—and nothing but. The first festival was launched in 1994 and saw crowds swell up to 40,000 people. The festival's reputation for smooth organization explains its growing popularity and why performers such as Cheap Trick, Foreigner, Lynyrd Skynyrd, and other classic rock staples are booked regularly. Campgrounds are available on-site and are encouraged for anyone who plans on attending all three days.

For more information: info@rock-fest.com

Camping: Yes

Accommodations

■ **Countryside Motel**

Jct. State Hwys. 29 & 27
Cadott, WI 54727
(715) 289-4000

♪ ROCK 'N' WHEELS FESTIVAL

July

Auburn, Michigan

www.rock-n-wheels.com

Admission: $

This festival celebrates two of America's most prominent obsessions: cars and rock 'n' roll. Rock 'n' Wheels honors music's golden era with a series of sock hop-style dance contests and karaoke competitions and bands perform classic songs from the 1950s and 1960s. The Charity Car Cruise is usually the festival highlight, with a wide range of pristine classic and muscle cars lining the city streets. This festival has been going strong since 1992 and brings a healthy dose of adolescent fun to the town of Auburn.

For more information: info@Rock-N-Wheels.com

Camping: No

Accommodations

■ **Super 8 Auburn**
4955 Garfield Rd.
Auburn, MI 48611
(517) 662-7888

♩ ROSKILDE FESTIVAL

June
Roskilde, Denmark
www.roskilde-festival.dk
Admission: $$$

Denmark's Roskilde festival began in the early 1970s and was known for featuring big names such as the Kinks and Fairport Convention. By the end of the '70s, it was booking edgy, youth-oriented talent and snagged artists such as U2 and Elvis Costello early in their careers. The festival has continued to book the best in new acts and has seen artists such as My Bloody Valentine, the Cure, Radiohead, and Flaming Lips take the stage.

For more information: (45) 463-66-613 or bigbox@roskilde-festival.dk

Camping: Yes, included in the ticket price.

Artist Submissions

Havsteensvej 11
4000 Roskilde
Denmark

Accommodations

■ **Gershoj Kro**
Havnevej 14
Roskilde
Denmark
(45) 470-52-8041

■ **Skuldelev Kro Hotel**
Ãstergade 2A
Roskilde
Denmark
(45) 470-52-0308

SAN DIEGO STREET SCENE

September
San Diego, California
www.street-scene.com
Admission: $$

The San Diego Street Scene, California's largest music festival, presents some of the best live bands around in a great outdoor environment and has done so for nearly two decades. Traditionally taking place the weekend after Labor Day, this event has drawn more than 100,000 people to the streets. James Brown, the Black Crowes, En Vogue, and Jurassic 5 have all recently performed here, which just shows what a great cross section of popular rock, R&B, and hip-hop acts will perform on the event's dozen stages.

For more information: info@street-scene.com

Camping: No

Accommodations

■ **San Diego Marriott**
333 W. Harbor Dr.
San Diego, CA 92101
(619) 234-1500

■ **Hilton Gaslamp District**
401 K St.
San Diego, CA 92101
(619) 231-4040

SAN FRANCISCO ALTERNATIVE MUSIC FESTIVAL

May
Oakland and San Francisco, California
www.sfalt.org
Admission: $–$$

Although the phrase "alternative music" has become a catchall for a lot of popular, radio-friendly music, the organizers at the San Francisco Alternative Music Festival manage to offer a true alternative. Performances at this event range from electronic soundscapes to free jazz to freak-outs to any other type of improvised music. The music comes from all over the West Coast, with several performers making a special visit from overseas.

Camping: No

Accommodations

■ **Phoenix Hotel**
601 Eddy St.
San Francisco, CA 94109
(800) 248-9466

■ **Hotel Ibiza**
10 Hegenberger Rd.
Oakland, CA 94621
info@hotelibiza.com

SAN FRANCISCO POP FESTIVAL

July
San Francisco, California
Admission: $–$$

This event began in 2001 with the title "2001: A Pop Fantasy." Since then the biennial event has brought together several well-known independent bands from the Bay Area and the United Kingdom who excel at creating sugary pop that combines circa-1960s melodies with the guitar buzz of bands like the Ramones. The Aislers Set, the Lucksmiths, and Boyracer might not be known to everyone, but this event goes a long way toward proving that there is something (besides lead) in the water in San Francisco.

Camping: No

Accommodations

■ **Phoenix Hotel**
601 Eddy St.
San Francisco, CA 94109
(800) 248-9466

■ **The Red Victorian**
1665 Haight St.
San Francisco, CA 94117
(415) 864-1978

CHRIS PRUITT *is one of the organizers involved with the San Francisco Pop Festival. He loves pop music, friendly faces, and breaking even.*

Why in the world would you want to help organize a music festival?

The whole idea of organizing a pop music festival in San Francisco came about because we were too poor to travel to the Kindercore Pop Fest in 1998, which was held in Athens, Georgia. We decided to throw our own—on our own turf in San Francisco in 1999. But I guess the main reason for organizing a festival is the love of the music. If we didn't put one together, nobody else would.

What is it about the music that inspires you to keep doing this?

Well, indie pop music is such a huge part of my life that it almost comes naturally. The music and friendly faces inspire us to keep putting on these pop fests.

What is the hardest part?

I guess the hardest part of planning the pop fests would have to be narrowing down the list of bands to ask. If it were possible, I would pick hundreds of bands. The truth of the matter is that we have to cram as many bands as possible into a four-day event.

Is it worth it?

Even though we put in almost a year's worth of work for a four-day event, it is totally worth it.

How do you decide the lineup?

We have a team of four to six people. We all generate a list of bands we would love to see perform. From that list we discard bands such as the dB's and Big Star. Although we would love to see them, we know it's just not possible. Then we ask away! It's like a birthday party. Obviously some bands won't be able to make it (especially if they are from overseas), so from there the list narrows down. Then we ask a handful of local bands and we have a complete lineup.

Do any of the proceeds from the festival go to charity or a cause?

Sadly, we do not donate any money to charity. All the money goes to the bands. Since most of them travel from so far away, it is the least we can do to help them out. We don't make any money either. It's only fair for the money to go to the bands that draw the fans. We always have all-ages shows. For those that don't know, that means the bar usually takes a percentage of the door money. At a local venue such as the Bottom of the Hill (with a maximum capacity of 276), they take thirty percent of ticket sales.

Do you have a good anecdote about last year's event you think people ought to hear?

At the end of Boyracer's amazingly energetic set, they completely smashed the majority of their equipment, even though they still had a few shows left on their tour. Some in the crowd just dropped their jaws while others were left in complete pandemonium. It is hard to use words to describe their destruction; it was something you just had to see.

Which acts do you think put on the best show?

You know, this is nearly impossible to answer. Every single band that has ever played has helped to make these events so amazing. I guess if I had to list a few of my personal favorites they would include Rocketship, Aislers Set, Ciao Bella, the How, Boyracer, Aerospace, Tullycraft, Marine Research, Dressy Bessy—I could go on and on. It really isn't fair to leave anyone out.

What advice would you give to potential festival organizers?

Be prepared to work your ass off! This is no simple task. The rewards are great, but only if you put every bit of effort into making the festival the best it can be.

♪ SCHWAGSTOCK

May
Lake Ozark, Missouri
www.theschwag.com
Admission: $$

Schwagstock is organized by the Missouri-based Grateful Dead tribute band, the Schwag. For the past six years, Schwagstock has provided an outlet for those who just haven't been the same since Jerry Garcia passed on. This event happens in the spacious Ozark Outdoors River Resort, where camping, river rafting, hiking, and swimming are all widely available. The two-day event is highlighted by the Schwag's evening performances, but the bands leading up to them also provide a fine mixture of blues, reggae, and roots rock. There is an open vending area for those desiring to sell food and wares, but be advised that the sale of alcohol and fireworks is strictly prohibited.

For more information: (314) 838-5248
Camping: Yes
Accommodations

■ **Cuba Super 8 Motel**
28 Hwy. P
Cuba, MO
(800) 800-8000

■ **Wagon Wheel Motel**
901 E. Washington St.
Cuba, MO 65453
(573) 885-3411

♪ SEATTLE IMPROVISED MUSIC FESTIVAL

June
Seattle, Washington
www.seattleimprovisedmusic.com
Admission: $

Fans of improvised music eagerly await this festival, which has been staged every year since 1985. It's one of the longest-running showcases for improvised music in the United States and regularly features spontaneous music from all over the world in a variety of forms, including jazz, world music, and rock. Past performers have included artists such as Nels Cline, Henry Kaiser, and violinist Eyvind Kang.

For more information: (206) 447-6144 or info@seattleimprovisedmusic.com
Camping: No
Accommodations

■ **Mayflower Park**
405 Olive Way
Seattle, WA 98101
(800) 426-5100

■ **Hotel Vintage Park**
1100 5th Ave.
Seattle, WA 98101
(800) 624-4433

♪ SHENANDOAH VALLEY MUSIC FESTIVAL

May–September
Orkney Springs, Virginia
www.musicfest.org
Admission: $

The Shenandoah Valley Music Festival has nearly four decades of experience in bringing quality music to local music fans and visitors. Held in Orkney Springs, Virginia, the festival is set up in a secluded resort area with a mineral springs spa nearby. A large pavilion provides an outdoor setting in which to enjoy a mixture of classical and popular music. The event is spread out over five different weekends during the summer, so there's plenty of time to enjoy this long-running event.

For more information: svmf@shentel.net
Camping: No

Accommodations

■ **Comfort Inn Shenandoah**
1011 Motel Dr.
Woodstock, VA 22664
(540) 459-7600
cis@shentel.net

■ **Cross Roads Inn Bed & Breakfast**
9222 John Sevier Rd.
New Market, VA 22844
(888) 740-4157
freisitz@shentel.net
www.crossroadsinnva.com

SOUTH BY SOUTHWEST (SXSW)

Mid-March
Austin, Texas
www.sxsw.com
Admission: $$$

Along with the CMJ Music Marathon in New York, SXSW is one of the top industry showcases in the world. Musicians fly in from all parts of the globe in hopes of coming away with a recording deal. It's a fair bet that the bands you see performing this year will be the ones exploding all over the press the next. Seasoned veterans play impromptu shows and you never know who you'll see walking down Austin's famed Sixth Street. This is a place where you can watch the Black Crowes and Jurassic 5 rock the house and then slip into a local café to watch the Strokes perform. You can eat barbecue chicken and watch the White Stripes for an afternoon. Tom Waits might be doing an impromptu gig on the back of a pickup truck. Industry schmooze-fest though this may be, it's also an incredible amount of fun. In addition to the vast number of musical performances, the film and interactive elements of the festival make sure that no aspect of the media is left untouched.

For more information: sxsw@sxsw.com
Camping: No
Accommodations

■ **Crowne Plaza**
500 N. IH-35
Austin, TX 78701
(512) 480-8181
sales@crowneplazaaustin.com
www.crowneplazaaustinhotel.com

■ **Omni Austin Hotel**
700 San Jacinto at 8th St.
Austin, TX 78701
(512) 476-3700

♪ SUMMERFEST

June–July
Milwaukee, Wisconsin
www.summerfest.com
Admission: $

Summerfest is a massive event that comes to Milwaukee once a year and spreads itself out over 90 acres of the Lake Michigan shoreline. The first festival began in 1968 after then-mayor Henry W. Maier attended Germany's Oktoberfest and realized how a large event of that nature can benefit both the town and its inhabitants. Over the years, Summerfest has welcomed artists such as Sly & the Family Stone, Bob Dylan, REM, and the Dave Matthews Band to its music stages, and the comedy stage has hosted stand-ups such as Billy Crystal and Adam Sandler.

If you tire of watching people perform, check out the amusement park. If the kids don't seem interested in Ted Nugent, you can take them to the Children's Theater and Playzone. Feeling hungry? Sit a spell and have a bite to eat from any of the almost 50 different restaurants that supply food for this event. Not enough? Well, don't forget about the skate park and the fireworks show. If you're looking for an experience that goes beyond the realm of your usual music festival, Summerfest is just the right destination for you.

Artist Submissions
Summerfest
attn: Entertainment Department
200 North Harbor Dr.
Milwaukee, WI 53202
production@summerfest.com

For more information: information@summerfest.com

Camping: No

Accommodations

■ **Astor Hotel**
924 E. Juneau Ave.
Milwaukee, WI 53202
(800) 558-0200

■ **County Clare Inn**
1234 North Astor St.
Milwaukee, WI 53202
(888) 94-CLARE
ctyclare@execpc.com
www.countyclare-inn.com

SUNDOG SUMMER SHAKEDOWN

October

East Troy, Wisconsin

http://sundogsummershakedown.itgo.com/index2.html

Admission: $$–$$$

The Sundog Summer Shakedown began in 2000 as an event "by Deadheads, for Deadheads." No doubt, the tie-dye is in full force here, but this friendly event is also perfect for families and all others who feel the need to lie back in the sun for a few days. The music maintains the same standards of country/rock/improvisational excellence that the Grateful Dead established, while also providing a large outdoor space that's ideal for after-hours jam sessions.

Artist Submissions

Shawn Moonrise Cemer

1412 Greenfield Cir.

Sun Prairie, WI 53590

shawn-moonrise@excite.com

For more information: timsundog@yahoo.com

Camping: Yes. Camping is highly encouraged.

Accommodations

■ **Pine Ridge**
W3895 Timberlake Rd.
East Troy, WI 53120
(414) 594-3269
BMalewicki@aol.com

■ **Pickwick Inn**
2966 Union St.
East Troy, WI 53120
(262) 642-5529
info@pickwickinn.com

TERRASTOCK

Fall

Various locations

www.terrascope.org

Admission: $$–$$$

The Terrastock Festival takes place every year in a different location, usually in the early fall. (Past events have been held in London, Rhode Island, Boston, and San Francisco.) The event is put together by the magazine *Ptolemaic Terrascope* and generally holds one of the most creative and fascinating lineups of alternative music you'll find that year. The festival pays tribute to the past while exploring psychedelic music and how it is defined in this current age. The bands range from tried-and-true alt-rock darlings (Sonic Youth) to lost favorites of yesteryear (Tom Rapp). Here you can see old-timey Country Joe McDonald rub shoulders with the Japanese act Acid Mothers Temple. Or you might catch the seventies Welsh rockers, Man, checking out a show by the Athens group the Sunshine Fix. From electronic knob twiddling to guitar drones to pure pop music, Terrastock is a wonder to behold.

Camping: No

• • • • 🎼 • • • •

BOB RUDELL *is a co-organizer for the Terrastock Music Festival, one of our favorite festivals ever (see page 416). We asked him to explain how "three grueling days" of work combined with a lack of ego are making the music festival relevant again.*

What is the allure of attending a music festival as opposed your basic rock show?

The allure of Terrastock comes from the atmosphere that's created when like-minded fans and musicians congregate for an intense weekend. "Three grueling days of music" is how I describe it, and it is wonderful. The bands and fans are pretty much one and the same, no rock star egos anywhere. Every forty-five minutes a different batch of people steps out of the audience and plays for their friends. I attend lots of basic rock shows too, but Terrastock has spawned a community that gathers wherever Phil [McMullen, Terrastock founder] decides to hold the event.

• • • • • • • • • • • •

• • • • • • • • • • • •

What is the biggest problem in organizing Terrastock?

The biggest problem is dealing with all the last minute challenges that crop up. Dealing with venues, ticketing services, hotels, etc.

How rigid are the lineups at Terrastock? What chance does a no-name band have of playing a show?

The bands in a Terrastock lineup all come at the invitation of Phil McMullen, usually after he's written about the band in the *Terrascope* (*Ptolemaic Terrascope* is the fanzine that begot the festival). A "no-name" band has a good chance of receiving an invite if they make sure Phil knows about them and, more importantly, if they fit in with the indefinable spirit of Terrastock. (Indefinable except to Phil, that is.)

What have been some of the musical highlights of the festival?

The number one highlight for me was at the first Terrastock in Providence when Tom Rapp did his comeback show. He was an unannounced performer and did a wonderful set. As a dedicated Pearls Before Swine fan in the sixties, it was surreal to hear that voice doing those wonderful songs after all those years. Getting to know Tom over the years since then has been a lot of fun, too.

Another highlight for me has been to see the respect between audience and artist. Quieter bands can expect a quieter audience that will listen to them—rather than shout over them from somewhere near the bar.

Other highlights . . . Roy Montgomery at Terrascope 2 in San Francisco, the semi-Velvets reunion of Moe Tucker and Doug Yule in Seattle, all the one-off gigs in London (Carl Hultgren—of Windy & Carl—with the Lothars, Tom Rapp, and Bevis Frond)—and the Acid Mothers Temple freak-out to close the Sunday psych-fest in Boston.

What place do you think a music festival has in today's musical climate?

The world needs events like Terrastock. The corporatization of music demands that Terrastock exist so that aspiring artists and musicians have a means to perform for an audience that will appreciate their work. In my opinion, the best music is created by people who don't know or care what the rules are—they have a sonic vision they need to communicate. So Terrastock is essential in this musical climate, maybe even more now than when it began in 1997.

• • • • • • • • • • • •

THREE RIVERS MUSIC FESTIVAL

April
Columbia, South Carolina
www.3riversmusicfestival.org
Admission: $

Year after year, the Three Rivers Music Festival does its part to encourage music interest through live performances and family activities. Organizers book an eclectic mix that covers Cajun, gospel, bluegrass, rock, hip-hop, and R&B. Over a three-day period, you can expect to be joined in the audience by 75,000 other people. Artists as diverse as country legend George Jones, jam rockers Vertical Horizon, funk master George Clinton, and hip-hoppers OutKast have been featured on previous bills. Potters, painters, and jewelry-makers are sure to be on hand as well.

Artist Submissions
Programming
3 Rivers Music Festival
P.O. Box 3638
Columbia, SC 29230
For more information: (803) 401-8990
Camping: No
Accommodations

■ **Adam's Mark Columbia**
1200 Hampton St.
Columbia, SC 29201
(800) 444-2326
www.adamsmark.com

■ **Clarion Hotel Town House Hotel**
1615 Gervais St.
Columbia, SC 29201
(866) 827-9330
www.clariontownhouse.com

TRIPTYCH SCOTLAND

April
Scotland
www.redt.co.uk/triptych
Admisssion: $$

Triptych encompasses several different events in a variety of venues in towns such as Glasgow, Aberdeen, and Edinburgh. Some of the best acts in Scotland perform here, with a smattering of rare performances from the fields of rock, jazz, and beyond. Scottish popsters Teenage Fanclub, punk/funk divas ESG, Philip Glass, Pharoah Sanders, and roots-reggae artist Dennis Alcapone performed at the 2002 festival, so you can see that eclecticism and quality go hand-in-hand.

For more information: (44) 870-220-1116

Camping: No

Accommodations

■ **The Point Hotel**
34 Bread St.
Edinburgh EH3 9AF
Scotland
(44) 131-221-5555
style@point-hotel.co.uk
www.point-hotel.co.uk

■ **Devoncove Hotel Glasgow**
931 Sauchiehall St., West End
Glasgow, Strathclyde G37TQ
Scotland

♪) V FESTIVAL

Mid-August
Weston Park and Hylands Park, United Kingdom
www.vfestival.com
Admission: $$–$$$

England's V Festival takes place in August in two different sites simultaneously. It's one of the region's most eagerly awaited events and generally attracts the biggest names in alternative rock and electronic music. Multiple stages come alive with electrifying sets and thousands of enthusiastic fans pack the grounds to hear music by bands such as Pulp, Stereophonics, Coldplay, Chemical Brothers, and the Red Hot Chili Peppers.

For more information: info@vfestival.com

Camping: Yes

Accommodations

IN WESTON PARK

■ **Bridge House**
Great Hay, Sutton Hill
Telford TF7 4DT
United Kingdom
(44) 1-952-585-642

IN HYLAND PARK

■ **Ramada Chelmsford**
Rivenhall End
Chelmsford CM8 3HB
United Kingdom
(44) 1-376-516-969

VERDUR'ROCK

June
Charleroi, Belgium
www.verdur-rock.be
Admission: $$

Verdur'Rock's unique approach to music festivals has been bringing audiences to Belgium since 1985. Mixing up relative unknowns from the region with popular international artists, the event fosters musical interest on all levels. The 2002 headliners were the ever-popular, English pub-rocking punks, the Stranglers.

For more information: verdur.rock@ville.namur.be
Camping: No
Accommodations

■ **Best Western**
Boulevard Mayence 1A
6000 Charleroi, Belgium
(32) 71-30-24-24

■ **Hotel Ibis**
Quai de Flandre, 12
6000 Charleroi, Belgium

VIVA LAS VEGAS

April
Las Vegas, Nevada
www.vivalasvegas.net
Admission: $$$

A combination of highly glossed, sleazy all-night debauchery and great music, the Viva Las Vegas festival is a celebration of rockabilly music that started back in 1998. The event takes place at the Gold Coast Hotel and you can expect to see a cavalcade of vintage cars, clothes, and amps as fans of the genre come out to play. The festival is known for digging up some of the lost legends of the 1950s and presenting them alongside current revivalists. Past performers have included the Royal Crown Revue, Lustre Kings, and Deke Dickerson.

For more information: TIngram@charter.net
Camping: No

Accommodations

■ **Palms Hotel**
4321 W. Flamingo Rd.
Las Vegas, NV 89103
(866) 725-6773
info@palms.com
www.thepalmslasvegas.com

■ **The Orleans**
4500 W. Tropicana Ave.
Las Vegas, NV 89103
(800) 675-3267
orleansinfo@coastcasinos.net
www.orleanscasino.com

♪ WHAT IS MUSIC? FESTIVAL

July

Melbourne and Sydney, Australia

www.whatismusic.com

Admission: $

As you might surmise from its name, this Australian event attempts to define the limits of music as we know it. Electronic cutups, nonlinear rock music, noise, and skewed folk are just some of the categories you'll experience during this uncompromising event. Artists such as Jad Fair, K. K. Null, Christian Fennesz, and the puzzling comedian Neil Hamburger have been on past bills.

Artist Submissions

What Is Music? Demos
98 Bunnerong Rd.
Pagewood NSW 2035
Australia

For more information: (61) 404-170-201 or ?@whatismusic.com

Camping: No

Accommodations

■ **Ibis Melbourne Hotel**
15-21 Therry St.
Melbourne 3000
Australia
(61) 396-392-399

■ **Ravesi's Hotel**
Corner Campbell Parade and Hall St.
Bondi Beach
Sydney 2026
Australia
(61) 293-654-422

♪ WICKER MAN FESTIVAL

July
East Kirkcarswell, Dundrennan, United Kingdom
www.thewickermanfestival.co.uk
Admission: $$

Based on the seventies cult film of the same name, the Wicker Man Festival is built around the more fun aspects of the movie (the burning of a wicker man, music, dancing) but leaves out some of the more frightening bits (human sacrifice, pagan rituals). In fact, the Wicker Man Festival has very little in common with the film (save for the man made out of wicker). Instead, you'll find a two-day event populated by a mixture of sweaty punk rockers and techno DJs. All in all, it's a fun, eclectic festival whose most recent lineup was highlighted by punk rock stalwarts UK Subs and the Stiff Little Fingers. Attendees are invited to spend the night, so bring a tent. Only 5,000 tickets are available, so be sure to purchase yours ahead of time.

Camping: Yes. Camping is available (and encouraged) on-site. You can purchase tickets for both the event and camping through www.lastyearsmen.com.

♪ WNED BUFFALO NIAGARA GUITAR FESTIVAL

Mid-June
Buffalo, New York
www.buffaloniagaraguitarfestival.com
Admission: FREE–$$

As you might imagine, the Buffalo Niagara Guitar Festival is a celebration of all things guitar. Concerts showcasing the versatility of this beloved instrument take place all week. Free events are offered daily, while the evening's shows tend to be ticketed and bear an admission price. The featured artists can range from the jazz guitar of John Scofield to the influential yet streamlined sounds of Bo Diddley to shredding showcases from the likes of ex-Triumph guitarist, Rik Emmett.

Artist Submissions
Guitar Festival
P.O. Box 1263
Buffalo, NY 14240

Camping: No

Accommodations

■ **The Hampton Inn & Suites**
220 Delaware Ave.
Buffalo, NY 14202
(716) 855-2233
www.hamptoninnbuffalo.com

■ **Best Western Inn**
510 Delaware Ave.
Buffalo, NY 14202
(866) 809-9330

YO-YO A GO-GO

July
Olympia, Washington
Admission: $–$$

This five-day event typically takes place at the Capitol Theatre in Olympia, Washington, and is one of the most respected in underground and independent music circles. Yo-Yo a Go-Go keeps ticket prices as low as possible while making sure that the bands they book are nothing less than stellar. You can expect to hear a wide range of indie pop and punk rock acts from all over the States (and beyond). Money is a secondary issue at this event; bands perform here because they want to. Even CDs and T-shirts are offered at reasonable prices. This inspires a great atmosphere for experiencing live music. Typically, the roster draws from famed, favorite local labels such as K Records and Kill Rock Stars, but the lineup is not limited to their stable of artists. In the past, artists such as Elliott Smith, Beck, Built to Spill, Sleater-Kinney, and Unwound have performed here.

For more information: yoyo@olywa.net

Camping: No

Accommodations

■ **Golden Gavel**
909 Capital Way
Olympia, WA 98501
(360) 352-8533

■ **Aladdin Motor Inn**
900 Capital Way
Olympia, WA 98501
(360) 352-7200

WORLD AND REGGAE

♪ AFROCARIBBEAN MUSIC FESTIVAL

July
Veracruz, Mexico
www.manos-de-oaxaca.com/afrocaribe/index.htm
Admission: $$$

The Afrocaribbean Music Festival is a package deal that includes six days of live music and a jungle tour to the ancient ruins and beaches surrounding the city of Veracruz in Mexico. More than a dozen styles of Afrocaribbean music are on display, encompassing pretty much anything with a beat that you can dance to: merengue, salsa, mambo, samba, rumba, calypso, soca, reggae, Brazilian jazz. . . . The city streets are filled with dancing in a true carnival atmosphere, with countless sales booths and food vendors representing the four corners of the earth. Performers have included Ruben Blades, Cuban singer Victor Lay, and Venezuelan group Teatro Negro de Barlovento.

For more information: rayeric@rnet.com.mx
Camping: No
Accommodations: Included with reservation

ATLANTIC WAVES: EXPLORATORY MUSIC FROM PORTUGAL

November
London, United Kingdom
www.atlanticwaves.org.uk
Admission: $$

Atlantic Waves, first held in 2001, presents a selection of Portugal's most acclaimed music in a wide variety of venues throughout London. You can expect to hear many variations of fado—the traditional Portuguese folk song—in addition to that country's musicians' eclectic take on jazz, hip-hop, electronic, and folk music. Outside of Portugal, London's Atlantic Waves festival is the premier place to explore the rhythms and subtleties of Portuguese music.

For more information: (44) 020-7908-7622 or info@atlanticwaves.org.uk
Camping: No
Accommodations

■ **Best Western Shaftesbury London Hotel**
165-73 Shaftesbury Ave.
London W1D 6EX
United Kingdom
(44) 020-7871-6000

■ **Regent Palace Hotel**
1 Glasshouse St.
London W1B 5DN
United Kingdom
(44) 870-400-8703

BELLINGEN GLOBAL CARNIVAL

First week in October
Bellingen, Australia
www.globalcarnival.com
Admission: $$

The phrase "global carnival" should clue you in to the fact that this is going to be a lot more than your typical music festival. For three days, this Australian festival mixes up theater, dance, and music to evoke a deeper understanding and appreciation for the arts. It's a time for Australians to discover the richness of their cultural history, while other visitors are sure to gain a greater understanding not only of Australia, but also of the many cultures they're surrounded by everyday. You can expect to hear Tibetan monks, traditional Chinese music, Aboriginal music, hip-hop, techno, and just about everything else under the sun. Be sure to come with open ears.

Artist Submissions

Festival Director

P.O. Box 350

Bellingen, NSW 2454

Australia

Camping: No

Accommodations

■ **Koompartoo Retreat**

Dudley St.

Bellingen, NSW 2454

Australia

(61) 02-6655-2326

koompartoo@midcoast.com.au

■ **Bellinger Valley Motor Inn**

1381 Waterfall Way

Bellingen, NSW 2454

Australia

(61) 02-6655-1599

motorinn@bellingen.com

www.bellingen.com/motorinn

BOB MARLEY DAY FESTIVAL

Mid-February

Long Beach, California

www.bobmarleydayfestival.com

Admission: $$

Long Beach Arena has hosted this event every year since 1981, bringing together reggae acts from Jamaica and the States to pay tribute to the great Bob Marley—the most popular reggae artist of all time. The festival consists of two days of performances by renowned artists such as Beenie Man, Bounty Killer, and Damian Marley & the Ghetto Youth Crew. The vendors at the International Food and Crafts Fair provide further reggae-themed fun.

For more information: (310) 515-3322 or press@bobmarleydayfestival.com

Camping: No

Accommodations

■ **Aquarium Inn**

848 E. Pacific Coast Hwy.

Long Beach, CA 90831

(562) 591-3929

■ **Alamo Motel**

1827 Pacific Ave.

Long Beach, CA 90806

(562) 591-8117

■ **All 8 Motel**
2400 Pacific Ave.
Long Beach, CA 90806
(310) 494-5178

CALIFORNIA WORLDFEST

July
Grass Valley, California
www.californiafestival.com
Admission: $–$$$

Pop rock, Australian harmony singing, Sikh vocalists, and former Grateful Dead drummer Mickey Hart highlight this three-day outdoor event held at the Grass Valley fairgrounds in California's historic gold rush country. Here you'll find an open stage for the unpolished performer; workshops instructing folks in dance, musical instruments, and the percussion of various international cultures; and food from around the world. Besides Mickey Hart, Australian favorite the Waifs, blues harmonica player Charlie Musselwhite, folk singer Iris Dement, and Hawaiian slack-key guitar player George Kahumoko, Jr., have performed at recent festivals.

Artist Submissions
Send a press kit and CD, along with references regarding your participation at other events, to:
California World Music Festival
P.O. Box 5198
Chico, CA 95927
For more information: (530) 891-4098 or info@worldmusicfestival.com
Camping: Yes, on-site.
Accommodations

■ **Alta Sierra Village Inn**
11858 Tammy Way
Grass Valley, CA 95945
(530) 273-9102

■ **Elam Biggs Bed & Breakfast**
220 Colfax Ave.
Grass Valley, CA 95945
(530) 477-0906

■ **Coach N Four Motel**
628 S. Auburn St.
Grass Valley, CA 95945
(530) 273-8009

EUGENE CELEBRATION

September
Eugene, Oregon
www.eugenecelebration.com
Admission: $

Billed as "Northwest of Normal," the town of Eugene, Oregon, takes a few days each September to make that phrase a statement of fact. An eclectic lineup of rock, reggae, hip-hop, and country acts perform in the streets downtown, while horseback rides, parades, a foot race, and countless food and arts and crafts booths are provided for festivalgoers' amusement. Recent festivals have featured the neo-funk rock of Fishbone, the progressive blue-grass stylings of the Austin Lounge Lizards, and the somewhat schizo-phrenic swing/ska band Cherry Poppin' Daddies.

For more information: (541) 681-4108 or info@eugenecelebration.com
Camping: No
Accommodations

- **Excelsior Inn**
754 E. 13th Ave.
Eugene, OR 97401
(800) 321-6963

- **Quality Inn & Suites**
2121 Franklin Blvd.
Eugene, OR 97403
(541) 342-1243

- **Campbell House, A City Inn**
252 Pearl St.
Eugene, OR 97401
(800) 264-2519

FLOYD WORLD MUSIC FEST

September
Floyd, Virginia
www.floydfest.com
Admission: $$–$$$

The Neville Brothers, Rhoda Vincent, Doc Watson, and Nordic import Gar-marna performed at the 2002 edition of this festival (the first one, to boot). In subsequent years you can be sure to expect plenty of acts from the States and abroad playing everything from modern rock to reggae, electronica to

African drum music. Considering the festival's setting in the middle of the Blue Ridge Mountains, you can also expect to hear authentic Virginian mountain music. Sponsored by the grassroots organization Across-the-Way Productions, the Floyd World Festival features 15 bands and is run very well. There's plenty of camping and a separate tent with kid friendly activities.

Artist Submissions

Send physical promo material by January 1 to:

Across the Way Productions

114-B South Locust St.

Floyd, VA 24091

For more information: (540) 745-FEST or erika@floydfest.com

Camping: Yes, on-site.

Accommodations

■ **Holiday Inn Express**
2725 Roanoke St.
Christiansburg, VA
(540) 382-6500

■ **Fairfield Inn and Suites**
2659 Roanoke St.
Christiansburg, VA 24068
(540) 381-9596

■ **Microtel Inn and Suites**
135 Ponderosa Dr.
Christiansburg, VA 24068
(540) 381-0500

GREEN MOUNTAIN MUSIC FESTIVAL

August

Hardwick, Vermont

www.greenmountainmusicfest.com

Admission: $$

This highly spiritual one-day festival offers yoga and tai chi, in addition to the live music, from noon until dusk. No drugs, alcohol, or camping are permitted, but plenty of tantalizing vegetarian food and fun crafts are sure to keep you happy. This event is extremely family friendly, and kids under 12 get in free.

For more information: (802) 350-4217 or info@greenmountainmusicfest.com

Camping: No

Accommodations

■ **Village Motel**
P.O. Box 375
Hardwick, VT 05843
(802) 472-5211

♪ INTERNATIONAL FESTIVAL OF NEW MUSIC & THE ARTS

July
St. John's, Newfoundland, Canada
www.sound.nf.ca/home.html
Admission: $

This Newfoundland event is an exciting combination of live performance and audience participation. Countless music-related activities fill the weekend, from African drum workshops to musical collages to something mysterious called a "Sound Massage Parlor." The music is not bound to any one style and you're just as likely to see old-time country singers as classically trained string quartets. But, in the end, experimentation and innovation reign. Each year offers a number of world premieres both from up-and-coming and established contemporary music artists, almost all of them from the region. Perhaps the most interesting event in conjunction with this festival is the "Harbour Symphony." Each day, at a specified time, the ships in St. John's Harbor sound their horns in sequence to produce music that can be heard all over the city.

For more information: soundart@nfld.com
Camping: No
Accommodations

■ **Comfort Inn**
41 Maple Valley Rd.
Corner Brook, NF A2H 6T2
Canada

■ **Delta St. John's**
120 New Gower St.
St. John's, NF A1C 6K4
Canada

■ **Quality Hotel Downtown**
2 Hill O'Chips
St. John's, NF A1C 6B1
Canada

♪ IRISH MUSIC AND ARTS FESTIVAL

September
Altamont, New York
Admission: $$

A small children's carnival with rides and games of chance adjoins the grounds of this festival, which is centered on, as the name suggests, Irish music of all kinds, from traditional Irish folk to modern rock. Artists such as the Prodigals, Tommy Makem, the Clancy Brothers, and the Ellen Ivers Band are imported from Ireland to perform on four stages alongside a handful of American acts playing their own interpretations of Irish music. Exhibits focusing on Irish arts and crafts are offered, and spontaneous open jams are anything but rare, so if you're a player, bring your instrument.

Artist Submissions

Send a CD along with a press package by January 1 to:
Irish Festival
c/o Matt Nelligan
125 Sherman St.
Schenectady, NY 12303

For more information: (888) 414-3378

Camping: No

Accommodations

■ **Ramada Limited**
1630 Central Ave.
Albany, NY 12207
(518) 456-0222

■ **Cocca's Inns and Suites/Buckshots**
Route 7
Latham, NY 12110
(518) 785-5571

■ **Albany Quality Inn**
3 Watervliet Ave.
Albany, NY 12206
(518) 438-8431

♪ IRISH SUMMERFEST

August
Euclid, Ohio
http://homepages.bw.edu/~scoyne/summerfest/
Admissions: $$

This summer weekend festival imports groups from abroad to entertain fans of both traditional and modern Irish music. In operation since 1993, the festival offers a look at Irish bands such as Blackthorn, Hair of the Dog, and the Prodigals, who'll play everything from jigs and reels to rock.

For more information: (440) 942-0935 or Pat_Coyne@irishsummerfest.org

Camping: No

Accommodations

■ **Euclid Motel**
18327 Euclid Ave.
Euclid, OH 44112
(216) 481-8666

♪ ISLAND FESTIVAL

Mid-June

Kalamazoo, Michigan

www.islandfestkalamazoo.com

Admission: $$

Dedicated to the reggae cause since the early 1980s—when Kalamazoo was a hot spot for touring reggae acts such as Toots & the Maytalls, Pato Banton, the I-Tals, among many others—the Islands Festival offers two days and nights of skankin' riddims and authentic Jamaican food.

Artist Submissions

Send press kit to:

Paul Toth
920 Fairbanks Ave.
Kalamazoo, MI 49048

For more information: wdeering@chartermi.net

Camping: No

Accommodations

■ **Comstock Motor Court Motel**
6302 King Hwy.
Kalamazoo, MI 49008
(616) 349-4353

■ **Downtowner Motel**
739 W. Michigan Ave.
Kalamazoo, MI 49008
(616) 349-6743

♪ LOTUS FESTIVAL

September
Bloomington, Indiana
http://home.bluemarble.net/~lotus/lotusfest/festival.html
Admission: $$

This heartland festival in Bloomington, Indiana, celebrates folk music and performers from around the world in addition to artists born and bred in the United States. Past performers include Habib Koite of Bamako, Malcolm Dalglish and the Ooolites, and a tribute to the festival's namesake, California folksinger Quinten Lotus Dickey.

For more information: (812) 336-6599 or lotus@lotusfest.org
Camping: Yes
Accommodations

■ **Fourwinds Resort**
9301 S. Fairfax Rd.
Bloomington, IN 47401
(812) 824-9904

■ **Days Inn**
200 Matlock Rd.
Bloomington, IN 47401
(812) 336-0905

♪ MONTEREY BAY REGGAE FEST

September
Monterey, California
Admission: $$

Monterey Bay hosts this rambunctious event every Labor Day weekend, attracting big reggae stars as well as obscure acts and cult favorites. Approximately 30 groups perform on three stages situated near the water in downtown Monterey. Artists have included Steel Pulse, President Brown, the Abyssinians, and Israel Vibration, a physically handicapped group. Activities for kids are provided, as well as a "Reggae Lounge" area for adults.

For more information: (831) 755-4899 or mbrf98@aol.com
Camping: Yes.
Laguna Seca Recreation Area
Monterey Salinas Hwy./Hwy. 68
Monterey, CA 93908
(888) 588-2267

Accommodations

■ **Arbor Inn**
1058 Munras Ave.
Monterey, CA 93940
(831) 372-3381

■ **Bayside Inn**
2055 N. Fremont St.
Monterey, CA 93940
(408) 372-8071

■ **Bay Park Hotel**
1425 Munras Ave.
Monterey, CA 93940
(831) 649-1020

MONTEREY WORLD MUSIC FESTIVAL

September
Monterey, California
www.montereyworldmusic.org
Admission: $$

The highly exotic selection of performers sets the Monterey World Music Festival apart from the pack. Their roster avoids pop music of any kind and instead brings the festivalgoer a broad palette of innovative music from around the globe. Acclaimed Indian vocalist Kiran Ahluwalia performed in 2002, alongside saxophonist Yuri Yunakov from Bulgaria and the haunting Swedish folk-rock band Garmarna. Half a dozen or more outstanding artists appear each year. Dance and instrument workshops are also available, but the real reason to go to the Monterey festival is the opportunity to catch rarely seen international musicians live and in person.

For more information: (831) 622-9595 or (800) 465-5575 or ccmc@culturalmonterey.org

Camping: No

Accommodations

■ **Arbor Inn**
1058 Munras Ave.
Monterey, CA 93940
(831) 372-3381

■ **Bayside Inn**
2055 N. Fremont St.
Monterey, CA 93940
(408) 372-8071

■ **Bay Park Hotel**
1425 Munras Ave.
Monterey, CA 93940
(831) 649-1020

NEW ENGLAND REGGAE FESTIVAL

July

Providence, Rhode Island

http://newenglandreggae.com/NewEnglandReggae.htm

Admission: $$

Griffiths, Yellowman, and a host of lesser-known reggae bands have appeared at this event, which is generally held at the Stepping Stone Ranch in Escoheag, Rhode Island. It offers two days and nights filled with live music, food from around the world, arts and crafts booths. Other activities such as horseback riding, hiking, and swimming are available as well.

For more information:

New England Reggae Festival Co.

c/o Lions Eye

163 Brook St.

Providence, RI 02906

Camping: Yes, both on-site and nearby. Contact:

Oak Embers

219 Escoheag Hill Rd.

Escoheag, RI 02864

(401) 397-4042

Accommodations

■ **Church House Inn**

122 Fountain St.

Providence, RI 02912

(401) 351-5505

■ **Providence Bed & Breakfast**

75 Weybosset St.

Providence, RI 02912

(401) 273-8833

■ **Old Court Bed & Breakfast**

144 Benefit St.

Providence, RI 02912

(401) 751-2002

NORTHWEST REGGAE FEST

September

Seattle, Washington

Admission: $$

The Northwest Reggae Fest features two days of live reggae acts and one day of fabulous DJs who are sure to get you barefoot and dancing. Help spread the reggae message of love and brotherhood while having a smokin' good time. This rain-or-shine event provides camping, food, and great entertainment.

For more information: (206) 230-7841 or rickj@ncia.com

Camping: Yes, on-site.

Accommodations

■ **Eastlake Inn**
3101 E. Madison
Seattle, WA 98102
(206) 322-7726

■ **A-1 Motel**
4450 Green Lake Way N.
Seattle, WA 98103
(206) 632-3733

OLD SONGS FESTIVAL

June
Altamont, New York
www.oldsongs.org/festival/index.html
Admissions: $$

With a name like Old Songs Festival, you might think this is a strictly traditional American folk and country festival. But annual lineups usually have just as many African drum and vocal groups as Irish and Celtic groups playing alongside American roots rockers and contradance callers. Eclecticism rules the day, all the way down to the wide selection of international food booths, workshops, and artists exhibiting pieces representative of their homelands. While the roster is far from single-minded, it's not exactly star-studded (Tom Paxton is the biggest American name to have appeared in recent years).

For more information: (518) 765-2815 or oldsongs@oldsongs.org

Camping: No

Accommodations

■ **Denny's Motel**
RR 3 Box 137
Altamont, NY 12009
(518) 456-4430

PANGAEA WORLD MUSIC FESTIVAL

Early May
Jonesborough, Tennessee

www.pangaeafest.com

Admission: $$

The town of Jonesborough, Tennessee—a favorite with tourists and the home of the National Storytelling Festival—hosts the Pangaea Festival for one weekend a year. Festival organizers seek to bring the cultures of the world together and to enrich the lives of both attendees and performers. Activities for kids and workshops are offered, while the concerts happen on four different stages under giant tents.

Artist Submissions

Send press kit or info to:

World Music Festival

P.O. Box 5

Jonesborough, TN 37659

For more information: Contact Steve Cook at (866) 401-4223 or email@jwcheritagealliance.org

Camping: No

Accommodations

■ **Blair-Moore House Bed & Breakfast**

201 West Main St.

Jonesborough, TN 37659

(888) 453-0044

blairmoorehouse@aol.com

■ **Cherokee Mt. Llama Bed & Breakfast**

201 Charlie Hicks Rd.

Jonesborough, TN 37659

(423) 913-2781

llamajo@aol.com

QUEBEC CITY INTERNATIONAL SUMMER FESTIVAL

Mid-July

Quebec City, Quebec, Canada

www.infofestival.com

Admission: $$

Quebec City, the oldest French city in North America, comes to vibrant life each year with the rich tapestry of music and arts known as the International Summer Festival. The festival's roots go back 35 years and the event remains one of the key celebrations for anyone interested in French song—or international music in general. Three stages showcase everything from French country singers to Slavic chants to traditional Vietnamese music. Even the streets get into the act with dancers and acrobats performing around the historic thoroughfares.

For more information: infofestival@infofestival.com

Accommodations

■ **Hilton Quebec**
1100 Rene Levesque E.
Quebec, PQ
Canada
(418) 647-2411
www.quebec.hilton.com

■ **Hôtel Clarendon**
57 rue Sainte-Anne
Vieux-Québec QC G1R 3X4
Canada
(888) 222-3304
reservation@hotelclarendon.com
www.hotelclarendon.com/
    introang.html

REAL DEAL REGGAE FESTIVAL

June
Bakersfield, California
www.a415production.com
Admission: $

This one-day festival features five acts on one stage in the Stramler Complex in Bakersfield, California. It's more of a large concert than a traditional festival, with past performers including Eek-a-Mouse, Lion Heart, and a selection of typically Irie beats.

For more information: (661) 335-0415 or tim@web-effx.com

Camping: No

Accommodations

■ **American Hotel**
910 Baker St.
Bakersfield, CA 93302
(805) 324-7007

■ **Bakersfield Lodge**
1219 S. Union Ave.
Bakersfield, CA 93302
(661) 327-7901

■ **Bakersfield Hotel**
1202 19th St.
Bakersfield, CA 93302
(661) 324-4814

REGGAE DESTINY FESTIVAL

June
Wilmington, North Carolina

http://musicorner.com/nightnurse

Admission: $

Now that she has 10 years of reggae promotion under her belt, Night Nurse Kimberly McLaughlin has finally decided to throw her own party. A handful of American and Jamaican reggae bands perform at this one-day event at the Greenfield Lake Amphitheater in Wilmington, North Carolina. Yellowman, Burning Spear, and the Night Nurse herself have appeared at recent festivals.

For more information: (910) 762-0477 or nnpromo@aol.com

Camping: No

Accommodations

■ **Worth House**
412 S. 3rd St.
Wilmington, NC 28403
(910) 762-8562

■ **Beau Rivage Plantation**
213 Small Dove Ct.
Wilmington, NC 28403
(910) 392-9024

■ **Azalea Inn**
P.O. Box 195
Wilmington, NC 28403
(910) 763-0121

REGGAE INLAND FESTIVAL

July

San Bernardino, California

www.reggaeinland.com

Admission: $$

This daylong concert features such top-flight reggae acts as the Wailing Souls and the Dancing Children. The venue has a designated children's area, and no one will go hungry thanks to the great food vendors. Booths selling art, crafts, and handmade clothing will also be available on-site.

For more information: reggaeinland2001@earthlink.net

Camping: No

Accommodations

■ **Arrowhead Motel**
24955 Redlands Blvd.
San Bernardino, CA 92415
(909) 796-0518

■ **Astro Motel**
111 S. E St.
San Bernardino, CA 92415
(909) 889-0417

■ **Central City Motel**
395 N. H St.
San Bernardino, CA 92415
(909) 888-6575

REGGAE ON THE RIVER

August
Piercy, California
www.reggaeontheriver.com
Admission: $$

Reggae on the River is a major California festival, each year providing a giant crowd the opportunity to witness their favorite reggae acts, from Dancehall to Roots, performing live. The summer weekend event (in its twentieth year in 2003) takes place on the grounds of French's Camp in Piercy, California—which is, appropriately enough, within the borders of Humboldt County, so bring your tie-dye and an open mind. Thousands of people descend on this festival each year, so make your reservations early and be prepared for a loud, friendly, three-day bash featuring reggae stars such as Sly & Robbie, Steel Pulse, and Burning Spear.

For more information: (707) 923-4583 or people@humboldt.net
Camping: Yes, on-site.
Accommodations

■ **Benbow Inn**
445 Lake Benbow Dr.
Garberville, CA 95542
(707) 923-2124 or (800) 355-3301

■ **Brass Rail Inn**
3188 Redwood Dr.
Redway, CA 95560
(707) 923-3931

■ **Best Western/Humboldt House Inn**
701 Redwood Dr.
Garberville, CA 95542
(707) 923-2771

REGGAE SUMFEST

July
Montego Bay, Jamaica

www.reggaesumfest.com
Admission: $$

Not surprisingly, the Montego Bay Reggae Sumfest is one of the premier reggae festivals in the world, featuring the genre's biggest names performing on multiple stages over the course of five days. Gregory Isaacs, Shaggy, Ninja Man, and Dennis Brown are just a few of the headliners of the past, with a host of lesser acts filling out the rest of the lineup. Festival nights are broken down into themes: Dancehall Night, Singers Night, Stereo System Night (DJs), Beach Party Night, and so forth. This is where you'll be exposed to the reggae acts that never make it to the States, which makes this a particularly good festival for hardcore reggae fans. As far as other activities go, Montego Bay is a major tourist spot and there are tons of things to do, from sunbathing to snorkeling to mountain climbing. There are also a great many stories of a mysterious plant that grows in abundance there and is a remarkably effective time killer.

For more information: (876) 953-2933 or info@reggaesumfest.com
Camping: No
Accommodations

■ **The Jamaica Grandiosa Resort**
3 Ramparts Close
Montego Bay, Jamaica
(876) 979-3205

■ **Holiday Inn Sunspree Resort Rose Hall**
P.O. Box 480
Rose Hall
Montego Bay, Jamaica
(876) 953-2485

■ **Caribic House**
69 Gloucester Ave.
Montego Bay, Jamaica
(876) 979-9387

SIERRA NEVADA WORLD MUSIC FESTIVAL

June
Angels Camp, California
www.snwmf.com
Admissions: $$

The Sierra Nevada World Music Festival takes place in Frogtown, California, within the borders of Calaveras County (made famous, of course, by Mark Twain's short story, "The Celebrated Jumping Frog of Calaveras County"). Located in the heart of gold rush country, visitors will have plenty of history to explore, in addition to the breathtaking beauty of the Sierra Nevada Mountains. And then there's the festival itself, which offers a smorgasbord of international attractions. Here you'll find live music, educational workshops, hands-on crafts, dance exhibitions, and food booths selected by the festival's promoters to ensure the maximum in both eclecticism and quality. The performers often manifest a heavy reggae slant, with dub reggae master Lee "Scratch" Perry, Toots & the Maytalls, and the Abyssinians appearing frequently. Cuban dance band Bamboleo, North African spiritualist Hassan Hakmoun, and world/hip-hop fusion experimentalists Ozomatli have appeared at recent festivals as well.

Artist Submissions

Submit artist packet to:

SNWMF 2003

attn: Artist Submissions

P.O. Box 208

Ryde, CA 95680

For more information: (916) 777-5550 or info@snwmf.com

Camping: Yes, on-site.

Accommodations

■ **Angels Inn Motel**
P.O. Box 1121
Angels Camp, CA 95222
(209) 736-4242

■ **Gold Country Inn Motel**
P.O. Box 188
Angels Camp, CA 95222
(209) 736-4611

■ **Jumping Frog Motel**
330 Murphy's Grade Rd.
Angels Camp, CA 95222
(209) 736-2191

SNOW MOUNTAIN MUSIC FESTIVAL

End of August
Lijiang, Yunnan, China
Admission: $$

China's Snow Mountain Music Festival has the honor of being the country's first outdoor music festival. It began in 2002 and was a resounding success. The event takes place about 10,000 feet up Jade Dragon Snow Mountain, probably the only festival in the world at such a high altitude. The thinning air did not dissuade the 10,000-some folks who attended the first time out.

Performers include a mixture of Chinese pop stars as well as a variety of harder-edged acts, ranging from hip-hop to heavy metal.

Camping: Yes

Accommodations

■ **Guanfang Hotel**
Middle-Snow Mountain Road
Lijiang, Yunnan Province, PRC
(86) 518-8888-6210-6212
gfhotel@public.km.yn.cn

♪ SPLASHY FEN MUSIC FESTIVAL

April
Drakensberg, South Africa
www.splashyfen.co.za
Admission: $–$$

The Splashy Fen Music Festival is a well-attended event at Splashy Fen Farm in the South Drakensberg Mountains of South Africa that brings in about 10,000 folks annually. Regional rock, folk, and Afro-pop groups play on multiple stages over the course of four days. Horseback riding and paragliding are offered, as are guided hikes into the Drakensberg mountain range.

For more information: splashyfen@futurenet.co.za

Camping: Yes, on-site.

Accommodations

■ **Sani Pass Hotel**
P.O. Box 44
Himeville 3256
KwaZulu-Natal, South Africa
(27) 033-702-1320
info@sanipasshotel.co.za
www.sanipasshotel.co.za

■ **Eagles' Rock Mountain Retreat**
P.O. Box 495
Underberg 3257
KwaZulu-Natal, South Africa
(27) 033-701-1757
eagles@futurenet.co.za
www.eaglesrock.co.za

■ **Himeville Arms Hotel**
P.O. Box 105
Himeville 3256
KwaZulu-Natal, South Africa
(27) 033-702-1305
himevillearms@futurenet.co.za
www.himevillehotel.co.za

SUMMER JAM

July
Cologne, North Rhine-Westphalia, Germany
www.summerjam.de/infos.php
Admission: $$

Approximately 30 internationally recognized reggae acts perform on three stages at Germany's Summer Jam. A crafts bazaar, a chill tent, and a large camping area are all set up on a small island that sits just off shore of the Rhine River in Cologne, Germany. Buju Banton, Max Romeo, Eek-a-Mouse, Beenie Man, and the Wailers have all appeared at recent festivals.

Artist Submissions
Contour Music Promotion
Alexanderstr. 78
70182 Stuttgart
Germany
For more information: (49) 07-11-238-5050 or office@contour-music.de
Camping: Yes, on-site.
Accommodations

■ **Flandrischer Hof**
Flandrische Strasse 3-5
Cologne, North Rhine-
  Westphalia 50674
Germany
(49) 22-125-2095

■ **Classic Hotel Santo**
Dagobertstrasse 22
Cologne, North Rhine-
  Westphalia 50668
Germany

■ **Comfort Hotel Central**
An den Dominikanern 3
Cologne, North Rhine-Westphalia 50668
Germany
(49) 22-113-5088

UCLA JAZZ REGGAE FESTIVAL

May
Los Angeles, California
www.studentgroups.ucla.edu/jazzreggae
Admission: $$

No, this isn't a festival devoted to the potentially frightening new genre of jazz-reggae music. It's a two-day series of concerts that features top-flight jazz artists on one day and equally acclaimed reggae artists the next. Jimmy Smith, Pharaoh Sanders, and Christine McBride represent the kind of jazz talent the festival attracts, while Barrington Levy and Junior Kelly are a sampling of the reggae acts that have appeared here in the past. Concerts are held in Drake Stadium on the UCLA campus. Buy your tickets well in advance; this festival, which celebrated its 16th year in 2002, regularly sells out.

For more information: jazzregg@ucla.edu

Camping: No

Accommodations

■ **Full Moon Inn**
8803 S. Figueroa St.
Los Angeles, CA 90003
(213) 753-6669

■ **108 Motel**
10721 S. Broadway
Los Angeles, CA 90061
(323) 779-7000

VIVA CHICAGO LATIN MUSIC FESTIVAL

August

Chicago, Illinois

Admission: *FREE*

The Chicago Mayor's Office organizes this two-day affair as a part of its ongoing program "Music Everywhere: Summer in Chicago." (Other events include the Chicago Blues Festival, the Chicago Gospel Festival, and the Chicago Country Music Festival.) Concerts take place downtown in Grant Park and offer more than 20 groups that run the gamut of Latin music—including cumbia, tropical, norteño, merengue, salsa, ranchero, and mariachi. Past performers include Latin rock sensation Malo, Puerto Rican salsa band El Gran Combo, and Mariachi Vargas de Tecalitlán.

For more information: (877) CHICAGO

Camping: No

Accommodations

■ **1011 Building**
1011 N. Clark St.
Chicago, IL 60610
(312) 944-4290

■ **Abbott Hotel**
721 W. Belmont Ave.
Chicago, IL 60657
(773) 248-2700

■ **Acacia Hotel**
725 W. Grand Ave.
Chicago, IL 60610
(312) 421-4597

♪ WORLD MUSIC FESTIVAL: CHICAGO

September
Chicago, Illinois
www.cityofchicago.org/WorldMusic
Admission: $–$$

This festival takes over the city for ten days and features artists from all over the world—Turkey, Spain, Bulgaria, Poland, and more. For some reason, a handful of American punk and noise rock bands often appear here as well. Most shows are performed for sold out crowds, so register in advance. Concerts take place in small and medium-sized venues all over the city, but most of them are concentrated downtown and are somewhat close to each other. Past performers include heavy noise rock band US Maple, the Cracow Klezmer Band, and Indian maestro Ali Akbar Khan.

For more information: (312) 742-1938 or WorldMusic@cityofchicago.org

Camping: No

Accommodations

■ **1011 Building**
1011 N. Clark St.
Chicago, IL 60610
(312) 944-4290

■ **Acacia Hotel**
725 W. Grand Ave.
Chicago, IL 60610
(312) 421-4597

■ **Abbott Hotel**
721 W. Belmont Ave.
Chicago, IL 60657
(773) 248-2700

TOP TEN FESTIVALS

The Authors Give Their Humble Opinion as to What Are the Top Ten Festivals in the Whole Wide World (in Alphabetical Order)

APPALACHIAN UPRISING (see page 65)

This rambunctious festival makes the grade because the grounds on which it is held are beautiful, you can experience an excellent combination of rock, bluegrass, and partying there, and the guy in charge was really nice to me when I asked him some questions.

BUMBERSHOOT (see page 324)

Bumbershoot makes our top ten thanks to its diverse array of activities and performers; the free-love, freak-out vibe of the whole weekend; and, most importantly, because the name of the festival sounds vaguely dirty.

DISCOVER JAZZ FESTIVAL (see page 254)

The Discover Jazz Festival in Burlington, Vermont, manages to have a firm grasp on what jazz is today. The event decidedly electrifies the city. Maybe it's the scenic setting, maybe it's the collection of people who show up, maybe it's the general vibe, or maybe it's a combination of all three; but, there's no doubt that the diverse lineup both educates and entertains. Anyone who thinks jazz festivals have lost their urgency or are simply an exercise in party throwing have yet to spend a day in the sun here.

FUTURESONIC (see page 231)

With its art installations and truly adventurous music programming, the Futuresonic festival in Manchester, England, provides one of the best insights into the world of electronic music. The most respected (and soon-to-be-respected) names in hip-hop, house, and beyond convene here. You should, too.

INTERNATIONAL MILITARY MUSIC FESTIVAL
(see page 51)

I don't know how a military music festival held in Berlin could *not* make our top ten. Weirdness counts.

PUCKERAMA: A WHISTLING FESTIVAL (see page 184)

Puckerama is not the largest festival in the world, nor does it offer the widest scope of musical entertainment. What it does offer, we'd like to remind you, is a festival dedicated to whistling. It is without peer.

TALKEETNA BLUEGRASS FESTIVAL (see page 204)

A notorious and over-the-top gathering in Talkeetna, Alaska—a town which is approximately 500 miles from nowhere. Talkeetna is a biker paradise, sure, but all are certainly welcome. The prevailing vibe at this festival is one of true communality. Though not for the fainthearted, it is essentially good-natured. Its organizers do their best to foster a safe form of chaos by providing their own special brand of on-site security officials.

TERRASTOCK (see page 382)

Each year Terrastock offers a glimpse into the startling and thunderous world of heavy psychedelic rock. This is where you will catch legendary Japanese noise masters Acid Mothers Temple and the resurrected sixties electro-psyche giants Silver Apples.

ULRICHSBERGER KALEIDOPHON (see page 307)

This Austrian event focuses on the outer limits of jazz and also happens to take place inside a house. But this is not your average house party—unless previous guests at *your* house parties have included Sun Ra, Cecil Taylor, Peter Brotzmann, and Evan Parker.

WOODFORD FOLK FESTIVAL (see page 222)

Woodford is where all those people got the idea for Burning Man. The fact that they set a massive humanoid structure on fire as a grand finale makes it a must-attend, in our book. The difference is that there are fewer ravers from San Francisco present at this one, thank God.

RESOURCES

BOOKS

Berger, Bruce. *Music in the Mountains: The First Fifty Years of the Aspen Music Festival*. Boulder, Colo.: Johnson Books, 2001.

Bianchi, Anne and Adrienne Gusoff. *Music Lover's Guide to Great Britain & Ireland*. Chicago: McGraw-Hill/Contemporary Books, 1995.

Campbell, James R. *Festival Fever: The Ultimate Guide to Musical Celebrations in the Northeast*. Glen Ridge, N.J.: FestPress, 1995.

Clynes, Tom. *Music Festivals: From Bach to Blues*. Canton, Mich.: Visible Ink Press, 1996.

Hopkins, Jerry. *Festival! The Book of American Music Celebrations*. London: MacMillan, 1970.

Minor, William and Bill Wishner. *Monterey Jazz Festival: Forty Legendary Years*. Los Angeles: Angel City Press, 1997.

Pincus, Andrew L. and Phyllis Curtin. *Tanglewood: The Clash Between Tradition and Change*. Boston: Northeastern University Press, 1998.

Santelli, Robert. *Aquarius Rising: The Rock Festival Years*. New York: Dell Publishing, 1980.

WEB SITES

www.bluegrass.com

Billing itself as "Planet Bluegrass" and cranking up a midi file jittery banjo music upon entry, www.bluegrass.com is an excellent resource for lover's of not just the music of bluegrass but the culture surrounding it. An excellent place to find out about bluegrass happenings all over the United States.

www.festivalfinder.com

We used this one quite a bit. At this site you'll find an archive of festivals all over the country. Be careful though, because not all of them are up and running anymore. Still this is a good spot to start researching if you're looking for a particular festival. Or you could try reading our book.

www.festivals.com

A search box in the upper left-hand corner of the page allows you to dial up a festival if it happens to be in the archive. Chances are it is and you get a blurb and some contact information if there is any. Pretty good source (if you know what you're after) with a link to expensive hotel referral sites and the sort of graphics that would brighten any grumpy goose's day.

www.jambase.com

Are you wearing a String Cheese Incident T-Shirt? Do you know what a stick bass is? Or Devil Sticks for that matter? If you answered yes to these questions then you either need to kill yourself or check out this site to find others like you.

INDEXES

Festivals, on the whole, are wily beasts. Trying to successfully categorize a festival that juggles Bulgarian hip-hop with old-timey string bands makes everyone look silly. The categories presented below are general guides and, to be honest, not entirely accurate. (You'll also find some festivals double listed where appropriate.) However, these are the best that we can do—and you cannot fault us for that.

INDEX BY GENRE

∞ Avant-Garde Jazz

∞ Bluegrass

∾ Blues

∽ Cajun & Zydeco

∾ Classical

∾ Country

∞ Electronic

∽ Gospel

∽ Hip-Hop

∽ Indie/Punk Rock

∽ Irish/Celtic

∞ Jam Rock

∞ Latin

∞ Mainstream Jazz

∞ Reggae

∞ Rock

∞ Smooth Jazz

∞ Soul/R&B

INDEX BY LOCATION

INDEX BY MONTH

∞ July

∽ September

∞ December

ALPHABETICAL INDEX